DUXFORD AND THE
BIG WINGS
1940–45

DUXFORD AND THE
BIG WINGS
1940–45

RAF AND USAAF FIGHTER PILOTS AT WAR

BY
MARTIN W. BOWMAN

Pen & Sword
AVIATION

First published in Great Britain in 2009 by
Pen & Sword Aviation
An imprint of
Pen & Sword Books Ltd
47 Church Street
Barnsley
South Yorkshire
S70 2AS

Printed and bound in England
by the MPG Books Group

Pen & Sword Books Ltd incorporates the Imprints of Pen & Sword Aviation,
Pen & Sword Family History, Pen & Sword Maritime, Pen & Sword Military,
Wharncliffe Local History, Pen & Sword Select, Pen & Sword Military Classics,
Leo Cooper, Remember When, Seaforth Publishing and Frontline Publishing

For a complete list of Pen & Sword titles please contact
PEN & SWORD BOOKS LIMITED
47 Church Street, Barnsley, South Yorkshire, S70 2AS, England
E-mail: enquiries@pen-and-sword.co.uk

Website: www.pen-and-sword.co.uk

Contents

The author gratefully acknowledges permission to use extended quotations from:

Airfield Focus 1: Duxford by Andy Height (GMS 1992); *Target of Opportunity: Tales & Contrails of the Second World War* by Lieutenant Colonel R.A. 'Dick' Hewitt (privately published, November 2000); *A Mississippi Fighter Pilot In WWII* by Lieutenant Colonel Ernest E Russell (Trafford Publishing (UK) Ltd 2008); *Historic Tales of the Wild Blue Yonder* by Larry Nelson (privately published 2006); *Wandering Through World War II* by Pete Keillor (privately published 2003). And I am no less grateful for the help given by Bob Collis; Air Commodore James Coward AFC; Andy Height; Lieutenant Colonel Richard Dick Hewitt; IWM Duxford; Pete Keillor; Huie Lamb; Lawrence 'Larry' W Nelson; and Lieutenant Colonel Ernest 'Ernie' Russell.

CHAPTER ONE

'We Shall Defend Our Island'

*Even though large tracts of Europe and many old and famous States have
fallen or may fall into the grip of the Gestapo and all the odious apparatus
of Nazi rule, we shall not flag or fail. We shall go on to the end, we shall
fight in France, we shall fight on the seas and oceans, we shall fight with
growing confidence and growing strength in the air, we shall defend our
island, whatever the cost may be, we shall fight on the beaches, we shall
fight on the landing grounds, we shall fight in the fields and in the streets,
we shall fight in the hills; we shall never surrender...*

Winston S Churchill

On a raw November day in 1932 a young RAF fighter pilot drove his little
red MG sports car along the winding A505 in Cambridgeshire to take up a
new posting at Duxford airfield just south of the University City of
Cambridge. This RAF fighter station forty miles north of London was home to 19
Squadron flying Bristol Bulldog IIA biplane fighters. At weekends the airfield
hosted undergraduate members of the Cambridge University Air Squadron who
were learning to fly and to become officers in the RAF. Duxford would normally
have been a Mecca too for the twenty-two-year-old ex-RAF College Cranwell
graduate, accomplished pilot and all-round sportsman who had flown Gloster
Gamecocks in tied together aerobatics at Hendon air displays. But for Douglas
Bader his posting to 19 Squadron was a bitter pill to swallow. Both his legs had
been amputated following a horrific crash during low-level aerobatics at Reading
Aero Club at Woodley airfield on 14 December 1931 when the wingtip of his
Bulldog clipped the grass and the aircraft smashed into the ground. Lesser men
would have died but expert medical care and his own tremendous fighting spirit
and a strong will to live pulled him through. He endured the long ordeal of

operations and rehabilitation and when given artificial legs Bader confounded the doctors who said that he would never walk unaided again. He not only proved them wrong, he proved to his RAF superiors that he could still fly aircraft, but the service was unable to pass him fit for flying because 'there was nothing in King's Regulations which covered his case'. Instead, he was posted to Duxford and on his arrival the wing commander in charge of the Station told him, 'Glad to have you here Bader. You're taking over the Motor Transport Section.'

In the 1930s Duxford was one of a few RAF stations that boasted permanent hangars and other buildings, brick barracks and mess sites and a large grass runway area. It was a far cry from 1914–18 when during the Great War military aviation really came of age and developments in weaponry and aircraft design made great strides and airfields had to be found to house the aircraft of the Royal Flying Corps. In England hundreds of potential sites were surveyed. One of them was on land north-west of the village of Duxford comprising 223 acres of land on the south side of the Newmarket to Royston road and fifteen acres on the other side of the road. Most of the land belonged to Temple Farm and College Farm. Once the survey was complete, the land was declared suitable and was requisitioned, as the RFC wanted to use Duxford as a training station. Tenders were invited from companies for the construction of the airfield, to include hangars, service buildings and living quarters for up to 800 personnel. In the summer of 1917, P & W Anderson, a Scottish civil engineering company, was given the contract to build the airfield and work began that October, at an estimated cost of £90,000. The buildings on the airfield site were mostly of brick and timber construction, but those on the domestic site on the north side of the road were mainly timber only. All materials were brought to the site from Whittlesford railway station, either by steam-driven lorries or horse-drawn wagons. The work progressed slowly and some of the roads showed signs of subsidence. Local people looked on with mixed feelings and complaints were made about the roads to the County Council and the Police. As the work progressed, more and more men were employed and at one stage it was estimated that a thousand men were working on the project. The cost of the work also began to rise but still progress was slow. In March 1918, United States Army personnel of the 159th Aero Squadron arrived to erect Bessonneaux hangars as a temporary measure to protect aircraft while the main hangars were completed. The permanent hangars would consist of three double-bay and one single-bay Belfast types with wooden concertina-type doors at each end. These buildings took the name from the wooden root trusses they incorporated.

As soon as the Bessonneaux hangars had been completed, the airfield was used as a mobilisation Station and 119, 123 and 129 Squadrons arrived in March and April 1918 with their DH 9 bomber aircraft. They were followed by the arrival of the American 151st, 256th and 268th Aero Squadrons but mostly they were put to work assembling aircraft and like Douglas Bader, fourteen years later, to running the Motor Transport Section. In July 1918 129 Squadron, now part of the Royal Air Force as the RFC had become on 1 April, disbanded. That July 35 Training Depot

Station with a complement of 450 men and 158 women (the latter engaged in clerical and domestic work) opened as part of a new system of RAF pilot training. RAF Duxford did not open officially until September 1918 though the contractors' work was still not finished. The Americans departed soon after Armistice Day, 11 November 1918, and the RAF and Britain's other services were severely reduced in size and equipment. At Duxford building work was more or less complete but the cost had risen to £460,000 and an inquiry was convened to determine what had caused the delay in construction. Duxford remained a permanent post-war RAF station, however, to be used for flying training, and a survey carried out during late 1919 led to a further £355,000 being made available to update the station. Work involved re-roofing the hangars, constructing extra buildings and refurbishment of existing ones. While this work was in progress the aircraft was placed on a 'care and maintenance' basis although in late 1919 No. 8 Squadron arrived from France to disband.

Despite some local opposition the land occupied by the airfield was purchased by the authorities for permanent military use. In April 1920 Duxford re-opened as No. 2 Flying Training School under the command of Wing Commander (later Air Chief Marshal) Sir Wilfred Freeman DSO MC. Flying training using Avro 504s and Bristol Fighters began but there was a shortage of experienced instructors and training suffered as a result. In 1921 Wing Commander Sidney Smith DSO AFC succeeded Sir Wilfred Freeman and pilot training was improved but there were many accidents, some of them fatal. In 1921 flights were made over East Anglia in aircraft fitted with cameras and the photographs taken were used for map making. That same year at the RAF Air Pageant at Hendon, Duxford beat the School of Photography, Farnborough, to take first place in the photographic mapping competition. By 1923 various courses had been devised for pilot training and all places filled. Many of the student pilots who later became famous gained their wings at the school. Among them were Acting Pilot Officer Jim Mollison, who proved to be a 'natural' when in an aircraft and Charles W.A. Scott.[1] At about this time it was decided that Duxford would become a fighter station and on 1 April 1923 19 and 29 Squadrons reformed there to fly Sopwith Snipes. In June 1924 2 FTS left for Digby in Lincolnshire. In January 1925 the Meteorological Flight formed at Duxford with two aircraft initially, but later equipped with Siskins, Hawker Woodcocks, Bristol Bulldogs, Westland Wallaces and Gloster Gauntlets.

The RAF had effectively redrawn the map in defence terms. Duxford's biplane fighters would now be defending the East Midlands and East Anglia. 19 and 29 Squadrons, once settled in at Duxford, were soon joined by 111 Squadron, which reformed on 1 October 1923, flying Gloster Grebes, with which 19 and 29 Squadrons also began to re-equip and 'Treble One' Squadron exchanged its Grebes for Armstrong Whitworth Siskin IIIs. The Squadron used these to carry out trials in high-altitude air combat. This task was carried on for several years, changing aircraft at intervals for variation and improvement reasons. By 1926 111 Squadron was using Siskin IIIAs and in 1927 Squadron Leader Keith B. Park, a New

3

Zealander who was to make his name in the Second World War, took command. In March 1928 111 Squadron left for Hornchurch. Meanwhile, 19 Squadron had re-equipped with Siskin IIIs and later Siskin IIIAs. 29 Squadron was also flying Siskin IIIs and in April 1928 moved to North Weald. 19 Squadron remained at Duxford and began to practise the formation flying and aerobatics for which it later became well known. 111 Squadron had started this trend while at Duxford and 19 Squadron carried on the tradition, flying Bulldog IIAs, which trailed smoke while engaged in formation aerobatics. When in 1935 19 Squadron became the first in the RAF to change to the Gloster Gauntlet, they soon became famous for flying three-aircraft formations with wings tied. The display team, led by Wing Commander (later AVM Sir) Harry Broadhurst, performed displays during the annual air exercises and at Hendon Pageants. By now, Squadron colours were carried and 19 Squadron's light blue and white chequerboard was eye-catching. In 1931 the RAF aerobatic team of Flight Lieutenant Harry Day and Pilot Officer Douglas Bader of 23 Squadron thrilled a tumultuous crowd of 175,000 people with a display of synchronised aerobatics in their Gloster Gamecocks that *The Times* said was 'the most successful of the Hendon displays yet held'. Another future Duxford luminary, Geoffrey Stephenson, was No. 3 in reserve.

At Duxford after Christmas 1932 when the wing commander was away Douglas Bader took the controls during a flight in an Armstrong Whitworth Atlas Army co-operation biplane booked out to Flying Officer Joe Cox, one of the instructors training the Cambridge undergraduates. There had been a link between Duxford and the University of Cambridge since 1 October 1925 when the Cambridge University Air Squadron was formed. An office was set up in Cambridge and by February 1926 flying training had begun at Duxford using Avro 504s. Bader had become friendly with Cox and had persuaded him to let his passenger do most of the flying from his seat in the back. These surreptitious flights continued until one day Bader made a landing on the tarmac runway. These were difficult and not officially approved of and therefore popular. Bader landed the Atlas perfectly with Cox holding his arms high out of the back cockpit to demonstrate that Bader was doing the flying. Just as he landed the biplane onto the runway the wing commander walked round the side of the hangar and saw Cox with his arms aloft and Bader at the controls. Both airmen were severely rebuked but the wing commander took no further action.

Towards the end of April 1933 Bader was sent for by Squadron Leader Sanderson, the 19 Squadron CO and acting station commander who had been 23 Squadron Adjutant at Kenley before Bader lost his legs. Bader walked into Sanderson's office and saluted. Sanderson told him that he had just received a letter from the Air Ministry who he said, had presented him with the most onerous task he ever had to do in the Air Force. In fact, he could not bring himself to read it out. Instead he said to Bader, 'Here, you'd better read it yourself.' The letter said that following the results of his final medical board the Air Council had decided that 'he could no longer be employed in the General Duties Branch of the Royal Air

Force' and that he therefore revert to the retired list 'on the grounds of ill-health'. Sanderson offered his apologies; Bader saluted and stumped out totally dejected. Two weeks later the flying officer donned his sports coat and flannels, dumped his two suitcases in the back of his beloved red MG sports car and drove to the Station Headquarters to present his papers to the adjutant. Minutes later Bader was gone, driving straight past the guardroom out of the gates and turning left on the road to London. Duxford had not seen the last of Douglas Bader but during his unwelcome period of peacetime obscurity the Station became well known to all and sundry.

On Empire Air Day 1934 the airfield held its first air display. Such events were becoming popular and profits were given to the RAF Benevolent Fund. An interesting day was planned, with static exhibitions and flying displays. One of these was 19 Squadron's display team, which left the crowd spellbound, and at the end of the day 2,385 people had passed through the gates, raising £108 and three shillings for the Fund. As impressive as the Empire Air Day was, it was transcended on Saturday 6 July 1935 when King George V carried out the Jubilee Review of the Royal Air Force. After an inspection at Mildenhall, the King and his guests, who included Marshal of the Royal Air Force Lord Trenchard, were driven to Duxford to watch a flypast of all the aircraft from Mildenhall. The King wore the uniform of the RAF for the first time, as did his sons, the Prince of Wales (later King Edward VIII) and the Duke of York (later King George VI). On the drive from Mildenhall, the roads were lined with people eager to see their King, and by the time the procession neared Duxford the crowd had grown to enormous numbers. On arrival, the King and his guests sat down to a lavish lunch in the Officers' Mess, while other guests and senior officers had lunch in one of the hangars, which had been laid out with tables and chairs and decorated. A raised stage was in the centre and on it stood the prototype Gloster Gladiator, the most modern type of RAF aircraft, which was about to enter service. After lunch, His Majesty and guests took their places in a purpose-built stand in front of the hangars. At 2.30 pm the King took the salute as the flypast comprising 182 aircraft, including 19 Squadron's Gauntlets prominently arrayed, flew overhead, the squadrons returning in a wing formation that stretched for nine miles across the Cambridgeshire sky. After the Review, which lasted just thirty minutes, the King and his entourage returned to London by road and an estimated 100,000 people, equally impressed, began heading home.

On the formation of Fighter Command in July 1936, Air Fighting Area became 11 Group and that same month a new expansion squadron, 66, was formed at Duxford from 'C' Flight of 19 Squadron, with Gloster Gauntlets. The two Duxford squadrons used the biplane fighters to perfect combat tactics. When in 1937 12 Group was formed with a headquarters at Watnall, Duxford became its southern station in the new command. Earlier in the 1930s the RAF had instigated an Expansion Plan, which affected Duxford in several ways. New brick-built barracks replaced the old wooden barrack blocks on the north side of the A505. In addition, a new Officers' Mess and Station Headquarters, both of permanent brick construction, were built to the designs approved by the Royal Fine Arts Commission, as was a group of married quarters. RAF Station Duxford was transferred from 11 Group to 12 Group, the Group charged with the defence of the whole of the Midlands area.

On the afternoon of 4 August 1938 Duxford entered into the history books with the arrival of the Spitfire, the world's first monoplane fighter. Vickers Senior Test Pilot, Jeffrey Quill, a small, lean man, just twenty-five with a puckish face that seemingly always had a half-smile, flew K9789 to Duxford for delivery to 19 Squadron. Quill flew down the downwind leg upside down, pumped the wheels up so they came upwards and rolled out to make a beautiful landing!

Reginald Joseph Mitchell's legendary design had flown for the first time on 5 March 1936. Two days later Hitler defied the 1919 Treaty of Versailles and sent a handful of battalions to occupy the demilitarised Rhineland. A few days later he completed his *Anschluss* (union) with Austria. The British Government continued to drag its feet militarily. On 29 September 1938, with Britain and France on the brink of war with Germany, Prime Minister Neville Chamberlain and France's Edouard Daladier met Hitler in Munich and caved in to the dictator's demands. Back home the Munich crisis caused Duxford and all the other RAF Stations to be placed on two hours' alert. Emergency procedures were put into practice, all leave was cancelled and steps were taken to implement the evacuation of service families but within a fortnight, life was back to almost normal. Chamberlain and Daladier had shamefully turned their backs on Czechoslovakia and signed an accord with Hitler who annexed the largely German-speaking Czechoslovakian Sudetenland. Chamberlain returned to Hendon Airport proudly waving a piece of paper signed by Hitler promising that the Sudetenland was the last of his territorial ambitions. Triumphantly the feeble first minister declared that it was 'Peace in our time'. Even if he did not show it, Chamberlain was delusional. Hitler's armies marched in and occupied all of Czechoslovakia on 15 March 1939. No one in Government wanted to shatter the illusion of appeasement and no country it seemed was prepared to stand up to Germany with its Army of 500,000 men and 2,000 aircraft it had secretly built up for three years. Chamberlain simply told the House of Commons that His Majesty's Government would continue to pursue its policy of appeasement. Fighter Command was in no condition to take on the German *Luftwaffe*, being equipped largely with obsolete biplane fighters, although there was at least a newfound sense of urgency to replace them with monoplane fighters.

For 19 Squadron, the remaining months of 1938 were spent converting to the Spitfire, joined by a select few of young pilots – the pick of their squadrons – who beat a path to Duxford to fly the sleek new monoplane. At Hornchurch in December Pilot Officer Roland Robert Stanford Tuck of 65 Squadron was called in and given an early Christmas present. He was to present himself at Duxford to be checked out on the Spitfire by Jeffrey Quill. On one or two occasions Tuck had visited Eastleigh, the Vickers Supermarine Company's experimental airfield in Hampshire, and had watched Quill and his colleagues test fly the first production examples, officially still on the Secret List. He could hardly believe his eyes – 'such speed, such manoeuvrability in a *mono*plane!' Sleek, strong and incredibly high-powered, the Spit represented the fighter of his dreams and he had fallen in love with her at first sight. 'Thirty feet of wicked beauty...'[2] At Duxford, Quill personally took Bob Tuck out to a parked Spitfire I (K9796) and began to teach him the cockpit drill. For over an hour Tuck sat in the thoroughbred fighter while Quill, standing on the wing peering in, ordered him to place his hands on various controls. When he had memorised the precise position of each knob, switch and lever and dial – there seemed to be at least three times as many as in the Gladiator – and could flash a hand to it unerringly, Quill made him do it with his eyes tightly closed. Tuck memorised the sequence – BTFCPUR (brakes, trim, flaps, contacts, petrol, undercarriage and radiator). Finally he took off and Tuck realised that the Spitfire was 'no relation to any of the aircraft he'd flown previously'. Tuck remained at Duxford for just over a week and returned to Hornchurch on 9 January 1939 as one of the RAF's first qualified Spitfire pilots.[3]

A steady stream of Spitfires continued to arrive at Duxford, and 66 Squadron also began to convert onto the type. Gauntlets, Gladiators and other outdated aircraft began to fly into history and the Spitfire reigned supreme at Duxford. Training on the new aircraft continued into 1939. Various problems were overcome, but there was the usual crop of accidents, which happened when new types were introduced. Nevertheless, the pilots and ground crews liked what they had been given. The summer wore on and tension mounted again. 611 (West Lancashire) Squadron of the Royal Auxiliary Air Force arrived on 4 August for summer camp, bringing its Spitfires. The Auxiliaries included pilots who had joined the RAF on short service commissions a year or so earlier and some, like William Johnson Leather, who had read mathematics at Clare College, had been members of the Cambridge University Air Squadron. The Auxiliaries learned that they had been embodied in the RAF for the duration. Squadron Leader James Ellis McComb, the thirty-one-year-old commanding officer who was educated at Stowe and had trained as a solicitor was given command on 3 September. Leather became one of the flight commanders. All three squadrons went to half-hour readiness on 24 August and personnel away from the Station were recalled. Perimeter security was stepped up and on 29 August all reservists were called up. Emergency procedures were once again implemented, including the sandbagging of various installations around the airfield. The day that Hitler's forces invaded Poland, 1 September, saw the general mobilisation of the RAF. Two days later, on Sunday morning the nation turned on their wireless sets and instead of the normal programmes serious music was being played. It was then solemnly announced that the Prime Minister, Neville Chamberlain, would make an announcement. His address began:

> This morning the British Ambassador to Berlin handed the German Government a final note saying that unless we hear from them by 11

o'clock that they were prepared, at once, to withdraw their troops from Poland, a state of war would exist between us. I have to tell you that no such undertaking had been received and that, consequently, this country is at war with Germany.

While Britain and France did nothing, Poland was crushed 'like a soft-boiled egg' and by October ninety per cent of her operational aircraft and seventy per cent of her aircrews had been all but eliminated.

The Station received Signal A34 announcing that war had been declared and security became even tighter. Work began on modification of barracks and other buildings in readiness for WAAF personnel. A false air raid alarm on 6 September kept everyone on their toes and flying movements became hectic. Camouflage paint was applied to the hangars, no civilian clothing was allowed on the Station and air raids or an invasion, or both, were expected at any minute. Neither happened, and life became routine again, but an air of expectancy prevailed. As winter arrived, training flights carried on in the cold and snowy weather, and secret new equipment was sent to Duxford for evaluation. 611 Squadron having departed, 19 and 66 Squadrons were involved in the trials, 66 Squadron working on experiments with VHF radio. These proved to be very successful, but it was found that production problems delayed bulk delivery, severely hampering the RAF's plans to ensure that its pilots had the best equipment available.

By now, patrols were flown daily, and 19 Squadron was even sent on detachment to Catterick, Yorkshire. 66 Squadron spent some time at Horsham St Faith in Norfolk, from where it carried out patrols over the North Sea in connection with shipping and fishing fleet protection. Back at Duxford, 222 Squadron was formed on 5 October 1939 to fly Blenheim Ifs, another new type for Duxford, in the shipping protection role. At the end of the year the weather became intensely cold, but 66 Squadron took its turn to fly patrols out of Horsham St Faith. On days at Duxford, gunnery practice missions at Sutton Bridge (on the Wash) and formation flying went on and life was hectic.

On 11 January 1940, Duxford-based squadrons were involved in their first action of the war. 66 Squadron, while on duty at Horsham St Faith, was scrambled to catch a Heinkel He 111 bomber, which had attacked a trawler. Three Spitfires found and intercepted it, damaging the port engine. The Heinkel was then lost in cloud and the Spitfires returned to base, but the enemy aircraft was later reported to have crashed in Denmark. By the beginning of February 1940, Duxford was snowed in, the winter turning out to be one of the worst on record. All flying ceased, but the newly built, centrally heated barrack blocks were much appreciated by their occupants. One of them was Douglas Bader, who on 7 February 1940 received a telegram telling him that he was posted to 19 Squadron at Duxford. His wife Thelma packed his kit and within two hours the highly elated airman was motoring to Cambridgeshire in his MG once again.[4] Bader arrived around tea time and reported to the new and bigger guardroom he had last seen in 1933 and eight years, one month and twenty-seven days after he had been critically injured and lifted from the wreckage of his Bristol Bulldog at Woodley.

In the time since he had been invalided out of the service, Bader had obtained a job with the Asiatic Petroleum Company (later renamed Shell) and had married. When war had broken out Bader began pestering the RAF and eventually his way back to pilot status came about though his own sheer persistence and refusal to give up. Quite simply, Fighter Command needed pilots, and trained pilots at that. Bader had finally managed to persuade the RAF to take him back and to let him fly operationally following an air test at Central Flying School, Upavon, in October 1939. When he flew the Harvard advanced trainer off the grass at Upavon with Rupert Leigh whom he had last known as a junior cadet at Cranwell, it was the first time that Bader had flown a RAF aircraft since his crash in the Bulldog seven years earlier. Bader flew superbly but as he could not operate the foot brake pedals with his artificial legs, Leigh took care of the braking. Bader flew the trainer around in circuits and landings and then climbed for a roll and a loop before landing again. He was exultant. Leigh said he would ask for Bader to return to the CFS for a full refresher course. In the interim when nothing more was heard, Bader had lobbied people such as his old Cranwell chum Squadron Leader Geoffrey D Stephenson who was leaving a desk job at the Air Ministry to take command of 19 Squadron at Duxford. Towards the end of November the Air Ministry envelope arrived informing Bader that they would take the former flying officer back, as a regular officer re-employed in his former rank and seniority. The refresher flight on 27 November in an Avro Tutor went well – even a little too well. On the first twenty-five-minute flight he flew dual and then went solo again and Bader flew the biplane inverted in the circuit area at 600 feet! On 4 December he piloted a Fairey Battle. Early in the New Year he flew the Miles Master and the Hawker Hurricane. The eight-gun monoplane fighter first flew on 6 November 1935 but it had not entered service until January 1938 and squadrons had become operational as soon as they could. Bader made up for lost time too, so quickly that it was as if he had never been away. At the end of January 1940 Joe Cox said, 'Well you might as well crack off to a squadron'. Bader immediately rang Geoffrey Stephenson, now in command of 19 Squadron at Duxford, where in 1933 he had left under cloud. Stephenson was glad to welcome him 'home'. Not for the first time, history was repeating itself again.

Douglas Bader was two weeks short of his thirtieth birthday and he noted that just about all the other pilots on 19 and 222 Squadrons were younger, by a few years. The last time he had known H.W. 'Tubby' Mermagen, an old friend with whom he used to play rugby, he was a pilot officer. But he was now a squadron leader in command of 222 Squadron, which was flying Blenheim Ifs but would soon convert to Spitfires and move to Lincolnshire, only returning south later to forward airfields for the battles ahead. Stephenson, who like Bader had first been commissioned in July 1930, soon got him fixed up on the Spitfire and a 'boy of twenty' showed Bader the cockpit layout. Bader flew the Spitfire before landing neatly.

On 13 February Flight Lieutenant Philip 'Tommy' Pinkham led Bader up for his first formation flying in a Spitfire. The twenty-five-year-old flight commander, born in Wembley and educated at Kilburn Grammar School, had worked for an insurance company and was a part-time soldier in the London Yeomanry before entering the RAF on a short service commission. Like Bader, he had flown Bulldogs, on 17 Squadron, and later, Gauntlets of the Met Flight at Mildenhall in 1937 before becoming an instructor. Bader was determined to show him and everyone else for that matter, what he was made of and he tucked his wing in about three feet behind Pinkham's and remained there for the rest of the flight. Coming into land Pinkham dipped low beside a wooden hut. Fortunately Bader was astute enough to take his eyes off his leader and look ahead for a second. At the last moment he saw the hut beneath the long mullet-head cowling that housed the Merlin engine, shoved on throttle and yanked back on the stick. His tail wheel ploughed through the roof of the hut but the Spitfire remained airborne and he landed safely. Pinkham came across the field laughing. He said, 'Awfully sorry ol' boy. Most extraordinary thing – d'you know not long ago I landed a chap in a tree just the same way.' Bader tore him off a strip and left him in no doubt about his 'character'.[5] A few days later Bader made his first operational flight with a convoy patrol off the East Coast. The Squadron flew patrols from Horsham St Faith near Norwich.

Most days were spent practising the three officially approved methods of attacking bombers known as 'Fighter Command Attack No. 1, 2 and 3'. In 'Attack No. 1' for instance, the fighters were supposed to swing into line astern behind the leader and follow him in an orderly line up to the bomber. Then they fired a three-second burst when their turn came in the queue before swinging 'gracefully' away after the leader again, presenting their bellies predictably to the enemy gunner. The magnificent CO of 74 Squadron, Adolph Gysbert 'Sailor' Malan, whose nickname came about as a result of service as a Third Officer with the Union Castle Steamship Line and who was one of twenty-three South African pilots in the Battle of Britain, was disgusted with this outdated theory. So too was Douglas Bader. Bob Stanford Tuck, who was posted to 92 Squadron as a flight commander on 1 May 1940, saw what he called the 'tight "guardsman" formations as counter productive because pilots were too preoccupied watching each others wingtips to keep their eyes peeled for enemy fighters'. Fighter Command theoreticians' long-held belief was that modern fighters were too fast for the dogfight tactics employed in the First World War but Bader's steadfast opinion was that nothing had changed. Height was everything and the old adage 'Beware the Hun in the sun' was as true as it ever was when his heroes, McCudden, Billy Bishop and Albert Ball, had hunted Fokkers over the Western Front. 'He who has the height controls the battle. He who has the sun achieves surprise. He who gets in close shoots down them down.' This was the credo in 1914–18 and it would be the same in this war. Bader told Stephenson that the only way to shoot down a bomber was for everyone to 'pile in together' from each side as close to the enemy aircraft as they could and then let him 'have the lot'; all sixteen or twenty-four machine-guns instead of just eight. Stephenson simply said that he might be right but that they had to keep on doing what they were told until they 'found out for themselves'.

Where flying was concerned Bader certainly kept on doing things the way that he had always done them, such as on one March evening, flying low-level straight and level slow rolls over a deserted Duxford just before dusk when he thought no one was looking. The rolls, one to the right followed by one to the left, continued right down to just below hanger height level. However, it did not escape the attention of Wing Commander 'Pingo' Lester, the Duxford station commander, who rebuked him with 'I do wish you wouldn't do that. You had such a nasty accident last time'.[6] A few days later, on 31 March, he took off in a Spitfire from Horsham St Faith but the fighter would not leave the ground. He had forgotten to change the pitch of the propeller from coarse to fine and the Spitfire simply refused to take off. It cart wheeled and hit the boundary fence at the far end of the airfield at some speed. Bader was unhurt but the same could not be said of his pride. The Spitfire was a write-off, as were his artificial legs but he immediately put on a spare pair and carried on flying. On 1 June he scored the first of his twenty aerial victories when he shot down a Bf 109E over Dunkirk and also was awarded a half share in an He 111 'probable'. On 13 June, having been promoted to flight lieutenant and given command of 'A' Flight in 'Tubby' Mermagen's 222 Squadron, he overshot the flarepath at Duxford in bad weather and his Spitfire finished up in a heap at the edge of the airfield.[7]

The Advanced Air Striking Force and 70 Wing RAF had gone to France to support the British Expeditionary Force (BEF) but generally speaking Germany had been content to carry on preparing and planning for her forthcoming Blitzkrieg.[8] The Allies on the other hand, would not allow themselves to believe that the war would ever really start in earnest. Leaders like Neville Chamberlain, Britain's Prime Minister, seemed to believe that his appeals to the German people for peace would be accepted. The period became known as the 'Phoney War' or the Sitzkrieg; when either side in the conflict took little aggressive action. Chamberlain claimed that 'Hitler has missed the bus' but on 9 April Norway was invaded by the Germans and on 10 May the Phoney War ended with the German western offensive and the invasion of Holland, Belgium and Luxembourg. Chamberlain resigned that same day and Winston Churchill took over as British Prime Minister. German armour penetrated the French line near Sedan and began its thrust to the coast. At Duxford on that same day 264 Squadron, which flew Defiants, arrived. Douglas Bader motored over to the 'Red Lion' at Whittlesford where his wife Thelma was staying and brought her back to Duxford for lunch in the Mess. Squadron Leader Rupert Leigh, another of Bader's Cranwell chums, who now commanded 66 Squadron, told them excitedly that the real war had begun. Bader was elated. Soon there were rumours that 19 Squadron would be sent to France in support of the BEF.[9] On 22 May 'Tubby' Mermagen's Squadron received orders for a posting to Kirton-in-Lindsey just south of the Humber and they and their eighteen Spitfires had to leave by 1500 hours.[10] A few days later armour plate for 19 Squadron's Spitfires arrived by road. When on 26 May the order was given to evacuate as many British troops as possible via the 1,000-year old port of Dunkirk, 19 Squadron was ordered to Hornchurch, 264 Squadron to Manston. Both were to fly covering patrols for the BEF.[11] Their place at Duxford was taken temporarily, for ten days at the end of the month, by 92 Squadron's Spitfires. When 66 Squadron returned they began sending detachments to Martlesham Heath.

At Hornchurch 19 Squadron began ten days of covering Operation *Dynamo*, the BEF's withdrawal from France, which began early on 26 May. Only a dozen Spitfires were available and more men than machines so the Squadron pilots drew lots to see who would fly them. Squadron Leader Geoffrey Stephenson led his Squadron off at breakfast time and over the French coast near Calais they saw twenty Ju 87s apparently unescorted attacking the troops on the beaches. When one section, led by Flight Lieutenant George Eric Ball, broke off to engage the *Stukas* about thirty quicksilver Bf 109s appeared. Stephenson ordered a 'Fighting Area Attack No. 2', which meant a very slow overtaking speed in formation 'vics' of three, attacking with a very slow overtaking speed so that pilots could get a very good burst of fire at the enemy aircraft. The German dive-bombers were fairly easy prey and 19 Squadron's pilots claimed ten *Stukas* shot down before the Messerschmitts intervened. A cannon shell hit the Spitfire flown by Pilot Officer P.V. 'Watty' Watson who baled out and disappeared. The twenty-year-old Canadian-born pilot was never seen again. Squadron Leader Stephenson's Spitfire was reportedly seen making a copybook Fighter Command Attack No. 2 on a *Stuka* whose single rear gun had stopped his engine, forcing him down, heading inland in a shallow glide, trailing blue glycol smoke. He was later reported to be a prisoner. Flying Officer Bell received head and arm injuries. George Ball was awarded a confirmed Bf 109E shot down.[12] Flight Lieutenant Brian John Edward 'Sandy' Lane, at twenty-two years old, one of the flight commanders on the Squadron, claimed a Ju 87 and two Bf 109Es but only one of the Messerschmitts was confirmed.[13] Lane oozed energy and a cheerful personality and the tall good looking pilot with permanent dark circles under his eyes, which gave him a misleading slightly dissolute look, was given temporary command of the Squadron. There were many who believed that he should have been given the command on a permanent basis. Despite his obvious lack of combat experience, though none would doubt his sense of duty and diligence, Squadron Leader 'Tommy' Pinkham became 19 Squadron's new commanding officer.

On the second patrol a large force of Bf 109s was engaged, three being claimed for the loss of two Spitfires. Sergeant CA Irwin was killed. Pilot Officer Michael D. Lyne, who was shot in the knee, nursed his Spitfire back across the Channel and crash-landed on Walmer Beach near Deal. Irwin was an ex-fitter who had retrained before the war as a pilot. Before the war many ex-riggers and fitters successfully retrained to become sergeant pilots and the best three Halton apprentices each year were offered a cadetship at Cranwell. Nevertheless, apprentices who received flying training did so on the understanding that they would return to their trades after five years. By the time war broke out about a quarter of the pilots in the RAF squadrons were NCOs. One of them was Flight Sergeant George Cecil Unwin. He was twenty-five years old and from Bolton-on-Dearne in South Yorkshire where his father was a miner. Unwin's mother encouraged her son's education and he won a scholarship to Wath Grammar School and aged sixteen passed his Northern Universities matriculation exam. Money was short, however, and it seemed the only option was to follow his father down the mine but in 1929 the determined youngster enlisted in the RAF instead. He chose Ruislip administrative apprentice school rather than the technical school at Halton as the course was shorter by a year and he passed out in 1931 as a leading aircraftsman, becoming an apprentice clerk in Records. In November 1935 he was selected for pilot training. Finally, in August 1936 the sergeant pilot was posted to 19 Squadron at Duxford where his flight commander was Flight Lieutenant Harry Broadhurst, an ex-Army officer and veteran of the North-West Frontier who figured largely in building 19 Squadron's reputation for aerobatic excellence at Hendon in the 1930s. Unwin became one of the first pilots in the RAF to fly Spitfires. On 3 March 1939 Unwin deliberately crashed his Spitfire following an engine failure, to avoid hitting some children playing in a field in which he was attempting to force-land. One of his best friends on the Squadron was Flight Sergeant Harry 'Bill' Steere, an ex-Halton apprentice who had attended secondary school in Wallasey. Steere had volunteered for pilot training and had also joined 19 Squadron as a sergeant pilot. By 1940 he was a flight sergeant and on 11 May he had shared in the Squadron's first victory when a Ju 88 was shot down about forty miles east of the Dudgeon lightship. Over Dunkirk he achieved some considerable success, destroying a *Stuka*, a Bf 109E and a Do 17 and half shares in two other victories.

Unwin had been left out of the first patrol on 26 May due to the shortage of Spitfires. His anger gained him the nickname, 'Grumpy', which remained with him thereafter. Unwin, who flew forty hours over Dunkirk in ten days, thought that it was a 'frightful nonsense' to send such inexperienced pilots against the French front.

> Flying in threes turned out to be crazy. If you weren't flying in threes and you want to turn quickly you can't without running into the other fellow. The Germans knew all this and they flew in twos [a *Rotte*]. We had to pick all this up and reorganise our attacks accordingly.

On 27 May when three of 19 Squadron pilots attacked a Henschel 126 near Ypres the victory was awarded to the dour Yorkshireman, who recalled later:

> The most dangerous period, certainly in my life and in many, many others, was my first fight, because despite all my experience, I admit I was in trouble. The first time you're shot at and most of the fighter pilots agreed with me, you freeze. I did. I suddenly saw a Messerschmitt coming up

inside me and I saw little sparks coming from the front end of him. I knew he was shooting at me and I did nothing, absolutely nothing. I just sat there, in a turn, not petrified but frozen for I don't know – ten or fifteen seconds. But never again did I do that. After that you don't hesitate; you've been blooded. But despite all my experience I just sat there and watched him shoot at me. Stupid thing to do I know, but fortunately he knocked a few little holes in the back of my aircraft and did no damage at all. And didn't hit me luckily. From then on, of course, you realise what a mug you were and you never do it again. But I suppose it's just one isn't used to being shot at in any walk of life and I suppose most people finding someone shooting at them would freeze anyway wondering what on earth's happening. From then on it never happened again. I was hit again, quite often, not for the same reason, not my own fault; put it that way.

In all, 19 Squadron claimed five victories, two of them unconfirmed. On 28 May Flying Officer John Petrie's altimeter was shot away and small pieces of metal lodged in his leg during a fight with Bf 109s. 'Grumpy' Unwin was credited with the destruction of a Bf 109E. He recalled, 'You were there to destroy the aeroplane, that was the target, you never thought of the bloke in it. Actually, if ever a man had a hot seat it was the poor Messerschmitt pilot, because he was sitting on his petrol tank! His aeroplane was flying perfectly in all right in a turn and then suddenly, it was a ball of flame.' On 1 June Unwin scored his third victory when he downed a twin-engined Messerschmitt Bf 110 north-east of Dunkirk. Claims for another Bf 110 and a He 111 were unconfirmed.

Sergeant John Alfred Potter's oil cooler was hit and when the engine seized at 4,000 feet, fifteen miles from the English coast, the twenty-five-year-old from Wallasey in Cheshire was forced to ditch in the Channel. After leaving school Potter had worked for his uncle, a builder, in Liverpool before he had been posted to 19 Squadron, early in 1937. Over Dunkirk on 26 May he had destroyed a Bf 109. Now, he was heading for the beleaguered French seaport once again. A small French fishing boat picked him up and as they approached Dunkirk, HMS *Basilisk*, a Royal Navy destroyer, was seen, stopped in the water. Its engines had been put out of action by the bombing and the French crew agreed to tow the destroyer further out to sea. Towing was interrupted when German bombers appeared overhead but towing began again after 19 Squadron's Spitfires drove them off. Ju 87 *Stukas* then appeared and their bombs sank the destroyer. The French fishing boat took off 200 men and another destroyer arrived to pick up more survivors. Potter was transferred to a coastal patrol boat and he was eventually landed at Dover. In all, 19 Squadron flew eleven patrols over the Dunkirk area until the evacuation from the port was completed[14] and they flew back to Duxford on 6 June having claimed twenty-four German aircraft for the loss of six Spitfires. Between 26 May and 2 June *Luftwaffe* bombers had flown just over 1,000 sorties, losing forty-five aircraft.

In a speech to the House of Commons on 4 June Winston Churchill said:

Even though large tracts of Europe and many old and famous States have fallen or may fall into the grip of the *Gestapo* and all the odious apparatus of Nazi rule, we shall not flag or fail. We shall go on to the end, we shall fight in France, we shall fight on the seas and oceans, we shall fight with growing confidence and growing strength in the air, we shall defend our island, whatever the cost may be, we shall fight on the beaches, we shall fight on the landing grounds, we shall fight in the fields and in the streets, we shall fight in the hills; we shall never surrender...

The Dunkirk evacuation had shaken the British people out of their complacency and a new sense of urgency was in the air. Security at sector airfields like Duxford was tightened up though it was possible to obtain a pass to visit Cambridge or the local pubs. The Home Guard (Local Defence Volunteers) manned a guard post at the junction of the main road and Flowerpot Lane, the road to Duxford village and the 'Flowerpot' and 'Plough' public houses. It was sometimes more difficult to pass the LDVs than the guards on Duxford airfield's main gate. In the summer of 1940, people expected Hitler's army to arrive at any time but Churchill refused to consider peace on German terms and Hitler realised that he might have to invade Britain. He code-named his invasion *Seelöwe* (Sea Lion). If the *Luftwaffe* failed to win control of the skies, an invasion would be impossible because German invaders would be under constant air attack. *Reichsmarschall* Hermann Göring, the chief of the *Luftwaffe*, believed that the *Luftwaffe* would easily defeat the RAF, and so the German *Wehrmacht* and *Kriegsmarine* prepared to invade.

On the night of 5/6 June the *Luftwaffe* carried out the first raids on England since the Zeppelin attacks of the First World War. The very next night German raiders attacked the Cambridge and Duxford area, dropping one incendiary bomb in a field at Thriplow, a mile and a half north-west of Duxford airfield. 19 Squadron began flying night patrols but this was very much a hit-and-miss affair with little success. Around midnight on 18/19 June four pilots of 'B' Flight were ordered to engage He 111P bombers of 4th *Staffel*, KG 4 in the Mildenhall area. Flying Officer John Petrie, who was almost killed in the fighting above Dunkirk when an explosive bullet from a Bf 109 he never even saw had shattered his instrument panel, spotted one of the Heinkels held in a searchlight near Newmarket. The ex-Cranwell cadet followed the bomber as it headed for Honington. Searchlights repeatedly lighted the Heinkel and Petrie fired, just as a Blenheim night fighter from 23 Squadron also closed to attack. Smoke billowed from the bomber and the upper gunner returned fire and ignited Petrie's fuel tank. Petrie, his face and hands badly burned, baled out and the Spitfire crashed at Whelnetham station. The Heinkel jettisoned its bomb load east of Newmarket before crashing on the Newmarket to Royston road near Fulbourn. All four crew baled out but *Unteroffizier* Paul Gorsh's parachute got caught on the tail and he went down with the aircraft and he was killed. *Feldwebel* Maier was apprehended by a Cameron Highlander who ordered the German pilot to surrender. Maier said that it was pointless taking him prisoner, as the *Führer* would be in London within the week. His Scottish captor replied, 'Prisoner? Who said anything about taking prisoners?' Maier, however, was entertained in the Officers' Mess at Duxford, as was the custom, at least according to 'Ace' Pace, one of the pilots on 19 Squadron, who had studied the aces and traditions of the RFC pilots in the First World War. Maier reiterated that the *Führer* would be in London soon to which one of the Spitfire pilots said that he had been in the capital an hour earlier and all looked perfectly normal. *Feldwebel* Maier broke down in tears and he had his pint of beer in the 'ladies'.

Eric Ball followed another He 111 to ten miles north of Colchester where, helped by searchlights, he set the Heinkel on fire and it in turn crashed near Margate with all the crew killed. In all, the *Luftwaffe* lost five Heinkel 111s to the combined night defences of the area. Toward the end of the month the night raids diminished, but the night patrols continued. On 18 June in a speech delivered first to the House of Commons and then broadcast over the BBC later that evening Winston Churchill said:

> What General Weygand called the Battle of France is over.[15] I expect that the Battle of Britain is about to begin. Upon this battle depends our own British life and the long continuity of our institutions and our Empire. The whole fury and might of the enemy must very soon be turned on us. Hitler knows that he will have to break us in this island or lose the war. If we can stand up to him, all Europe may be free and the life of the world may move forward into broad, sunlit uplands. But if we fail, then the whole world, including the United States, including all that we have known and eared for, will sink into the abyss of a new dark age made more sinister and perhaps more protracted, by the lights of perverted science. Let us therefore brace ourselves to our duties and so bear ourselves that, if the British Empire and its Commonwealth last for a thousand years, men will still say: 'This was their finest hour'.

The Prime Minister's rhetoric with its Shakespearean overtones produced loud and prolonged cheers in the chamber and boosted morale as well as showing the world that Britain was not finished. Two days later the House went into Secret Session to hear his statement on the situation following the French debacle. Most knew that Mr Churchill's inspiring and uplifting words in public could not conceal a stark reality that Britain was open to invasion, although the 'thin blue line' would have to be overrun first before German troops could land. The battle for survival that lay ahead could not be fought by RAF Fighter Command without the chain of twenty-nine radio location (radar) stations situated around the approaches to Britain that stood like sentinels between the Bristol Channel and Land's End and the Orkneys. Each had about 150 miles' range at 18,000 feet and almost all the south and east coasts were covered down to about 600 feet at forty miles' range.[16] The early warning system was backed up by the 'mark one eyeballs' of the Observer Corps made up of thirty-two centres whose 30,000 volunteers manned over 1,000 posts around the clock monitoring the height, speed and strength of the enemy formations overhead. All of the information detected by radar and the Observer Corps watchers was passed to the sector stations and to Bentley Priory enabling the sector controllers in the bomb proof sector Operations rooms deep underground to have a complete picture on the large plotting tables in front of them.

The sector control rooms were presided over by experienced career officers like Wing Commander Alfred Basil Woodhall at Duxford. 'Woody' Woodhall was a South African who in 1914 had been a lance corporal in the Witwatersrand Rifles before joining the Royal Marines. During the early twenties he had flown biplane torpedo bombers before transferring to the RAF in 1929. When war came, Woodhall had a desk job at the Air Ministry and he was posted to Duxford on 12 March 1940 as senior controller. Ubiquitous WAAFs wearing headsets plotted the raids on table maps, dutifully moving each one around the grids like in a board game with croupier rakes as the enemy raids developed. On the wall, a five minutes coloured change clock ticked away and a 'tote' recorded all details of enemy raids and fighters sent to intercept. Sector station Operations rooms were the nerve centre and crucial but above all else, the Battle ahead was ultimately in the skilled hands and sharp eyes of the fighter pilots, or Dowding's 'chicks' as they came to be called. No one was counting their chickens, certainly none more so than AOC himself.

1   Mollison and his wife, the famous aviatrix Amy Johnson, flew *Black Magic*, one of three DH 88 Comet Racers in the MacRobertson Air Race from Mildenhall to Australia in October 1934. Tom Campbell Black and Charles W.A. Scott won the race in *Grosvenor House*. Amy Johnson made several record flights including those to Cape Town and back in 1936 before she met her death as an Air Transport Auxiliary (ATA) pilot in January 1941 while ferrying an Airspeed Oxford in bad weather from Prestwick in Scotland. HMS *Hazlemere* patrolling off Herne Bay, spotted a parachute coming out of the clouds and dropping into the sea. The CO jumped overboard and tried to reach her but both were drowned and Amy's body was never recovered. Jim Mollison, who also served in the ATA, remained convinced right to the end of his life that she had been shot down. Campbell Black was killed at Liverpool Aerodrome in 1936 when an incoming plane struck his stationary aircraft. See *Mildenhall: Bombers, Blackbirds and the Boom Years* by Martin W Bowman (Tempus 2007).

2   *Fly For Your Life* by Larry Forrester (Frederick Muller Ltd 1956)

3   *Fly For Your Life* by Larry Forrester (Frederick Muller Ltd 1956)

4   Later Bader brought his wife down to stay at the 'Red Lion' at Whittlesford

just outside Duxford. 'Her landlady was a formidable woman known as "The Sea Lion" because of a tendency to a straggling black moustache. She dominated everyone and Thelma was getting a little restive until Douglas gave The Sea Lion the benefit of his overwhelming personality, fixing her eyes with his glittering eyes and speaking a few forceful words. The Sea Lion and he became great friends after that and Thelma was happy.' *Reach For the Sky* by Paul Brickhill (Collins 1954).

5   See *Reach For the Sky*. Pinkham has been described by Wing Commander D.G.S.R. Cox, a sergeant pilot in 1940, as a 'real gentleman'. 'He treated a sergeant pilot the same as he would treat an air marshal.' (*Fighter Boys* by Patrick Bishop (Harper Perennial 2004).

6   *Flying Colours: The Epic Story of Douglas Bader* by Laddie Lucas (Hutchinson 1981).

7   On 24 June 1940 ACM Trafford Leigh-Mallory gave Douglas Bader command of 242 (Canadian) Squadron languishing at RAF Coltishall. On 11 July Squadron Leader Bader claimed his second victory, a Dornier Do 17Z off Cromer. It was the first of eleven victories Bader scored while leading 242 Squadron before he was promoted to Wing Commander Flying of the Tangmere Wing in March 1941.

8   In late September when Lord Gort's BEF moved across the English Channel to France, four Hurricane squadrons – 1, 73 85 and 87 – went with them. By mid-November two more squadrons – 607 and 615, equipped with Gloster Gladiators – were sent to reinforce them. All political attempts to persuade the RAF to send Spitfires to France were resisted but the movement of the Hurricanes and the Gladiators left Dowding with about thirty-five on paper for the defence of Britain. On 15 May Winston Churchill promised France's Premier, Paul Reynaud, ten fighter squadrons. On 16 May any thoughts of sending fighter squadrons to France was vetoed emphatically by Sir Cyril Newall, Chief of the Air Staff. He told Churchill that he did not think that a few more fighter squadrons would make any difference between victory and defeat in France. By then the ten Hurricane squadrons in France had lost 195 Hurricanes. Some squadrons were down to two and three fighters and another had lost twenty-six pilots. One of the worst hit was 242 Squadron. Between May and June 1940 the all-Canadian fighter squadron had lost every pilot of flying officer rank and middle echelon officers, over enemy territory. Flying Officer Russ Wiens had noted: 'The war in the air today makes shows like *Dawn Patrol* look like Sunday School.' *The Few, Summer 1940, the Battle of Britain*, by Philip Kaplan and Richard Collier (Orion 2002).

9   Holland capitulated on 15 May in the face of the German onslaught and on

28 May Belgium surrendered.

10   Mermagen joined 266 Squadron on 12 September 1940 to assume temporary command. He was awarded the AFC and retired in 1960 as Air Commodore CB CBE AFC.

11   264 Squadron was stood down at Duxford on 31 May. 264 Squadron's claims for May were fifty-six enemy aircraft destroyed for the loss of fourteen Defiants.

12   George Eric Ball, from Tankerton, Kent, joined the RAF in April 1937. After training he was posted to 19 Squadron in February 1938.

13   Brian John Edward 'Sandy' Lane was born on 18 June 1917 in Harrogate, North Yorkshire. He attended St Paul's public school, joining the RAF on a short service commission in 1936 when he lost his job as a supervisor in an electric bulb factory. On completion of training he was posted to 66 Squadron in January 1937, but in June moved to 213 Squadron. Shortly after the outbreak of war he was posted to 19 Squadron as a flight commander.

14   By 4 June over 338,226 troops had been rescued from France.

15   On 22 June France concluded an Armistice with Germany. France capitulated on 25 June, freeing more than 400 *Luftwaffe* prisoners of war. The campaign in the West had cost the German Air Force 147 *Stukas* and 635 bombers.

16   *Battle Over Britain* by Francis K. Mason (McWhirter Twins Ltd 1969).

CHAPTER TWO

Dowding's Chicks and Bader's Boys

Why marry now when there is only England left?
Marry later to celebrate the victory.

Werner 'Vati' (Daddy) Mölders JG 51, 6 August 1940

On 14 July 1936 Air Marshal Sir Hugh Caswall Tremenheere Dowding, a fifty-four-year-old widower wedded to the service, had become the first Air Officer Commander in Chief of Fighter Command at the 166-year old Bentley Priory, atop a hill at Stanmore just north of London. Three days later civil war broke out in Spain. While the German *Legion Kondor* put the war to good use, sending 370 handpicked pilots and aircrew, devised tactics and honed its skills, Dowding set about making good 'some lamentable deficiencies' at Fighter Command. Appearing remote and aloof earned him the nickname 'Stuffy' but he had the interest of his pilots at heart and no detail escaped his attention, even the need for bullet-proof glass for fighter aircraft. His requests were met with the customary penny pinching arguments until he reminded them that if it was seen as essential for cars owned by Chicago gangsters then it was equally essential for his pilots. Dowding recognised the potential afforded by new fighters and radar and to this he soon introduced Operations rooms at all Commands. (In November 1940 he said that 'The war will be won by science thoughtfully applied to operational requirements'.) He also saw the need for all-weather runways. In 1938 the Air Council had informed Air Chief Marshal Dowding that his retirement date was set for the end of June 1940. In July 1940 the Air Staff asked him to defer retirement until the end of October. As of 1 July, RAF Fighter Command Order of Battle, on paper at least, stood at fifty-six operational squadrons in three Groups. However, the attrition in France and unserviceability of machines meant that over the south of England just 312 RAF fighters (twenty-nine squadrons in 11 Group) were available to face 2,000 *Luftwaffe* fighters and bombers. Eleven more fighter squadrons, equipped with only 113 serviceable Spitfires, Defiants, Hurricanes and Blenheim Ifs, were in 12 Group, with 19 and 264 Squadrons at Duxford and the rest stationed at four more airfields from Norfolk to Lincolnshire.[1]

If the situation regarding the number of aircraft available was parlous the shortage of available pilots was critical. Many experienced pilots had been lost in France where the fighting over Dunkirk alone had cost four squadron commanders, seven flight commanders and about twelve section leaders killed or taken prisoner.[2] The wounded and battered remnants of the squadrons returned to England, to be re-equipped (patched up might be a better term) and to receive newly trained airmen. Some had to be taken out of the front line altogether and moved north to quieter backwaters to begin again. Two squadrons were soon regarded as non-operational through lack of aircraft. Another had only seven pilots fit to fly operationally while another had twenty-three pilots on operational strength but only half its ground crew were available. On 1 July 19 Squadron's strength, officially, was only eight Spitfires and five of these were unserviceable. On the same date 264 Squadron had eleven Defiants available, only seven of which were serviceable. On 3 July 19 Squadron again moved to Fowlmere complete with sleeping huts for the pilots and tents for the ground staff, cooking tender, PBX telephone exchange and the Welch Regiment to guard them, for what amounted to a twenty-one-day sojourn. The village had no shop and only two pubs. The officers frequented the 'Chequers' and the landlord did not want the ground staff. Their abode was the 'Black Horse' where they had beer and played a lot of cards including gambling games, which were illegal but everyone turned a blind eye to it.[3]

'Fowlmere had many good features', recalled Wallace 'Jock' Cunningham, 'including a reduction in red tape, the main snag being that their kit was still at Duxford, where they had to go once a week for a real bath.' The twenty-four-year old Glaswegian had joined the RAFVR at the time of Munich and flew at weekends at Prestwick flying school. Their instructors were ex-RAF gathered around the nucleus of the 1933 Mount Everest Flight – Squadron Leader the Marquess of Douglas and Clydesdale, Flight Lieutenant D. MacIntyre, Capper and Ellison. 'All like characters from *Boy's Own Paper*.[4] The Tiger Moths and Hawker Harts that they flew from a grass field were single engined biplanes, open cockpit and with all the nostalgic smells of dope (fabric), hot oil and antiquity.'[5] At the same time Cunningham was studying at the Royal Technical College in the last year of his diploma in mechanical engineering, which he completed in May 1939. In the spring of 1940 he gained his wings and at the end of familiarisation, in June 1940, he was posted to 19 Squadron – 'a glum posting'. Passing through London on the train journey to Duxford he encountered dome soldiers returned from Dunkirk. Their comments about the absence of the RAF over the beaches made him feel personally responsible for the evacuation. At Fowlmere Sub-Lieutenant Arthur

Giles Blake, a twenty-three-year-old FAA pilot from HMS *Daedalus* at Lee-on-Solent who converted to fighters at 7 OTU, Hawarden, before joining 19 Squadron in July, became messing officer. 'Admiral' Blake joined the Royal Navy in early 1939 and had passed out from the Royal Naval College, Greenwich. Peter Howard-Williams ran the bar. The problem for the latter was keeping the beer cool enough to prevent it going off during the warm weather; a case of 'Drink up, gentlemen'.[6] Howard-Williams was a twenty-one-year-old Cranwellian – a foreshortened course here in 1939 allowed him to be posted to 19 Squadron in March 1940. In early 1941 he joined 118 Squadron and he finished the war with four enemy aircraft destroyed flying Spitfires in 118 and 610 Squadrons. His brother Jeremy was a night-fighter pilot with 604 Squadron and also received a DFC.

After the defeat of their homeland in March 1939 many of the Czech Air Force pilots had escaped to France where they flew with the *Armée de l'Air* until the fall of France and had then escaped to England to join the RAF. At Duxford, on 10 July, 310 Squadron (Czechoslovakia) had become the first unit to be formed in the RAF with foreign nationals, being equipped with Hurricane Is. On 18 July Squadron Leader George Douglas M. 'Bill' Blackwood, an old Etonian and an Edinburgh publisher in peacetime, arrived from 213 Squadron to take command of the three dozen Czech pilots.[7] Apart from Flying Officer Cesek, the interpreter, none of the Czechs on the unit could speak a word of French or English. Yet from 18 June onwards, when the first contingent of Czechs emerged from a heavy bomber in southern England, they took infinite pains to demonstrate their willingness. When the contractor assembling their hutted camp at Duxford bemoaned the shortage of hands, 310, under Squadron Leader Alexander 'Sasha' Hess, one of the oldest pilots in the Battle of Britain having been born in 1899, weighed in as builders' labourers. Then they donated the £10 they received in wages from the contractor to the Czechoslovak Red Cross in London. Language, one flight commander, Flight Lieutenant Gordon Leonard Sinclair, was to recall, proved a problem so acute that 'We just put them into the cockpit and said "Fly". Only that way could we find out whether they were navigators, bomb aimers or – what we badly wanted – pilots'.[8] The twenty-four-year-old, whose hometown was Eastbourne, was a pre-war entrant who had joined the RAF on a short service commission in March 1937. He had previously served on 19 Squadron since November 1937 and had seen considerable action with 19 Squadron over Dunkirk in May and June, destroying two Bf 109Es, a couple of Bf 110s, a He 111 and a Do 17. At the end of June he had been awarded a DFC. Blackwood's other British flight commander was Flight Lieutenant Jerrard Jeffries, who while flying with 17 Squadron had downed a Hs 126 over France on 11 May.[9] 'Jock' Cunningham, one of three Scottish pilots in 19 Squadron, which was also composed of New Zealanders, Canadians, South Africans, Rhodesians, English and Czechs, recalls:

Our friends from overseas tended to be mature and experienced pilots. In particular, the Czechs had a healthy hatred of the enemy and – despite some difficulties with the language – they also made a great contribution to the social life of the Duxford area. I recall Stanislav Plzak.[10] writing to his girlfriend in Cambridge and asking, 'Jock, what is the difference between "beautiful" and "bloody fool"?' I cannot vouch for it but a young WAAF requested an interview with her section officer to discuss a problem she had. The SO asked if she had a check-up and got the answer, 'No, it was a wee Glasgow laddie.'

When General Karel Janousek later presented Cunningham with the Czechoslovakian Air Force wings, which he was very proud to receive, he was told by the Czechs he flew with that the wings gave the recipient free admittance to the underground and the brothels of Prague. Cunningham says, 'That was untrue – at that time Prague did not have an underground.'[11]

Eighty-seven Czechoslovaks flew with the RAF during the Battle of Britain. Determined never to lose face in front of their RAF hosts, the Czechs (and the Poles) had a summary way with anyone who 'let the side down'. On one occasion a Czech NCO in an abortive take-off tipped a Hurricane clumsily on its nose. Immediately Squadron Leader 'Sasha' Hess led the miscreant summarily behind a hangar, prompting Bill Blackwood to intervene. Fisticuffs between officers and NCOs he stressed were strictly forbidden in the RAF. 'Fists?' echoed Hess, appalled by such a plebian suggestion. 'I shoot him!'[12] Despite their undoubted fighting prowess, there were language problems to overcome and ACM Dowding was at first reluctant to pitch the Czech, and Polish, squadrons into the battle.[13]

As the air war over England entered its first phase, at Duxford and Fowlmere Squadron Leader Philip C 'Tommy' Pinkham AFC and his pilots and armourers had more pressing problems. Since the beginning of July 19 Squadron had been receiving the first of the 20-mm Hispano Mk I cannon-armed Spitfire Ibs issued to RAF Fighter Command. This gun was in full production at the BSA factory at Sparkbrook, which delivered the first of 42,582 Hispano cannons built during the war on 12 April 1940. At this time the Browning Mk II guns normally fitted were being converted to Mk II (Star) to give an increased rate of fire. The first three aircraft, which were armed with a single 20-mm gun in each wing, were received with great excitement. Enthusiasm soon waned, however, when it was soon found that the early cannon were fitted with an unreliable feed mechanism and an ejector, which caused frequent jamming of spent cases and stoppages of the gun. Lord Beaverbrook had recognised the great potential of the 20-mm gun. Unfortunately, he had authorised priority for thirty Mk I Spitfire wing sets to be fitted with a cannon on each wing and attached to airframes on the production lines before completion of full trials at the Aircraft and Armament Experimental Establishment and the Air Fighting Development Unit. These were tested and processed under special arrangements by No. 6 Maintenance Unit at Brize Norton and delivered to 19 Squadron, as they became available for service trials.[14]

Pinkham and his pilots had been enthusiastic about the tremendous destructive power, accuracy and range the guns promised but stoppages were too frequent for operational use. If only one of the guns stopped, it was difficult to make a steady sighting with the other because the asymmetric recoil of the remaining gun made it impossible to aim. Fitting the cannon in the Spitfire's thin wing had meant resting them on their sides, which caused rounds to jam in the breach. The magazines held only sixty rounds each and pilots considered that the fire period of just six seconds was too short for prolonged combat. With the spread of the eight machine-guns replaced by the muzzle power of the 20-mm cannon, new engagement tactics involving dive attacks had to be invented. Pinkham devised a new method of attack whereby Sections of four flying in line astern were to try to get to a position about 2,000 feet above and to the side of enemy aircraft, dive down in echelon to a point behind the enemy and open fire in turn. This method was practised over the Duxford area from 4 July onward with Spitfire Is acting as target aircraft but these tactics would be of little use. Pinkham also introduced a new formation abandoning the unsatisfactory vic of three aircraft and substituting it with Sections of two fighters flying in line astern. It was 'at once attractive to watch and easy to manoeuvre' said the squadron diarist.[15]

Frequently the cannon-armed Spitfires were flown to 3 ATS at Sutton Bridge near King's Lynn for firing trials after each successive modification was made to the feed and ejection systems. One Spitfire Ib was flown to the Air Fighting Development Unit at Northolt for development trials but it was found that the Squadron's armourers had already acquired an experience of the Hispano superior to the AFDU staff![16] The air-gunnery tests proved very unsatisfactory with the cannon misfiring constantly. Pilots discovered that they could only fire when straight and level and even the mildest 'g' forces could cause the nose of the bullet to dip and jam in the breech when the firing button was pressed. On the plus side, the Spitfire Ibs were fitted with constant speed propellers, which gave a shorter take-off run, allowed longer duration from less fuel consumption and avoided 'surge'. For six weeks 19 Squadron persevered with the cannon-armed Spitfires during which time they engaged *Luftwaffe* formations on five occasions with extremely indifferent results.[17]

On 23 July 19 Squadron returned to Duxford and on 2 August the Squadron flew its first combat patrol with its cannon-armed Spitfire Ibs. It was not a great success, as the cannon still tended to jam and overheat. Wilfred Greville Clouston, who on 24 June had been awarded a DFC, was leading Blue Section on patrol off the Norfolk coast in a machine-gun armed Spitfire Ia. The twenty-four-year old New Zealander and former clerk from Auckland had joined the Squadron in June 1937. In constant action over Dunkirk in May and June, he had destroyed two *Stukas*, a couple of Bf 109s and a Dornier Do 17 as well as being awarded half shares in three other victories. Pilot Officers Eric Burgoyne and nineteen-year old Raymond André Charles Aeberhardt in his Section flew Ibs. Aeberhardt had joined the RAF on a short service commission in August 1939 and had been posted to 19 Squadron on 9 June 1940. At 1115 hours the Section intercepted a Heinkel He

111H of II/*Kamfgeschwader* (KG) 55 near the Cromer Knoll light vessel and all three pilots got in a short burst before the bomber dived into a convenient cloud.[18] Clouston's machine-gun bullets disabled the Heinkel's starboard engine and it was thought that he might have killed the mid-upper gunner, although the bomber did make it back and the crew were unhurt. The two cannon-armed Spitfires suffered stoppages and no results were observed. Clouston was awarded a half share in an He 111 damaged. A half share in a Bf 110 victory would follow on the very last day of the month.

On 6 August Hermann Göring had told his *Führer* that the RAF would be destroyed in time for Operation *Sea Lion* to be launched on 15 September, when 'German soldiers will land on British soil'. In the second week of August the *Luftwaffe* launched Phase 2 – *Adlerangriff* or 'Eagle Attack'. Its aim was to destroy RAF Fighter Command on the ground and in the air. On 12 August Squadron Leader Pinkham led the six cannon-armed Spitfires of 'B' Flight to Eastchurch aerodrome in Kent, which was intended as a forward airfield for mounting strafing sorties against invasion barges in French ports. Ironically, on 13 August a raid by thirty Do 17s of KG 2 *Holzhammer*, which were wrongly given the Coastal Command aerodrome as their target, rendered the runways inoperative. *Kommodore* Johannes Fink, *Kanalkampfführer*, who led the raid by seventy-four Dorniers on Eastchurch and the naval base at Sheerness, commanded KG 2 who were based at Arras and Epinoy. When his back was turned, Fink's grandiose title was more commonly referred to as, 'Chief Sewer Worker'. KG 2 claimed ten Spitfires destroyed on the ground but only one Spitfire of 266 Squadron and five Blenheims of 35 were destroyed. None of 19 Squadron's aircraft were damaged. Fink lost five Dorniers and five more were damaged.

Two days later the airfield at Martlesham Heath was bombed by Bf 109s and Bf 110s of *Eprobungsgruppe* 210, an experimental unit based at Calais-Marck commanded by Swiss-born Walter Rubensdörffer. All of 19 Squadron's available Spitfires were scrambled to meet the raid but they were ordered off too late and the enemy force was long gone by the time the Spitfires reached the Suffolk coast. The Suffolk airfield was put out of action for forty-eight hours. Returning to Duxford in the early evening of 16 August after a standby on convoy duty at Coltishall at 1735 hours, 'A' Flight's seven cannon-armed Spitfires led by Flight Lieutenant 'Sandy' Lane were given a point to intercept some Heinkel bombers thirty-five miles east of Harwich at 12,000 feet. The investigation proved to be 150 German bombers and fighter escorts flying southwards. The bombers were in front and the forty Bf 110C-2 escort fighters of ZG 26 and ZG 76 were behind, stepped up. The nine *Zerstörer gruppen* that took part in the Battle of Britain had long since been regarded as an elite and the Bf 110 had performed well in Poland, as a long-range escort. However, it was simply too heavy to dogfight with the Spitfire or Hurricane. A further escort of fifty Bf 109Es of II./JG 26 *Schlachtgeschwader* was about 1,000 to 1,500 feet above. Operating in Sections line astern, 'A' Flight attempted to fly in unobserved under the fighter escort to attack the bombers but the Spitfires were spotted by the Bf 110s, who immediately attacked allowing the bombers to escape. It was time for 'Yellow 4', Pilot Officer Wallace 'Jock' Cunningham, to stand up and be counted. When he had joined the Squadron he realised that he had to become useful as quickly as possible in order to become operational and this involved formation flying and dogfighting practice so that he could fly without thinking about it. This is what he and the other Spitfire pilots did on 16 August. They waded into the Bf 110s off Harwich in two sections of three and four respectively. Cunningham attacked a Bf 110, which stall turned to the right and presented its underside as a sitting target. He fired a long burst at the Messerschmitt, which rolled over and dived vertically through cloud. It was confirmed by Flight Lieutenant 'Sandy' Lane who saw the Bf 110 still in a vertical dive out of control as it entered cloud at 2,500 feet and that the base of cloud was only 1,000 feet. Lane's port gun fired only five rounds. Cunningham suffered a stoppage on his starboard cannon after just thirty-six rounds but all sixty were fired from the starboard gun.

Flight Sergeant George Unwin flying as 'Red 3' in Lane's Section, claimed two Bf 110s destroyed though he was credited with only the one, and one probable. His starboard cannon had jammed after firing just nine rounds but he had emptied the shells remaining in his port magazine into the second Bf 110 at 100 yards' range. His victim went into a steep dive and its tail came off. Unwin followed it through a low cloud layer and saw it hit the sea. Sergeant John Potter was able to fire 120 rounds of ammunition without any stoppages and claimed hits on the starboard engine of a Bf 110, which flicked over to port and a large part of the cockpit canopy broke away. Potter claimed it as destroyed. Two more German aircraft were badly damaged and losses might have been higher if the cannon on five of the Spitfires had not suffered stoppages. Henry Adrian Charles Roden, twenty-four years old and from Bradford, suffered stoppages in both cannon after firing about fifty shells. Roden had been educated at Bellahouston Academy in Glasgow and in July 1937 had joined the RAFVR, being called up on 1 September 1939 and joining 19 Squadron on 6 May. He had crashed in his Spitfire on 28 July at Duxford after a combat with a Ju 88. He made no claim for German aircraft destroyed and his own Spitfire was slightly damaged by return fire. Flying Officer Francis Noel Brinsden, a twenty-one-year-old New Zealander from Auckland, leading Yellow Section, saw a Bf 110 diving to attack the leading Section. Brinsden had been educated at Takapuna Grammar School and after leaving had worked as a bank clerk before being provisionally accepted for a short service commission in 1937. He sailed for England in the RMS *Arawa* in mid-August 1937 and on 9 July 1938 he joined 19 Squadron at Duxford.[19] Brinsden pulled into a climb to engage the fighter but both his cannon stopped after just nine rounds fired. Sergeant Bernard James Jennings, a twenty-five-year-old who had joined the RAF as an aircraft hand on 1 May 1933 before learning to fly in 1938 and joining 19 Squadron in August, also had stoppages in both cannon. Pinkham was of the opinion that the poor performance of the cannon in combat was the result of the effects of 'g' in the violent manoeuvring during dogfighting. The magazine was only properly supported under conditions of positive 'g' and any violent actions or negative 'g' manoeuvres could cause a stoppage. The armament of five of the Spitfires engaged had performed satisfactorily under test and the 12 Group Armament Officer who visited Duxford on 18 August endorsed the squadron leader's view. Trials were begun immediately to establish the facts. Brinsden took up the same Spitfire that he had flown in combat on 16 August and pulled the aircraft into a loop, opening fire when in the recovery dive and continuing to press the firing button, while pulling out of the dive. Both the port and starboard cannon stopped after firing only two and eight rounds respectively. On the 18th Brinsden repeated the experiment flying the Spitfire used so successfully by Sergeant Potter on 16 August. Again both cannon suffered stoppages after only a few rounds had been fired. The tensioning of the magazine springs was re-adjusted but still the cannon stopped during firing. Pinkham was of the opinion that nothing could be done to correct the problems unless the guns were positioned in the upright position and the magazine replaced by a belt feed.[20]

By 17 August losses in Spitfires and Hurricanes over the past ten days had reached 218 (183 in combat, thirty destroyed on the ground and five in accidents) but the replacement of pilot casualties was causing grave concern. In the heat of battle identification was confusing if not impossible. This was none more so apparent than on Monday 19 August when the Hurricanes and Spitfires got in each other's way trying desperately and determinedly to break up formations of fleeing Dorniers attacking the railway viaducts at Battersea. At 1810 hours Green Section in 19 Squadron were scrambled from Fowlmere. Flying Officer Leonard Archibald Haines, a Dorsetshire lad who hailed from Melcombe Regis near Weymouth, led the Spitfires. Haines had joined the RAF on a short service commission in September 1937 and on completion of training had been posted to 19 Squadron. After seeing action over Dunkirk in the first few days of June 1940, he was promoted to flying officer and he remained active throughout the Battle of Britain. At 1845 hours Haines' formation intercepted a single Dornier Do 17Z of 7./KG 2 flown by *Leutnant* Hamp, which had just bombed RAF Honington, eight miles east of Aldburgh. Flight Sergeant 'Bill' Steere ('Green 2') who had been awarded a DFM in June after his victories over Dunkirk, opened the attack with a 2½-second burst, which stopped the enemy's port engine. Haines then opened fire but he had to break away when both cannon stopped firing. Steere and twenty-year-old Sergeant David George Samuel Richardson Cox applied the *coup de grâce*, although Steere's port cannon stopped after firing about thirty rounds. Cox, who hailed from Southsea in Hampshire and was educated in Bournemouth, had commenced work in a solicitor's office and on his first attempt to join the RAF he failed his medical, so he worked as a fish porter in Billingsgate Market to get fit. He was accepted into the RAFVR in April 1939 and had been called up on the outbreak of war, joining 19 Squadron on 23 May 1940 on completion of this training. The Dornier went down and Leonard Haines saw Hamp and his three

27

crew bale out before it hit the sea. All four men were killed. Haines, Steere and Cox shared in the victory. On the way home Steere noticed a Spitfire of 66 Squadron from Coltishall in trouble. He followed it until about four miles short of landfall it began pouring smoke and lost height rapidly. Pilot Officer John Alnod Peter Studd baled out but it was fifty minutes before the Aldburgh lifeboat reached him. By then he was unconscious and Studd died soon after. He was twenty-two years old.

By now the *Luftwaffe* was averaging unacceptable losses of forty-nine aircraft a day and the RAF, nineteen a day, excepting 17 August when there was no significant fighting. Six days of poor weather also gave Fighter Command a breathing space. Even so, the odds were stacked in the enemy's favour, a point forcibly made on 20 August by British Prime Minster Winston Churchill.

> The gratitude of every home in our island, in our Empire and, indeed, throughout the world, except in the abodes of the guilty, goes out to the British airmen, who, undaunted by odds, unweary in their constant challenge and mortal danger, are turning the tide of the world war by their prowess and their devotion. Never in the field of human conflict was so much owed by so many to so few.

The 'Few' were getting fewer. The odds were stacked in the *Luftwaffe*'s favour and while British factories could replace the aircraft losses, Fighter Command needed every pilot it could get. Three days earlier the mounting losses of pilots in Fighter Command forced Dowding to seek thirty-two replacements from four Fairey Battle squadrons and Lysander Army Co-operation squadrons in 22 Group, all of whom were sent on a six-day OTU course prior to joining their new squadrons.[21] Some pilots in the Fleet Air Arm volunteered for attachment to RAF Fighter Command. Douglas Bader, who had been promoted and was now commanding 242 Squadron, lost his first pilot on 20 August during a North Sea convoy patrol. Twenty-nine-year-old Midshipman Peter John Patterson, who had joined the Hurricane squadron from Lee-on-Solent on 1 July, dived vertically into the sea and his aircraft exploded five miles north-east of Winterton. Bader recalled:

> With Fighter Command short of pilots in the frantic build up after Dunkirk the Royal Navy seconded to us fighter pilots from the Fleet Air Arm. They were without exception well-trained, disciplined and great characters. I had three in 242 Squadron – Midshipman Patterson and Sub-Lieutenants Cork and Gardner.[22] The first two were RN while 'Jimmy' Gardner (the sole survivor of the war) was 'Wavy Navy' (RNVR).[23]

Richard John 'Dickie' Cork and Arthur Blake had attended Slough Grammar School and they became lifelong friends, playing in the Windsor Rugby Club and in 1936 they also rowed together in the Eton Excelsior Rowing Club. Two years earlier Blake had followed Cork to work for Naylor Brothers of Slough, having remained at school for two years more than his best friend. In 1938 both men applied for commissions in the Royal Navy together with a view to flying in the

Fleet Air Arm. They were both offered short service commissions and they entered Greenwich Naval College together for basic training and then attended Pilots' Course No. 6 as midshipmen in 1939. Both became sub-lieutenants and in late August they were posted to 20 EFTS, Gravesend, and in early November 1 FTS at Netheravon. Both gained their pilot's badges in March 1940 and they were posted to HMS *Raven* at Southampton for deck landing and other training with 759 and 760 Squadrons. In June 1940 they were sent with a group of other newly qualified naval pilots, including Dennis Jeram, Francis Dawson-Paul and 'Jimmy' Gardner, to 7 OTU at Hawarden for operational training on Spitfires.[24] While Cork and Gardner were sent to 242 Squadron, Blake had been posted to 19 Squadron.

Bader continues:

> The Royal Air Force seems to breed unusual characters. When I first took over 242 Squadron in June 1940. I encountered Pilot Officer Percival Stanley Turner. When Air Vice Marshal Leigh Mallory had given me the job he had warned me that the squadron was composed mainly of Canadians. They'd had a rough time in France; they lacked a squadron commander and both flight commanders; they were touchy, ill disciplined and bloody-minded. With his final exhortation 'Good luck' I hastened to Coltishall, in Norfolk, on my new assignment. I arrived late at night and made contact with the pilots of 242 early the next morning. Leigh Mallory had understated the situation. After my initial shock, I had my adjutant Peter Macdonald (a World War I veteran and Member of Parliament for the Isle of Wight) assemble all the pilots in my office. I then told them in reasonable words (or so I thought) how members of a good squadron should dress, behave, and generally conduct themselves. Having finished, I asked if anyone had anything to say. There was silence. Then a strong Canadian voice commented 'Horse-shit'. After a long pause, the same voice added 'Sir'. For some reason, which even now I cannot define, this made the monstrously insubordinate interjection from Stan Turner entirely acceptable. Stan was simply one of those people who was 'agin' authority. Any suggestion from a senior officer was automatically resisted, and then carried out loyally and thoroughly. We became life-long friends. After a magnificent wartime career, not entirely free from incident (depending on whether the particular senior officer he'd just insulted knew him or not), Stan ended the war a much-decorated Group Captain. He fought in both the Hurricane and Spitfire with equal ability.

The new intake who joined the brotherhood that made up the RAF fighter squadrons that summer were the happy few, a band of brothers unique in British military history from all walks of life and from all over Europe and the far flung reaches of the Empire. Canadians, Australians and New Zealanders, some of them fed up with their dead end jobs, answered the call to arms with gusto. Pilot Officer

Kirkpatrick MacLure Sclanders, who was born in Saskatoon, Saskatchewan, and brought up in St John's, Newfoundland, had learned to fly at age fifteen. When he was old enough, he took part in air shows in Canada, acting as a Boy Scout who accidentally starts an aircraft engine and then takes off and performs aerobatics. He had first ventured to England in 1935 and joined the RAF that September, being posted to 25 Squadron at Hawkinge in August 1936. A year later, in September 1937, he resigned his commission because of bad health and had returned to Canada where he became a reporter. He underwent surgery and regained his fitness but he was unsuccessful in trying to get into the RCAF. He applied to fly in the Russo-Finnish War but it finished and he went to France. When the collapse came he escaped to southern France by boat with Polish refugees. He reached England and rejoined the RAF and was commissioned, joining 242 Squadron on 26 August.

On 24 August at 1545 hours Flight Lieutenant Brian 'Sandy' Lane leading a dozen of 19 Squadron's Spitfires took off from Fowlmere with orders to intercept a force of fifty Dornier Do 17Zs and Bf 110s and a *Staffel* of Bf 109s north of the Thames Estuary. However, the Dorniers had already bombed RAF North Weald before the Spitfires could engage them. At 1610 hours Lane spotted the formation above and climbed beneath the Bf 110s with the sun at his back. The Messerschmitts saw the Spitfires shortly before the RAF fighters got in range and they turned to engage the six Spitfires of 'A' Flight. Meanwhile, Green Section of 'B' Flight took on the Bf 109s. 'Sandy' Lane opened fire on the nearest Bf 110 but had to break away as tracer fired from behind flew past his cockpit canopy and appeared to hit the Bf 110. He lost sight of his quarry and picked out another Bf 110 approaching it from below and he scored hits on the port engine. The Bf 110 dived into the sea. Lane had fired all 120 rounds of ammunition without a stoppage. Sergeant Bernard Jennings flying as No. 2 in Yellow Section picked out a loose formation of four Bf 110s and attacked the rearmost aircraft. His opening burst put the starboard engine out of action and knocked the propeller off before the Bf 110 went down in a steep dive. Jennings broke away beneath the three remaining Bf 110s before climbing again to re-engage. He fired a fairly long burst at another Bf 110 and saw a large part of the tailplane, including he starboard rudder and tail fin, break off before the aircraft swung to port and went down in a dive. Jennings tried to follow but he lost sight of the doomed enemy fighter. He soon saw two more and he opened up with one cannon as the other had stopped after thirty-one rounds. A Bf 109 went right across his sights and the Bf 110 and thinking that there could be more fighters behind him, Jennings broke off the action. He fired the rest of his ammunition at a Bf 110 but failed to score any hits.

Following raids by German bombers on London and other English cities the previous night, the War Cabinet sanctioned the first RAF raid on Berlin on 25/26 August. Just over 100 Whitleys, Hampdens and Wellingtons bombed the German capital, which was to become known to RAF crews as 'The Big City'. On Monday 26 August the *Luftwaffe* delivered three main attacks on airfields in Kent and Essex and Portsmouth and the aerodromes in 10 Group. In the afternoon the objectives for the bombers of KG 2 and KG 3 were North Weald and Hornchurch with diversions in the east London area. Ten squadrons in 11 Group were scrambled and they managed to disrupt proceedings, although over 100 bombs fell on the sector station at Debden seven miles from Duxford. Finally, in the mid-afternoon, the Hurricanes of 310 (Czech) Squadron, which had became operational on 17 August with a patrol along the Thames Estuary, were sent off from Duxford in an attempt to catch the raiders as they left the Debden area. Instead of taxiing round the airfield they took off 'riskily downwind – a manoeuvre that won them an extra two minutes of precious combat time'.[25] Even though the wrong radio crystals had been fitted in some aircraft, the Czechs managed to intercept the main northern formation and several successful combats ensued in what was their first combat in the Battle. Sergeant Eduard Maxmilian Prchal claimed the first of three aircraft he destroyed during the Battle of Britain.[26] The experienced Czech pilot chased a Dornier Do 17Z-3 of 7./KG 2 for thirty miles and shot it down fifteen miles south-east of Harwich.[27] Heading for the coast near Clacton-Southend stretch the Czech saw, over to the left, what he thought was a Spitfire, but when he got closer he saw that it was a Bf 109. Prchal levelled out at 5,000 feet just as another Bf 109 fired a short burst of cannon and machine-gun fire at his Hurricane, which holed his glycol tank, port wing and rudder, filling the cockpit with vapour from the glycol. Prchal was hit in the shoulders, left arm and neck by splinters but he decided to crash-land rather than bale out. He turned steeply to starboard and tried to get his bearings but he could not see his compass, so he flew by the sun, intending to land as soon as he saw an airfield. Undercarriage up and three and a half miles south-east of Hornchurch, Prchal force-landed near Upminster. His Hurricane was later written off.

East-south-east of Chelmsford Pilot Officer Emil Fechtner destroyed a Messerschmitt Bf 110C-4 with a burst of 1,200 rounds closing to 100 yards. The twenty-four-year-old Czech pilot and ex-French Foreign Legionnaire was lucky to be in the battle at all. On 1 August his Hurricane stalled and crashed and two weeks later he had been involved in a collision with Pilot Officer A. Navratil at 25,000 feet. Heavy black smoke emitted from one of the Bf 110's engines left a trail from 15,000 feet downwards.[28] Suddenly, six Bf 109s appeared and Fechtner had to find sanctuary in the clouds before leaving the action. He flew east for four minutes and crossed over the railway line and the road leading to Chelmsford and Colchester before heading home to Duxford. Pilot Officer Vaclav Bergman meanwhile, who was one day short of his twenty-fifth birthday, was shot down by a Bf 110. He baled out unhurt at Southminster, his Hurricane crashing and burning out at a farm not far away. Flight Lieutenant Gordon Sinclair returned with slight damage to his glycol system following an attack on Do 17s over Clacton.

Squadron Leader 'Bill' Blackwood saw a Dornier Do 17Z-3 slightly apart from the rest. It was a 7./KG 2 machine flown by *Leutnant* Krieger. Blackwood attacked, closing to 300 yards before firing and Krieger's bomber started to go down. It crashed at Cole End, Wimbish, north-east of Chelmsford, after the crew had baled out.[29] Blackwood suddenly smelt burning. He looked around his cockpit but when he looked to starboard he could see that his right wing tank was blistering on the topside of the wing. He broke off the engagement, realising that his petrol tank was burning inside the wing and about ten seconds later the tank flared up. Blackwood undid his harness, disconnected his oxygen tube and turned the Hurricane onto its back before dropping out of the cockpit. He landed in a freshly harvested field of stubble at Wickham Bishops near Maldon and was unhurt.

On Friday 30 August the *Luftwaffe* began a forty-eight-hour assault on Fighter Command's Sector stations with attacks by 1,345 aircraft. 11 Group was threatened with being overrun by sheer weight of numbers and 12 Group was called upon to act as an airborne reserve for Park's hard-pressed squadrons. It was decided to bring 242 Squadron, which was flying Hurricanes at Coltishall, to Duxford daily on a reserve basis. Early that morning 242 Squadron was scrambled but was recalled while *en route* to Duxford. Squadron Leader Douglas Bader and his pilots had been champing at the bit for some time at the Norfolk backwater and they were convinced that the Battle was passing them by.

Bader, his English flight commanders and his pilots, made up largely by Canadians, had spent many frustrating days at Readiness waiting for 11 Group's call. In a short space of time Bader had characteristically licked the battered Squadron into shape and morale had soared. The regally named 'B' Flight commander, George Ffolliott Powell-Shedden was only twenty-four years old but he was beginning to go bald. He was shorter than Eric Ball whom Bader had 'pinched' from his old Squadron at Duxford, and had a tendency to stutter when excited but he was a 'solidly built, steadfast type with thoughtful eyes'. Like his commanding officer he was also an ex-Cranwell man.[30] On completing his education at Wellington School, George Shedden Ffolliott Powell as he then was, had taken the examination for the Royal Military Academy at Woolwich, since his father wanted him to become a gunner, the family having had five generations of military and naval service. Powell wanted to fly, however, and when Woolwich could not accept him because of a stammer from which he suffered all his life, he took the examination for the RAF College at Cranwell, gaining the highest marks. On 9 August 1938 he had changed his name by deed poll when he became the heir of his grandfather, Sir George Shedden of Springhill.

The 'B' Flight commander could not have been more different than Bader's 'A' Flight Commander. Flight Lieutenant Eric Ball, a lean, firm-jawed man with a little moustache above good smiling teeth, had a scar furrowed through the fair curly hair where a bullet fired by a Bf 109 had creased him at Dunkirk. On 26 May Ball had scored his first victory flying a Spitfire on 19 Squadron, destroying a Bf 109 in the Calais-Dunkirk area. He had even destroyed a Heinkel He 111 at night on 18/19 June when the bomber was knocked down ten miles north of Colchester. His first victory on 242 Squadron had come on 30 August when west of Enfield he had destroyed another Heinkel damaged a Bf 110 and had been awarded a half share in another He 111 victory at Rochford. Apart from Bader and the two flight commanders, the only other English pilot on the unit was Pilot Officer Denis W Crowley-Milling, an Old Malvernian and former Rolls-Royce apprentice who would also make quite a name for himself.[31] The 'sturdy blond Pilot Officer who looked about 17 but was in fact 21', was to remain with 242 Squadron until the spring of 1941, receiving a DFC on 11 April.

All the Canadians seemed fearless and none more so than Pilot Officer Willie McKnight, 'a flinty-eyed little dead shot of twenty from Calgary, who had already knocked down several German aircraft in the shambles in France'.[32] 'Under the tender lips' was a 'tough little man with a DFC [awarded on 14 June]. He had a weakness for soft music; he had a large collection of Bing Crosby records and played them endlessly in the mess in the evenings, being greatly irritated when Lawrence Cryderman, a former school teacher from Islington, Ontario, sang over the top of the velvety Crosby.'[33]

Already Bader had his eye on several pilots as future section leaders, especially 'the handsome firm jawed' Pilot Officer Hugh Tamblyn, a 23-year old ex-Defiant pilot who had a steady eye and 'dry good humour' who had 'an air of utter reliability about him.'[34] Percival Stanley 'Stan' Turner from Toronto was a first class pilot and was both fearless and decisive. His new responsibilities as a section leader had curbed his wild streak.[35] Noel Karl Stansfeld, of fair, curly hair and good looks also had an air of utter reliability about him. The twenty-five-year-old Canadian from Edmonton, Alberta, had two confirmed victories, a half share in one other victory and a *Stuka* victory unconfirmed, all achieved in May and June during the Dunkirk fighting. Another half share had been awarded for downing a Heinkel He 111 west of Enfield on 30 August.[36] In 1938, Laurie E Cryderman, a pilot officer who had just joined the Squadron, on 31 August, was tall and slight with crinkly hair and a cheerful charm. He had been leading a jazz band and he was still only about twenty-four years old. Pilot Officer Norris 'Norrie' Hart, twenty-five years old from Montreal, who had scored his first victory on 30 August when he had downed a He 111, was shorter, firm-faced, quick of wit and speech delivered in a hard, dry accent. On the side of his Hurricane he had painted a chamber pot with swastikas falling into it. Pilot Officer John Blandford Latta, a dark and slight twenty-six-year-old Canadian from Victoria, British Columbia, had been a salmon fisherman who had also served in the 16th Canadian Scottish Territorial Regiment before joining the RAF in 1939. Latta 'had a drawly voice and occasionally showed the dourness of Scottish forebears'.[37] Pilot Officer Marvin Kitchener 'Ben' Brown has been described as 'very handsome, very brave and a very bad shot'. Brown, who was from Kincardine, Ontario, had joined the RAF in March 1939. In May 1940 he was attached to 85 Squadron and was shot down in France, suffering bullet wounds in his right leg. He was evacuated to England and had rejoined 242 Squadron on 13 July. Twenty-seven-year old Pilot Officer Norman Neil Campbell of St Thomas, Ontario, who had joined 242 Squadron on 1 July, was 'even more handsome'.[38] Robert 'Bob' Davidson Grassick was 'compact and blithely imperturbable' but after scoring some victories during the fighting over Dunkirk he was injured in a motorcycle accident late in August and missed the September fighting.[39] Yet apart from accents no one noticed nationality any more; they were too busy training as a team and life under the new CO was stimulating, though no fighting seemed in sight. All that was to change on the afternoon of Saturday 31 August.

1   13 Group, which covered Scotland and the north-east, had seventeen squadrons. On 5 June 19 Squadron had moved to Fowlmere, Duxford's main satellite airfield, three miles away on top of a hill for a twenty-day sojourn. 'Fowlmere (known officially as G.1), like Duxford, had been a prominent First World War airfield, but had been closed, and all buildings demolished, soon afterwards. In 1940 the site was brought back into use, but the new buildings were hastily erected and equipment was sparse. The luxury of Duxford's accommodation was sorely missed in the Nissen huts of Fowlmere!' *Airfield Focus 1: Duxford* by Andy Height (GMS 1992).

2   The fighting in France and over Dunkirk cost the lives of 110 fighter pilots. Another forty-seven were wounded and twenty-six taken prisoner. Worst affected was 85 Squadron, which lost eight pilots killed and six wounded in just eleven days.

3   *The Battle of Britain July–October 1940: An Oral History of Britain's Finest Hour* by Matthew Parker (Headline Book Publishing 2000).

4   On 3 April 1933 the Marquess and his observer Colonel L.V.S. Blacker in a Westland Wallace powered by a supercharged Bristol Pegasus engine, were the first to fly over Mount Everest. MacIntyre and his observer, a Gaumont British News photographer, in another Wallace, filmed the epic event.

5   *Memories of a British Veteran* by Wallace Cunningham, *The Burning Blue* (Pimlico 2000).

6   *Memories of a British Veteran* by Wallace Cunningham, *The Burning Blue* (Pimlico 2000).

7   A sister Czech Hurricane Squadron, 312, was formed at Duxford on 29 August, moving to Speke near Liverpool in September. It did not become operational until 2 October. In late May 1941 the unit moved to Kenley, received Hurricane IIs and commenced offensive operations.

8   *The Few, Summer 1940, the Battle of Britain.*

9   Jeffries had joined the RAF on a short service commission in October 1936 and he was posted to 17 Squadron in August 1937. He had been posted to 85 Squadron but on 12 July he was promoted to become a flight commander on 310 Squadron.

10 26-year old Stanislav Plzak, who was born in Pilsen, had served in Fighter Flight 32 of Air Regiment 1 until 1938 and then in 1940 had flown the Morane 406 in the *Groupe de Chasse* II./2, being awarded three half shares in three victories during early June. He had been attached to 19 Squadron from 310 Squadron since 29 August.

11 *Memories of a British Veteran* by Wallace Cunningham.

12 *The Few, Summer 1940, the Battle of Britain*

13 303 '*Warsaw-Kosciuszko*' Squadron, which became fully operational on Hurricane Is on 31 August, became the most successful Hurricane equipped fighter squadron in the Battle with around fifty confirmed victories. (303 Squadron was officially credited with 126 victories, but historians now quote between forty-four and fifty-eight kills that can be verified. Few point out that the Polish squadrons were not committed to the Battle much before the end of August.) A total of 154 Polish pilots served with Fighter Command during the Battle of Britain and no fewer than thirty had been killed by 30 October. Eighty-six Czech nationals flew in the Battle of Britain for the loss of eight pilots.

14 *Spitfire; The Story of a Famous Fighter* by Bruce Robertson (Harleyford Publications 1960). The Air Fighting Development Unit had been set up to evaluate new aircraft and systems alongside the Air Gun Mounting Unit, which concentrated on armament. Both units started to move into Duxford in late 1940. Alongside them was the Naval Air Fighting Development Unit, 787 Squadron, which flew shipboard types such as the Fulmar and Martlet.

15 *RAF Fighter Squadrons in The Battle of Britain* by Anthony Robinson (Brockhampton Press 1999).

16 *Spitfire; The Story of a Famous Fighter.*

17 On 11 August 19 Squadron received X4231, which was armed with two cannon and four machine-guns and though judged to be rather overloaded was at least a step in the right direction.

18 *Jagdgeschwader* (JG) indicated single-seat fighters, *Kamfgeschwader* (KG), bombers, and *Zerstörer Geschwader* (ZG) twin-engined fighters. (The *Lehrgeschwader* (LG) and *Erprobungsgruppe* 210 (EprGr210) were two operational evaluation units, each *Gruppe* flying a different type.) *Schlachtgeschwader* indicated 'attack unit'. Each *Geschwader* was dived into a *Stab* (staff) unit (with usually four aircraft) and three or four *Gruppen*; these latter being identified by Roman numerals eg. II./KG 55. Each *Gruppe* was itself divided into three or four *Staffeln* of about ten to twelve aircraft each, depending upon serviceability. These *Staffeln* were identified by Arabic numerals eg. 2./KG 55. Thus a full-strength *Geschwader* had an establishment of about ninety to 120 aircraft.

19   *Men of the Battle of Britain* by Kenneth G Wynn (CCB Associates 1999).

20   *RAF Fighter Squadrons in The Battle of Britain.*

21   During July seventy-four pilots were killed and forty-nine wounded and in August the numbers rose to 148 killed and 156 wounded.

22   Richard John 'Dickie' Cork was born in London on 4 April 1917, attending the Royal Naval College, Greenwich. He commenced flying training in August 1939, receiving his wings on 20 January 1940. He received advanced training with 759 and 760 fighter training squadrons of the Fleet Air Arm, and was then seconded to the RAF on 7 June 1940 due to the shortage of fighter pilots. After a brief course at 7 OTU, Hawarden, he was posted to 242 Squadron on 1 July, remaining with this unit until 8 December. In that time he claimed five victories.

23   Richard Exton Gardner joined the Royal Navy VR, training as a pilot for the FAA, and being posted to 780 Squadron in September 1939. After attending 7 OTU at Hawarden he had been posted to 242 Squadron at the start of July 1940. He was to claim four and one shared victories with 242. His first was on 10 July when he destroyed a He 111 twenty-five miles off Lowestoft. A half share in a Dornier Do 17 followed on 21 August and he destroyed a Do 17 on 7 September and two more on the 18th plus being awarded a Do 17 probable. On 5 November his Hurricane, P3054, was damaged in combat with Bf 109s, although he escaped unhurt. He left 242 Squadron at the end of November with a brief posting to 252 Squadron, Coastal Command, but then rejoined the FAA and was sent to 807 Squadron, newly equipped with Fulmars on HMS *Ark Royal*. This carrier escorted the *Tiger* convoy through the Mediterranean to Egypt during May 1941, when he made several further claims, an award of the DSC following late in July. Further sorties into the Mediterranean in support of convoys to Malta followed. His total score was six and four shared destroyed and one probable. In December 1942 he commanded 889 Squadron land-based in Egypt and Libya, but returned to the UK at the end of the year. In 1943 he joined the School of Naval Air Warfare at St Merryn in Cornwall, becoming commanding officer in November 1944. Awarded an OBE in June 1945, he retired as a Commander in March 1946.

24   Dennis Mayvore Jeram retired as a lieutenant commander in 1954 having destroyed four enemy aircraft on 213 Squadron in 1940 and a fifth flying the Martlet II on 888 FAA Squadron. Dawson-Paul destroyed seven German aircraft and shared one destroyed flying with 64 Squadron in July 1940. His final victory was on 25 July when he destroyed a Bf 109 over the Channel before he too was shot down into the sea and severely wounded. Jeram was picked up by a German E-boat but died five days later.

25 *The Few, Summer 1940, the Battle of Britain.*

26 The twenty-nine year old, who was from Dolni Brezany, north of Prague, had served in the Czech Air Force from 1929 to 1936 and had flown for Bata Co on international flights until 1939 and in June that year he arrived in Poland. In September when the tiny *Lotnictwo Woljskowe* (Polish Air Force) could not hold back the *Luftwaffe* any longer, Prchal and other Czech and Polish personnel fled to France and joined the *Armée de l'Air*. Prchal served in the *Groupe de Chasse* I./8 flying Bloch MB 152 fighters and on 6 June he shot down a Bf 109E and was awarded a half share in a Do 17 victory. Next day he destroyed a Henschel 126. With the fall of France, he escaped to England and joined 310 (Czech) Squadron.

27 Do 17Z-3 U5+LR crashed at Highams Farm, Thaxted. *Oberleutnant* Heidereich and *Unteroffizier* Panczack were killed. *Feldwebel* Hohenstadter and *Unteroffizier* Gussmann baled out wounded and were captured.

28 At around the time of Fechtner's combat Bf 110C-4 2N+AK of 9./ZG 26 crashed and exploded on Crabtree Farm, Great Bentley, near Chelmsford. *Feldwebel* Opper and *Unteroffizier* Nick were killed. Bf 110D 3U+CM of 4./ZG 26 crashed and burst into flames at Great Tey. *Oberfeldwebel* Rosler and *Unteroffizier* Heinrich were killed. Bf 110C-4 3299 of 9./ZG 26 was also shot down in the Chelmsford area and it crashed in the Thames Estuary. *Unteroffizier* Reinhold and his *bordfunker* were killed.

29 *Leutnant* Krieger and *Unteroffizier* Illing who were both wounded were captured as were *Unteroffizier* Winter and *Gefreiter* Schneider. U5+TR was a write-off.

30 He was born on 1 April 1916 in East Cowes on the Isle of Wight. He entered Cranwell in 1935, was commissioned on 19 December 1936 and posted to 47 Squadron at Khartoum in the Sudan. In September 1939 he was posted to Egypt as a flight commander in 33 Squadron, but in June 1940 returned to the UK, being posted to 242 Squadron early in July.

31 Crowley-Milling was born on 22 March 1919. He attended Malvern College and then became an apprentice engineer with Rolls-Royce. He joined the RAFVR in 1937 as a sergeant and was called up at the outbreak of war, joining 615 Squadron in France on completion of his training and receipt of a commission. Following the withdrawal of the unit to England he was posted in June 1940 to 242 Squadron.

32 *Reach For the Sky.* William Lidstone 'Willie' McKnight was born in Edmonton, Canada, on 18 November 1918, attending the University of Alberta and serving as a private in the militia from 1935 to 1938. In

February 1939 he halted his medical studies to join the RAF on a short service commission, completing his training and joining 242 Squadron, which was forming with predominantly Canadian pilots, in November 1939. With the outbreak of the *Blitzkrieg* on to May 1940, he was posted out to 607 Squadron as a reinforcement, but two days later, moved to 615 Squadron, gaining his first victory with that unit on 19 May when he shot down a Bf 109E at Cambrai. On 28 May he returned to 242 Squadron and was at once in action over Dunkirk, shooting down a Bf 109E over Ostend. On 29 May he destroyed Dornier Do 17, nine miles east of Dunkirk and a Bf 109E and an unconfirmed Bf 109 N-NNW of the port. On 31 May he destroyed two Bf 110s E and NNW of Dunkirk and a Bf 109E two miles west of the town. On 1 June he destroyed two Ju 87s off the French coast near Dunkirk and two other *Stuka* victories were unconfirmed. He then returned to France with 242 Squadron on 8 June, taking part in the retreat to the Biscay ports and the withdrawal to England. On 14 June he destroyed two Bf 109s south of Champagne to take his score to eleven.

33   *Reach For the Sky*. Lawrence Ellwood Cryderman had joined the RAF in December 1938. He had little experience on Hurricanes and was posted to 5 OTU on 5 September 1940, rejoining 242 Squadron three weeks later. He was lost over the North Sea on 8 February 1941. On 30 August McKnight had notched his twelfth, thirteenth and fourteenth confirmed victories when he destroyed two Bf 110s and a He 111 at Hatfield-North Weald.

34   *Reach For the Sky*. Hugh Norman Tamblyn was born on 5 September 1917 in Watrous, Saskatchewan, joining the RAF on a short service commission in April 1938. He was posted to 7 Bombing and Gunnery School as a staff pilot but in December 1939 he joined 141 Squadron, one of the first two Defiant units. On 19 July his was one of only three aircraft from a formation of nine from Hawkinge to survive an attack by a *Staffel* of about ten Bf 109Es of II./JG 2, the *Richthofen Geschwader*, south of Folkestone. Five of the Defiants were shot down, a seventh with a dead engine crashed at Hawkinge and an eighth was severely damaged, the gunner baling out and presumed drowned. Tamblyn's gunner, Sergeant Sydney William Martin Powell, claimed one of the attackers shot down. Tamblyn had been posted to 242 Squadron on 8 August and by the end of September had been promoted to flying officer. Powell was commissioned in May 1941 and he left the RAF with the rank of flight lieutenant in 1946.

35   Turner was born in Ivybridge, Devon, on 3 September 1913, but emigrated to Canada with his family as a child, settling in Toronto. He joined the RAF on a short service commission in October 1938, being posted initially to 219 Squadron in October 1939 and then to the new 242 Squadron the following month, when it was formed mainly with Canadian pilots. With

the outbreak of the *Blitzkrieg* on 10 May 1940, he was posted out to reinforce 607 and 615 Squadrons for a brief period. He soon rejoined 242, seeing action with the unit over Dunkirk and then in the retreat to the Biscay ports after the evacuation of the BEF. Promoted flying officer during September, he was at once made a flight commander.

36   Born in Edmonton, Alberta, on 25 February 1915 Stansfeld worked as an accountant on the Vancouver Stock Exchange from 1936 to 1939, before travelling to England to take up a short service commission in the RAF from May 1939. On completion of training he was posted to 242 Squadron in February 1940. In April he was attached to 85 Squadron in France, but returned to his own unit before the *Blitzkrieg* began. He then saw action throughout the chaotic fighting in France, over Dunkirk and during the Battle of Britain.

37   *Reach For the Sky.* On 14 June he destroyed two Bf 109Es near Paris and two more Bf 109Es over Dunkirk and a half share in a Do 17 shot down on 21 August. Born on 6 August 1914 in Vancouver, British Colombia, Latta joined the RAF on a short service commission in February 1939, being posted to 242 Squadron in November. He first saw action over Dunkirk in May 1940, before moving to France with the squadron and taking part in the withdrawal to the Brittany coast.

38   *Reach For the Sky.* Campbell was killed on 17 October 1940. Ben Brown was killed on a local flight on 21 February 1941.

39   Bob Grassick was born in London, Ontario, on 22 May 1917. He travelled to the UK from Canada to join the RAF in October 1938, completing his training in September 1939 and being posted to 3 Squadron. In November he was moved to 242 Squadron. On 14 May 1940 he was sent to France on attachment to 607 Squadron. On 16 May he moved to 615 Squadron and on the 19th he returned to England. He was believed to have claimed two Bf 109s and a Ju 88 shot down on 15 and 16 May, although it was feared that the latter might have been a Blenheim of 59 Squadron. Upon rejoining 242 Squadron he destroyed a Bf 109E and damaged another on 25 May over Dunkirk and downed another two Bf 109Es on 29 and 31 May. He returned to France with 242 on 8–16 June. Grassick returned to 242 Squadron to take part in the early cross-Channel sweeps and in June 1941 he became a flight commander, receiving a DFC the following month. He was then posted to the Middle East in late September, where he served as an instructor at 73 OTU, Aden, until February.

CHAPTER THREE

Big Wing

*And there was the aerodrome, mostly grassed and the big hangars there
and you could see the main gate. To the right was what looked like a little
housing estate, which was the previous married quarters for the airmen
and their families. And suddenly as we looked there had obviously been
something going on because planes seemed to be landing from all
directions. And as we looked one of them appeared to hover for a moment
and then it nose dived straight down into the ground. And there were
smoke trails rising. The noise just stopped absolutely instantaneously and
we looked at each other a bit shocked. And the mood changed and we were
all very much sobered up. And I think we then realised that it wasn't a
great lark and it was quite serious business that we were in for. Actually,
we were reminded of this because the pilot was killed of course, and he'd
owned a large Alsatian dog, which for the next few days just seemed to
roam the camp looking for him all the time until somebody else took him
over. It was quite sad.*

Jean Mills WAAF[1]

The weather throughout the remainder of 31 August, which before the war
would have been a Bank Holiday weekend with time to laze, remained
mainly fair with haze in the Thames Estuary and the Straits of Dover, so
there was still a chance of action. Finally, at around half past four, 242 Squadron
were ordered off again. Wing Commander 'Woody' Woodhall, the Duxford
Controller, ordered '242 Squadron scramble! Fly vector 190 degrees for North
Weald. Angels 15'. North Weald is thirty miles south of Duxford and the usual way
to have covered the airfield would be to patrol over the airfield and wait for the
enemy to appear. The Hurricanes took off and took fifteen minutes to reach 15,000
feet but Bader ignored the request to 'Vector one-nine-zero. Buster'. Instead he led
the formation further west to get up-sun and climbed them to nearer 20,000 feet to

gain full advantage of the attackers who he guessed correctly would approach from the west with the sun at their backs. The target for the Heinkel He 111H-2s of KG 53 escorted by Bf 110s of II./ZG 2, II./ZG 26 and II./ZG 76 was not North Weald as was thought, but the Vauxhall Motor Works at Luton. Just north of North Weald Bader received directions to vector 340 degrees. At about the same time he saw three unidentified aircraft below and to the right of the Squadron and ordered the three Hurricanes of Blue Section to investigate. At around 1700 hours Bader spotted a tight enemy formation stepped up from about 12,000 feet with their escort fighters at 15,000 to 20,000 feet, which he thought was fifty Dorniers escorted by a similar number of Bf 110s. Bader led his remaining Hurricanes down into the German formation west of the reservoirs at Enfield, heading for the Hatfield-North Weald area. He ordered Flying Officer George Patterson Christie, leading Green Section, to attack the top of the lower formation of Bf 110s. Christie, a twenty-three-year-old from Westmount, Quebec, who had joined the RAF in June 1937, was a former PRU pilot who had forced a Fiat BR 20 *Cicogna* (Stork) bomber down in the Mediterranean on 13 June despite his Spitfire being unarmed.[2] He had joined 212 Squadron and was posted to 242 Squadron on 21 July. Christie made a head-on attack on a Bf 110[3] of 5./ZG 2, which was being flown by *Hauptmann* Schuldt. The German pilot dived down off to starboard pursued by the Canadian from Calgary who kept on his tail and sprayed a burst from fifty yards astern. Oil began pouring from Schuldt's starboard engine and the petrol tanks burst into flames. Doomed, the Bf 110 went into a vertical dive from 6,000 feet and hurtled straight down into Rochfords nursery garden at the rear of Nos 16–22 Durrants Road about 500 yards from the reservoir at Ponder's End, killing the *Hauptmann* and his *bordfunker*, *Unteroffizier* Dyroff.

Red Section (Bader, McKnight and Crowley-Milling) and Yellow Section (Eric Ball, Dickie Cork and Sergeant Robert Henry Lonsdale) formed into line abreast to dive down through the middle of the bomber formation. Heavily outnumbered, Bader's only aim was to try to break up the Heinkel formations and take the Bf 110s on individually in dogfights. It seemed to work because the tightly packed enemy formation immediately broke up fan-wise and they were badly mauled by the Hurricanes. 242 Squadron claimed eight Bf 110s destroyed, one probably destroyed and one damaged. The Squadron also claimed five Heinkels shot down.[4]

As McKnight veered left Bader went right to attack two Bf 110s who made climbing turns to a nearly stalled position to try and get on the Hurricane leader's tail. Bader reached the top of the zoom and pumped a short three-second burst at one of the Bf 110s at almost point blank range and the enemy fighter seemed to burst into flames. Bader then picked out another Bf 110 below and to his right just beginning its dive after a stalled turn. He turned in behind the Messerschmitt and fired a burst from about 150 yards' range. The Bf 110 pilot tried to squirm out of it by pushing his stick violently backwards and forwards but the second time he tried it, Bader got in another burst, which knocked pieces off the starboard wing near the engine and then the whole of the starboard wing caught fire. The Bf 110 fell away to the right in a steep spiral dive. Bader was too busy looking around to notice if any of the crew got out and he noticed in his mirror another Bf 110 coming up from behind. He did a quick turn as six white streams of tracer poured from the fighter's guns. Bader turned and the Bf 110 put its nose down. He tried to catch up but he could not so he did not fire any further bursts at it.

Pilot Officer Willie McKnight, the nose of whose Hurricane had a sharp-edged scythe dripping blood to symbolise death, the grim reaper, claimed three of the Messerschmitts. He recalled:

> While patrolling with the squadron over North Weald, enemy were sighted on the left at about 1705 hours. The enemy aircraft were in a vic formation, stepped up from 12,000 to 18,000 feet. Attacked middle section of Me 110s and two enemy aircraft broke off to attack. Succeeded in getting behind one enemy and opened fire at approximately 100 yards. Enemy aircraft burst into flames and dived towards the ground. Next attacked He 111 formation and carried out a beam attack on nearest one, opening fire at approximately 150 to 20 yards. Port engine stopped and aircraft rolled over on back, finally starting to smoke, then burst into flames and crashed to earth. Lastly, was attacked by an Me 110 but succeeded in getting behind and followed him from 10,000 feet to 1,000 feet. Enemy aircraft used very steep turns for evasive action but finally straightened out. I opened fire from approximately thirty yards. Enemy's starboard engine stopped and port engine burst into flame. Enemy crashed in flames alongside large reservoir.[5] No return fire noticed from first two enemy but last machine used a large amount.

Crowley-Milling scored his first victory when he shot the belly out of a He 111H-2. He attacked the bomber alone and from astern, giving it a five-second burst. The rear gunner returned fire but he soon stopped as the doomed bomber went down. Crowley-Milling began following it but he had to break off to port when tracer bullets from a Bf 110 passed his starboard wing. Norrie Hart saw 'Crow's' Heinkel go down. Hart attacked another Heinkel of 5./KG 1 piloted by *Unteroffizier* Burger and shot it down north of London. Burger and his four crew were all killed.[6]

Yellow Section, led by Flight Lieutenant Eric Ball, also drew blood west of Enfield. Ball spotted a solitary Heinkel circling, diving and turning and he approached from behind out of the sun, closing to 100 yards and firing one-third of his ammunition. Both the Heinkel's engines caught fire and the pilot crash-landed the bomber on an aerodrome full of cars near North Weald. With the sun still at his back Ball chased a straggling Bf 110 and knocked out one of the engines. The enemy fighter lost height rapidly and went down for his second victory. His No. 2, Dickie Cork, carried out a beam attack on a Bf 110 and set the port engine on fire. The enemy pilot frantically put the fighter into a stall turn but seconds later the Messerschmitt exploded on the ground. Sergeant Robert

Lonsdale ('Yellow 3') got a lone Heinkel 111 with a ten-second burst from 300 to 50 yards range and it crashed in about the same area as Cork's victim.

Green Section had gone for the Heinkels after the Bf 110s had quickly dispersed. Norrie Hart came across three He 111s in line about 1,000 feet below him and as he began his dive, he saw Eric Ball attacking the last one in the formation. Hart picked out the second Heinkel and a burst of fire from his guns sent it into a dive. Hart was about to follow the enemy down when he noticed that the first Heinkel was making a steep right-hand turn. He turned inside it and used all his remaining ammunition on the He 111 and it went down, crashing in a field with all the crew still aboard. Hart did not hang around because three Bf 110s began chasing him.

Noel Stansfield ('Black 1') saw a straggling He 111 and in the first of three attacks he silenced the rear gunner who had returned fire with cannon. The Heinkel's port engine began smoking and the starboard motor stopped altogether. The Heinkel crashed on the same aerodrome near North Weald where Ball's victim had come down. Three of the crew staggered out of the wrecked bomber. Meanwhile Sergeant George William Brimble ('Black 2'), who was from Ward End, Birmingham, had followed Stansfield during the attack on the Heinkel and had fired at it from 250 yards. After watching Stansfield follow the Heinkel almost into the ground Brimble broke away and saw a Bf 110 making a gentle turn to port. He carried out a quarter-attack and it went down and soon crashed. As Brimble flew across to rejoin Stansfield a Bf 110 got him in his sights and opened fire. Brimble returned fire at 350 yards' range and the enemy machine dived violently down but he lost sight of it when another Bf 110 got on his tail.

On the way home to Duxford Bader picked up Green Leader (George Christie)[7] and Blue Section, who were highly disgruntled having missed the battle and not even firing a single round in anger. Six Heinkels were actually lost and two returned to base badly damaged while four Bf 110s were actually lost and three returned to base damaged. The Heinkels that did get through to their target badly hit the Vauxhall Works and fifty-three civilians were killed and sixty were injured. Bader felt that 242 Squadron had had a 'successful' first engagement with the *Luftwaffe* 'under favourable circumstances'. 'Although, as was usual in 1940, heavily outnumbered, we had the height, the sun, and controlled the fight. We felt that with more aeroplanes we would have been even more successful.' Altogether, the day's fighting cost the RAF twenty-six fighters shot down with fifteen pilots saved and the *Luftwaffe* had lost thirty-six.

Back at Coltishall the AOC 12 Group, AVM Sir Trafford Leigh-Mallory, telephoned his congratulations to Bader who replied that if he had had thirty-six fighters they could have shot down three times the number of German aircraft. In theory, a large fighter formation could be brought to bear on the enemy 'Balbo'[8] thereby increasing the chances of 'knocking down' more aircraft than smaller formations were capable of doing. (On 21 June 85 Squadron had flown a wing practice with 66 Squadron, Duxford.) Trafford Leigh-Mallory had long held the belief that a 'Wing' could achieve greater killing potential than the squadron formations favoured by ACM Sir Hugh Dowding at Fighter Command and by AVM Keith Park at 11 Group, who had much less time to form up squadrons into Wings.

On Saturday 31 August *Luftwaffe* attacks began early that morning with raids coming in over Kent and the Thames Estuary and six squadrons in 12 Group were put at readiness. The airfields at Debden, Biggin Hill, Manston, West Malling, Hawkinge, Hornchurch, and Lympne were the main *Luftwaffe* targets. North Weald got off lightly but Debden was particularly badly hit with about 100-kilo high-explosive bombs and incendiaries being dropped by Dornier 17s of KG 2. The sick quarters and barrack block received direct hits and the WAAF quarters was flattened while other buildings were damaged but the Operations rooms continued to function throughout the attack. Eleven Spitfires of 19 Squadron were scrambled from Fowlmere to intercept a large force of German bombers and fighters to the south and they took up station at 20,000 feet south of Fulbourn. Flying Officer Francis Brinsden was late taking off.[9] Trying to catch up with the Squadron, the former bank clerk, who over Dunkirk on 26 May had destroyed a Ju 87 and shared another, met a Bf 109 head-on at 22,000 feet. The German pilot fired first and the Spitfire went into a dive. Brinsden baled out at 5,000 feet over Newton and landed unhurt.

At 0830 hours fourteen Do 17s of II./KG 2 escorted by six Bf 110s of 8./ZG 26 were approaching Duxford and the attack went in as the sector station's anti-aircraft guns opened up on the raiders. Fortunately, Wing Commander Woodhall had urgently requested cover for his airfield and AVM Keith Park diverted nine Hurricanes of 111 Squadron led by Squadron Leader John Marlow 'Tommy' Thompson, who had been on patrol since 0810 hours, to intercept the raid. The Hurricane pilots sighted the enemy and as fate would have it, they were in an ideal position to deliver a head on attack, first against the Dorniers, shooting Do 17Z-3483 of II./KG 2 down, before turning their guns on the Bf 110s, one of which was destroyed. One Hurricane was lost but Sergeant 'Bobby' Craig DFM who was wounded, baled out safely.[10] Treble One Squadron pressed home their attacks with such ferocity that the Dorniers scattered and turned for home jettisoning their bombs as they fled while the Bf 109E pilots in desperation, adopted the now familiar defensive circle.

The Spitfires of 19 Squadron meanwhile intercepted the *Gruppe* of Dorniers, which had attacked Debden. Flying Officer James Baird Coward was leading Green Section in 'B' Flight. The twenty-five-year old had joined the RAF on a short service commission in October 1936. On 29 December 1939 he had married Cynthia Bayon, who lived at her parents' huge house at King's Farm at Little Shelford, four miles from RAF Duxford. After a spell in hospital to have his tonsils removed, her husband had rejoined 19 Squadron, then at Fowlmere. Over Dunkirk on 2 June 1940 he had claimed a Bf 109 probably destroyed. After Dunkirk seven or eight exhausted soldiers were billeted at King's Farm for a spell. Cynthia's sister

Joan and her husband, Bill Smith, a 66 Squadron fighter pilot, and their brother Michael H.A.T. Bayon, who wanted to be a fighter pilot, all lived at the house, which soon became known as 'RAF King's Farm'.[11] Every morning after breakfast Cynthia would give her husband a farewell kiss, saying, 'See you later'. Exhausted after flying for hours a day James and Bill would arrive for the three course evening meal served on a white damask table cloth with its huge silver soup tureen. Mike Bayon well remembers both of them falling asleep on the dinner table between courses.

Ten miles east of Duxford Coward was hit in the left leg by an explosive bullet from one of the Dorniers. Looking down he could see his foot hanging loose on the pedal. He still went in to open fire on a Dornier but immediately his cannon jammed. He instinctively ducked as the top of his Spitfire grazed the underside of the enemy bomber. His cockpit hood was ripped away and the Spitfire spiralled down out of control, petrol spilling all over him. He baled out at 22,000 feet and got caught on the back of the cockpit as he went. He finally freed himself and was going to free fall for a bit in case the enemy aircraft shot him in his parachute. But his foot was 'thrashing around' by his thigh and the pain was too much to bear so he pulled the ripcord and swung there in a figure of eight. 'It was amazing how bright it was so high up' he observed.

His Spitfire crashed in flames near Little Shelford where his wife Cynthia, now seven months' pregnant, was bathing her sister's baby at King's Farm. Mike Bayon, who was in a field feeding chickens, vividly recalls the events of that clear, dewy Saturday morning.

> The German planes came winging over in tight formation, pretty high. Three Spitfires beamed into attack. I could hear the gunfire and see the absurdly pretty cotton wool bursts of the cannon shells. One of the Spitfires was hit. I was not to know that it was James. He was pressing home an attack on a Dornier when a Messerschmitt from behind completely removed his foot with a cannon shell. Glycol from burst hydraulics was burning his face and hands and soon he realised that the plane was out of control. He baled out and with every heartbeat he could see a gush of blood from his severed foot and at that height and in that cold thin air, the blood spread out almost pink in curious spirals, rather like a long sinuous chiffon scarf. He decided not to pull the ripcord yet or he would have bled to death before he could land.

As Coward came down blood was pumping out of his left leg and he thought he would bleed to death so he used the radio wire from his helmet to put a tourniquet around his thigh. After that he felt no pain apart from the petrol that had drenched him and was stinging his armpits and crotch. He drifted across Duxford towards Fowlmere and then the wind took him back again and he landed in a stubble field behind the roundabout on the Royston–Newmarket Road near the Red Lion at Whittlesford. A young lad of sixteen came dashing up with a pitchfork, obviously thinking that he was a German. He was told to 'piss off' and 'fetch a doctor!' In due course a medical officer from the local AA unit who was *en route* to Duxford for breakfast, turned up but he was unable to administer any morphine because the orderly corporal had gone on leave and taken the key to the poisons' cupboard with him.[12]

Mike Bayon finished feeding the chickens and came in from the field.

> Cynthia was standing very straight, very tense, in the hall, listening to the RAF doctor. He had decided to 'break it gently'. He took an eternity, constantly urging her to be brave and so, of course, she thought James was dead. He would have done better to say, 'Your husband is alive, and is in no danger of dying; but he has been wounded' and take it from there. And, as the doctor finished talking, the baker's wife ran in from next door to tell our cook the news in detail. We were never able to unravel how the village grapevine had been so quick and so accurate.[13]

James Coward was eventually taken by ambulance to Addenbrooke's Hospital in Cambridge where his leg was later amputated below the knee. Three weeks later he was discharged from Ely RAF Hospital just in time for the birth of his first child, a daughter, Janice. Coward was later on Winston Churchill's staff and then an instructor at 55 Operational Training Unit where, incidentally, he taught the young man who had found him.[14]

Flying Officer Ray Aeberhardt's Spitfire was damaged but still flyable. Aeberhardt left the fight and made it back to Fowlmere where he tried to land his damaged Spitfire at 0850 hours but he had to land without flaps. The aircraft flick rolled and caught fire. Aeberhardt died in the flames. A contingent of about a dozen WAAFs that had just arrived in an open-backed lorry from the little railway station at Whittlesford where they lugged their kit bags, and gas masks and tin hats behind them up the platform witnessed the accident. Jean Mills, a plotter and tracer, recalls:

> We were clinging onto the sides and laughing and talking. We were quite excited because we were all pretty young, eighteen or nineteen I suppose, and most of us hadn't been away from home before and life was a great big adventure and we were feeling very hyper I should imagine. And the truck bumped over the country roads and suddenly we reached the brow of a hill and we could see Duxford stretched out before us and it was a very sunny day. And there was the aerodrome, mostly grassed and the big hangars there and you could see the main gate. To the right was what looked like a little housing estate, which were the previous married quarters for the airmen and their families. And suddenly as we looked there had obviously been something going on because planes seemed to be landing from all directions. And as we looked one of them appeared to hover for a moment and then it nosed dived straight down into the ground. And there were

smoke trails rising. The noise just stopped absolutely instantaneously and we looked at each other a bit shocked. And the mood changed and we were all very much sobered up. And I think we then realised that it wasn't a great lark and it was quite serious business that we were in for. Actually, we were reminded of this because the pilot was killed of course, and he'd owned a large Alsatian dog, which for the next few days just seemed to roam the camp looking for him all the time until somebody else took him over. It was quite sad. There were moments like that, but most of the time you were so busy that you just didn't let it get at you.[15]

South of Colchester two Sections attacked the Bf 110s but spent rounds jammed many of the Spitfires' cannon and prevented firing. Wilfred Clouston and Eric Burgoyne shared in the destruction of a Bf 110 and David Cox was awarded a Bf 110 probable. He recalled:

I hadn't fired my guns or anything and then I heard over the radio that the enemy formations were making for the Thames estuary, withdrawing. So I climbed up and just near Clacton I saw about twenty Messerschmitt 110s going round in a circle, which they used to do, partly for defence and partly to be at the rear of any withdrawing bombers. So I, with cannon which I hadn't fired, climbed above them. And of course the 110's a fairly big aeroplane and when there's twenty of them I thought to myself, 'Well, if I dive on them there's a chance of hitting something'. I always think it was a bit of an Errol Flynn effort. Anyway, I dived firing away with my six seconds of ammunition, and used that up very quickly, as you can imagine. And then one of them broke away. I couldn't say its engine was on fire but it was smoking. I went to follow it down but the others then attacked me so I carried straight on down. I didn't see what happened to the 110 and I only claimed it as a probable.[16]

Just after lunch twelve Hurricanes of 310 (Czech) Squadron led by Gordon Sinclair were scrambled and ordered to patrol Hornchurch at 10,000 feet. Pilot Officer Jaroslav Sterbacek, a twenty-seven-year old born in Dolni Lhota, flew one of the Hurricanes. He had joined the Squadron earlier that day. The Czech Squadron sighted a dozen Dornier 17Zs and their Bf 109E escorts and attacked. Sinclair scored his first victory since assuming command of 'A' Flight when he downed a Do 17Z. At around the same time Flight Lieutenant Jerrard Jeffries, who was leading his flight against some Dorniers at 11,000 feet, downed one of the Do 17Zs for his second victory of the war. Pilot Officer Emil Fechtner poured machine-gun fire into the engine and cockpit of another Dornier. Part of the cockpit snapped away and the Do 17Z dived on its port wing to the ground.[17] Squadron Leader 'Sasha' Hess was set upon by several Bf 109Es and as one of them overshot he fired and hit from below. The German fighter spun crazily down to the ground. Another *Rotte* suddenly appeared on the scene and Hess broke off. He and other

Hurricane pilots spotted a Dornier on the left outskirts of its group. It was a 4./KG 3 machine[18] piloted by *Unteroffizier* Bock and the Czech squadron leader gave it a four to five-second burst. At 1,000 feet the German bomber straightened out from a dip and Hess fired more rounds into the doomed aircraft, which careered down near the River Roach south of Burnham-on-Crouch and crash-landed on Eastwick Farm. Bock, who was mortally wounded, died three days later, but *Oberleutnant* Gahtz, *Oberfeldwebel* Bulach and *Gefreiter* Neumann clambered out of the wreckage and surrendered to their captors. Pilot Officer Jaroslav Maly claimed a Do 17 before the twenty-five-year old from Prague had his Hurricane set on fire ten miles north-east of London by Bf 109Es attacking from the rear and out of the sun. Turning left he met three Bf 109Es and after watching one of them go down he saw a parachute opening four to five miles away. Jaroslav Sterbacek was shot down and killed by Bf 109s without having the chance to prove himself on his debut. Pilot Officer Miroslav Kredba, twenty-six years old, from Libichov in Czechoslovakia, was shot down but baled out safely.[19] Pilot Officer Stanislav Zimprich, twenty-four years old, from Havlickuv Brod who had joined 310 Squadron on 10 July, shook off a Bf 109 and turned the tables on him, firing into the fighter until it dived away but nothing further was seen and he did not claim it.

Fighter Command lost thirty-nine fighters on 31 August, when the RAF flew 2,020 sorties and the *Luftwaffe* almost 2,800 sorties against London's sector airfields. These were the worst losses of the Battle so far and they brought the number of RAF pilots killed and wounded that week to 115 with sixty-five of the fighters downed on the 30th and 31st. South of the Thames only two RAF Sector stations were still operational. That night, seventy-seven RAF bombers hit back at Berlin again. At Coltishall 242 Squadron had been scrambled three times to patrol North London but they had found no sign of the *Luftwaffe*. More RAF fighters had to be brought to bear against the enemy raids. AVM Trafford Leigh-Mallory landed at the Norfolk station and talked 'Wings' to Bader between two patrols. The commander told Bader that, starting on the morrow, 242 and 310 Squadrons' Hurricanes would use Duxford daily. Together with 19 Squadron operating out of the satellite at nearby Fowlmere, they would form the 'Big Wing'. At first there was no 'trade' for Bader to pursue and he practised with the Duxford Wing for four days, reducing take-off times to just three minutes, the same as a squadron, climbing 242 Squadron on a straight course followed by 310 and 19 Squadrons. Though they were not called into action on 1 September, Fighter Command sent up 147 patrols involving 700 fighters and lost fifteen aircraft from which nine pilots survived. The *Luftwaffe* lost fourteen aircraft.

On Tuesday 3 September *Luftflotte* 2 began assembling over the Pas de Calais at eight o'clock that morning and headed for the airfields at Hornchurch, North Weald and Debden. By 0940 hours sixteen squadrons totalling 122 fighters had been ordered into the air to meet the threat. Five minutes later a group of fifty-four Dorniers and about eighty Bf 110 escorts flying at 15,000 feet approached their target at North Weald from the north-east. More than 200 bombs were released over the airfield with aircraft on the ground refuelling but despite widespread destruction the airfield remained operational. As the German bombers turned for home eight cannon-armed Spitfires of 19 Squadron led by Squadron Leader Pinkham were ordered to patrol between Duxford and Debden at 20,000 feet. All the Spitfires except Leonard Haines, Green Leader, who had eight machine-guns, were armed with two cannon. They were still climbing to their height of 20,000 feet when the sector controller warned them that the enemy raiders were approaching from the south-east and later that they were over North Weald. On reaching 20,000 feet they saw explosions and clouds of smoke from the Essex airfield. There were fifty to sixty bombers at 'Angels 20', escorted by 100 fighters stretching from 20,000 to 25,000 feet, with a single fighter ahead of and above the whole formation. Pinkham tried to make a front quarter attack on the bombers but his Spitfires were headed off by a group of Bf 110s and they broke up into pairs line astern to engage them. Three of the Bf 110s were shot down[20] but six of the Spitfires suffered gun stoppages. 'Jock' Cunningham for instance, followed his leader into the attack but fired only nine rounds from the port cannon and four from the starboard gun before they jammed. The 19 Squadron pilots could do little but fly off and leave the bombers to six Hurricane squadrons and eight Spitfires of 603 Squadron.

310 Czech Squadron claimed six Bf 110s and a Dornier destroyed between North Weald and Chelmsford before they ran low on fuel. Pilot Officer Emil Fechtner shot down a Bf 110C-4 of I./ZG 2[21] and it crashed south-east of North Weald with the loss of *Unteroffizier* Korn and *Oberleutnant* Müller. At the same time Flight Lieutenant Jerrard Jeffries chased and shot down another Bf 110C-4,[22] which crashed ten miles north of North Weald. *Unteroffizier* Schuberth and *Feldwebel* Wagenbroth were killed. Five minutes later Flying Officer Gordon Sinclair using height and the sun at his back to good advantage, destroyed a Bf 110C-4,[23] which also crashed near North Weald. *Oberfeldwebel* Winkler and *Gefreiter* Weller were killed. Sergeant Josef Koukal, who also destroyed a Bf 110, saw the port mainplane of a Dornier cut off a yard from the engine. One of the crew baled out from 10,000 feet. Pilot Officer Jaroslav Maly shot down a Bf 110[24] near North Weald at about the same time. *Oberleutnant* Messner and *Unteroffizier* Santoni were killed. Sergeant B Furst destroyed a Bf 110 with a single burst before he ran out of ammunition and the enemy fighter crashed south of Chelmsford. Sergeant Josef Kominek, twenty-seven years old, from Prague, claimed a Dornier probably destroyed. Jeffries also ran low on ammunition and was almost out of petrol when he reached Duxford but he glided down onto the grass perfectly.

Back at Fowlmere 19 Squadron had had more than its fill of the cannon-armed Spitfires. The same day 616 'South Yorkshire' Squadron, AAF, at Kenley was withdrawn to Coltishall following two weeks of heavy losses and some of 19 Squadron's pilots, including Johnnie Johnson, were sent to the Norfolk station to bolster their depleted numbers. Johnson, who was a young civil engineer and a weekend flyer with the RAF Volunteer Reserve before the war, had joined 19 Squadron at the end of August with twenty-three hours on Spitfires. He wrote:

> …The squadron adjutant sent for us. 'You chaps are to report to 616 Squadron at Coltishall at once. They've just been pulled out of the front line and will have time to train their new pilots. It's probably the best thing. You can see what the form is here. We must have experienced pilots who can take their place in the squadron.'

The phone rang and the adjutant listened for a few moments before he slowly replaced the receiver. 'They've found the CO [sic], probably dead when he crashed.'[25] For a moment he brooded. 'Well good luck with 616.'[26]

On Tuesday 3 September 611 Squadron's Spitfires arrived at Fowlmere from Digby to take over 19 Squadron's place in the Order of Battle for a day while they rearmed with the machine-gun armed Spitfire Is. On 4 September the *Luftwaffe* attacked aircraft factories and airfields in Kent in two phases. 19 Squadron returned to the Battle Order again and Sergeant Stanislav Plzak claimed a Bf 109E probably destroyed over South London.

On Thursday 5 September the weather was fine and warm and the *Luftwaffe* carried out airfield attacks in two phases. AVM Park ordered special cover for fighter factories. At about 10.00 am raids developed over Kent heading for Croydon, Biggin Hill and Eastchurch while others were made on North Weald and Lympne. Fourteen fighter squadrons were scrambled and most of the German bomber formations were forced way from their intended targets. In all, the *Luftwaffe* launched twenty-two separate formations over a period of eight hours in an attempt to swamp the defences. Most of these raids were intercepted and in these engagements Fighter Command lost twenty fighters to the *Luftwaffe*'s twenty-three throughout the twenty-four-hour period, although five RAF pilots were saved. At 0947 hours 19 Squadron were scrambled and ordered to patrol Hornchurch at 15,000 feet. The eleven Spitfires were led by Squadron Leader 'Tommy' Pinkham AFC with his six in 'B' Flight and the other five of 'A' Flight led by Flying Officer Brinsden bringing up the rear. About forty Dornier Do 17Z bombers were sighted approaching the Thames Estuary from the west flying in stepped up vic formations with the same number of Bf 109s slightly astern and 5,000 feet above the bombers. The Spitfires were still climbing to reach their assigned patrol height and another fighter squadron attacked the bombers as the enemy formation turned south into the sun. This turn of events meant that 19 Squadron now had to attack with insufficient height and the added disadvantage of attacking into the sun but Pinkham led his three sections into an astern attack on the Dorniers regardless, ordering 'A' Flight to take on the enemy fighters. Brinsden put his five Spitfires into line astern and began a climbing turn up to the Bf 109s' altitude but in turning into the sun he lost sight of the enemy fighters and they did not regain contact. The enemy fighters ignored 'A' Flight and went instead for 'B'

Flight. 'Tommy' Pinkham was last seen engaging a vic of Dornier Do 17Zs. It is believed that he was shot down and killed near Hornchurch by the Bf 109s in their initial attack. What is certain is that his Spitfire crashed at Birling in Kent. Pilot Officer Eric Burgoyne, his No. 2, lost contact with his CO when turning into the sun and so he attacked alone. He opened fire on one of the rearmost Dorniers and was then attacked from behind by a Bf 109 and he was forced to break off with damage to his tailplane, elevator and rudder. Burgoyne, who was awarded a Dornier probable, landed safely at Fowlmere.

'B' Flight's second (Black) Section made attacks on the enemy bombers before the intervention by the Bf 109s. Pilot Officer Walter John 'Farmer' Lawson, a twenty-seven-year old from Somerset who had joined the RAF as an aircraft apprentice in 1929, claimed his first victims, a Dornier probably destroyed in the Maidstone area and another as damaged. Lawson had passed out as a fitter and in December 1936 had re-mustered as a pilot, being commissioned on 1 April 1940 when he joined 19 Squadron. Almost immediately, Bf 109s fired at Pilot Officer Frantisek 'Dolly' Dolezal ('Black 2')[27] and Lawson's Spitfires. Lawson's was severely damaged though he managed to return unhurt. 'Dolly' was awarded a Bf 109 probable. Flying Officer Leonard Haines ('Green 1') and Sergeant Stanislav Plzak ('Green 2') destroyed a Bf 109 apiece. Haines saw the enemy pilot climb to 800 feet and bale out in the vicinity of Ashford. Flight Lieutenant Brian 'Sandy' Lane downed a Bf 110. Back at Fowlmere the 'A' Flight commander took command of 19 Squadron. Lane had been awarded a DFC at the end of July. 'Farmer' Lawson was promoted to take over 'A' Flight. One of Lane's immediate problems was the question of the cannon-armed Spitfires his Squadron had been lumbered with. He was given notice to prepare for withdrawal to Digby in Lincolnshire to allow further trials uninterrupted by battle, a situation that did not sit well with the Squadron. They wanted their eight-gun Spitfires back even if it meant that they were 'ex-OTU junk or perhaps from the Caledonia market' as 'Jock' Cunningham described them.

Douglas Bader recalled:

The armament experts at Fighter Command had been trying to improve the weight of fire-power of the Spitfire and had decided that two 20-mm cannons plus four machine guns would be an ideal mixture. 19 Squadron were the unlucky recipients of these first cannons. I well remember the occasion when 19 Squadron's Spitfires were fitted with these cannons, since we were on the same aerodrome, Duxford. The cannons would fire about two rounds and then stop. The reason was that the wings had been adapted to accept cannons instead of being built for cannons. The stoppage occurred on recoil. After a couple of sorties with no cannons working in close combat with the enemy, the pilots were not best pleased. The armament 'experts' at 12 Group and Fighter Command tried to insist that the 19 Squadron armourers did not know their job. 'Stuffy' Dowding heard about this and came, with his armament 'experts' to see for himself. I was present on this occasion. 'Sandy' Lane, the 19 Squadron commander, was an old chum, a fine leader and pilot. Dowding said: 'Hullo Lane, I hear you're in trouble with your cannons. Tell me.' 'Sandy' replied: 'They fire one round, sir, and that's all.' At this point one of the armament 'experts' mistakenly intervened to say: 'There's nothing wrong with the cannons, sir, I think the armourers do not fully understand them.' Courteously, Dowding turned to him and said: 'I want to hear what Squadron Leader Lane thinks.' He looked at 'Sandy' and said: 'What do you recommend?' Without pause, 'Sandy' answered: 'Remove the cannons and put back the machine guns, sir.' Stuffy said: 'Thank you, Lane.' He then turned to his staff and said: 'You will arrange to do that straightaway, please.' That was typical of the C-in-C Fighter Command in 1940. I was present once when he told one of his staff officers: 'Our job in this Headquarters is to look after the squadrons in the field.'

Eventually, the unsatisfactory magazine was replaced by a belt-fed system, which had been made a requirement as early as 1938. It was much less bulky and easier to install. In 1941, when the Spitfire VB was in production the wing had been designed to take cannons and they worked perfectly.

The Duxford Wing began to operate on the morning of Friday 6 September but no contact was made with the enemy. Six of 11 Group's seven sector stations and five of its advanced airfields were very badly damaged during three main attacks by the *Luftwaffe*, which were largely broken up. Even so, only seven out of eighteen squadrons despatched engaged the enemy formations. It was obvious that some controllers were ordering squadrons intended to engage the enemy bombers to patrol too high. When Group ordered a squadron to 16,000 feet, sector controller added on one or two thousand, and the squadron added on another 2,000 feet in the vain hope that they would not have any enemy fighters above them. As a result some of the enemy bombers slipped in under 15,000 feet and bombed without interruption. The majority of the formations were only intercepted after they had dropped their bombs. Fighter Command lost twenty-three aircraft, the pilots of twelve fighters being saved. *Luftwaffe* losses were thirty-five.

On Saturday 7 September the sector stations expected annihilation and a signal (Invasion Alert No. 1) was sent that an invasion was 'imminent'. The *Luftwaffe*, however, switched its daylight attacks, sending 348 bombers drawn from five *Geschwader*, escorted by 617 single and twin-engined fighters to hit London in the first of their 'reprisal' attacks on the capital following raids by RAF Bomber Command on Berlin.[28] This vast aerial armada, the greatest yet seen, assembled eighty-eight miles away over the Pas de Calais and headed towards the Thames Estuary on a twenty-mile front stepped up from 14,000 to 23,000 feet. The more than a mile and a half high formation, which was led by *Kommodore* Fink with KG 2, covered an astonishing 800 square miles. The sight must have sent shock waves throughout Fighter Command when the radars first picked up the mass formation. The RAF pilots who were sent up to intercept became embroiled in melees and attacks that might begin and be pressed home at any height from 25,000 feet down to near the ground. One moment there could be as many as 140 separate fights going on at the same time, the next pilots were seemingly alone. It was a situation that must have frozen the blood of even the bravest of men, if they had time to dwell on it. The situation demanded the utmost alertness and once sighted, the RAF pilots opened fire at an average of 200 yards, closing sometimes to less than fifty yards. By a curious irony it was a quarter of a century before, on 8 September 1915, that *Zeppelins* had made their first big raid on London.

At 1617 hours AVM Park ordered eleven squadrons into the air and six minutes later he brought all remaining Spitfires and Hurricanes to Readiness. By 1630 hours all twenty-one squadrons stationed within seventy miles of the capital were in the air or under take-off orders.[29] As the first four squadrons of RAF fighters attacked the southern flank of the huge formation it was soon apparent to Dowding and Park that the *Luftwaffe* was heading for London and not the precious Essex and Kentish fighter airfields. Despite the spirited and strong resistance put up by the fighter squadrons, not least the Poles of 303 Squadron, many of the bombers had a clear run over the capital, which was heavily bombed. Nineteen Fighter Command pilots were lost from the twenty-eight fighters shot down and forty-one German aircraft were destroyed.

At Coltishall 242 Squadron had spent another frustrating day at Readiness waiting for 11 Group's call. To them 7 September must have seemed like another opportunity missed as the cosmopolitan squadron spent most of the day kicking its heels as reports filtered through of waves of German bombers attacking London. Pilot Officer John Benzie, from Winnipeg, who had joined 242 Squadron at Church Fenton in January, was among those who waited impatiently for action. The twenty-five-year-old had served in Princess Patricia's Canadian Light Infantry before joining the RAF on a short service commission. Over France on 23 May Benzie had been attacked by Bf 109s near Ypres and he baled out south of Dunkirk, wounded, and was evacuated to England by sea. Benzie had rejoined his Squadron on 11 July and was still to make his mark, having been sent on a parachute course at Weeton, Lancashire, in early August.

Finally, at 0445 hours Ops rang and Bader and his pilots, straining at the leash, at last got the order to 'Scramble!' Once airborne 'Woody' Woodhall at Duxford calmly told Bader that there was some 'trade' heading in over the coast. The South African asked Bader to 'Orbit North Weald. Angels 10' and added, 'If they come your way you can go for them'. Bader went instead to 'Angels 15'. Nearing North Weald Woodhall called Bader again. 'Hallo, Douglas. Seventy plus crossing the Thames east of London, heading north.' In the distance Bader saw black dots staining the sky. They were not aircraft. They were anti-aircraft bursts. This could mean only one thing. Over the radio Willie McKnight called out, 'Bandits. 10 o'clock'. Bader recalled, 'We had been greatly looking forward to our first formation of thirty-six fighters going into action together, but we were unlucky. We were alerted late, and were underneath the bombers and their fighter escorts when we met fifteen miles north of the Thames'. All Bader could do was attack the formation of about seventy Dorniers of KG 76 and Bf 110s of ZG 2 heading for North Weald as best they could while eight Spitfires of 19 Squadron tried to hold off assaults from the Bf 109s flying high cover. Behind Bader's Hurricanes the rest of the Duxford Wing strained to catch up. 'Jock' Cunningham in 19 Squadron at Fowlmere recalled:

> Perhaps he was not the most skilful of pilots but Bader carried the confidence of his squadron and they followed him into the attack. He used to complain of having cold feet at high altitude. Evidently the nerve ends send a misleading message. It was said also that he was more resistant to the effects of 'g' in a tight turn. The tin legs did not provide a place for the blood to go – thus no blackout.[30]

Squadron Leader Brian Lane ('Red 1') had led his eight Spitfires off from Fowlmere but though they were faster they did not climb as well as the Hurricanes and he took up position behind 310 Squadron from Duxford. They never did catch up with Bader and the rest of 242 Squadron to form the Wing. Lane's small formation consisted of three Spitfires of Red Section leading and two aircraft of Yellow Section tacked on behind with a three-aircraft vic of 'B' Flight (Blue Section only) bringing up the rear. They were about 5,000 feet lower than the force of twenty bombers escorted by fifty Bf 110 fighters flying east at 15,000 feet. So the pilots of 'A' Flight had to climb to attack in what became a thirty-minute running fight from North Weald to Deal in Kent. 'B' Flight could not climb quickly enough and largely failed to get within range of the enemy. Wilfred Clouston and 'Bill' Steere in Blue Section had to return to Duxford but north of Margate Pilot Officer 'Dolly' Dolezal ('Blue 3') claimed a Bf 110 destroyed and a He 111 damaged. All five Hurricanes in 'A' Flight singled out one of the Messerschmitt fighters and 'had fun shooting it to pieces'.[31] It crashed about a mile east of Hornchurch and south of a railway line. The crew baled out but one parachute failed to open. The other man landed in a field and appeared to be taken prisoner by two women from a nearby house.

'Jock' Cunningham, who was 'Yellow 2', attacked a Bf 110 and as he broke off he 'blacked out' and lost formation. He climbed and joined up with some Hurricanes. They flew east and attacked a formation of twenty-four Heinkel He 111s of I and II./KG 53. The Scot singled out one of them and attacked from astern. He set it ablaze and he attacked again from below, after which the Heinkel began to lose height rapidly and it crashed ten miles inland of Deal or Ramsgate. Cunningham climbed again and found three He 111s proceeding east. He attacked from astern again and fired two bursts at the leader. Whitish smoke began coming from the tail but the enemy bomber did not lose height. Unable to continue the attack because he had run out of ammunition, Cunningham returned to Fowlmere.

'Grumpy' Unwin ('Red 3') meanwhile, had become separated from his Section and he climbed to 25,000 feet where he found and joined a Hurricane squadron. They went after a formation of sixty bombers and fighters and while Hurricanes took on the bombers, Unwin suddenly found himself surrounded by Bf 109s. He fired at five and two went down west of London. He used up the rest of his ammunition on some unescorted bombers before heading home. The main attack over and with nothing to fire at, 19 Squadron began returning to Duxford.

Bader recalled:

Some of the Spitfires and indeed the Hurricanes were caught on the climb by the German fighters, but our casualties were less than might have been expected. To be attacked by an enemy fighter when you are climbing is fatal if your opponent is experienced. You are flying slowly and are thus virtually unmanoeuvrable as well as being a sitting target for an opponent above you and flying faster.

Bader found himself positioned below some Bf 110s with only Sub-Lieutenant 'Dickie' Cork ('Red 2') anywhere near. Undeterred, Bader opened full throttle and boost and climbed and turned left to cut off the Messerschmitt with Cork on the beam slightly in front. Bader gave a very short beam burst at about 100 yards at the Bf 110s, which were flying a section of three in line astern in a large rectangle. Bader, accompanied by Cork, picked out a Bf 110 in the back section and gave it short bursts. The Bf 110 started smoking and caught fire. Bader did not notice the result, which was later confirmed by Pilot Officer Stan Turner ('Green 1') who saw the aircraft diving down in flames from the back of the bomber formation. At the time of Bader's attack on the Bf 110 he noticed a yellow-nosed Bf 109 in his mirror and he turned to avoid the enemy fighter. He heard a 'big bang' in the cockpit of his Hurricane as an explosive bullet came through the right-hand side of the fuselage touching his map case and knocking the corner off the undercarriage selector quadrant. The bullet finished up against the petrol-priming pump. Later four bullets were found in the self-sealing petrol tank. Bader executed a steep diving turn and found a lone Bf 110 below him, which he attacked from straight astern and above him. He saw the aircraft go into a 'steepish straight dive' finishing up in flames in a field at Downham Hall just north of the railway line west of Wickford and due North of Thameshaven. Both crewmembers, *Leutnant* Hans Dietrich Abert and *Unteroffizier* Hans Scharf, were killed.

Dickie Cork, meanwhile, had climbed to meet the enemy aircraft and carried out a beam attack of the leading section of bombers, firing at a Do 17 on the tail end of the formation. Its port engine burst into flames after two short bursts and crashed vertically. German aircraft from the rear then attacked Cork and gunfire hit his starboard mainplane. He broke away downward and backward nearly colliding head on with a Bf 110 before giving the Messerschmitt a short burst. Pulling away Cork saw the front cabin of the Bf 110 break up and go into a vertical dive. Two of the crew baled out. Whilst following the Bf 110 down it was stalling

55

and diving. A Bf 109 attacked Cork from the rear, one round from the enemy aircraft going through the side of his hood and hitting the bottom of his reflector sight and bullet-proof windscreen. Cork received a number of glass splinters in his eyes so he broke away downwards with half roll and lost sight of the enemy aircraft. Both his and Bader's Hurricanes were so badly shot up that they were now unflyable and Cork was sent to the Sick Bay to have his bleeding face attended to.

Bader's two Bf 110s were confirmed as were Cork's Do 17 and a Bf 110. Denis Crowley-Milling, who was flying as 'Red 3', flew in to meet the enemy just above the AA fire but he had to bank sharply left and away when he was attacked from the rear by a Bf 110. He came in again and spotted a Bf 110 just behind the last bomber. Over the Thames Estuary 'Crow' fired a four-second burst and hit the enemy fighter's port engine. He could also see smoke coming from the other motor. It was his second victory. At that instant he was fired on from behind by a Bf 109 and his Hurricane received a shell in the radiator and another in the left aileron while a third lodged behind his seat. His armoured glass windscreen was shattered by a cannon shell but incredibly he was not hit. 'Crow' made a successful forced-landing at Stow Maries near Chelmsford.

Pilot Officer Stan Turner picked out another Bf 110 before opening fire from close range. A Bf 109 came after him and opened fire on his Hurricane but Turner turned the tables on his opponent and fired a short burst into it. The Bf 109 flicked over and Turner turned his attention to the bombers, getting a few short bursts in before some more Bf 109s attacked him again. He claimed a Bf 109 damaged. Willie McKnight got two and Eric Ball one Bf 110 destroyed and one Bf 110 damaged. Pilot Officer Hugh Tamblyn claimed a Bf 110 destroyed – his first victory on the Squadron – and he also chased a yellow-nosed Bf 109E, firing at it from 150 yards' range. The Messerschmitt veered off to the right and went down and he was later credited with a probable. Noel Stansfeld picked out a Dornier and the gunner fired a burst of about fifty rounds at him that fortunately missed his Hurricane. Stansfeld went below the bomber and came up again and this time he caught the Dornier in the port beam sending it down into a roll. The German attempted a second roll but it was going too slow and it crashed. Stansfeld was awarded a Do 215 but it was a Dornier 17, possibly of *Stab*/KG 2, which was damaged by fighters near London and two crew members wounded.[32] Charles Roy Bush 'a steady-eyed New Zealander' from Wellington, was credited with damaging a Bf 110 and a He 111.[33] Eric Ball claimed a Bf 110 destroyed and another damaged and 'Jimmy' Gardner downed a Dornier with three short bursts at 250 to 50 yards' range. The port engine stopped and the oil tank burst into flames. The crew baled out before the Dornier crashed in a field about three miles north-east of Shell Haven. The sub-lieutenant got a hole in his wing and engine cowling but he managed to land back at Duxford. Powell-Shedden destroyed a Bf 109E-4 of I./JG 27 flown by *Leutnant* Genske in combat over the Thames Estuary. Genske baled out and he was captured. His Messerschmitt crashed and burned out at Park Corner Farm, Hacton Lane, Cranham.

Flight Lieutenant Gordon Sinclair led 310 (Czech) Squadron from up sun and he put 'A' Flight into line astern to attack the Bf 110s as he saw 242 Squadron attacking the bombers. Sinclair picked out a Messerschmitt and shot it up with a full deflection shot before climbing into the sun and attacking another with a long burst. The port engine stopped but Sinclair ran out of ammunition before he could finish it off. 'Red 2', Sergeant Pilot Bohumir Furst and 'Red 3' Sergeant Karel Seda fired at one of the Bf 110s attacked by Sinclair. Furst attacked another Bf 110 over Whitstable and smoke poured from the port engine and he claimed it as a probable. Minutes later he chased a group of bombers north of Canterbury and Furst found himself fifty yards behind a Bf 109. He fired a burst and the enemy pilot baled out. It was the Pole's third victory of the war having shared the destruction of an Hs 126 and downing a Do 17 on 21 May while flying with the *Armée de l'Air*. A pair of Bf 110s then attacked Furst and he had to break away. Seda, meanwhile, followed Sinclair as he led their section in a curve towards the bombers and he closed to fifty yards' range and fired at a Bf 110. White smoke poured from the engines but the thirty-two-year-old former commercial airline pilot from Ujezd in East Bohemia did not see the *Luftwaffe* machine crash. Pilot Officer Stanislav Janouch, who was leading Yellow Section at 25,000 feet over Grays Thurrock, took the Section towards the enemy, level out of the sun. A Bf 110 appeared just in front and Janouch fired five bursts at 400 to 50 yards' range, which produced smoke from both engines. It was Janouch's fourth victory of the war. In May 1940 flying with *Groupe de Chasse* I./6 he had shared a He 111 victory and claimed a Bf 109 and a Hs 123 biplane shot down.[34]

Jerrard Jeffries ('Blue 1') leading 'B' Flight climbed into the sun and fired all his rounds at a Messerschmitt and saw pierces of metal flying off but he could not get closer to finish it off. Over Southend Pilot Officer Vilem Goth ('Blue 2'), a twenty-five-year-old Czech pilot who had joined 310 Squadron on 10 July, picked out two Bf 110s and out of the sun. He dived on one of them firing from 200 to 50 yards' range. The cockpit broke up in the air and the Bf 110 fell vertically towards the Thames Estuary between Southend and Foulness Island. As Goth broke away, he felt that his Hurricane had been hit. Then another Bf 110 was on him. In the ensuing combat the return fire ceased and the port engine was badly hit. The Bf 110 veered to the right and spun down over the sea. Goth could see nothing more since his cockpit was covered in oil and with his engine cutting out and the glycol tank emitting white smoke, it cut out altogether and he had to shut the throttle and dive towards the coast. He belly-landed at Whitman's Farm, Purleigh, about two miles south-east of Maldon in Essex. Posted to 501 Squadron at Kenley on 17 October, Goth was killed on 25 October, when he collided with Pilot Officer K.W. MacKenzie during a combat over Tenterden in Kent. Goth's Hurricane crashed in Bridgehurst Wood, Marden. MacKenzie was unhurt.

Pilot Officer John Eric Boulton ('Blue 3') attacked a Bf 110 over the Thames Estuary from below and behind without result before he saw a Heinkel heading south-east over Kent. After crossing the coast the twenty-one-year-old who before joining the RAF in 1937 had worked for the Buick Motor Co. in London, carried out two stern attacks at 15,000 feet. Boulton fired all his remaining rounds at the Heinkel and the port engine began to smoke and lost height diving down into the Channel near the Goodwin Sands. It was Boulton's first victory[35] since being attached to 310 Squadron on 11 July. He had asked for and been granted permission to fly with the Czechs on operational sorties.

Pilot Officer Emil Fechtner ('Green 1') fired at one of the bombers from below and set an engine smouldering before he took after a Bf 110 and fired at it. The Messerschmitt climbed and then fell off into a spin before crashing into the mass of dense smoke over the oil refineries. A bullet hit Fechtner's main tank but did not explode. While trying to reach some Dornier 17s Pilot Officer Stanislav Zimprich ('Green 2') saw a Bf 110 below. He fired at 300 to fifty yards' range, hitting the port engine, which sent the fighter gliding to the ground below. Zimprich followed another Bf 110 just above the beach-line near bombed oil tanks and the fighter folded and crashed into the inferno. An enemy bullet struck the 'footstep' of Zimprich's Hurricane, but he was unhurt. Sergeant Josef Koukal was shot down over the Thames Estuary at 20,000 feet and was grievously burned. He made a delayed drop to 11,000 feet to extinguish his burning clothes but after he landed they blazed again and he suffered seventy per cent burns to his face and body. His Hurricane crashed near Capel Fleet, Harty Marshes, on the Isle of Sheppey. Koukal was taken to Queen Victoria Hospital at East Grinstead and he became one of Archie McIndoe's guinea pigs. The Czech pilot was later commissioned and he left the RAF as a flight lieutenant. After the war he returned to Czechoslovakia and he became State Test Pilot.

When the claims were totted up they totalled eleven enemy aircraft and two probables,[36] all for the loss of two Hurricanes. By dusk their pilots were still missing. Then Denis Crowley-Milling, with nothing worse than a cut face, called to say that he was unhurt (although he would not fly again until the 15th). No word was received from Pilot Officer John Benzie who had gone down in the fighting over the Thames Estuary. The young Canadian airman was dead. Bader recalls:

> I lost one pilot killed, a second shot down but unhurt, a third untouched but his Hurricane badly shot up, while the CO (myself) got a cockpit-full of bullets and the right aileron shot off his Hurricane. We destroyed eleven aircraft, but it was windy work, let there be no mistake. On landing, I rang the Operations Room in a fury to be told that we had been sent off as soon as 11 Group had called for us from Duxford. This was one of the recurring problems during this heavy last period of the Battle. 11 Group, which guarded the southeast of England, was nearest to the enemy operating from northern France. Its controllers had an impossible task. When the German armadas started across the Channel for London, half or more of 11 Group's airfields were too close for the fighters to gain height to intercept the enemy, with the result that their pilots had to climb northwards. Duxford

was forty-three miles north of Tilbury, an ideal position for intercepting an enemy approaching London from eighty miles southeast of our capital. Quite naturally, the 11 Group controllers, who bore the heaviest burden of responsibility during the Battle of Britain, committed all their own squadrons before calling on Duxford in 12 Group.

Next morning 242 Squadron flew to Duxford, where Bader and his pilots again spent a frustrating day waiting in vain to be summoned by 11 Group as the German bombers returned to bomb London again. Fighter Command had flown 817 sorties on 7 September and on the 8th they flew 305 losing just two aircraft with one pilot saved. The *Luftwaffe's* losses, which made only some small attacks on airfields but made a heavy and concentrated attack that night on London, were fifteen.

On Monday 9 September Bader and his pilots again waited at Readiness throughout the day, as the German raids only really reached a tempo during the late afternoon when their targets were aircraft factories in the South London suburban area. At 1700 hours radar had detected a build-up of German aircraft over the Pas de Calais. They were twenty-six He 111s of II./KG 1 escorted by twenty Bf 110s of III./ZG 76 and sixty Bf 109s of JG 3. Nine squadrons engaged the enemy bombers but only when they headed in were 242 and 310 Squadrons' Hurricanes and 19 Squadron's Spitfires permitted to 'Scramble'. 'Woody' Woodhall asked Bader 'Will you patrol between North Weald and Hornchurch, Angels 20?' Anticipating that the enemy formation would swing west and come out of the sun Bader disregarded this and climbed south-west to 22,000 feet over the reservoirs at Staines, still climbing. When he sighted the bombers at around quarter to six, he ordered 19 Squadron's Spitfires to climb higher and provide cover as the Hurricanes attacked a formation of Dornier 17s in line astern through the middle of the enemy bomber formation. Powell-Shedden fired at one of the Dorniers and shouted, 'F-f'f'flamer', as it blew up. Bader claimed a Dornier and two Do 17s damaged. Back at Duxford Sergeant Pilot George William Brimble and Roy Bush, who had destroyed a Bf 110, said that they had seen their CO's Dornier go down in flames and that only one of the crew had baled out.[37] Willie McKnight and Hugh Tamblyn each downed two Bf 110s and Eric Ball had got a Bf 109E. Sergeant Eric Richardson, a twenty-eight-year old former RAF apprentice who had passed out in December 1931 as a fitter, destroyed a Dornier south of the Thames for his second victory, having destroyed a Ju 88 on 1 August. After being selected for pilot training he had joined 242 Squadron and had gone to France in June 1940, returning home after the defeat with no maps and landing on a beach near Minehead after running out of petrol. Richardson was commissioned later and awarded the DFC.

On 19 Squadron there were eight claimants for six aircraft destroyed, three probably destroyed and two damaged. Flight Lieutenant Wilfred Clouston climbed and the New Zealander put his Squadron in position to attack seven Bf 110s. Just as he was about to attack two Bf 109Es crossed his sights so he turned on them.

The rear one emitted glycol fumes after a short burst and then burst into flames. The fighter was from I./JG 53 and probably the one[38] flown by *Feldwebel* Heinrich Höhnisch, whose unit had been tasked with giving direct fighter cover to the rear of a He 111 formation attacking the London docks. One *Kette* of Heinkel bombers had become separated so Höhnisch's *Staffel* had covered them but they had only seven Bf 109s and he was the tail end Charlie with *Oberfeldwebel* Müller. The Bf 109s had made no contact with the RAF fighters but Höhnisch was certain that they could expect fighter attacks out of the sun as soon as they turned 180 degrees for their return flight. To his surprise he saw six Spitfires on a reciprocal course in a line abreast fifty metres above him. To avoid the inevitable attack Höhnisch tried to climb with his *Staffel* flying in front and below him and when he was level with his *Staffelkapitän* he thought he had made it but he was wrong. There was a rattle like an explosion in his fighter when Clouston's bullets hit home. Höhnisch was hit in the face by flames 'with the pressure of a blow torch'. The German pilot baled out with severe burns and bullet wounds to his right calf. The Messerschmitt crashed at Cherry Lodge Farm in Old Jail Lane, Biggin Hill. Höhnisch stayed in Woolwich for two months.[39] Clouston then attacked the second Bf 109 and fired the rest of his ammunition. He could see his shots hitting the German fighter and when his ammunition had finished he saw him going down in a left-hand gliding turn 'looking rather the worse for wear'.[40] Clouston was awarded a Bf 109E and another Bf 109E probably destroyed.

Sub-Lieutenant Arthur 'Admiral' Blake who destroyed a He 111 in the London area returned to Duxford with bullets through the windscreen and the gravity tank but he was unhurt. Flight Lieutenant Francis Brinsden landed at Detling with claims for two He 111s probably destroyed. One of them was probably a He 111H-3 of 3./KG 1 flown by *Oberleutnant* Kiunka, which Brinsden approached from dead astern when he saw another Hurricane attacking it. Brinsden emptied all his remaining ammunition into the bomber, which when he finished was down to 1,000 feet with both engines stopped and the flaps and undercarriage down. Kiunka put the badly damaged bomber down at Sundridge near Sevenoaks. All the crew were captured.[41] Sergeant David Cox engaged some Bf 109s but broke off to attack a Dornier, which sought safety in a convenient cloud. The former solicitor's clerk carried on determined to 'shoot something down'. He had plenty of ammunition and flew south a bit until to his right he saw six single aircraft that he thought were Hurricanes but as he got nearer he realised that they were Bf 109s. Four of the Messerschmitts dived away and he never saw them again. One of the other Bf 109s climbed behind his Spitfire and the other climbed above and in front. Then the one behind opened fire and Cox turned very violently while the Bf 109 carried straight on. The other Bf 109 turned and as he approached at right angles to the Spitfire Cox fired a 90-degree deflection shot and he went down. In the London area Pilot Officer Wallace 'Jock' Cunningham also destroyed a Bf 109. Pilot Officer Arthur F. Vokes, a twenty-three-year-old pre-war RAF Volunteer Reserve pilot from Edgbaston in Birmingham also got on the score sheet when the former bank clerk damaged a Dornier over north London.

In all the Duxford Wing had routed the bombers and claimed eleven of the twenty-eight officially destroyed this day.[42] Two of 242 Squadron's pilots failed to return. Pilot Officer Kirkpatrick Sclanders was shot down in combat with Do 17s and Bf 110s over Thames Haven at 1745 hours. The twenty-four-year-old Canadian, who had been a pilot since the tender age of fifteen, was killed, his Hurricane crashing at Marden Park Farm, Caterham. Sergeant Robert Lonsdale meanwhile, had managed to bale out safely. He later telephoned to say that he had been shot down by return fire from a Do 17 over the Thames Estuary. Lonsdale was used to adventures of this sort. He had joined the RAF on a short service commission in November 1935 and two years later he was serving with 25 Squadron and was a member of his Squadron's display team. He had resigned his commission on 30 November 1938 and rejoined the RAF early in 1940 as a sergeant. He served with 46 Squadron in Norway in late May to early June before being posted to 242 Squadron on 20 July. After the action over the Thames Estuary and taking to his parachute, Lonsdale had landed in a tree in the grounds of a girls' school at Caterham, hurting his leg, and he could not get down because of his injury. Uncomfortably, he had 'roosted in the branches for half an hour while the girls stood underneath giggling until the local constable arrived and brought him down a ladder'.[43]

Three of 310 Squadron's pilots failed to return although two were safe. After colliding with Pilot Officer John Boulton of 310 Squadron during an attack over Croydon, Flying Officer Gordon Sinclair DFC baled out of his Hurricane. Boulton's Hurricane hit a Do 215 amidships and crashed in Woodmanstern Lane, Woodmanstern, and he was killed. Sinclair was unharmed apart from a sprained ankle. He telephoned Bader and when his CO asked him how he was, he is reported to have said, 'Utterly amazed sir. D'you know, I lobbed straight into Caterham High Street and I was picking my parachute out of the gutter when a chap walked up and said, "Hallo Gordon, old boy. What are you doing here?" And I'm dammed if it wasn't a chap I was at school with.'[44] The third man lost, Pilot Officer Frantisek Rypl, was unhurt after crashing near Oxted out of fuel.

Despite the high claims for victories Bader was still not satisfied, still feeling that with more fighters the Duxford Wing could have destroyed more enemy aircraft than it had. He later said:

> Tactics were not for the Battle of Britain. All the fighter pilots could do was to get at the German bombers the quickest way possible, risking interference from Me 109s. These enemy fighters took a heavy toll particularly of 11 Group squadrons based in Kent and Surrey, which were too near the Channel to climb to the enemy height in time. As a result they were frequently clobbered on the way up.

But when Bader flew to 12 Group Headquarters at Hucknall, Leigh-Mallory told his impatient squadron leader that he would be getting two more squadrons – 302 'City of Poznan' with Hurricane Is and 611 'West Lancashire' AAF, with Spitfires. On paper this was the equivalent of sixty or more fighters.

Even the normally ebullient Bader, who was also awarded the DSO, was dumbfounded.[45]

1   *Spitfire Summer: When Britain Stood Alone* by Malcolm Brown (Carlton Books Ltd 2000).

2   Christie recalled: 'While over Genoa a Fiat biplane fighter carried out a quarter attack on my right. So I descended into the clouds. While returning to base I observed a twin-engined bomber approaching the coast about thirty miles east of Vannes. It had Italian markings, a rear top turret and front turret. I could not see if it had a 'dustbin' underneath. I carried out three attacks almost out of range from the beam, then as the turrets appeared to be unable to turn through more than 45 degrees I carried out full beam attacks passing over the top very low. After two attacks he descended and force-landed on the water. The crew of five climbed onto the wing and swam towards the shore. They had no lifebelts or dinghy. The machine sank in about three minutes, nose first.' *Above All Unseen: The Royal Air Force's Photographic Reconnaissance units 1939–1945*. Edward Leaf (PSL 1997)

3   Bf 110D/O 3315 A2+HK.

4   Hurricanes of 56 Squadron, who claimed three Bf 110s and two Heinkels east of North Weald, joined 242 Squadron in the battle. 'B' Flight of 303 *Warsaw-Kosciuszko* Squadron were at 10,000 feet *en route* to *rendezvous* with six Blenheims for an interception exercise when they ran into a formation of what was thought to be sixty Dornier Do 17s and sixty Bf 110s. Over St Albans one of the Polish pilots claimed a Do 17 destroyed for the unit's first victory in the Battle although the victim was actually a Bf 110 of 4./ZG 76. *The Luftwaffe Fighters' Battle of Britain: The Inside Story: July–October 1940* by Chris Goss (Crécy Publishing Ltd 2000). After the defeat of Poland and then France, where Polish fighter pilots distinguished themselves in action against the *Luftwaffe*, they made their way to England to join the British cause in its hour of greatest need. On arrival in the UK they were 'processed' through No. 3 Polish Wing at Blackpool and sent to Operational Training Units before being posted to fighter and bomber squadrons. The earliest arrivals were absorbed into Regular and Auxiliary squadrons and several saw action with the RAF by the end of July. It was only when their numbers grew too large to be absorbed that it was decided to form special squadrons almost entirely composed of Poles and Czechs.

303 *Warsaw-Kosciuszko* Squadron was formed at RAF Northolt on 22 July 1940 from pilots of the 111 *Kosciuszko* and 112 *'Warsaw' Eskadra* of the *Lotnictwo Woljskowe* (Polish Air Force) evacuated from France. As such they became the second Polish fighter squadron to form in the RAF. 302 'City of Poznan' Squadron had begun forming on 17 July with Hurricane Mk Is. At Church Fenton 306 'City of Torun' Squadron formed from personnel in the 3rd (Poznan) and 4th (Torun) Air Regiments of the Polish Air Force but it did not become operational with Hurricane Is until November 1940.

5   Bf 110C 3257 M8+BM of 4./ZG 76 crashed at Enfield Sewage farm, Wharf Road, Ponder's End at 4.55 pm. *Hauptmann* Heinz Wagner, *Staffelkapitän* 4./ZG 76, and *Stabsfeldwebel* Heinrich Schmidt both killed.

6   He 111H-2 5125 V4+MV made it as far as the coast and was forced to ditch in the sea off Folkestone harassed by Sergeant Beardsley of 610 Squadron. Burger, *Gefreiters* Hildebrand, Feierabend, Roggermann and Klappholz were all picked up by the ASR and landed at Dover. Another 5./KG 1 Heinkel He 111H-2 5444 V4+GV flown by *Oberleutnant* Wächter is also thought to have been destroyed by 242 Squadron over London at 1449 hours. Wächter and *Gefreiter* Mahl were killed and three others were missing.

7   Christie was awarded a DFC on 21 August 1940. Squadron Leader Christie was killed near Point Quebec on 6 July 1942 in a Hudson.

8   A 'mass formation', named after Marshal Balbo, Italian Minister for Air during the 1930s, who favoured mass tactical formations. Balbo, as Governor of Libya, was shot down and killed by his own anti-aircraft guns near Tobruk on 28 June 1940.

9   In R6958.

10   Sergeant John Teasdale Craig was a former Halton Apprentice. He was KIA (killed in action) on 2 June 1941 in a mid-air collision at 56 OTU aged twenty-seven. He had six victories and four probables.

11   William Alexander Smith was born at Lucknow, India, on 18 November 1915 and was educated in Scotland where he read engineering at Edinburgh. He joined the RAF on a short service commission in June 1937. After training his initial posting was to 2 AACU in March 1938 on target-towing duties. On 1 February 1939 he was posted to 66 Squadron at Duxford on Spitfire Is. On Christmas Eve 1939 he was promoted to flying officer. On 13 May 1940 he damaged a Ju 87 at Streefkerk and over Dunkirk on 2 June he damaged a Bf 109. He was posted to 229 Squadron flying Hurricane Is at Digby on 11 June, where he became a flight

commander. He claimed a He 111 destroyed on 11 September at Reigate, which was shared with three Spitfire pilots. On 15 September he damaged two Heinkels and probably destroyed another on the 26th near Southampton. Next day he attacked some Ju 88s, damaging one but being hit himself by crossfire. He was had to force-land his Hurricane at Linfield, writing off P3603. On 30 September he damaged a He 111 at Woking. On 6 October he made a crash-landing in Hurricane P3716 near Leatherhead after a routine patrol, out of fuel and with his radio not working. He damaged a Do 17 near Staines on the 24th. On Christmas Eve 1940 he was promoted to flight lieutenant. In May 1941 229 Squadron was sent to the Middle East aboard HMS *Furious*, flying off to Malta on the 21st, from where the aircraft were flown on to Mersa Matruh. Initially the pilots were attached to 73 and 274 Squadrons in the Western Desert until the end of August, when 229 Squadron was ready to operate in its own right. On 15 July he destroyed a Ju 87 of II./SrG2 in the Tobruk area and probably destroyed another. On 1 September 229 Squadron began to operate its own aircraft and in October he was promoted to command the squadron. On 23 November in the Tobruk area he destroyed a Ju 87 of *Stab* I or II./StG1 and claimed another as a probable. On 29 November he damaged a G50 at Tobruk and on 3 December he damaged a SM84 at Gabr Saleh. He followed this on 14 December with the destruction of a Bf 109 south-east of Tmimi and a Ju 88 of III./LGI destroyed on the 27th at Gazala. On 9 January 1942, whilst on a bomber escort operation over Agedabia, four of 229 Squadron's Hurricanes were shot down by Bf 109Fs of I./JG 27, one of them being that flown by Smith, who was wounded. He returned on 7 February and ten days later he claimed a Cant Z1007bis as damaged over the Mediterranean but it was later discovered that he had shot it down. It was his sixth confirmed victory. At the end of February his tour finished. He was promoted to squadron leader on 1 March and he was awarded a DFC on 17 March. He then became an instructor at one of the Middle East OTUs. In January 1943 he took command of 1435 Squadron on Malta, but his stay here was brief, and by the end of February he had gone. He remained in the RAF after the war, retiring in November 1962 as a wing commander. He died in the RAF Hospital, Ely, on 21 November 1990. *Men of the Battle of Britain* by Kenneth G. Wynn (CCB Associates 1999)/ *Aces High* by Christopher Shores and Clive Williams (Grub Street 1994).

12   *Memories of a British Veteran* by Wallace Cunningham.

13   Mike Bayon wanted to be a fighter pilot but he eventually became a Mosquito navigator in 8 Group and flew fifty-two Mosquito raids before the war in Europe ended. He was awarded the DFC.

14   Coward was born in Teddington, Middlesex, on 18 May 1915 and educated
      at Sutton High School. After completing elementary, intermediate and
      advanced flying training from February to September 1937, he was posted
      to 19 Squadron at Duxford. On 6 November 1939 Coward was appointed
      'A' Flight Commander in 266 Squadron, then forming at Sutton Bridge.
      Men of the Battle of Britain. After receiving an artificial limb and fit again,
      James Coward was posted to Mr Churchill's personal staff, in charge of roof
      spotting (watching for enemy aircraft) at Chequers and Chartwell. In early
      January 1942 he went on a three months' refresher course at Hullavington,
      after which he was posted to 52 OTU Aston Down to command a squadron.
      In October 1942 Coward went as CFI (Chief Flying Instructor) to 55 OTU.
      On 21 November 1943 he took command of 1 ADU at Croydon. Coward
      was sent on a course at RAF Staff College on 17 June 1944, following
      which he was posted to the Air Ministry, in charge of Fighter Operational
      Training. After the war he held a series of staff appointments and
      commands and was awarded the AFC in 1954. He retired from the RAF on
      8 September 1969, as an Air Commodore. *Men of the Battle of Britain*.

15   *Spitfire Summer: When Britain Stood Alone*. Aeberhardt, who was from
      Walton-on-Thames, was buried in the churchyard of St Mary and St
      Andrew at Whittlesford near the airfield.

16   *Spitfire Summer*. Years after the war Cox found out that it had crashed and
      that the crew were taken prisoner. Cox's victim was Bf 110D 3396 3U+HS
      of 8./ZG 26, which crashed in the sea between Colne Point and Clacton at
      0830 hours. *Oberleutnant* von Bergen and *Unteroffizier* Becker were
      captured. 14./LG 1 lost two Bf 110s. One was shot down by fighters over
      the Thames estuary and crashed in the sea off Forness, Thanet. *Leutnant*
      Eichorn was rescued unhurt and captured. *Unteroffizier* Growe was killed.
      A second Bf 110 L1+AK ditched in the sea near the Nore Light, Thames
      Estuary; *Feldwebel* Gottlob and *Obergefreiter* Doepfer were both rescued
      and captured. A Bf 110C-2 of 1./ZG 2, a Bf 110C of *Stab* ZG 26, a Bf
      110C-4 of *Stab* III./ZG 26, and a Bf 110C of 6./ZG 76 all crash-landed in
      France on their return after being damaged in fighter attacks.

17   Dornier Do 17Z 2669 5K+LM, which was also damaged by ground
      defences, force-landed at Princes Golf Club, Sandwich. *Oberfeldwebel*
      Lange, *Unteroffizier* Krostoptsch, *Feldwebel* Berndt and *Feldwebel*
      Wuensch were all wounded and captured. Do 17Z-3 3414 of 5./KG 3
      crashed in the sea near the South Goodwins. *Feldwebel* Nickel drowned,
      Unteroffizier Blasche, *Feldwebel* Gutat and *Unteroffizier* Sonntag were
      captured. Six other Dorniers of KG 2 and KG 3, which were damaged by
      the fighters near Colchester, returned safely to their bases in France.

18   Do 17Z 3264 5K+KM.

19 Kredba was killed on 14 February 1942 on a night training flight.

20 Bf 110D 3U+EP 3310 of 6./ZG 26 was shot down by Leonard Haines near North Weald at 1048 hours. *Leutnant* Manhard and *Unteroffizier* Driews were killed. Despite a jammed starboard cannon, Sergeant George Unwin destroyed Bf 110C-2 3U+KR 3225 of 7./ZG 26 near North Weald at about 1045 hours. *Unteroffizier* Ucker was killed and *Feldwebel* Grau was wounded. Sub-Lieutenant Arthur Blake RNVR damaged Bf 110C-2 3U+GT 3378 of 7./ZG 26 at about 1045 hours before both his cannon failed and it crashed at Wissant. Sergeant Roden, who made no claim, had no problems with stoppages.

21 Bf 110C-4 3M+JHL 2133 of I./ZG 2.

22 3M+EK 2065.

23 3M+EL 3113.

24 3M+CB 3120.

25 Squadron Leader M. Robinson was posted away on 3 September 1940.

26 *Wing Leader* by Group Captain (later AVM) Johnnie Johnson CB CBE DSO* DFC* (Chatto & Windus 1956). Wing Commander 'Johnnie' Johnson finished the war as the top scoring British fighter pilot with thirty-four confirmed victories.

27 Born in Ceska, Trebova, on 14 September 1909, Dolezal joined the Czech Air Force in 1937, serving in the 36 Fighter Flight of Air Regiment 2 before escaping on 20 June 1939 to France where he joined *Groupe de Chasse* II./2. Flying the Morane 406, he claimed one victory and figured in other shared claims during May–June before he escaped to England. In August 1940 'Dolly' was commissioned into the RAF and he was posted to 310 (Czech) Squadron before being attached to 19 Squadron on 24 August.

28 By 6 September, a huge German invasion fleet appeared to be ready to sail. British forces were put on 'Alert No. 2' meaning that an attack was probable in the next two days.

29 On 7 September 984 Hurricane and Spitfire pilots were flying with the squadrons, a deficiency of nearly twenty-two pilots per squadron and of these 150 were only partly trained.

30 *Memories of a British Veteran* by Wallace Cunningham.

31 *Battle Over Britain.* Bf 110D-0 A2+NH of *Stab* II./ZG 2. *Leutnant* K Schonemann and *Unteroffizier* H Mescheden baled out too low and were killed. This aircraft was also attacked by Hurricanes of 1 and 310 Squadrons.

32   Dornier Do 17 2674 A5+CA.

33   Born in Wellington on 7 February 1918, Roy Bush worked initially for an insurance company, but joined the RAF on a short service commission early in 1939. After attending 5 OTU, Aston Down, he was posted out to France in mid May 1940 to join 615 Squadron at Abbeville, where he flew Gladiators on airfield defence until the unit was withdrawn to England on the 21st. At the start of June he was posted to 242 Squadron and returned to France, where he was involved in the Allied retreat until this unit too was withdrawn on 18 June.

34   Originally designed as a dive-bomber, the Henschel Hs 123 was the *Luftwaffe*'s last operational biplane remaining in service until mid-1944. With its radial engine overspeeding it made a shattering noise, which demoralised troops under attack.

35   He shared the victory with Sergeant D.A. Hekke of 504 Squadron.

36   The Duxford Wing destroyed three Bf 110s of I./ZG 2 over North London that evening. Bf 110C-4 3117 3M+FL crewed by *Oberfeldwebel* Otterbach and *Hauptfeldwebel* Ohligschlager who were killed. Bf 110C-4 3246 3M+BB flown by *Oberleutnant* Granz and *Feldwebel* Schutel, both killed. Bf 110C-4 2216 crewed by *Leutnant* Kislinger and *Unteroffizier* Dahnke, who were killed.

37   Brimble had destroyed a Bf 110 on 30 August. He scored another victory on 18 September when he destroyed a Dornier Do 17.

38   Bf 109E-4 1508 'White 5'. *The Luftwaffe Fighters' Battle of Britain: The Inside Story: July–October 1940.*

39   *The Luftwaffe Fighters' Battle of Britain: The Inside Story: July–October 1940.*

40   *The Luftwaffe Fighters' Battle of Britain: The Inside Story: July–October 1940.*

41   In October 1940 Brinsden went to 303 Squadron at Leconfield, as RAF Liaison Officer. He returned to operations on 26 March 1941, when he joined the newly formed 485 Squadron at Driffield, as a flight commander. He went to the MSFU at Speke on 22 July as Port Loading Officer. He took command of 3 ADU at High Ercall in mid-August 1942. He was posted to 54 OTU Charter Hall in February 1943 for a night-fighting conversion course and then joined 25 Squadron flying Mosquito *Intruder* fighter-bombers at Church Fenton. On a sortie to Westerland on 17 August 1943 on the night of the Peenemünde raid he bombed Sylt airfield and successfully attacked the hangars at rooftop height. He was then picked up and blinded

by searchlights. With vision almost lost he headed out to sea but struck the surface of the water and broke both airscrews. Brinsden ditched the aircraft and he and his navigator Flying Officer P.G. Fane-Sewell, got into their dinghy and attempted to sail out of the bay under an offshore breeze. Dawn brought a wind change and at mid-day on 18 August they were blown ashore into the arms of German troops who had been watching them for six hours. Eventually Brinsden found himself in *Stalag Luft III. Men of the Battle of Britain*.

42 He 111 H-3 5713 V4+BL of 3./KG 1 was shot down by Sub-Lieutenant Arthur Blake RNVR of 19 Squadron over north-east London at 1750 hours. *Unteroffizier* Marck, *Oberfeldwebel* Heidrich, *Gefreiter* Reinecke and two other crew were killed. Bf 109E-4 1394 of *Stab* I./JG 27 was shot down by Pilot Officer Wallace 'Jock' Cunningham of 19 Squadron near London at 1750 hours. *Oberleutnant* Bode was killed. Cunningham was also awarded a Do 17 probable. The Hurricane flown by Pilot Officer J.E. Boulton of 310 Squadron struck He 111 H-2 2630 A1+ZD of III./KG 53, which was falling after collision with another Hurricane south of Croydon at approximately 1800 hours. Boulton was killed, as were *Feldwebels* Endorff, Wenninger, Dorig and Broderich and *Oberleutnant* Melnecke. Bf 110C 2137 2N+FM of III./ZG 76 was shot down by Squadron Leader Douglas Blackwood of 310 Squadron near Croydon at 1740 hours. *Unteroffizier* Bierling and *Unteroffizier* Weiher were killed. Bf 110C 3207 2N+EP of II./ZG 76 was shot down by a 310 Squadron Hurricane near Croydon at 1750 hours. *Feldwebel* Ostermuncher and *Gefreiter* Zimmermann were killed.

43 *Reach For the Sky*. Lonsdale had destroyed a Heinkel He 111 on 30 August and he downed a Do 215 on 9 September. He was posted to 501 Squadron on 12 October 1940. In January 1941 he was posted to Canada as an instructor. In October he was promoted to warrant officer. He returned to the United Kingdom in 1943 and converted to Lancasters.

44 *Reach For the Sky*. However, *The Battle of Britain Then and Now*, edited by Winston G Ramsey (After the Battle 1980) says that Sinclair landed in a wood at Caterham and the Hurricane crashed off Purley Way, Wallington. *The Battle of Britain* by John Frayn Turner (Airlife 1998) says that Sinclair's parachute descent took nearly thirteen minutes and he landed in a wood just off the Purley Way at Coulsdon. He was picked up by Lieutenant G.D. Cooper of the Irish Guards from Caterham. Cooper had been watching the whole action through his field glasses and told Sinclair what had happened. Sinclair was awarded a Do 17 victory, his tenth and final victory of the war.

45 302 'City of Poznan', the first of the Polish fighter squadrons to form in England, had begun forming at Leconfield on 17 July from Polish pilots who had served with the III./3 Poznan Fighter *Dyon* in Poland and with GC

I./145 in France. Initially, they were equipped with Hurricane Is and coastal operations began in August. The Poles began the move further south on 11 October when the 'Poznan' Squadron was stationed at Northolt. 611 Squadron had been stationed at Duxford in September 1939 equipped with Spitfire Is. In October it had moved to Digby from where on 2 June 1940 a detachment had been sent to operate over the Dunkirk evacuation from Martlesham Heath. In the one day eight victories were claimed for the loss of two Spitfires. From August to October 1940 611 Squadron was equipped with some of the first Spitfire IIAs.

CHAPTER FOUR

In the Teeth of Odds

All the great struggles of history have been won by superior will-power wresting victory in the teeth of odds or upon the narrowest of margins.

Winston S. Churchill

After his visit to Hucknall Douglas Bader was buoyed and excited at the prospect of getting two more squadrons. Now he could field three Hurricane squadrons, which would fly together at the lower level of 20,000 feet if the Wing were called in time, with the Spitfires protecting them 5,000 feet higher. Bader was always looking to 'clobber' the enemy at every opportunity but early morning patrols from Duxford over the next two days, 10 and 11 September, proved frustrating with no sightings of enemy aircraft. The same could not be said of Duxford's Spitfires however. Tuesday 10 September was quiet over England until late in the afternoon when the *Luftwaffe* took advantage of cloud cover and attacked some airfields of 10 and 11 Groups. The Spitfire flown by 'Grumpy' Unwin was believed damaged in combat with a Bf 110 east of London and he force-landed unhurt. The following day some bombs fell on London and there were three large raids on Portsmouth and Southampton. Fighter Command flew 678 sorties and lost twenty-nine aircraft, seventeen pilots killed and six wounded while the *Luftwaffe* lost twenty-five aircraft. Though 242 Squadron sat out the action Squadron Leader 'Sandy' Lane led an all-Spitfire wing made up of 19, 611, and 74 Squadrons who used Duxford as a forward base. The three Squadrons were in the thick of it at just after four o'clock in the afternoon. 'Sandy' Lane had just eight Spitfires made up of Red Section with four and Blue and Green Sections operating as pairs. At about 1615 hours Lane who was at 23,000 feet, spotted anti-aircraft fire south of Gravesend and this drew his attention to a formation of about fifty Heinkels followed by two other large bomber formations. Lane dived his formation down in a head on attack on the dozen or so leading Heinkel 111s 3,000 feet below. Red Section followed with the four Spitfires echeloned to port. The attack made the enemy scatter. Lane saw three Bf 110s flying near the Heinkels and he opened fire on the rearmost aircraft from astern. It was last seen diving down with its starboard engine on fire. He then carried out head-on and beam attacks on the Heinkels, finishing his ammunition in an astern attack, which set fire to a Heinkel's starboard engine. 'Grumpy' Unwin, who damaged a Dornier over east London, singled out a Heinkel He 111. Unwin recalled:

> This Heinkel was flying around. There was a very thin layer of cloud no more than fifty feet thick and I was wandering around above this, having lost everybody. An incredible thing this in air warfare. You go in as a squadron or a wing and you get mixed up and then, two minutes later, you are on your own. You can't see an aeroplane anywhere. It's amazing how suddenly the sky seems to clear. You can find them eventually but it was rather strange, it always happened. I'd got split up on this particular occasion and I was above cloud looking for some fun and what have you and I suddenly saw this Heinkel come out of the cloud, climbing. He was smack in front of me. So I closed in and gave him a burst whereupon he promptly went back into the cloud. I thought, 'Damn it' and I was about to go down again when he came up again. And he did this some four or five times. And I was rather puzzled on one occasion, about the third or fourth time, because he went down apparently unhurt and when he came up he had one engine blazing. I thought, 'That's bloody funny, he didn't have that when he went into the cloud'. Anyway, when we got back for debriefing 'Sandy' Lane repeated exactly the same story. But he was the one underneath the cloud. And so what was happening was that this Heinkel was being shot at by me above the cloud, went for cover into the cloud, which was so thin he went through it. Below it happened to be Lane and he shot at him and he went back up again. And this went on until eventually he was shot down. It was a bit puzzling why he kept coming up for more. But that was the reason.[1]

Six other pilots in 19 Squadron claimed victories. David Cox was awarded a Do 17 probably destroyed and Leonard Haines a confirmed Bf 110 victory. Pilot Officer 'Dolly' Dolezal got a Bf 109 probable at Gravesend before he had to break away and return to base slightly wounded by a splinter in his right knee and with his Spitfire severely damaged. Sergeant Bernard Jennings ('Red 2') made a head-on attack on a Bf 110 and then fired two bursts from astern at a He 111, which went down apparently out of control near Gravesend. Next he found a formation of Bf 110s and he attacked the rearmost machine. It fell behind with a smoking engine and he finished it off firing from above and behind. The Bf 110 crashed between Sittingbourne and Maidstone. 'Farmer' Lawson was credited with a He 111 destroyed. Sergeant Henry Roden made a lone attack on a formation of Bf 110s, which had gone into a large defensive circle. He dived from out of the sun from 1,000 feet above them and pulled up beneath one of them in an astern position before giving it a five-second burst. He then had to break away as other Bf 110s were turning into a firing position behind him. The twenty-four-year-old's victim was last seen in a shallow dive with one engine smoking.

611 Squadron claimed two enemy aircraft shot down and three probably destroyed. Flight Sergeant Herbert S Sadler, a former aircraft apprentice who had joined the RAF in 1932, claimed a Bf 110 destroyed over Gravesend. He had joined 611 Squadron at Duxford on 21 September 1939 and over Dunkirk on 2 June 1940 had destroyed a Bf 110. Sergeant Stephen Levenson, who came from Taynuilt, claimed a Ju 88 destroyed in the London area. He was also awarded a Bf 109 probably destroyed. Levenson's Spitfire was damaged by return fire from a He 111 over Croydon and he crashed with a dead engine at Bletchingley unhurt. Pilot Officer John Wilfred Lund, a twenty-one-year-old from Norton in Yorkshire, got a Bf 110 probably destroyed over south London. The son of a Methodist minister, Lund had read history at Oriel College, Oxford, and was a member of the University Air Squadron before joining the RAF. He had shared in the destruction of two Dornier Do 17s during July and August. Sergeant Alfred Denmark Burt, a twenty-four-year old former aircraft apprentice, got a He 111 probably destroyed in the area south-east of London/north-west Dungeness. Burt was posted to 603 Squadron on 4 October. Over the capital and the London Docks 74 Squadron claimed five aircraft destroyed, two bombers probably destroyed and three enemy aircraft damaged. KG 26 had lost six Heinkels and eleven damaged while ZG 26 lost five Bf 110s and one damaged.

Winston Churchill made the following broadcast to the nation:

> The effort of the Germans to secure daylight mastery of the air over England is of course the crux of the whole war. So far it has failed conspicuously... For him [Hitler] to try and invade this country without having secured mastery in the air would be a very hazardous undertaking. Nevertheless, all his preparations for invasion on a great scale are steadily going forward. Several hundreds of self-propelled barges are moving down the coasts of Europe, from the German and Dutch harbours to the ports of northern France, from Dunkirk to Brest, and beyond Brest to the French harbours in the Bay of Biscay.

In Germany Hitler postponed Operation *Sealion* until 14 September and when that day arrived he postponed it again until the 17th. Over the past two weeks 231 RAF fighter pilots had been killed or badly wounded and 295 Hurricanes and Spitfires destroyed or badly damaged. It was going to be a close run thing.

On Thursday 12 September it was cloudy in the Channel and there were only small raids in the south of England and even a reduced effort by the German raiders at night when the main force raided the capital. At Duxford 19 Squadron received eight additional Spitfires. During the past three engagements, 19 Squadron had been operating at reduced strength with eight or nine Spitfires instead of twelve. Another handicap was the need to re-fit the Spitfire Ia aircraft with VHF radios in place of the older HF units, which had been carried out on the now-departed Mk Ibs. During the changeover Spitfires with both types of radio had to fly in mixed formations with all the attendant problems with communication.[2] Three operational Spitfire pilots, Pilot Officer Richard Leoline Jones, Sergeant Henry Walpole Charnock and Sergeant David Edward Lloyd were transferred in from 64 Squadron, which was now a Category 'C' unit, a reinforcement scheme having been introduced by Dowding five days earlier. Jones had joined the RAFVR in 1938 before becoming a pilot in the RAF. Charnock, who at thirty-five was a few years older, had been educated at Harrow School and was a graduate of the RAF College, Cranwell, in 1924. He had been commissioned at the end of 1925 and posted to 32 Squadron, flying Grebes, Gamecocks and Siskins and in August 1930 was posted to 1 Squadron, seemingly destined for a brilliant career, but in December he was court martialled for a low flying offence and he was cashiered. Charnock had rejoined the RAF at the outbreak of war in 1939 as a sergeant and had crashed a Spitfire during a routine patrol on 6 September.[3] Lloyd, who came from Wanstead, Essex, had joined the RAFVR in 1939, joining 64 Squadron on 28 August 1940. The weather was still unsettled on 13 September with bright intervals and showers and rain in the Channel while the Straits were cloudy. That night 105 German bombers raided London again. Next day 302 'City of Poznan' and 611 'West Lancashire' AAF joined 242, 310 and 19 Squadrons at Duxford and Fowlmere as a succession of afternoon raids were made on London. Mainly they were composed of fighters and twice the Duxford Wing patrolled North London but to no avail. Sergeant Frantisek Marek, a twenty-seven-year-old from Ceske Budejovice, who had joined 19 Squadron from 310 Squadron on 29 August, was killed when he crashed near Horndon-on-the-Hill at Orford, Sussex during a routine patrol. It was presumed that he was a victim of an oxygen system failure aboard his Spitfire. The Czech was one of fourteen RAF pilots who were lost this day when Fighter Command flew 860 sorties, although six were saved. The *Luftwaffe* also lost fourteen aircraft.

Then came the day that is forever etched in RAF folklore and the glorious annals of world history. Sunday 15 September dawned misty with the promise of fine weather throughout the rest of the day but with cloud patches. Göring intended that his bombers carry out two heavy attacks on London in an attempt to further sap and perhaps finally break the morale of its long suffering inhabitants. The first wave of twenty-five Dornier Do 17s of I and III./KG 76 and 160 Bf 109s plotted heading for the capital were engaged by 11 Group. The III *Gruppe Kommandeur*, Aloise Lindmayr, a Slovenian-born *Ritterkreuzträger* or Knight's Cross holder led the bombers. At 1122 hours the Duxford Wing's fifty-six Hurricane and Spitfire fighters were scrambled to meet the returning waves of Dorniers and Bf 109s leaving the London suburbs. Flight Lieutenant Wilfred Clouston, who should have led 19 Squadron, took off late because his oxygen bottle had not been refilled. Squadron Leader Lane had trouble starting his engine and so he, 'Jock' Cunningham and 'Admiral' Blake also took off late. What was left of the

Squadron, led by 'Farmer' Lawson, joined up with the rest of the Wing as 242, 302 'City of Poznan' and 310 (Czech) Squadrons headed south at 25,000 feet with 19 and 611 Squadron's Spitfires stepped up behind them at 26–27,000 feet.

At quarter past twelve the Wing saw the German formations 3,000 feet below and down-sun south of the capital. For once the Wing had position, height and numbers. Once again, Bader practised what he and the RFC pilots preached. 242 Squadron's Hurricanes tore into the composite *Gruppe* of KG 76 and their Bf 109 escorts without mercy, Bader aiming his guns directly at the 'beetle-eye' glazed nose of the Dornier for maximum effect. Bader recalled:

> During this period of mass formation raids the methods of attack adopted by the British fighter leaders were decided according to the situation. There were one or two rare occasions when a leader found himself approaching an enemy formation head-on at the same height. This was a splendid moment for the leading section of fighters because the enemy bomber crews were sitting in a 'glass-house' in the front end, with no protection. Facing an eight-gun fighter. The worst sufferer in this respect was the Heinkel 111, which had three people in the front consisting of two pilots and a gunner lying on his stomach between them – the latter had to manipulate a single machine-gun which fired out of the nose. Both the Spitfire and the Hurricane were each so instantly responsive to the pilot's whim that this hazardous head-on attack was perfectly possible since, having fired a short burst, the pilot pulled up over the bomber.

As usual when under attack from fighters the Dorniers closed into tight formation to concentrate their feeble defensive fire. As Bader's Hurricanes made their eye-level, head-on attacks, *Feldwebel* William Raab, pilot of one of the Do 17Zs in the 9th *Staffel* who had survived a low-level attack on Kenley less than a month earlier, on 18 August, was understandably scared. 'They came in fast, getting bigger and bigger. It was very frightening: in the glass noses of our Dorniers there was not even a molehill to hide behind!'

'Here come those last fifty Spitfires,' joked one of the crew. (For some time now German Intelligence claimed that Fighter Command was down to its 'last 50 Spitfires'.) Could the words have come from the lips of *Unteroffizier* Malter? Or did *Feldwebel* Teuffert speak them? Perhaps it was *Oberfeldwebel* Streit. Raab never found out for the crew was doomed, hit by a fusillade of fire from one of Bader's Hurricanes south of London. The stricken Dornier[4] staggered across Sussex where finally it crashed into the sea just off the coast. Malter was killed, Teuffert was wounded and Streit and Raab were listed as 'missing'. Just who got the Dornier is hard to say. All told, 242 Squadron claimed five Dorniers of KG 76 with two more damaged. Over south London Noel Stansfeld and Dickie Cork each claimed a Do 17, as did Stan Turner. Hugh Tamblyn claimed a Do 17 destroyed and one damaged while Pilot Officer Neil Campbell claimed a Dornier damaged south of the Thames and Flight Lieutenant Powell-Shedden was awarded a half share in a Dornier victory. Norrie Hart claimed a Bf 109 destroyed.[5]

At around the same time as Bader's Hurricanes were attacking the Dorniers, 19 Squadron's pilots were meting out death and destruction in the turbulent sky over the London area. 'Grumpy' Unwin destroyed a Bf 109 near Westerham. Five minutes later Pilot Officer 'Jock' Cunningham – 'Blue 3' – broke away from his Section to attack a solitary Bf 110. His first attack from above and right rear quarter set the German aircraft's starboard engine on fire. He broke away, turned in from the left and delivered another attack from the left-hand side. The Scot considered that the Bf 110 was as good as destroyed and he broke off the attack. The Messerschmitt was then attacked by two Hurricanes who more or less shot him from the sky. At the same time Flight Lieutenant Wilfred Clouston destroyed a Bf 110 over south London and 'Farmer' Lawson got a Do 17 probably destroyed in the London area.[6] Five minutes later Clouston destroyed his second Bf 110, in the South London area, and Flight Sergeant 'Bill' Steere destroyed a Bf 109. At half past twelve Sergeant David Cox destroyed a Bf 109 south of Tunbridge Wells. About twenty minutes later Leonard Haines, who was leading Green Section south of London, noticed AA fire just west of the capital and when he investigated he could see a force of forty German aircraft, which he could not identify. They were the bombers of I./KG 1, 5./KG 2, 6./KG 26 and KG 53, which were bombing London's Victoria Docks escorted by Bf 109Es, including those of 2./LG 2 from Calais Marck on the Channel coast. Their losses were always very high because the Messerschmitts flew on the furthest flank of the escort and they therefore had no rear cover.[7] Haines put his section into line astern and made for the AA fire when two Bf 109E-7s of 2./LG 2 appeared to his right. He turned and attacked them, giving the one flown by *Unteroffizier* August Klik ('Red 2') a burst and it half rolled and dived vertically to 12,000 feet where it straightened out. Haines dived after it and as the Messerschmitt finished its dive he recommenced his attack. Haines was going faster than the Bf 109 and he continued firing until he had to pull away to avoid collision. The Bf 109 half-rolled and dived vertically with black smoke apparently coming from underneath the Klik's seat. Haines followed it down until the fighter entered cloud at 6,000 feet. Klik did not want to bale out because German pilots had been warned that Polish pilots would shoot at them in their parachutes and he did not want to ditch because it was not worth the risk. He turned towards dry land and made a smooth landing on the Isle of Sheppey in the Thames Estuary where he was quickly apprehended by the Home Guard.[8]

West of London 310 Czech Hurricane Squadron saw enemy bombers heading north and they turned south to attack. At the same time the bombers took a turn southwards. In the brief fight that followed, 310 Squadron claimed four Dorniers destroyed. Flight Lieutenant Jerrard Jeffries who was leading 'B' Flight, dived on the bombers and figured in two Dornier victories, one of which was shared with a Spitfire pilot. The other was shared with Pilot Officer Hubacek, Sergeant Jan Kaucky and Sergeant Raimund Puda[9] and Sergeant R.T. Holmes of 504 Squadron and Flying Officer A.K. Ogilvie of 609 Squadron in combat over London at 11.50 am. The Do 17Z of 1./KG 76, which was flown by *Oberleutnant* Robert Zehbe, crashed in Victoria Station yard.[10] Flight Sergeant Josef Kominek who began an attack with Jeffries lost sight of his leader at 15,000 feet probably because he was four miles above Kingston on Thames while the Czech was by now overhead Tunbridge Wells. Kominek and three other Hurricanes attacked a Dornier 17Z of 9./KG 76,[11] which disappeared into a convenient cloud and the other Hurricanes flew off. Kominek continued after the elusive Dornier, which was being flown by *Oberführer* Wagner. The Czech pumped three more bursts into it, bits flew off the doomed bomber and smoke appeared. Wagner's crew jettisoned their bombs over the Kent countryside before the Dornier crashed three miles south-west of Tunbridge Wells at Red Lane Farm, Rotherfield.[12]

302 'City of Poznan' Squadron led by Squadron Leader William Arthur John Satchell, the thirty-two-year-old CO, had height advantage and claimed seven bombers destroyed and two more probably destroyed. As Bader had headed for the most westerly of the three formations of Dorniers, Satchell took the middle group, flying in vics. Satchell, who had joined the RAF ten years earlier, had taken command of 302 Squadron on its formation at Leconfield on 13 July 1940 and had scored the Squadron's first victory when he downed a Ju 88 on 20 July. He followed Bader's advice and dived from above almost vertically giving a full deflection shot, attacking the left leader who went straight down. As Satchell began an attack on another Dornier, a Bf 109 hit him but he was unhurt. Next he spotted a dozen Dorniers east of London flying east-south-east and Satchell made a beam and quarter attack from either side. One of them fell out of formation and went down between Rochester and the coast.

Pilot Officer Stanislav Jozef Chalupa, a twenty-five-year-old from Zaraz near Chrzanow in the Kracow region, who had served with the Polish Air Force, flying with 123 *Eskadra* in September 1939, claiming one shared victory, saw a formation of Dorniers through puffs of AA fire. He got in three bursts at the leading one in the second vic firing from 250 to thirty yards' range. The Dornier dived violently but Chalupa did not see what happened to it. He picked out a second Dornier and attacked from 100 yards. Smoke and flames were seen coming from the port engine and two crew jumped from the burning aircraft before another pilot cut off the tail of the aircraft with his own wing. It was the Pole's third confirmed victory of the war having destroyed a He 111 flying a Morane 406 in *Groupe de Chasse* I./2 in May 1940 and downing a *Stuka* on 8 June. He also shared in five other victories during his spell with the French and he was wounded in combat during June. After joining 302 Squadron in July, he damaged a Ju 88 and claimed a Ju 88 probable on 21 August. Flight Lieutenant Tadeusz Chlopik went for the furthermost section of Dorniers. The thirty-two-year-old Polish pilot hit one and saw the port engine smoking heavily with blue wisps coming from the starboard motor. The Dornier dived on its back and the three crew jumped out. By now Chlopik was flying at 14,000–17,000 feet over the south-eastern suburbs of London where he attacked and hit another Dornier from behind and above. Its port engine began spluttering and drew many more Hurricanes and two Spitfires to it.

Flying Officer Tadeusz Czerwinski approached a Dornier above and in front of him and fired three bursts, which set the port engine alight. Three other Hurricanes joined in the attack and by the time that Czerwinski had tried to attack again the crew abandoned the doomed Dornier. Flight Lieutenant Frantisek Jastrzebski, the thirty-five-year-old 'B' Flight CO, who had joined 302 on Squadron 26 July, flew down-sun and fired a few brief bursts at a Dornier before another Hurricane joined in. Jastrzebski turned 180 degrees to starboard and did not see the Dornier again but while climbing he saw five crew had taken to their parachutes. He landed at Henlow and refuelled before returning to Duxford. Jastrzebski had trained as a teacher before joining the Polish Army, transferring to his country's air force and attending officers' school at Deblin. He was commissioned as a 2nd lieutenant in 1928. Ten years later he was commanding 132 *Eskadra* in III./3 Fighter *Dyon* at Poznan. During the fighting in September 1939 he destroyed a Ju 86, a Bf 110 and a Bf 109 before he escaped to France via Hungary and Yugoslavia, reaching Lyon in January 1940. From 19 May he led a flight of six pilots in *Groupe de Chasse* II./1 defending the Chateaudun area. He claimed an enemy aircraft destroyed and shared in the destruction of another.

Flying Officer Julian Kowalski, a thirty-year-old from Nagornik, Kielce, fired two bursts at the last Dornier of a group and the bomber sought sanctuary in clouds. He could only claim a damaged. Below the clouds he saw two more Dorniers already being set on effectively by Hurricanes and they soon went down. Sergeant Jan Palak shared a Do 17 destroyed with another Hurricane. The twenty-nine-year-old climbed again and saw a Bf 109 diving towards another Hurricane so he turned towards the enemy fighter at full throttle and gave it two bursts. Pieces flew off the Bf 109 as it dived vertically down. Palak could only claim a probable although he believed that it would not have recovered. He landed at Maidstone at 12.35 pm. Though he did not score any victories on 302 Squadron Palak was posted to 303 Squadron on 23 September and he claimed a Bf 109 destroyed on 5 October.

Sergeant Edward Paterak, thirty years old, met a close formation of five Heinkel 111s at 270 mph and carried out a beam attack, which killed the rear gunner. Paterek aimed a long burst at very short range and the bomber hurtled down out of control from 5,000 feet and crashed soon after for his first victory since joining 302 Squadron at Leconfield on 23 July. Paterek landed at Wattisham. Sergeant Marian Wedzik meanwhile, got on the tail of a Dornier 17 and gave it a burst. Smoke poured from the port engine and port mainplane was set on fire before the bomber banked steeply to port. Paterek did not see what happened to it, as he returned over London trying to find his leader but he could not find him and he headed back to Duxford. Finally, Sergeant Antoni Siudak singled out a Dornier 17 at 240 mph and fired causing a cloud of black smoke appearing from the cockpit and port mainplane. The rear gunner returned fire and the thirty-one-year-old Pole lost the machine-gun panel of his port mainplane, while the whole mainplane looked to be badly torn. The Dornier spun down and Pilot Officer

Stanislav Lapka, twenty-five years old and from Borzyny, Warsaw, finished it off with a large piece flying off the underbelly of the fuselage. He was hit by return fire from the Dornier and smoke filled his cockpit. Lapka's starboard machine-gun panel then came undone and flew up, causing a heavy drag. At an altitude of 15,000 feet, he dived away and baled out with a minor foot injury. Antoni Siudak was posted to 303 Squadron at Northolt on 23 September. He claimed two Bf 109s and shared in the destruction of a He 111 on 5 October. Next day a lone raider bombed the airfield and Siudak was killed while taxying his Hurricane.

611 Squadron claimed three Dorniers destroyed. Flight Lieutenant William Leather destroyed his Dornier ten miles west of Canterbury. It was the flight commander's second victory, having downed a Bf 109E over Dunkirk on 2 June and sharing in a Dornier victory east of Withernsea on 2 July. He was awarded a DFC on 8 October. Sergeant Stephen Levenson got a Dornier in the London area. Flying Officer Philip S.C. Pollard downed a third Dornier in the Rochester–Herne Bay area for his first victory. Pollard, who was from Kingston, Surrey, had joined the RAF on a short service commission in September 1938.[13] Squadron Leader James McComb the commanding officer, claimed a Bf 110 probably destroyed south of London. He had claimed a Bf 109 and a He 111 probably destroyed over Dunkirk in May 1940 and had destroyed a Dornier Do 17 on 21 August.

The Duxford Wing landed, refuelled and was soon at Readiness again. A second German attack was picked up on radar at just after 1 pm and began to come in, in three waves an hour later. Twenty-three squadrons from 11 Group and three from 10 Group were committed to the battle. Finally, at 1412 hours forty-nine fighters of the five-squadron Wing were summoned to action by 11 Group, now badly in need of reinforcements but Bader again complained of being scrambled too late. Seven Hurricanes of 302 Squadron were last off and told to reach 20,000 feet as soon as possible and fly due south where an enemy formation was crossing the coast at Dover. 'Woody' Woodhall asked Bader to patrol Canterbury–Gravesend and Bader did. Two formations of bombers had been broken up before reaching London and the Duxford Wing and five pairs of squadrons from 11 Group engaged the remaining aircraft over the capital. Bader seeing the enemy bombers in disarray called it, 'The finest shambles I've ever been in'.

The CO Squadron Leader Brian J 'Sandy' Lane DFC, was leading 19 Squadron's Spitfires and he and eight of his pilots claimed aircraft destroyed or damaged in a twenty-minute running fight. Flight Sergeant 'Grumpy' Unwin, Lane's 'Red 3', reported sighting 'thousands of 109s'. At 1430 hours Sub-Lieutenant Arthur Blake ('Blue 3') damaged a Dornier 17Z and then spotted Bf 109s above. He climbed to engage them, shooting one of the Bf 109s down in flames. Then he joined three other RAF fighters in finishing off a stray He 111 over the London area. He was later awarded a half share in the He 111 victory. Blake's Spitfire had been hit during the fight with the Bf 109s and smoking badly so he forced-landed at RAF Rochford. He was unhurt and would return to action on the 17th. Ten minutes later 'Jock' Cunningham – 'Yellow 3' – attacked the main enemy formation but he was attacked from behind by Bf 109s. Sergeant Henry Roden's Spitfire was hit in the glycol tank by a Bf 109E in the attack and he force-landed unhurt. His luck finally ran out on 15 November following combat with Bf 110s off Harwich. He forced-landed in bad visibility and hit a tree. Roden died of his injuries the next day.

After an indecisive dogfight with a Bf 109 Cunningham had a Hurricane come up on his tail. They then attacked an enemy formation, opening fire at 300 yards on the left-hand aircraft. The Bf 109 dived through the clouds on fire. At about the same time over North London Pilot Officer Arthur Vokes ('Green 2') came under attack from a Bf 110, which had got onto his tail without being seen and the enemy fighter fired a burst of tracer at him. Most went over Vokes' starboard wing but one bullet went right through his main spar. Vokes climbed steeply and after a couple of turns he was able to get on the tail of the Bf 110 and fired causing the enemy's starboard engine to stream smoke. He claimed the Bf 110 probably destroyed. Ten minutes later over the Thames Estuary Leonard Haines ('Green 1') destroyed a Bf 109. He then climbed to 25,000 feet and patrolled the coast near Beachy Head hoping to meet more enemy aircraft on their way home. Spotting a returning Bf 110 straggling along he dived into the attack and followed it all the way to the French coast where it crashed on the beach in flames. 'Bill' Steere ('Blue 2') shot down a Do 17Z and saw the crew bale out before it went down into the clouds below. Wilfred Clouston ('Blue 1'), who had led Blue and Green Sections down on six Dorniers below him, singled out one of the Dorniers and chased it thirty miles out to sea east of Southend until his ammunition ran out.[14] Brian 'Sandy' Lane meanwhile, had his hands full.

At approximately 1440 hrs AA fire was sighted to the south and at the same time a formation of about thirty Do 215s was seen. I climbed up astern of the enemy aircraft to engage the fighter escort, which could be seen above the bombers at about 30,000 feet. Three Me 109s dived on our formation and I turned to starboard. A loose dogfight ensued with more Me 109s coming down. I could not get near to any enemy aircraft so I climbed up and engaged a formation of Me 110s without result. I then sighted ten Me 109s just above me and attacked one of them. I got on his tail and fired several bursts of about two seconds. The enemy aircraft was taking violent evasive action and made for cloud level. I managed to get in another burst of about five seconds before it flicked over inverted and entered cloud in a shallow dive, apparently out of control. I then flew south and attacked two further formations of about thirty Do 215s from astern and head on. The enemy aircraft did not appear to like the head on attack as they jumped about a bit as I passed through. I observed no result from these attacks. Fire from the rear of the enemy aircraft was opened at 1,000 yards. Me 110s opened fire at similar range but appeared to have no idea of deflection shooting.

Lane finished the day with a Bf 109E probably destroyed. Flight Sergeant 'Grumpy' Unwin fired a three-second burst at a Bf 109, which half-rolled and dived steeply into the clouds. Although the Spitfire pilot pursued his prey, he lost the Bf 109 at 6,000 feet when his windscreen froze up. Climbing back up to 25,000 feet, a *Rotte* of Bf 109s appeared above him, flying south. Unwin gave chase and caught both over the Lydd area. The first consequently burst into flames and went down vertically and the second crashed into the sea. It is likely that these two Bf 109s were from I./JG 77. *Oberleutnant* Kunze of the *Geschwaderstabschwarm* was killed when his aircraft crashed at Lympne, as was *Unteroffizier* Meixner who crashed into the sea off Dungeness.

Though 'Sandy' Lane's and 611 Squadron's Spitfires assailed the bombers, 242 Squadron and Bader's two other Hurricane squadrons were jumped by Bf 109s. Flight Lieutenant Powell-Shedden, who shot down a Do 17, was shot down by Bf 109s over Rye but he baled out of his Hurricane and dislocated his left shoulder.[15] Noel Stansfeld destroyed a He 111 between Kenley and Maidstone. Dickie Cork shot down his second Do 17 of the day, in the Maidstone area, and damaged two Bf 109Es.[16] His score since transferring to the RAF was now five destroyed and three damaged.[17] Douglas Bader was credited with a Do 17 destroyed and two more Dorniers damaged.[18] Stan Turner destroyed his second Dornier of the day and he was also awarded a Bf 109E probable in the Maidstone area. Denis Crowley-Milling and John Latta each destroyed a Bf 109 in the Maidstone area.

After the Bf 109s had jumped 310 Squadron and the Wing broke up Flight Lieutenant Jerrard Jeffries climbed his Hurricane formation to 24,000 feet into the sun east of London and the enemy fighters turned west. Jeffries waited and then led his fighters into a head-on attack with the sun behind him, diving straight through their first formation. He fired at one of the Messerschmitts in the leading section and its starboard engine caught fire, broke away and went down. Behind him Sergeant Josef Rechka and two other Hurricanes surprised a Heinkel He 111H-4 of KG 26 flown by *Leutnant* Streubel who was forced to put the badly damaged bomber down on the beach at Asplans Head near Foulness. Rechka, unmoved, watched as Streubel and his four crew clambered out of the wrecked Heinkel.[19] A Dornier Do 17Z-3 of 4./KG 3 flown by *Unteroffizier* Wien, which crashed on the Isle of Grain in the Thames Estuary, was downed by Pilot Officer Stanislav Fejfar.[20] The twenty-eight-year-old from Stikov had joined the Squadron on 7 September. It was his fifth victory of the war. Flying with *Groupe de Chasse* I./6 he had destroyed a Bf 109 on 20 May and on the 25th had shared a Heinkel 111 victory. On 5 June he downed an Hs 123.[21] Jeffries destroyed a Bf 109 east of London and Sergeant Jan Kaucky shared a Dornier destroyed with two Spitfires. Sergeant Prchal shared in a He 111 destroyed in the east London area with an unknown pilot. Pilot Officer Josef Hubacek was shot down by a Bf 109 near Chatham and he baled out with slight wounds to his right leg. He was taken to Chatham Hospital for treatment. Sergeant Brohumir Furst claimed a He 111 over the Thames Estuary. Squadron Leader 'Sasha' Hess was shot down by a Bf 109 over Billericay and he baled out unhurt.[22]

Seven Hurricanes of 302 'City of Poznan' Squadron had scrambled at 1410 hours and climbed to Angels 20 before flying south behind the rest of the Duxford Wing. Squadron Leader Satchell took his tiny formation towards fifteen bombers flying east. Satchell saw a Bf 109 in his mirror, flying above him. He waited until the Messerschmitt dived to attack and then pulled up sharply, letting the Bf 109 pass below him before getting on his tail and shooting it down with several long bursts. The Bf 109 went down on its back and crashed. Seeing that his leader was busy Pilot Officer Edward Roman Pilch, a twenty-five-year-old from Poland, dived for the Dorniers and he and a Spitfire shot one of the Do 17s down from 6,000 feet over the Thames Estuary. Pilch then spotted another Dornier and he attacked this one as the rear gunner took aim and fired briefly. Smoke started pouring from the port motor and Pilch finished it off after heavy AA fire burst all around his Hurricane. The Dornier went down in shallow waters not far from Margate. Flight Lieutenant Julian Kowalski damaged a Dornier and probably destroyed another when he closed to thirty yards and opened fire knocking its tailplane off and causing chunks of wing to fly off. His port machine-gun panel became loose. While it did not fly off completely, it caused very strong drag and prevented proper control of the Hurricane: the Hurricane and he dived away to find an airfield. He made it back to Duxford where his left undercarriage wheel got in a rut and broke away, the Hurricane finally coming to rest with a broken undercarriage. When Kowalski examined his fighter he found that his flap and undercarriage were not working properly and one of his wheels was punctured. Flying Officer Tadeusz Czerwinski, who destroyed a Dornier, was also forced to break off his attack when his engine failed but he managed to nurse the fighter back to Duxford.[23] Flight Lieutenant Tadeusz Chlopik destroyed a Dornier over the Thames Estuary but he was forced to bale out after being attacked by fighters. Unable to pull his parachute ripcord, he was killed, falling dead at Rawreth.

Julian Kowalski dived down on a lone Do 17 and only opened fire when he was within thirty yards of his prey. The tailplane disintegrated and large pieces of wing flew off as the bomber dived at about 45 degrees to the ground. Kowalski saw another Dornier ahead of him whose rear gunner was calmly firing tracer at him. He opened fire on the Do 17 and claimed it but it was not confirmed. When Kowalski finally landed at Duxford and examined his Hurricane he discovered that the flap and undercarriage were not working properly and one of his wheels was punctured. Pilot Officer Edward Pilch claimed two Dorniers destroyed. The first dropped out of formation at 6,000 feet on fire and crashed into the Thames Estuary. The rear gunner of his other victim took aim and fired briefly until Pilch fired at him and then nothing more was seen or heard though smoke had started to pour out of the bomber's port engine. Then heavy AA fire burst all around his Hurricane. Pilch waited for the barrage to stop and went in and finished the Dornier off. It dived into shallow waters not far from Margate.[24]

611 Squadron claimed five enemy aircraft shot down. Flight Lieutenant William Leather claimed two Dornier Do 17s for his second and third victories of

the day.[25] Squadron Leader James McComb downed a Dornier over south-east London. He was posted away for a rest on 19 October. He was awarded a DFC on 22 November. Flight Sergeant Herbert S Sadler shared in the destruction of a Dornier in the London area with another fighter pilot. Sadler, who was commissioned early in November 1940, was killed in action on 5 February 1941. He was twenty-four years old. Pilot Officer Maurice Peter Brown, a twenty-one-year-old from London, who had been a staff pilot at Cranwell before the war, shot down a He 111 at Tunbridge Wells and shared in the destruction of a Do 17. He had previously shared in the destruction of a Do 17 on 21 August over the sea at Mabelthorpe.[26] Sergeant Stephen Levenson was awarded a Dornier probably destroyed at Weybridge.[27] Pilot Officer John Lund was awarded another Dornier probable over London. He was posted to 92 Squadron on 2 October and was killed in action exactly a year later on a *Rhubarb* (low-level day fighter sweep) over France. Flying Officer Thomas Draper Williams claimed a Dornier probably destroyed over South London. Claims by the Duxford Wing at the end of the day were high: forty-four enemy aircraft shot down, with eight probables. Overall, Fighter Command claimed to have shot down 185 aircraft, but the true figure was fifty-six German aircraft shot down for the loss of twenty-six RAF fighters but thirteen pilots were saved. One of the pilots who failed to return following a combat with Bf 109s of JG 26 was Sergeant John Potter of 19 Squadron. Once again the twenty-five-year-old had ditched his severely damaged Spitfire in the Channel but this time he was picked up just off the French coast by a German naval launch and taken to St Omer with a foot wound caused by a bullet that came through the cockpit floor. After hospitalisation in Lille, Brussels and Malines and the loss of two toes, he was sent to *Stalag Luft* I at Barth in Silesia on 17 December. He was later moved to *Stalag Luft* III, Sagan, and he remained a prisoner until the end of the war.

On the night of 15/16 September 180 German bombers formed long processions from Le Havre and Dieppe-Cherbourg, all heading for London. Meanwhile, arguments ensued on both sides of the divide. Next day Göring called a conference of his *Luftflotten* and *Fliegerkorps* commanders in France and decided to return to a policy of attack on Fighter Command rather than industrial and residential targets by day. Bomber formations would now be reduced in size and *Gruppen* would bomb targets in the London area with maximum fighter escort to destroy as many RAF fighters as possible. Göring predicted that this would finish off Fighter Command in four to five days. In England the belief that 'Big Wings' were unwieldy seemed justified, especially when 11 Group's own three-squadron 'Wing' of thirty-two fighters, led by Squadron Leader Bob Stanford Tuck from Debden, had only eight fighters remaining by the time they intercepted the bombers.

There was only slight air activity on Monday 16 September when the weather prevented any heavy attacks on England. The few small attacks that penetrated to east London were intercepted and nine *Luftwaffe* aircraft were destroyed for the loss of one Spitfire and a Hurricane but both pilots were saved. On 17 September there was gloom in Germany where Hitler postponed Operation *Sealion* indefinitely. During the day seven to eight main raids totalling 250 aircraft crossed the south coast and these were intercepted by twenty-eight squadrons of RAF fighters. One of the raids was a large German fighter sweep in the afternoon. Squally showers and local thunder over England and drizzle in the Straits and Thames Estuary was in contrast to the bright intervals over the Channel where Sub-Lieutenant 'Admiral' Blake claimed two Bf 109E-4s of 9./JG 53 destroyed after he pursued them all the way from the Thames Estuary. One of the Messerschmitts was piloted by *Oberleutnant* Jacob Stoll, *Staffelkapitän*, and the other by *Oberleutnant* Herbert Seliger, both of whom were never seen again.[28] These victories took Blake's score to four and one shared destroyed during the Battle. He had also damaged two more enemy aircraft. RAF Fighter Command lost five aircraft with one pilot killed and two wounded out of 544 sorties flown. *Luftwaffe* losses totalled eight aircraft. That night 268 bombers hit London again.

Next day, Wednesday 18 September, the weather was bright and squally. At 9 am the first blips appeared on Fighter Command radar screens, showing a heavy build up over Calais. The enemy aircraft, mainly fighters, crossed the coast between North Foreland and Folkestone at 20,000 feet. They were split up over Maidstone and the Estuary and turned for home after running engagements with seventeen RAF squadrons. One was shot down by AA fire. Two hours later radar betrayed four raids that totalled 190 aircraft. They crossed the coast at Deal and attacked Chatham. At least sixty reached the centre of London. The rest roamed over Kent. At 2 pm *Luftflotte* 2 began to assemble 150 aircraft over Calais. As they climbed to 20,000 feet the Germans sorted themselves into neat formations and set course for Gravesend. Breaking cloud over Kent the Germans were met in force. Although some of them penetrated the defences, the majority of formations were broken up and repelled. The Duxford Wing had been scrambled three times during the day at 0900, 1250 and 1616 hours, the first two occasions without success.

On the third occasion while patrolling Hornchurch they spotted AA bursts to the south-west of London and found two enemy formations of between twenty and thirty bombers flying up the Thames, but they could see no escorts. Leaving 611 Squadron on patrol and 19 Squadron to look after the escorts, Bader led his three Hurricane squadrons into an almost vertical diving attack on the first formation of Junkers Ju 88s. The Germans scattered, leaving only four vics of five aircraft. 242 Squadron claimed twelve Ju 88s and Do 17s and four bombers probably destroyed for no loss. Bader damaged a Ju 88 and claimed a Do 17 south-east of Hornchurch. Willie McKnight destroyed a Do 17 and shared a Ju 88 victory with a Spitfire to take his score to seventeen and three unconfirmed destroyed.[29] Pilot Officer Neil Campbell claimed three Ju 88s destroyed, two of them shared with Spitfires, and damage to another.[30] Roy Bush was credited with a Ju 88 probably destroyed. Eric Ball destroyed a Ju 88 ten miles south of London for his fifth victory while Norrie Hart destroyed two Ju 88s south-east of Hornchurch to take his score to four.[31]

Hugh Tamblyn claimed two Do 17s, one of them south-east of Hornchurch and the other over the Thames Estuary. Sub-Lieutenant 'Jimmy' Gardner claimed two Do 17s probably destroyed and Sergeant George Brimble claimed a Do 17 destroyed over the southern suburbs of London. The remaining bombers soon turned for home.[32]

Meanwhile, the Spitfires of 19 Squadron, which were led by Flight Lieutenant Wilfred Clouston ('Blue 1') set about a group of ten Ju 88s flying in two vics of five south of the Thames Estuary. Clouston attacked the starboard outer Ju 88 in the second enemy vic and saw it drop out of formation. The crew baled out and the bomber went down west of Deal. This victory took the New Zealander's score to nine and three shared destroyed.[33] Flight Sergeant 'Bill' Steere ('Blue 2') closed in on a bomber he identified as a He 111 just as another RAF fighter was completing a beam attack on the enemy aircraft. Steere fired a five-second burst. He followed it down through cloud and he saw it hit the sea. He then climbed and met a Ju 88 diving over the mouth of the Thames. The ex-Halton apprentice fired a short deflection burst at it and he saw the bomber go vertically into the cloud with one engine on fire. Flying Officer Leonard Haines and 'Grumpy' Unwin ('Blue 3') above him had also fired at the bomber and all three shared in the victory. Unwin also attacked a Bf 110, which could not return fire from the rear, presumably because the gunner was dead, so he closed to just fifty yards and fired. The Bf 110 pilot baled out and the fighter crashed near Eastchurch. Close by Haines was set upon over the Isle of Sheppey by a pair of Bf 109Es but he managed to get one in his sights and he fired. The Bf 109 half-rolled and dived for cloud with black smoke pouring from it. It could have been engine exhaust and so Haines could only claim it as a probable. Sergeant Stanislav Plzak ('Green 3') fired a couple of bursts at a bomber he identified as a He 111 and stopped both its engines. The crew baled out and the bomber crashed near Gillingham, Kent. Pilot Officer 'Dolly' Dolezal ('Green 2') claimed a bomber twenty miles east of Sandwich.[34] Pilot Officer Frantisek 'Haddy' Hradil, a twenty-eight-year-old from Tesetice, who had been attached to 19 Squadron since 29 August, force-landed following an engine seizure. Flight Lieutenant 'Farmer' Lawson ('Red 1') led Red Section into an attack on nine Ju 88s. He attacked one of them – probably the Ju 88A-1 of 9./KG 77 flown by *Feldwebel* Wahl – and could see his tracers hitting the port mainplane and engine. He claimed a Ju 88 destroyed in the London area before he was forced down after his glycol tank was damaged in combat over the Thames Estuary. He and Hradil were unhurt.[35] 'Jock' Cunningham ('Red 2') had followed his leader and attacked the same Ju 88. Sergeant David Edward Lloyd ('Red 3') joined Cunningham in the attack on the Ju 88 and they both continued firing until Wahl and his crew went down in flames at Sandwich.[36] Lloyd was posted to 92 Squadron in November and on 1 December he damaged a Bf 109. Commissioned in January 1942 he was No. 3 in an OTU formation on 17 March when he was killed in a mid-air collision with the leader of a 315 (Polish) Squadron formation.

310 (Czech) Squadron claimed six Do 215s destroyed and one probably

destroyed by Pilot Officer Stanislav Zimprich.[37] Over the Thames Estuary Flight Lieutenant Jerrard Jeffries destroyed a Dornier for his fifth victory[38] and Sergeant Raimund Puda shared a Do 17 victory with Sergeant Miraslav Jiroudek to take his final score to one and four shared destroyed.[39] Pilot Officers Stanislav Janouch and Stanislav Fejfar also shared a Do 17 victory with the pilot of another Hurricane. Pilot Officer Emil Fechtner, like his compatriot Jiroudek, a former French Legionnaire, and Pilot Officer Vaclav Bergman and Sergeant Eduard Prchal all claimed a Dornier apiece.[40] Jiroudek, who had been born at Zibohlavy, Kolin, in March 1914 had served in the Czech Air Force from 1933 to 15 March 1939. He escaped to Poland on the night of 14/15 June and later he joined the Foreign Legion. He was seconded to III./7 *Groupe de Chasse* and after the French defeat he escaped to England via North Africa and had joined 319 Squadron on 6 August. Over Faversham on 5 November AA hit his Hurricane and he baled out as his fighter crashed at Graveney, Sittingbourne.[41]

Not to be outdone, 302 'City of Poznan' Squadron, scrambled at 4.50 pm and instructed to patrol Hornchurch at Angels 20, destroyed nine and claimed five probably destroyed. Squadron Leader Satchell closed to eighty yards and his victim, a Dornier, was enveloped in smoke and flame and disappeared. Before breaking away, Satchell had his Perspex covered with oil from the burning bomber. He then saw two enemy bombers crash – one in the sea off Sheerness and the other on the peninsula between the Medway and the Thames. Squadron Leader Mieczyslaw Mümler, a forty-one-year-old former Polish artillery officer, picked out another Dornier and fired at it before he had to get out of the way of other attacking Hurricanes. As he banked away he could see flames coming from the rear gunner's position. When Poland was invaded Mümler was commanding III./3 *Dywizjon Mysliwski* supporting the Poznan Army. In the fighting in September 1939 he claimed three victories including a Heinkel He 111 and an Hs 126 and shared in the victory over another Heinkel. His was the only fighter division to retain its operational capability until 17 September when the Soviet invasion from the east occurred. Mümler escaped to Rumania and made his way to France where he commanded 2e *Groupe de Chasse Polonnaise* and flew Morane MS 406s. After his pilots had been detached in sections and sent to French units he flew with *Groupe de Chasse* II./7 and on 1 June he shot down a He 111 near the Swiss border. He shared in the destruction of a Dornier Do 17 on 15 June and damaged a Heinkel. He reached England and was appointed joint CO of 302 Squadron at Leconfield.

Flight Lieutenant Julian Kowalski made successive attacks on two Ju 88s and at his last burst he saw a parachute open from the rear gunner's position and become entangled in the mainplane. Debris flew through the sky and forced him to break off. Behind came Yellow Section. Flight Lieutenant James Farmer chased a Dornier 17 and then he attacked a Ju 88. James Nigel Watts Farmer was twenty-five years old and had joined the RAF on a short service commission in August 1935 and had joined 57 Squadron in June 1936 before joining 302 Squadron and becoming the CFI (Chief Flying Instructor). Pieces peeled off the Junkers before it vanished into a convenient cloud, by which time Farmer had used all his ammunition. Farmer was awarded a DFC in March 1941. Flight Lieutenant Piotr Laguna could not focus his sights properly and so rather than risk hitting a Hurricane, the thirty-five-year-old Pole conserved his rounds. Laguna had distinguished himself flying for with *Groupe de Chasse Polonaise de Varsovie* I./145 flying Morane 406s. On 8 June he was one of five Polish pilots who attacked a formation of Bf 110s and destroyed five without loss. Laguna had taken command of the unit after the Polish CO was seriously wounded. On 19 June the Poles had left La Rochelle by boat for England where he became 'A' Flight commander of 302 Squadron. Laguna was killed on 27 June 1941 leading the Northolt Wing. Another of 302 Squadron's Polish pilots, Sergeant Marian Wedzik, chased a Ju 88 out to sea and forced it down to 1,000 feet. The twenty-seven-year-old from Guc, Lodz, and another Hurricane pilot attacked the Junkers alternately, with pieces breaking off at regular intervals but they could not claim it. Wedzik was to return home in 1946.

Pilot Officer Edward Pilch and the rest of Green Section broke up a group of Ju 88s and he made five attacks on one of them despite return fire from the rear gunner before it went down. Sergeant Edward Peterek closed to 100 yards and fired at another Ju 88, setting one engine on fire before the three crew baled out. It is quite probable that Pilch and Peterek's victims were two Ju 88A-1s of 8./KG 77.[42] Peterek's propeller and radiator were hit by flying debris from the doomed bomber and the reserve petrol tank ruptured, covering him in petrol. He switched off his engine immediately and glided southwards. He saw the Ju 88 crash and then forced-landed himself. It is believed that his Hurricane was hit by debris from the enemy aircraft causing him to make a forced-landing at Sandon Lodge Farm, Danbury. He was unhurt. Posted later to 303 Squadron, Peterak collided with another aircraft on a training flight on 28 March 1941. He crashed into the sea near the Bar Lightship and drowned.

Pilot Officer Stefan Wapniarek, who had destroyed three German aircraft in the air in the fighting in Poland before joining 302 Squadron on 30 July, made two attacks on a Ju 88 and saw the rear gunner jump out near Southend-on-Sea before firing at another Junkers. The enemy bomber fired tracer bullets at him but the twenty-four-year old Pole retaliated by firing all the remaining ammunition in his guns before it broke up and crashed into the sea. Wapniarek flew on for eight minutes over the sea before reaching the coast and by then he was virtually out of fuel, as well as ammunition, so he landed at Rochford, Essex. Pilot Officer Wlodzimierz Eugeniusz Karwowski, a twenty-eight-year old experienced pilot from Kielce, destroyed another Ju 88, his second victory of the war. Only one of the crew baled out before it crashed.[43]

In Blue Section Flight Lieutenant William Riley, an Irishman from Manorhamilton in County Leitrim destroyed a Ju 88 and claimed another as probably destroyed.[44] Flight Lieutenant Frantisek Jastrzebski fired at several bombers and claimed a Dornier 17 as probably destroyed. Sergeant Eugeniusz Jan Adam Nowakiewicz, twenty years old from Jaslo, claimed a Ju 88 probably destroyed.[45]

Altogether, the Duxford Wing claimed thirty destroyed, six probables and two damaged in the air battle. Ten were claimed by 242 Squadron while 19 and 302 Squadrons had claimed seven each and 310 Squadron, six. Despite the Duxford Wing's claims, only nineteen *Luftwaffe* aircraft had been shot down during that memorable afternoon with II./KG 77 losing nine Ju 88s over the Thames Estuary.[46] Twelve British fighters were lost but only three of the pilots were killed, in the course of 1,165 sorties.

1   *Spitfire Summer.*

2   *RAF Fighter Squadrons in the Battle of Britain* by Anthony Robinson (Brockhampton Press 1999).

3   *Aces High* by Christopher Shores and Clive Williams (Grub Street 1994).

4   Do 17Z 3322 F1+DT.

5   Actual KG 76 losses were six shot down, four damaged and almost all the remaining fifteen were damaged to some degree. *Luftwaffe Bomber Aces: Men, Machines, Methods* by Mike Spick (Greenhill Books 2001).

6   Do 17Z-3 2649 5K+HN of 5./KG 3 was damaged by Spitfires of 19 Squadron over east London at 1205 hours. One crewmember was wounded.

7   *The Luftwaffe Fighters' Battle of Britain: The Inside Story: July–October 1940.*

8   *The Luftwaffe Fighters' Battle of Britain: The Inside Story: July–October 1940.*

9   Twenty-eight-year-old Raimund Puda, who was born on 18 August 1912 at Brnik in Bynsk, had joined the Czech Air Force late in 1930 and in 1937 was Solo Acrobatic Champion at the International Meeting at Zurich, Switzerland. In September 1938 he joined Czech Air Lines and in July 1939 was accepted by the *Armée de l'Air* as a corporal pilot. He flew the American-built Curtiss H-75A with *Groupe de Chasse* II./4, destroying a Do 17 on 16 May and being awarded two half shares in two other unit victories before II./4 flew to Morocco. After the 22 June Armistice Puda took a ship to Gibraltar and from there to the UK to join the RAF and in August he was posted to 310 Squadron.

10   Dornier Do 17Z 2361 F1+FH. Zehbe, *Unteroffizier* Goschenhofer and *Unteroffizier* Hubel were killed. *Unteroffizier* Hammermeister and *Obergefreiter* Armbruster were captured. See *The Battle of Britain Then*

and Now. Jan Kaucky returned to Czechoslovakia in 1946 and became a pilot with Czech Air Lines, as did Josef Rechka and Eduard Prchal. In 1950 all three escaped to England with their families.

11   Do 17Z 2814 F1+AT.

12   *Oberführer* Wagner, *Obergefreiter* Böhme and *Gefreiters* Holdenried and Kottutsch were killed.

13   Philip Selwyn Covey Pollard was shot down and killed by Bf 109s on 22 June 1941 when 611 Squadron acted as high cover for bombers attacking the marshalling yards at Hazebrouck.

14   Dornier Do 17Z-3 2304 U5+HN of 5./KG 5 was shot down by Spitfires of 19 Squadron over London at approximately 1500 hours. *Unteroffiziers* Bohmel, Huber and Mobius and *Gefreiter* Birg were killed. Do 17Z-2 1135 U5+MN of 5./KG 5 was damaged by Spitfires of 19 Squadron over London at about 1500 hours.

15   On recovery he was posted to 258 Squadron in November and in April 1941 was given command of 615 Squadron. On 19 July he was posted to Malta, where he formed the Malta Night Fighter Unit. During August while flying Hurricane IIs, he shot down a BR 20M of 43° *Stormo* on the night of 11/12 August despite being blinded by searchlight and he was awarded a half share in two more BR 20 probables on 26/17 August. In December 1941 he was awarded a DFC and promoted to wing commander, Takali. He left Malta on 21 July 1942, returning to the UK via the Middle East. After a spell on staff duties at Air Ministry, he attended the Fighter Leaders' School. But as his stammer was proving very troublesome at this time, he trained instead for radar-controlled night fighting at Cranwell and Cranfield, joining 96 Squadron as a supernumerary in January 1944, then taking command of 29 Squadron in March. From April to July he commanded RAF Bradwell Bay, then returning to the squadron until December 1944. Promoted to group captain, he was awarded a DSO on 27 April 1945. He retired as a group captain in March 1961.

16   Two Dornier Do 17Zs of 8./KG 2 are believed to have been shot down near London by 242 Squadron at approximately 1500 hours. Do 17Z 2549 U5+FS was lost with *Feldwebel* Simon, *Unteroffizier* Flemming, *Feldwebel* Hirsch and *Gefreiter* Sandmann. Do 17Z 3401 U5+DS crashed in the Channel. *Gefreiter* Ertl and *Feldwebel* Dürtmann were killed. *Seenotflugkommando* picked up two NCOs. *Battle Over Britain*.

17   Cork was awarded a DFC by the RAF and remained with 242 Squadron until 8 December 1940. In January 1941 he returned to the FAA. On 14 April 1944 he was killed flying a Corsair, which was involved in a collision

with another Corsair. Cork's wartime score was nine and two shared destroyed, one probable, four damaged and seven destroyed on the ground.

18   Dornier Do 17Z 2549 U5+FS of 8./KG 2 was shot down by Hurricanes of 242 Squadron near London at about 1500 hours. *Feldwebel* Simon, *Unteroffizier* Flemming, *Feldwebel* Hirsch and *Gefreiter* Sandmann were killed. Do 17Z 3401 U5+DS of 8./KG 5 was also shot down near London by 242 Squadron Hurricanes at about 1500 hours. *Gefreiter* Ertl and *Feldwebel* Durtmann were killed. Two crew were picked up by *Seenotflugkommando*.

19   He 111H-4 6985 1H+1H. Streubel, *Feldwebels* Schwartz, Marenbach and Potenberg and *Gefreiter* Domes were all taken prisoner.

20   Wien, *Feldwebel* von Goertz and *Gefreiters* Schild and Weymar were all captured. Their Dornier Do-17Z-3 2879 5K+CM was a write-off.

21   In early 1942 Fejfar was on 313 Squadron; he damaged three enemy aircraft and destroyed a Fw 190. He was shot down and killed on an escort operation on 17 May 1942 for Bostons attacking a radio-location station at Freya near Wissant.

22   Hess went to the USA in 1942 as Czechoslovakian Air Attaché.

23   KIA on 22 August 1942.

24   Pilch was killed on a training flight on 20 February 1941.

25   By 7 December 1940 Leather, who was awarded a DFC on 8 October, had shared in four more victories to take his final score to three and four shared destroyed. He took command of 145 Squadron in 1941 and post war he returned to 611 Squadron and commanded the Auxiliary unit from 1946 to 1949.

26   On 28 September he went to 41 Squadron at Hornchurch. Two days later he damaged a Dornier Do 17. He shot down a Bf 109E-4 of 6./JG 52 on 20 October and *Oberfeldwebel* Walter Friedemann baled out near Ashford and was killed. Brown landed at West Malling and he collected Friedemann's lifejacket as confirmation of his victory. On 25 October Brown attacked a Bf 109 and claimed it as a probable when the Squadron jumped a formation of forty Messerschmitts. *Men of the Battle of Britain/Battle Over Britain*.

27   Sergeant Stephen Austin Levenson was promoted to warrant officer and he later converted to bombers and flew Stirlings on 214 Squadron. He was KIA on the night of 16/17 September 1942 when on the raid on Essen his Stirling I was shot down over Belgium by *Hauptmann* Walter Ehle, *Stab* II./NJG 1.

28   Bf 109E-4 5141 and Bf 109E-4 1228 respectively.

29   On 5 November McKnight was awarded a half share in a Bf 109E victory with Flying Officer Leonard Haines who had received a DFC on 8 October 1940. *Feldwebel* Erhard Scheidt of 1./JG 26 baled out and the fighter crashed at Birchington. He received a Bar to his DFC on 8 October. Promoted to flying officer in November, on 12 January 1941 McKnight took part in one of the first low-level *Rhubarb* sorties over France. He strafed some troops, but as he turned for a second attack, Bf 109s were seen and he vanished, whether shot down by the German fighters or by ground fire not being ascertained. Haines gained another half share in a Bf 110 victory on 15 November and scored his eighth and final victory on 28 November when he downed a Bf 109E five miles east of Ramsgate. Later in the year he was posted as an instructor at an OTU, but was killed in a flying accident here on 30 April 1941.

30   Killed on 17 October 1940.

31   Killed on 5 November 1940.

32   Brimble later joined 73 Squadron. He was killed on 29 November 1940 on a Middle East ferry flight.

33   In November he was posted to command 258 Squadron, which was forming with a majority of New Zealand pilots. In August 1941 he was posted to Singapore to command 488 Squadron, a new RNZAF unit to be formed with Buffalos. In January 1942 he was posted to the Singapore HQ as a wing commander, where he was captured the next month when Singapore fell, spending the rest of the war as a PoW.

34   Dolezal returned to 310 Squadron in January 1941 and became CO in April 1942, also being awarded a DFC during that year. In January 1943 he was promoted to lead the Czech 134 Wing. He left the RAF on 3 March 1945 to join the reformed Czech forces, returning to Czechoslovakia at the end of the war. He was killed in a flying accident on 4 October 1945 when an Si 204 in which he was a passenger, crashed.

35   Lawson's claim (Ju 88A-1 3173 3Z+ED of *Stab* III./KG 77, which crashed at Eastry Mill, south of Sandwich) was later reduced to a quarter share. (Major Kless, *Gruppe Kommander*, and *Oberleutnant* Lauth were killed. *Unteroffizier* Proebst and *Feldwebel* Himsel baled out and were captured.) 'Haddy' Hradil was shot down and killed by *Hauptmann* Rolf Pingel over Southend on 5 November 1940. *Battle of Britain: The Photographic Kaleidoscope: Vol., II* by Dilip Sarkar (Ramrod Publications 2000). Pingel was shot down on 4 July 1941 and he became a PoW.

Squadron pilots at Duxford, early 1938, in front of Gloster Gauntlet I K4097. Back Row L–R: F/O A.G. 'Pete' Gordon; F/L John Banham; S/L Henry Illiffe-Cozens; P/O Gordon Sinclair. Middle Row: George Eric Ball; P/Os James Coward, Wilf Clouston and 'Ace' Pace. Seated: Ian Robinson; F/O L. Carr 'Granny' Withall (KIA 12.8.40); F/O M.C.F. 'Mike' Mee (who died aboard HMS *Glorious*, which was sunk off Norway on 8.6.40); F/O Eric Hugh Thomas. (*Air Cdre Coward*)

Squadron pilots at Duxford, June 1939. Back Row L–R: Gordon Sinclair; F/O 'Mike' Mee; P/O James Coward. Middle Row: P/O 'Granny' Withall; F/O Eric Thomas; F/L John Banham; P/O Wilf Clouston; Ian Robinson. On the grass: Eric Ball; F/O 'Pete' Gordon; P/O 'Ace' Pace. (*Air Cdre Coward*)

Pilots of 19 Squadron run to their waiting Spitfire Is during a 'Scramble' on Press Day at Duxford o 4 May 1938. (*Central Press*)

P/O Leonard Archibald Haines (KIA 30.4.41) who hailed from Melcombe Regis near Weymouth joined the RAF on a short service commission in September 1937 and was posted to 19 Squadron. After seeing action over Dunkirk in the first few days of June 1940, he was promoted F/O and he remained active throughout the Battle of Britain. (*Central Press*)

Six Spitfire Is of 19 Squadron in formation led by the CO, S/L Henry Illiffe-Cozens in the nearest aircraft. Next are F/O Doug Genders, P/O James Coward; F/L John Banham; P/O Wilf Clouston and F/Sgt Harry 'Bill' Steere (KIA on Mosquitoes 8.6.44). (*Air Cdre Coward*)

L–R: P/O Wallace 'Jock' Cunningham, Sub Lt Arthur Giles 'Admiral' Blake RN (KIA 29.10.40) and F/O Francis Noel Brinsden at Fowlmere in September 1940. (*IWM*)

Utilizing an old kitchen table from one of the farm cottages, S/L Brian 'Sandy' Lane, 19 Squadron CO briefs his pilots at Fowlmere. (*IWM*)

The Sector G Operations Room at Duxford. In the cubicles behind the controller are the R/T operators in direct touch with the aircraft. (*IWM*)

Pilots of 310 (Czech) Squadron. Centre, squatting, is the CO, S/L 'Bill' Blackwood. To his left, arm on knee, is F/L Jerrard Jeffries. On the ground pointing finger at the map, cigarette in right hand, is S/L Alexander 'Sasha' Hess. On Blackwood's right, looking down at the map is F/L Gordon Sinclair. (*IWM*)

(*Left*) P/O Richard Leoline Jones of 19 Squadron who in April 1941 became a DH test pilot. (*IWM*)
(*Right*) P/O Raymond André Charles Aeberhardt (19) (KIA 31.8.40).

242 Squadron pilots at Coltishall, September 1940. Sgt John Ernest Savill on the wing with hand on cockpit sill. L–R: Pilot Officer's Denis Crowley-Milling, Hugh Tamblyn (KIA 3.4.41), 'Stan' Turner and Norman Campbell (KIA 17.10.40); F/L 'Willie' McKnight DFC (KIA 12.1.41); S/L Douglas Bader; F/L George Eric Ball (KIFA 1.2.46) and Pilot Officers Michael G. Homer DFC (KIA 27.9.40) and Marvin 'Ben' Brown (KIFA 21.2.41). (*IWM*)

P/O Michael Giles Homer DFC (KIA 27.9.40).

P/O John Benzie of 242 Squadron (KIA 7.9.40).

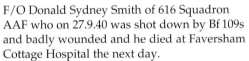

F/O Donald Sydney Smith of 616 Squadron AAF who on 27.9.40 was shot down by Bf 109s and badly wounded and he died at Faversham Cottage Hospital the next day.

P/O Jaroslav Sterbacek of 310 (Czech) Squadron (KIA 31.8.40).

Pilots of 19 Squadron on the wing (l–r): S/L Brian 'Sandy' Lane DFC; F/Sgt George 'Grumpy' Unwin DFM and F/O Francis Noel Brinsden. Standing (l–r): Sgt Bernard Jennings (19 Squadron); F/L Colin Hamilton Macfie (616 Squadron); S/L Howard Frizelle 'Billy' Burton (616 Squadron CO) and P/O Phillip Howard 'Uncle Sam' Leckrone (or 'Zeke) of 616 Squadron. Leckrone, from Salem, Illinois was the first Eagle to be killed (on 5.1.41 when he collided with P/O Edwin 'Bud' Orbison (22) a Californian, during a formation practice). *(IWM)*

Dornier Do 17Z-3 2669 5K+LM of II/KG 3 from Deurne near Antwerp, which was badly damaged by Hurricanes of 310 (Czech) Squadron during the attack on Hornchurch on 31.8.40. *Obfw* Lange tried to escape by flying low and avoid further damage but the Dornier was hit by AA fire and it crash-landed on the beach at Sandwich Flats at Pegwell Bay near Ramsgate. *(IWM)*

S/L Bader with P/O Willie McKnight DFC to his right and F/L George Eric Ball DFC to his left. *(IWM)*

S/L Bader and S/L Alexander 'Sasha' Hess, one of the oldest pilots in the Battle of Britain having been born in 1899. In March 1941 Bader was appointed Wing Commander Flying at Tangmere flying Spitfires on offensive sweeps over the continent. Awarded a DFC in January 1941 for ten victories, a bar to his DSO followed in July for 15 and a bar to his DFC came in September for four more. On 9.8.41 Bader was shot down over France on a fighter sweep and he spent the rest of the war as a PoW until finally being released from Colditz Castle in April 1945. *(IWM)*

Fighter contrails over southern England in the summer of 1940.

Arming a 19 Squadron Spitfire on 21.9.40. (*IWM*)

F/L 'Farmer' Lawson (KIA 28.8.41), S/L Brian 'Sandy' Lane DFC 19 Squadron CO and F/Sgt George 'Grumpy' Unwin DFM on 21.9.40. (*IWM*)

F/Sgt George 'Grumpy' Unwin DFM and 'Flash' his Alsatian. Unwin's DFC was awarded on 1.10.40, a Bar to this following on 6.12.40 after he had just been promoted Warrant Officer. Unwin was commissioned in July 1941. He joined 613 Squadron in April 1944 to resume operations flying Mosquito bombers. He was awarded a DSO on 21.3.52 for his actions during the Malayan Emergency. (*IWM*)

S/L 'Sandy' Lane DFC and other 19 Squadron pilots relaxing at Fowlmere, September 1940. (*IWM*)

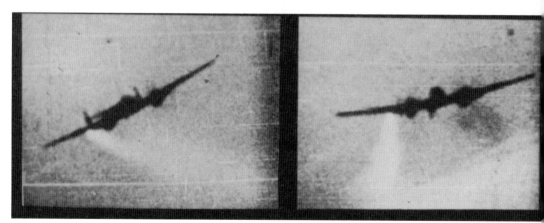

Camera gun film showing the end of a Bf 110. (*IWM*)

Line up of Spitfires of 19 Squadron at Duxford.

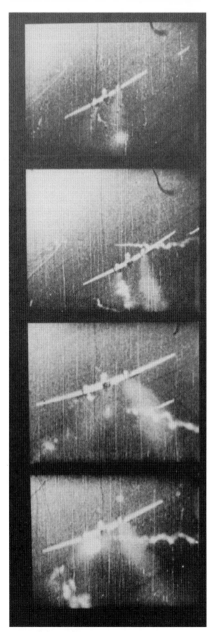

Camera gun film showing the demise of a Bf 110. (*IWM*)

WAAF plotters at RAF Duxford. (*IWM*)

F/Sgt George 'Grumpy' Unwin DFM returns from a sortie in September 1940. (*IWM*)

Spitfire II QJ-A of 19 Squadron. (*IWM*)

Spitfire II P7420 of 19 Squadron, which flew into a tree at Boxford, Sussex on 15.11.40 killing Sgt Henry Roden. (*IWM*)

Spitfire K9795 of 19 Squadron banks away from the camera. (*IWM*)

36   Ju 88A-1 3168 3Z+FT, which had been attacking Tilbury Docks, crashed in
        flames near Vange Creek, Pitsea Marshes near Basildon, Essex. Wahl,
        Gefreiters Buschbeck and Lesker and *Feldwebel* Graf were all killed. Ju
        88A-1 5104 3Z+DT of 9./KG 77, which was also adjudged to have been
        shot down by 19 Squadron, crashed at Cooling Court, Cooling, Kent.
        Unteroffizier Kurz, Gefreiter Köhn and *Feldwebel* Burkart were killed.
        Unteroffizier Gläsecker was captured.

37   The Czech was killed on 12 April 1942 when he collided with Flight
        Sergeant Halama near Perranporth.

38   In 1941 Jeffries, who was awarded a DFC on 1 October, changed his name
        to Latimer by deed poll. He was killed flying as second pilot of a Lancaster
        of 106 Squadron on 15 April 1943.

39   On 18 October Puda moved to 605 Squadron, where on 5 November 1940
        he was shot down by Bf 109s, baling out of Hurricane V6619 over the
        Thames Estuary. He was commissioned in June 1941 and posted to CFS,
        Upavon, on an instructors' course, then going to 9 FTS at Hullavington. In
        January 1942 he went as a staff pilot to I Signal School, Cranwell, but in
        August 1942 became an instructor again at 3 FTS. In October 1943 he went
        to 24 Squadron at Hendon, flying in the Communications Flight there. After
        the war he rejoined the Czech Air Force in July 1945, and in February 1946
        transferred once more to Czech Air Lines. However, when the Communists
        took power in 1948 he again fled to the West, rejoining the RAF in October
        1948, where he converted to Avro Yorks. He then flew multi-engined types
        until his retirement from the service in October 1954, being awarded the
        Queen's Commendation for Service in the Air. He settled in England in
        retirement.

40   Eduard Prchal was commissioned in December 1941 and posted to 68
        Squadron to become a night fighter, although he achieved no successes in
        this role. He was later posted to 511 Squadron, Transport Command,
        ferrying aircraft from Canada to the Middle East. On 4 July 1943 he was
        the pilot of a Liberator carrying the Polish General Sikorski from Gibraltar
        to London, but crashed on take-off and was badly injured, being the sole
        survivor. He returned to the squadron on recovery. After the war he returned
        to Czechoslovakia with his wife and daughter, serving with the air force
        there until January 1946, when he left and joined Czech Air Lines as a
        senior captain. In 1950 he sought asylum in the UK and in 1951 moved to
        the USA where he became Czech language instructor at the US Army
        Language School at Monterey, California. He retired in 1978 and died in
        California on 12 December 1984.

41   On 10 September 1941 Jiroudek was sent to RAF Kemble for rest. He converted to Beaufighters and flew with 68 Squadron from Coltishall in 1942. Later he flew transports and he returned to Czechoslovakia on 18 July 1945 where in 1946 he became a captain flying with Czech Air Lines.

42   Aboard Ju 88A-1 3162 3Z+FS *Oberleutnant* Georg Fuchs, *Obergefreiter* Baumann and *Gefreiter* Folinger were killed. *Feldwebel* Stier was wounded. On Ju 88A-1 3142 3Z+BS one crewmember was wounded and he and the rest of the crew were taken prisoner.

43   After a patrol in bad weather conditions on 18 October Wapniarek was killed attempting a forced-landing at Nutwood Farm at Thames Ditton. Karwowski had joined the Polish Air Force in 1934 and was commissioned as a pilot in 1937. At the time of the Polish surrender he was in Rumania taking delivery of an aircraft and he escaped to France on foot. Joining II./6 *Groupe de Chasse* he destroyed a Heinkel 111 on 10 May 1940 before escaping to England and joining 302 Squadron in July. He later flew fifty-one *Ramrods* with 306 Squadron, retiring as a squadron leader in 1947.

44   William Riley had joined the RAF on a short service commission in August 1935. He had been posted from 263 Squadron to join the Poles in July 1940 after flying Gloster Gladiator II fighters in Norway where he received a third share in a He 111 victory on 24 May and downed another He 111 on the 26th. His first victories on 302 Squadron came on 21 August when he was awarded a Ju 88 probable east of Bridlington.

45   Jastrzebski failed to return on 25 October 1940 from a patrol over the English Channel. His body was washed up at Sylt. Nowakiewicz, who was attached to 5 OTU during most of September, had flown to Rumania after Poland fell and reached France where he joined II./7 *Groupe de Chasse*. He was the top-scoring Polish pilot of the Battle of France with three and two shared victories. After the fall of France he flew to North Africa and finally England on 16 July, where he joined 302 Squadron on 20 August.

46   KG 2 lost eight Dorniers destroyed and five damaged. KG 3 lost six and four damaged. KG 26 lost one Heinkel He 111 and three damaged and KG 53, six and four damaged.

CHAPTER FIVE

Eagles With Gloves On

There is a popular song called 'They'll always Be An England'. There always will be, but you'll hardly recognize it; and I know damn well I'll not be around to be in it!

Joe Kennedy, defeatist Ambassador to Great Britain, in a conversion with his mistress, Clare Booth Luce. Badly shaken by the Blitz, Kennedy fled London in October 1940 and was soon replaced at the Court of St James by John Winant

Air operations on Thursday 19 September were much reduced by rain showers that spread across Britain from the west and *Luftwaffe* attacks were chiefly over the Thames Estuary and east London. Losses for the day were eight German aircraft for no RAF losses. Flight Lieutenant William Riley and Flying Officer Julian Kowalski of 302 'City of Poznan' Squadron destroyed a Ju 88 four miles north-east of Brandon.[1] In Germany Hitler finally ordered the assembly of the invasion fleet to be stopped and shipping in the Channel ports to be dispersed. The Battle was winding down and the threat of invasion had all but receded although British service chiefs were unaware that *Sealion* had been postponed and the German invasion was still awaited. The *Luftwaffe* continued to mount raids on southern England. On Friday 20 September it carried out a single powerful sweep in two waves, each of about thirty Bf 109s. They were engaged by four RAF fighter squadrons, which claimed two of the enemy fighters shot down while seven Spitfires were lost. On 21 September there was only slight activity with some German fighter sweeps in east Kent. Most of Fighter Command's 563 sorties were flown in the evening[2] when five raids crossed the south coast to attack airfields south of London. Twenty-one squadrons in 11 and 10 Groups together with the Duxford Wing were scrambled to intercept but only one of the squadrons engaged the enemy. Nine *Luftwaffe* aircraft were shot down for no losses to Fighter Command. Stanislav Chalupa of 310 Squadron was injured in a crash-landing and he was forced to cease operational flying. When he recovered from his injuries he returned to 310 Squadron as Operations Room Controller.[3]

Again on 22 September there was only slight activity and at night London was bombed although during the afternoon a lone Dornier Do 17Z took advantage of cloud cover and bombed Fowlmere destroying one of 'B' Flight's Spitfires. Red Section, which was on patrol over Duxford, claimed to have damaged the raider north of Fowlmere before it regained the clouds. On Monday 23 September German fighter sweeps were made towards London and eleven RAF aircraft and three pilots were lost while the *Luftwaffe* lost sixteen aircraft. Wing Commander 'Woody' Woodhall, who led 310 Squadron on at least three operational sorties during September, took twelve Hurricanes up to patrol the Duxford area and they were later vectored to patrol the Thames Estuary but no enemy aircraft were spotted.

Next day the *Luftwaffe* switched its attacks to the British aircraft industry and the Supermarine factory at Southampton was bombed. On 25 and 26 September German attacks were widespread with attacks on Bristol and Plymouth and Southampton while at night London and Merseyside were attacked. On 25 September 19 Squadron received its first few Spitfire II aircraft, which had a more powerful engine and a cartridge starter system to speed up scrambled take-offs. 74 Squadron flew down from Coltishall to operate from Duxford and joined Nos 19 and 611 Squadrons to intercept a raid coming in over London at 20,000 feet. By dusk Fighter Command had flown 668 sorties with thirteen *Luftwaffe* aircraft claimed shot down for the loss of four RAF fighters. On 26 September RAF Fighter Command flew 417 sorties losing six aircraft to the Germans' three.

The last 'Big Wing' 'thrash' came on Friday 27 September when the *Luftwaffe* mounted heavy attacks on London and one on Bristol and made phased attacks on airfields in Nos 10 and 11 Groups. At 0815 hours the Kent and Sussex radar stations had reported a number of fast raids approaching on a fifty-mile front. These had quickly materialised as six groups of Bf 110 *Jabos* (fighter-bombers) of V/LG 1 and II./ZG 76 together with Bf 109s from *Jafu* 2. Crossing in between Dover and Brighton, these formations were hit repeatedly by 11 Group fighters and the *Luftwaffe* made no apparent attempt to attack specific targets. They remained over Kent and Surrey for almost an hour, some penetrating to London. Their purpose was to exhaust the defending fighters' fuel and ammunition so that a subsequent heavy raid with a strong escort of Bf 109s could reach the capital without interference. However, German plans were dashed when the Messerschmitts were late at the assembly area off the French coast and the fifty-five Ju 88s of I and II *Gruppen* of KG 77 crossed the Channel almost entirely without escort. Twelve Ju 88s were shot down and the rest of the force got no further than central Kent where they were so severely mauled that they retreated in confusion. Some Ju 88s reached the outskirts of London and twenty slipped through to the centre.

At around noon the Duxford Wing was scrambled to patrol north London. The

Spitfires of 19 Squadron teamed up with Spitfires of 616 Squadron AAF from Coltishall to provide top cover for the Hurricanes of 242 and 310 Squadrons on patrol over Hornchurch. During the fighting and flying from Kenley 616 Squadron had been all but wiped out. Three of the Auxiliary Squadron's pilots who flew in the Wing this day were Pilot Officer K Holden, Sergeant P Copeland and Flying Officer Donald Sydney Smith, who came from the village of Highley near Bridgnorth, Shropshire. He attended Winchester College and had joined the RAF Volunteer Reserve. After graduation Smith had been appointed geography master at Droxford Senior School and later at Highley School where his father was headmaster. Eventually, the young pilot gave up teaching to make his career in the RAF and he was gazetted as a pilot officer in May 1938. A period of attachment to the Fleet Air Arm convinced him that his preference lay with fighters and so he applied for a transfer to Fighter Command and he arrived on 616 Squadron at Leconfield.[4]

'Woody' Woodhall came on the radio and said, 'Angels 15' and Bader, knowing that instruction came from 11 Group, climbed to 23,000 feet. Woodhall came on the air again and said, 'There's a plot of thirty plus south-east of the Estuary. They don't seem to be coming in.' Bader led his Hurricanes and Spitfires over Canterbury where he found no enemy activity. He flew on to Dover and headed west for Dungeness before winging around. Woodhall's voice kept ringing in his ears about bandits cruising about the south-east but the sky seemed empty. Finally Woodhall called up and said that Bader might as well return to Duxford. Bader had other ideas, however. He told him he was swinging around for one more look. Turning back from Dungeness he saw wings glinting in the sun at about 17,000 feet and an 'untidy' gaggle of about thirty Bf 109s milling around Dover at between 18,000 and 20,000 feet. Visibility was good with a cloud layer higher at 25,000 feet. With the sun at his back Bader ordered the Wing to break up and attack as they liked as he dived into the attack. Bader picked out a Bf 109, which was passing below him. He turned behind and above the enemy fighter and fired a two-second burst. The Bf 109 simply dissolved into thick white smoke, turned over slowly and went down vertically. Bader then went in behind a second Bf 109 that flew in front and below him. He fired a quick burst and the fighter began evasive action by rolling on to its back and diving away. Bader did the same but pulled out short and cut off the fighter on the climb. Bader began a long chase, which ended with him getting in a 'squirt' from 400 yards' range. There was a puff of white smoke and the Bf 109 slowed enabling Bader to get in more 'squirts' and black smoke began pouring from the port side of the fighter's fuselage and the front of Bader's Hurricane was covered with the German's oil. The Bf 109's propeller stopped dead and the doomed fighter glided down under control at a shallow angle until it hit the sea off the coast between Dover and Ramsgate. Bader had used up all his ammunition and he dived down to ground level into the haze heading for Gravesend where he landed safely. His Hurricane was rearmed and refuelled and the CO had lunch with 66 Squadron.

Pilot Officer Hugh Tamblyn who was Green Leader, had tacked on to another Bf 109, which he tried to follow all the way from Dover to mid Channel from 1,200 feet to 120 feet but the enemy machine was faster. The German pilot also tried to throw the Hurricane off the scent by making skidding turns, porpoising and making violent climbing turns to 500 feet. Tamblyn's shots were hitting the enemy machine because he could see petrol and glycol spewing from the fighter but he overshot on his last burst. He had just forty rounds remaining in one gun but a stoppage prevented him from firing them. Visibility was down to less than a mile and Tamblyn reluctantly had to turn for home where he put in a claim for a Bf 109 damaged.[5] 'Green 2', Pilot Officer Michael Giles Homer DFC, who had been posted to 242 Squadron just six days earlier, was shot down in combat with Bf 109s near Sittingbourne. Pilot Officer John Latta ('Green 3') was at 21,000 feet when he saw a Bf 109 3,000 feet lower. It was an opportunity too good to miss and as he got within range the enemy fighter levelled off and Latta fired a burst at him from astern, which hit the petrol tank. The Bf 109E crashed five to ten miles inland of Dover. Latta then spotted more Bf 109s heading back in 'some disarray' towards the French coast. Overtaking one of them he fired at it from fifty yards' range and was gratified to see the petrol tank explode and the fighter went into a steep dive from 10,000 feet before going straight down into the sea about five miles off Dover. These victories took the twenty-seven-year-old's score to seven and one shared destroyed. His Hurricane had been hit in the tail and one of the wings and he also had to put down at Gravesend.[6]

Noel Stansfeld ('Red 2') chased another Bf 109 across Dover and then lost sight of the enemy fighter. A Ju 88 crossed in front of his sight and he fired at it from 200 yards range. The Junkers flew on keeping parallel to the Kent coast heading eastwards and streaming smoke. The Canadian was unable to finish the damaged bomber off because at about fifty feet away he ran out of ammunition. He could not determine its fate because of bad visibility but he was convinced that it would not make it home. He was awarded a Ju 88 probable. Stansfeld and Stan Turner (Blue Leader) were also awarded the DFC and Willie McKnight received a bar to his DFC. Flight Lieutenant Eric Ball who was Yellow Leader, got on the tail of a Bf 109 near Dover–Canterbury and fired at it from 200 yards' range. He hit the enemy pilot's cockpit but his petrol tank had been hit and Ball had to break off the engagement. He had to get down quickly and he force-landed wheels up in a field near Sandwich with his engine on fire. He was unhurt and later he was awarded a Bf 109 damaged.[7]

Pilot Officer Roy Bush ('Blue 2') was at first unable to get into a firing position during his initial dive on the Bf 109s. Climbing to gain much needed height he saw six Bf 109s about 3,000 feet above and decided to go for the furthermost one but the enemy leader turned quickly and dived on the New Zealander's Hurricane. Bush put his fighter into a spin and dived only to find that the Bf 109 pilot was still in pursuit. He performed a quick turn and reverse action and got on the Bf 109's tail before he fired. The fighter went down into the sea between Dover and Gravesend but Bush was awarded only a Bf 109 'damaged'[8]

Sergeant Edward Paterak of 302 'City of Poznan' Squadron forced-landed unhurt at Chelmsford after an unequal fight with a bomber. Gordon Sinclair in 310 Squadron was shot down again, this time over Thanet, but he was unhurt and he landed by parachute at Chilham.[9] Near Dover, Sergeant Josef Kominek claimed a Bf 109E-1 destroyed. His victim was probably *Unteroffizier* Struwe of 9./JG 3 who went down five miles south-west of Dover, his fighter crashing at Owen's Court Farm, Selling. Struwe is believed to have baled out and been taken prisoner. Kominek was on patrol in his Hurricane on 2 November when it caught fire but he managed to bale out safely and the aircraft crashed on a bungalow at Warden, on the Isle of Sheppey. Kominek was killed on 8 June 1941 when his Hurricane stalled and spun in at Coe's Farm near Girton, Cambridgeshire, during low-level manoeuvres. Pilot Officer Emil Fechtner, who had had a similar experience and then on 15 August had been involved in a collision at 25,000 feet, landing unhurt at Upwood, claimed a Do 17 probably destroyed south-east of London. Fechtner was awarded a DFC in October. His luck finally ran out on 29 August when he was killed in a crash near Duxford after colliding with Jaroslav Maly during a patrol.

19 Squadron was to have flown in three sections of four aircraft but 'Sandy' Lane's take-off in one of the new Mk IIs was delayed and the leading section was reduced to three Spitfires. Lane eventually caught up with the Wing formation and he attempted to break up the enemy formations attacking Tilbury Docks but he was able to fire only two short bursts at fleeting targets during his initial dive. When he tried to pull up to regain height he found that his Spitfire was no longer responding to the controls. He had felt the aircraft skidding as he started his dive and he adjusted the rudder's trim tab but it failed to correct this movement. A 'bowed' rudder made worse by the trim control being wrongly adjusted was the cause of the problem and once fully developed, the skid caused the Spitfire's vertical tail surfaces to blanket one of the elevators, rending it inoperative. As his Spitfire passed through 10,000 feet Lane decided to bale out. Before doing so he made one last attempt to recover control and by exerting all his strength he managed to pull the nose up. By this time he was down to only 3,000 feet and he could take no further part in the fight.

Meanwhile, 'Farmer' Lawson ('Red 1') had picked out a Bf 109E-1[10] over the Thames Estuary. Lawson fired several short deflection bursts at the Messerschmitt, which dived away towards the French coast, reducing height to 3,000 feet. Lawson followed, firing his remaining ammunition into the Bf 109, which dived into the sea ten miles off Cap Griz Nez. It took his score to three confirmed.

By now other Messerschmitts were diving down to sea level and heading for France at top speed. Pilot Officer Frantisek 'Haddy' Hradil ('Red 3') made no claim but Sub-Lieutenant Arthur Blake ('Red 2') picked out one of the fleeing Bf 109s ahead of him and to his right. He turned and gave it a deflection shot, which sent the fighter straight down into the waters below. It is possible that it was the Bf 109E-4 flown by *Unteroffizier* Scheidt of 6./JG 27 who was killed.[11] On 29 October Blake, who had been recommended for the award of a DFC, was acting as 'weaver' for 19 Squadron to the south of London, when his Spitfire[12] was picked off by Bf 109s and crashed at Chelmsford, Essex. Blake was killed.

'Grumpy' Unwin, leading Yellow Section, had also seen the Bf 109s attacking from above and he decided to engage them. He claimed one of the fighters destroyed over south-east Kent but he had to use all his ammunition to down the Bf 109, which finally spun into the sea. His No. 2, Sergeant Bernard Jennings, carried on to attack the leading Bf 109 of a formation of four and saw the fighter that he had fired at begin to smoke. Jennings then had to break away when the other fighters dived on him.[13]

Sergeant David Edward Lloyd was unable to get an enemy aircraft in his sights and so made no claims but Sergeant David G.S. Cox was in the thick of it, as he recalls.

19 Squadron was the top squadron at about 28,000 feet and after about five minutes on the patrol line a large number of Bf 109s attacked from out of the sun. Although it was not long after noon the sun was at an angle, it being the end of September, and to the advantage of the Luftwaffe. 19 Squadron was flying in four vics of three – a useless formation as apart from the Squadron Commander everyone was concentrating on keeping in formation and not looking out for the enemy. The first I knew was a shout of '109s' over the radio and we made a 'split-ass' turn to port as the 109s burst in amongst us. Immediately the No. 3 of my vic on the left went down with smoke coming from his Spitfire. Later I learnt he was killed – it was Pilot Officer Burgoyne who joined 19 Squadron on the same day in May 1940 as myself.[14] After a few hectic moments spent avoiding the 109s I found myself alone. I was a few miles inland of Dover, and saw a lone Hurricane being attacked by seven Bf 109s. I started to go to his assistance, but before I could give him any effective help he went down in flames. I believe it was Pilot Officer Homer of 242 Squadron.[15]

The seven 109s then turned their attention to me. They were obviously top class – all yellow-nosed – as they formed into a circle around me, some above and some below to cut off any escape. After many hectic moments of turning into their attacks as soon as I saw one behind me and taking some pot shots at them – more to boost my morale than in the hope of hitting one – the end came. I had got near to one below me and momentarily concentrated too long on firing at him. There was a flash and a loud bang in the cockpit and at the same time I felt as if I had been kicked in the side. For a second or two I was stunned and let go of the control column. I remember dazedly thinking 'this is it', and wondering how long it would be before I hit the ground. Then suddenly I decided it was not it. I grabbed the control column and yanked it back. My Spitfire went into a vertical climb, and as it lost speed I levelled out, tore off my helmet, undid the hood, undid my straps, rolled the aircraft over on its back and thrust the control column sharply forward. The negative 'g' had the effect of shooting me out like a pea from a pod. I quickly pulled the ripcord on my parachute and was promptly jerked about in all directions as it opened. This was because in the panic take-off from Duxford I had not used my own aircraft but one used by a giant of 6 feet 4 inches. I am only 5 feet 7 inches. I was lucky I did not fall out!

As I slowly floated down I felt a lot of pain in my right leg. I looked down and I saw the flying boot on my right leg had many holes, out of which blood was appearing. I landed in the corner of a field and I was picked up by two farm labourers. They took me into the farm house[16] and laid me on a settee. I was feeling pretty grim by then and must have looked it, as the farmer got out a bottle of whisky, which he gave to me, with the comment he was keeping it for Victory Day (this in 1940!) But I looked as if I could do with it, although this is the worst thing for anyone with open wounds. I arrived at an emergency hospital near Ashford in rather a high state. I did not require much to put me under for the surgeon to take several pieces, some as large as two shilling [10p] pieces, of an explosive cannon shell out of my leg.[17]

Pilot Officer Kenneth Holden, who had joined 616 Squadron in early 1939, claimed one of the fighters destroyed. Over Dunkirk on 28 May he had destroyed a Bf 109 and claimed a probable. On 1 June he repeated the action and on 1 September he had damaged two Bf 109s.[18] Sergeant Percy Copeland claimed two Bf 109s damaged and another probably destroyed. Copeland, who had joined the RAFVR in 1937, had downed a Heinkel 111 over Dunkirk on 1 June 1940. On 26 August he was shot down in a surprise attack by a Bf 109 and he forced-landed his Spitfire at Wye. He was wounded and was taken to Ashford Hospital. On 14 October he was posted to 66 Squadron and was commissioned in November. Copeland was killed while flying a Kittyhawk in the Western Desert on 26 June 1941 when Italian MC 202s attacked the formation. He was twenty-five years old. Flying Officer Donald Smith was shot down by Bf 109s and badly wounded while acting as 'weaver' for the formation. The former geography master and Fleet Air Arm pilot crashed at Workhouse Cottage, Throwley. He was admitted to Faversham Cottage Hospital where he died the following day.[19]

Flying Officer Dennis Thomas Parrott ('Green 3') had joined the RAF in June 1937 and had been posted to 9 Squadron at Stradishall in July 1938 before transferring to 19 Squadron on 31 July. He broke formation when he saw three Bf 109s passing to starboard and turned on their tails. Parrott picked out one of the enemy fighters and followed it down in a vertical dive to 10,000 feet, firing intermittently before pulling up behind. He followed the fleeing fighter four miles out to sea where south of Folkestone the Bf 109 finally plunged into the Channel. Parrott was killed on 22 June 1941 on 29 Squadron at the age of twenty-four.

Total claims by the Duxford Wing for 27 September were twelve destroyed. This brought Bader's 'Big Wing' claims to 152 aircraft shot down for the loss of thirty pilots. The *Luftwaffe* lost fifty-five aircraft including twenty-one bombers and nineteen Bf 109s. The RAF lost twenty-eight fighters. As the Battle of Britain entered its final phase it was clear that the Duxford Wing was unlikely to see much further action as speed of reaction was essential when trying to intercept incoming high level fighter sweeps. For another fortnight the Duxford Wing assembled each day at Duxford and patrolled London, usually twice a day, but the *Luftwaffe* had been reigned in during the daylight hours and victories were few and far between. On 12 October Hitler postponed Operation *Sealion* until the following spring.

On the 15 October Flight Lieutenant William Riley and Pilot Officer Waclaw Krol of 302 'City of Poznan' Squadron each destroyed a Bf 109 at Canterbury and Maidstone respectively.[20] Krol had recorded several victories during the fighting in September 1939 over Poland and in May/June 1940 fighting with *Groupe de Chasse* II./7 before joining 302 'City of Poznan' Squadron on 21 August. His final wartime score was nine destroyed, three probables and four damaged. On 18 October Sergeant Jan Nowakiewicz and Squadron Leader Satchell shared a Ju 88 probably destroyed over the south coast.[21] At Boulogne on 26 October Satchell claimed a Bf 109 probably destroyed and Sergeant Anton Lucjan Markiewicz, a Bf 109 damaged. The twenty-five-year-old who had qualified as an aircraft mechanic in 1934 had destroyed several German aircraft, including a Henschel Hs 126 over his homeland on 1 September 1939. Two days later Squadron Leader 'Bill' Blackwood, Pilot Officer Vaclav Bergman and Pilot Officer Jaroslav Maly of 310 (Czech) Squadron shared in damaging a Dornier Do 17 five miles south-west of Duxford.[22]

In October the Duxford Wing was disbanded and the Hurricanes of 242 Squadron returned to Coltishall to fly convoy patrols again. The Hurricane I was clearly out of sorts in a fight with the sleek and powerful Bf 109, especially at 25,000 feet where the Hawker machine sagged and could rarely catch the Messerschmitt.

The Battle of Britain had been won but at a cost to Fighter Command of 915 aircraft and 733 pilots killed or wounded. 'Big Wing' controversy still reigned. The Duxford Wing, with Bader leading, had flown six major daylight attacks during the September battles with two on 15 September when five squadrons comprising twenty-seven Hurricanes and twenty Spitfires were engaged each time. However, of thirty-two 'Big Wings' launched from Duxford and Wittering by 12 Group, only seven met the enemy and only once did a 'Big Wing' arrive first at its intended point of interception.[23] Bader himself said later, 'It worked like a charm once or twice and the arrival of this large formation in support of hard pressed 11 Group squadrons as highly satisfactory. Unfortunately, it was too seldom.'

In the aftermath of the Battle, on 17 October, a famous conference took place in the Air Council Room at the Air Ministry in Whitehall to use the lessons learned to be 'applied generally to enable the fighter defence to operate at maximum efficiency' in the months ahead. At the meeting Squadron Leader Douglas Bader was asked for his views on leading and operating big formations. Bader did not speak for long and his contribution was officially recorded. He said that from his practical experience time was the essence of the problem. 'If enough warning could be given to bring a large number of fighters into position there was no doubt that they could get most effective results.'[24] Later that month Sir Archibald Sinclair, Secretary of State for Air visited Duxford to confer with Bader and Woodhall[25] and the squadrons. The minister satisfied himself that Lord Balfour, the Undersecretary of State for Air, should visit without delay and make a detailed on the spot practical assessment of the points Bader and the squadron commanders had raised about the 11 Group versus 12 Group 'Big Wing' controversy. On the morning of 2 November Captain Harold Balfour flew himself to Duxford to confer with the squadrons. The former First World War pilot who had also been a reporter on the *Daily Mail*, returned to London that evening, sat down in the Air Ministry and penned what became known as the 'Duxford memorandum'. He expertly recorded the arguments for and against the 'Big Wing' put forward by 11 and 12 Groups respectively and copies were later sent to the RAF Air Marshals including Sir Hugh Dowding and AVM Sholto Douglas, the Deputy Chief of the Air Staff. Acrimony ensued. Later, as the RAF turned to the offensive, the architects of victory, ACM Hugh Dowding at Fighter Command and ACM Sir Keith Park, AOC 11 Group, who was 'shot through with strain and fatigue'[26] handed over to ACM Sir W Sholto Douglas and ACM Sir Trafford Leigh-Mallory respectively. Dowding stepped down in November 1940 and embarked on a war aviation development mission to America. Having already been 'retired' once before, in the autumn of 1941, Dowding finally retired from the RAF in June 1942. In March 1941 Sholto Douglas established the post of wing commander flying at all main airfields, and Bader was given the Tangmere Wing.[27]

From November 1940 Duxford squadrons flew offensive patrols over France and shipping protection sorties returned to the daily workload. In the Dover–Deal area on 5 November 'Grumpy' Unwin destroyed a Bf 109 and Flight Lieutenant 'Farmer' Lawson of 19 Squadron claimed a Bf 109 probably destroyed. The latter then destroyed a Bf 109 in the Birchington area.[28] Leonard Haines shared in the destruction of a Bf 109 with Willie McKnight DFC of 242 Squadron.[29] Sergeant Henry Charnock scored the first of his three Bf 109 victories on 19 Squadron, when he downed one of the enemy fighters over Birchington. He would end the war with 72 Squadron and a total of eight enemy aircraft destroyed and one probable. On 15 November 19 Squadron was on a convoy patrol, twenty-five miles east of Deal at 20,000 feet, when two condensation plumes were sighted above at 35,000 feet. Squadron Leader 'Sandy' Lane ('Red 1') climbed after the leading enemy aircraft, a Bf 110, and when it sighted the Spitfires approaching, turned east and dived. Lane ordered line astern and at 8,000 feet opened fire. He then observed an object leaving the aircraft, which appeared to be a piece of cowling. At the same time a stream of coolant appeared from the port engine. Pilot Officer 'Jock' Cunningham ('Red 2') recalls that when his CO could not get his guns in line and 'kindly let him get his nose in', it was like 'hounds after a fox; a changed situation for the squadron'.[30] Cunningham saw smoke coming from the port engine of the Bf 110 after Lane's attack. He then attacked, firing three bursts and saw the starboard engine break into flames and eventually crash into the sea. A bullet from the rear gunner splintered Cunningham's windscreen. A second Bf 110 was shared destroyed between Leonard Haines, Arthur Vokes,[31] 'Grumpy' Unwin and Sergeant David Fulford. The young NCO pilot from Dinnington, Yorkshire, had been posted to 19 Squadron on 25 September from 64 Squadron at Kenley, having entered the RAF College, Cranwell, in September 1939 as a flight cadet. On 28 November between Ramsgate and Southend Leonard Haines and 'Bill' Steere shared in the destruction of a Bf 109 of I./JG 26.[32] 'Grumpy' Unwin and Sergeant David Fulford were also successful, the two Yorkshireman sharing in the destruction of a second Messerschmitt fighter. Fulford was commissioned in March 1941. He was killed in action on 611 Squadron on 2 November 1942 when Fw 190s shot down his Spitfire over Le Touquet.

The Hurricanes of 258 Squadron from Leconfield were also present at Duxford for a few days at the end of November. 242 Squadron left Duxford at the end of November 1940 and 19 and 310 Squadrons carried on with defensive patrols. These included night patrols by 19 Squadron from Fowlmere, as the flarepath lights there were far enough away from Duxford as to, in effect, act as a decoy. Night raids still occurred, and on the night of 25 February 1941 at about 11.00 pm eight bombs fell on the Duxford flarepath and one high-explosive bomb on 310 Squadron's dispersal. This bomb ignited a fuel bowser and two Czech airmen were killed and five injured. The two airmen are buried in the graveyard of Whittlesford church and constitute the only deaths caused at Duxford by enemy bombing. Hurricane Mk IIBs arrived on 310 Squadron in June to supplement the Mk IIAs received by the Czechs in March and in July the Squadron moved to Dyce in Scotland, to be replaced by 56 Squadron from North Weald. The Hurricane squadron had claimed eighty-eight victories in the Battle of Britain from September until the end of 1940. In September 1941 56 Squadron became one of the first two squadrons to be re-equipped with the Hawker Typhoon Mk IA.[33] Re-equipment of 266 'Rhodesia' Squadron followed in February 1942 and 609 'West Riding' Squadron AAF in March. These were the first 400-mph fighters in the RAF but the Sabre engine was proving unreliable with repeated engine failures during the first twelve months of service. It produced a disappointing performance at higher altitudes and an inferior rate of climb. Most problems were caused by the Napier Sabre engine, which was prone to cutting out in the air and there were several crashes. Tail wheel collapse and poor all-round vision were also listed as problems to be solved before the aircraft could enter operational service. By June the troubles seemed to have been overcome, and the three squadrons left for forward bases. A fourth squadron, 181, was formed at Duxford in August and equipped with Typhoons before also moving away. Structural failure of the tail assembly caused many accidents until this problem was rectified and the other problems were gradually overcome.[34]

19 Squadron left Duxford in August 1941, although it had been officially based at Fowlmere since February, bringing an eighteen-year association with the Station to an end.[35] The Spitfire squadron was replaced almost immediately by 601 'County of London' Squadron AAF.[36] The Squadron became the first and only RAF unit to re-equip with the American-built Bell Airacobra I, with conversion taking place at Duxford.[37] In RAF service Airacobras were limited to the ground attack role but unserviceability dogged their short service life with the RAF. 601 Squadron flew its Airacobras operationally on a *Rhubarb* on the French coast on 9 October but after its failure in action the RAF reduced its order to about eighty aircraft and the type was taken off operations in December. Replacement with Hawker Typhoons was planned but in January 1942 601 Squadron moved to Acaster Malbis in Yorkshire and in March Spitfire VBs were received. A move was then made to Digby to prepare for service overseas. The Spitfires were put aboard the US aircraft carrier *Wasp* and flown off to Malta in April, together with 603 Squadron. The pilots fought a desperate battle until June, claiming twenty-five victories before flying out in flights to Egypt.

On 1 August 1941 meanwhile, 133 Eagle Squadron was established at Coltishall and during the following weeks it was moved to three other stations – to Duxford, Collyweston and then Fowlmere. This Squadron was one of three American units – 71, 121 and 133 Squadrons – that were formed late in 1940. Prior to the United States' entry into the Second World War 244 Americans pilots flew in the Eagle squadrons of RAF Fighter Command. They came from the big cities and the backwoods, up state and down town, from California to Connecticut, the Deep South to Dixie; Delaware to Dakota; Frisco to Florida; Mid-West to Maine; the mighty Mississip' to Missouri; New York; New England; Ohio and Hawaii; the Pacific, Philly and the Rockies to the Rio Grande; from Texas to Tallahassee; Wyoming; Wisconsin; the Windy City and way beyond. Most had followed the Battle of Britain in the news and knew that, in time, the US would become involved in the war though it was the stories of the RAF pilots flying their Hurricanes and Spitfires that inspired many, keen for adventure, to join the RAF.[38] To equip 133 Squadron, motto 'Let us to the battle', eighteen Hurricane IIB fighters armed with four 20-mm cannon were flown in. Flight Lieutenant George A Brown DFC, who had been wounded in the fighting on 30 August 1940, was selected to lead the new Eagle squadron. His newly formed band of brothers, or should it be cousins, thought him 'stand offish' and reserved' but Brown understood Americans and how to get the best out of them. His opening words at the pilots' meeting the morning after they arrived were: 'Gentlemen, no Englishman is more appreciative than I am to see you American volunteers over here to assist us in our fight. It is going to get a lot tougher as time goes by, so take a good look around this room.

A year from now most of you will be dead.'[39] Shaken, the pilots glanced around the room at one another, each with the same thought in mind – 'You poor ignorant bastards, you've had it.'[40]

The Adjutant of 133 Squadron was Pilot Officer J.G. Staveley-Dick, an English lawyer:

…with the proverbial pipe clenched in his teeth, appearing always to be in a state of amazement at his close association with such oddball Americans. Commander of 'A' Flight was Flight Lieutenant H.A.S. Johnson, a former civil servant in the Foreign Office, 'a true bubble and squeak type'. Flying Officer J.M. Emerson, 'a fabulous character, millionaire cattleman from Argentina, playboy, polo player, became the squadron intelligence officer' and Flying Officer R.T. Wood, a 'quiet reserved Englishman' was appointed engineering and maintenance officer.[41]

One of the Squadron's many larger-than-life pilots, Pilot Officer Andrew 'Andy' Mamedoff, a twenty-nine-year-old Jewish-American whose family were White Russian émigrés from Siberia was made 'B' Flight commander. Andy was a Russian type with a full mane of dark hair and pale blue eyes in a puckish Mongol face, an inveterate gambler and womaniser, who had grown up in Thompson, Connecticut. After learning to fly he had performed at air shows. He then bought his own plane in order to develop a charter service in the Miami area but he upped sticks for southern California. Late in 1939 he and Eugene Quimby 'Red' Tobin and twenty-six-year-old Vernon Charles 'Shorty' Keough crossed into Canada, the three soldiers of fortune, some would have called them mercenaries, intending to head for Europe and fly for the Finns in the Russo–Finnish war. Tobin was a six foot redhead from Los Angeles, the son of a real estate broker, who had learned to fly in the late 1930s, paying for his lessons by working as a guide and messenger at the MGM studies in Hollywood. Keough was a 4 feet 10 inch New Yorker from Brooklyn. He had been a professional parachutist and stunt pilot, had made more than 500 jumps and had logged several hundred flying hours, scraping by as a barnstormer. Apparently he was so short because he had two vertebrae removed after a parachute accident.[42] When Finland fell they were told that they would be able to join the *Armée de l'Air* so they had set sail for St Nazaire on the French Atlantic coast, arriving in Paris on 4 June. From then on their escapades read like a Hemingway novel. Within a few days German Panzers had surrounded the French capital but the three Americans had taken a train to Tours, hoping to fly fighter aircraft. France was in complete turmoil and the fifth column, dressed as Czech soldiers, were everywhere. By now Paris too had fallen. The Americans realised that they only way they could fly and fight was to try to reach England. They joined two Czech pilots in an attempt to steal two Potez three-seat bomber aircraft but the plan failed when the Czechs were killed by French soldiers who thought that they were Germans dressed in Czech uniforms. The Americans hitchhiked south-west intending to reach the coast and catch a boat. On 17 June they arrived at the small town of Arcay, which was heaving with tens of thousands of refugees and deserters. Finally, at St Jean de Luz not far from the Spanish border, they boarded the British registered steamship, the *Baron Nairn*. It was the last ship leaving for England.

Despite attempts by the US Embassy to send them Stateside, they enlisted in the RAF. 'Shorty' Keough, who 'barring circus freaks', was the smallest man some men had ever seen, had to be given a leg up into his Spitfire and he almost failed his medical board because of his lack of height. They thought that he would never ever reach the rudder bar in a Spit but Keough produced two seat cushions that he had brought with him all the way from the States via France especially for the purpose. One went under his parachute and raised him up, the other he wedged in the small of his back. Now he was able to see out of the cockpit and reach the bar! The little New Yorker and the Californian Cossack and their tall wisecracking buddy were posted to 609 Squadron at Warmwell in Dorset where they took part in the fighting. Tobin shared in the destruction of a Do 17 on 8 August and Keough was awarded a share in the destruction of a Do 17 on 18 September.

On 26 September 1940 the three inseparable American soldiers of fortune were posted to Drem in Scotland where they became the proud founder members of 71 Eagle Squadron. During a protection convoy just off the east coast on 15 February Keough failed to pull out of dive and his Hurricane smashed into the sea at over 500 mph. 'Shorty's lack of height had never proved to be an impediment. Vertigo was suspected but he had simply forgotten to turn on his oxygen and had blacked out for lack of air. The twenty-nine-year-old died instantly he hit the water.

On 4 July Mamedoff and Tobin marked another death in the Eagle family when on that Independence Day afternoon they and the pilots of 71 Squadron bade their farewells to Billy Fiske, the first of the Eagles to fall, at a Memorial Service at St Paul's Cathedral in London. Mamedoff became the first of the Eagles to take a war bride when he married Penny Craven, one of the most eligible young women in England, the daughter in the wealthy Craven cigarette family. Vic Bono, his best man, persuaded several members of the squadron to fly two 'honour guards' of the cannon-armed Hurricanes after the church ceremony at Epping! The new bridegroom was posted to Coltishall on 1 August 1941 to be a flight commander in 133.

A month later, on 7 September, 'Red' Tobin went missing on 71 Squadron's first fighter sweep over France. It is possible that the gangly twenty-four-year-old tangled with twenty-two-year-old Joachim Müncheberg of JG 26 who downed the Spitfire near Montreuil for his 53rd *abschuss*. Gone too were Hilard Fenlaw, like Mamedoff, recently married and Pilot Officer Bill Nichols, who shot up and forced to crash-land, was soon captured. Tobin's sister Helen was visiting relatives in Denver when she received word that Gene was reported missing in action. His girlfriend in Los Angeles, twenty-four-year-old Anne Haring, a tall Irish beauty, contacted the International Red Cross as soon as she learned that he was missing. It was not until late October that she finally received confirmation that Tobin was dead. Mamedoff was now the only surviving member of the three brave, brash musketeers who had set out full of spirit and adventure to fight in Europe.

On a practice flight on 27 September Walt Soares, a Californian who had learned to fly in 1938 in a 40-hp Taylorcraft, and his wingman, Charles S Burrell of Hamilton, Massachusetts, collided while turning on final approach and they were killed. It was 133 Squadron's first fatal accident. Sent aloft daily in flight and squadron formations, the pilots of 133 Squadron quickly learned the rudiments of strict air discipline. One practice interception with a Duxford squadron developed into an explosive dogfight all the way down to the deck. Both commanding officers and all four flight commanders had to shout orders for their teams to break it off.[43] Early in October 1941 133 Squadron fled the Eagle's nest at Duxford and moved to Fowlmere. The Eagles' winter sojourn was short because on 8 October the fifteen Hurricanes piloted by American nationals left for Eglington, eight miles from Londonderry in Northern Ireland where they were to take further instruction amid rain, more rain and mud. At Fowlmere Mamedoff took off first and led them to Sealand to refuel. In less than hour they touched down at the transit station but overhead, storm clouds began rolling in from the Irish Sea. Only six of the Hurricane pilots that took off again reached RAF Andreas on the Isle of Man, a tiny pinprick in the Irish Sea, having missed several hilltops by only a few feet. Three landed at an intermediate airfield. Two more turned back for Sealand. The other four Eagles never arrived. One of them was Mamedoff. Local farmers found the twenty-eight-year-old's broken body and blazing Hurricane in a field near the village of Maughold, south-east of Ramsey. On 14 October a telegram arrived at Lev and Natasha Mamedoff's Russian Bear restaurant in Connecticut telling them of their only son's death and that he was to be buried in Brookwood Military Cemetery in Woking.[44]

From the time the first Eagle Squadron was formed in September 1940 until all three squadrons were disbanded and incorporated into the USAAF in September 1942 they destroyed 73½ German aircraft while seventy-seven American members were killed. Once America came into the war negotiations began to transfer the Eagle squadrons to the USAAF and most pilots were given a rank equivalent to their RAF rank. None of the Eagle squadron pilots had served in the USAAF and they did not have US pilots' wings so they received US pilots' wings upon their transfer. General Spaatz wanted to spread the experience of the Eagles amongst various new US fighter squadrons but the three Eagle squadrons wanted to stay together as units. The USAAF did not have any suitable aircraft so the new squadrons were equipped with Spitfire VBs. On 29 September 1942 the Eagle Squadrons were incorporated into the 4th Fighter Group, as the 334th (71), 335th (121) and 336th (133) Fighter Squadrons.

On 12 August 1942 1st Lieutenant J.A. Glenn of the 1st Fighter Group, USAAC, became the first American pilot to arrive at Duxford when he flew a Lockheed P-38F Lightning in from Goxhill on tactical trials. The fastest American fighter available when war began, the P-38 was the first twin-engine, single-seat fighter ever mass-produced.[45] On 14 September the 1st Fighter Group was assigned to the 12th Air Force destined for North Africa but continued to fly missions from England until 25 October.[46] That same month a nucleus of officers of the 350th Fighter Group arrived at Duxford.[47] This Group had the use of a number of Spitfires and P-39 Airacobras for working-up purposes, but the late arrival of ground crews from the USA slowed this process down. By January 1943 the Group was at full strength and soon began the journey to North Africa. On 20 December meanwhile, 169 Squadron, which had been formed in June as a tactical reconnaissance unit in Army Co-Operation Command with the North American Mustang I, arrived at Duxford from Clifton for shipping reconnaissance and ground-attack operations.[48] At Duxford throughout 1942 the Air Fighting Development Unit tested a variety of British and American aircraft. Chief among these was the Mustang, which had resulted after a visit made by the British Purchasing Commission officials to America in April 1940 and which, like the Airacobra and the P-38, was powered by the same Allison powerplant.[49]

Ironically, with all the comings and goings of American fighters and RAF Mustangs at Duxford in 1942 because of a lack of numbers and suitable long-range fighter escorts, B-17 and B-24 bombing missions were largely restricted to making pinprick raids on the U-boat pens and airfields in France. On 6 September Brigadier-General Ira C. Eaker, Commanding General of VIIIth Bomber Command, mounted his largest bombing mission so far sending three dozen B-17s to the Avions Potez factory at Meaulte. It was on this mission that the fighter unit that would soon become one of the American fighter groups' greatest adversaries, *Jagdgeschwader* 26 and their yellow-nosed Focke-Wulf 190s, confronted the American formations for the first time. Based at Abbeville-Drucat in northern France JG 26, or 'Abbeville Kids' as they became known to American fighter pilots and bomber crews alike, were among the *Luftwaffe* elite and had taken part in daylight escort sorties over England in the summer of 1940. II./JG 26 were encountered continuously from the French coast to the target and the escorting four squadrons of Spitfire IXs failed to rendezvous with the bombers. JG 26 intercepted the Spitfires and shot down three. About fifty Fw 190s and a handful of Bf 109s bounced the Fortresses and *Hauptmann* Conny Meyer, CO of II./JG 26 claimed the *Luftwaffe's* first American heavy bomber victory of the war. *Leutnant* Otto P 'Stotto' Stammberger was one of the few German fighter pilots who survived the battle of attrition in the West, 1942–3, first serving with 9./JG 26 and rising to the rank of *Oberleutnant* and command of 4./JG 26 from 26 February 1943 until he was severely injured in air combat on 13 May. He was to recall:

In the defence of the Reich during 1942 and 1943, we were only present in the West with two Fighter Wings, Jagdgeschwader 2 Richthofen and us, Jagdgeschwader 26 Schlageter. In all, we could muster 240 fighter aircraft, which could only be employed in Gruppen of 25 to 30 each, as the bombers came in using different routes all the time. Our 240 fighters were dispersed from Brest to the mouth of the River Scheldt, and the individual Gruppen of our Jagdgeschwader 26 had to cover a stretch of 250 kilometres along the Channel coast. Therefore, on each mission only one, sometimes two Gruppen could possibly be thrown against the enemy. It often happened that I took off during 1942 and 1943, for my third or fourth sortie on a day with only three or four serviceable machines, the rest having all being damaged, having crash-landed or being completely lost during the earlier sorties.[50]

Though the B-17 Flying Fortresses and B-24 Liberators hit their targets on almost every mission they were not in large enough concentrations to damage them seriously. This was especially true of the raids on the U-boat pens on the French Atlantic coast. Losses were high, mainly because for most of the route they were flown without escort and the bombers were sent in to bomb at heights that got progressively lower in a search for accuracy. The *Luftwaffe* day fighter arm had also developed new tactics to combat the bombers. At first they intercepted the B-17 Flying Fortresses and B-24 Liberators from the rear where enough guns could be brought to bear on enemy fighters. *Luftwaffe* experiments proved that the frontal area of the American bombers offered very little in defensive firepower. Despite the dangers of very high closing speeds this became the best method of shooting the bombers down. *Oberstleutnant* Egon Mayer, *Kommandeur*, III./JG 2 and *Oberleutnant* Georg-Peter 'Schorch' Eder, *Staffelkapitän*, 12./JG 2, are credited with developing the head-on attack, where the bomber armament was weakest. On 20 December when 101 B-17s struck Romilly-sur-Seine airfield twelve squadrons of fighters flew escort as far as Rouen. At this point II./JG 26 led by Major Gerhard 'Gerd' Schöpfel who had paralleled the American formation waiting for the escorts to leave, attacked the Forts from head-on[51] and two were shot down. For an hour the enemy fighters attacked in relays and JG 26 did not break off until the withdrawal escort appeared over the Channel.[52]

On early bombing missions most RAF officers remained sceptical when the press enthusiastically credited Fortress and Liberator gunners with several fighters destroyed and praised them for beating off scores of Focke-Wulf 190s. Few in the RAF believed that the 8th Air Force could succeed where they and the *Luftwaffe* during the Battle of Britain had failed. The British wanted the USAAF to join RAF Bomber Command in its night bombing offensive. The USAAF however, was not about to change its daylight precision bombing concept. Harrison Salisbury, a United Press Correspondent, put it very succinctly when he wrote:

By no means had the 8th Air Force been established to become an appendage of the RAF. That was not for the likes of General Ira C Eaker, or a young cigar-chomping, tough-talking colonel named Curtis LeMay, or the others. The 8th Air Force was a high-octane outfit. It was run by ambitious men and backed by an ambitious command in Washington. It had set up by a large public relations staff – men from newspapers, publicity firms, advertising agencies – and made use of Hollywood celebrities. They were not attracted to the air force because they thought it was going to take directions from the English.

Eventually the British, notably Winston Churchill, came to accept the American method of bombing and it would grow into a formidable 'round the clock' bombing strategy. But for now, the American high command persisted in sending combat boxes on bombing missions in daylight even though UK-based fighters did not have the range to accompany the bombers all the way to their targets and back again. Over the sub pens and airfields *Flieger Abwehr Kanonen* (flak) defences broke up the formations and the *Luftwaffe* fighters pounced on the disabled and crippled remnants and finished off the stragglers. On 16 February ninety-five bombers were dispatched to bomb the U-boat pens at St Nazaire. German fighter controllers simply waited until the escort fighters turned back before unleashing their fighters and six Fortresses were shot down. Thirty heavies returned battle-damaged. On 10 March when sixty-seven B-17s attacked the marshalling yards at Rennes, three squadrons of RAF Spitfires and, for the first time, the 4th Fighter Group's P-47C Thunderbolts escorted the bombers but several bombers were shot down by German fighters. Despite the mounting losses and with no long-range escorts available General Ira Eaker ordered maximum efforts on U-boat yards in Germany. Even when missions were flown to France with a Spitfire escort they fared no better. When the fighters failed to rendezvous with the Fortresses they flew a triangular course in mid-Channel, which allowed the *Luftwaffe* ample time to intercept. When the Spitfires finally arrived they had to return low on fuel, leaving the B-17s to fly on alone to the target where 2./JG 26 and 12./JG 2 tore into the unescorted bombers and damaged nine.

By mid-1942 heavy losses in the bomber groups made it obvious to all that long-range fighters would be required to escort even heavily armed phalanxes of USAAF Fortresses and Liberators flying in close formation in daylight in the European Theatre of Operations (ETO). The Airacobra was unsuitable; the P-38F began to be deployed in large numbers in the ETO. Although slightly slower and less manoeuvrable than most single-engined fighters then in service, the Lightning's greater range made it an excellent escort fighter. Other theatres of war had a bigger call on the P-38s[53] and the Mustang was still being touted by the Americans as a tactical fighter. There was only one other fighter that was suitable and available in potentially high numbers and that was the Republic P-47 Thunderbolt.

1   Ju 88A-1 2151 3Z+GH of I./KG 77. *Unteroffizier* Dorawa, *Gefreiters* Schulz and Scholz and *Unteroffizier* Etzold were killed.

2   Pilot Officer D.A. Adams of 611 Squadron destroyed a Do 215 at Hoylake-Dolgellau during an enemy reconnaissance sortie over Liverpool.

3   Chalupa was awarded the *Virtuti Militari* in February 1941 and remained with 302 Squadron until the end of July 1942. After the war he settled in Canada.

4   On the night of 7 August he had a lucky escape when he was forced to abandon his Spitfire, which crashed and exploded near the station. *The Battle of Britain Then and Now.*

5   Tamblyn was decorated with the DFC by HM the King on 1 April 1941. Two days later he was shot down and killed.

6   On 10 January 1941 Latta took part in the first *Circus* operation, escorting Blenheims to raid Guines airfield near Calais, but two days later took part in one of the early low-level *Rhubarb* operations. Four Hurricanes were sent out in pairs, both being intercepted by Bf 109s. Flight Lieutenant 'Willie' McKnight DFC was lost from one and John Latta from the other. Latta had nine confirmed victories and one shared destroyed.

7   At the end of January 1941 Eric Ball was posted out to the Middle East, joining 73 Squadron as a flight commander in the desert. On 12 April he flew into a sandstorm and was forced to land in Axis territory, spending the rest of the war as a PoW. On release in 1945 he joined 567 Squadron, an anti-aircraft co-operation unit, briefly, but in October was promoted to squadron leader and given command of 222 Squadron on Meteor F.3 jets. He was killed in a flying accident on 1 February 1946, aged twenty-seven.

8   Roy Bush was killed on 30 November 1948 during a photographic reconnaissance of the Gisborne area in an Oxford. The aircraft had crashed in the Ruahines, and was believed to have broken up in the air. All three aboard were killed.

9   In January 1941 he was posted to HQ, 12 Group, on staff duties, but in May helped form 313, another Czech squadron, which he commanded. He survived the war.

10   3369 11+? of 3./JG 27, which crashed at Mays Farm, Selmeston, near Lewes, has been attributed to Lawson. (*Battle Over Britain*). Gefreiter John baled out and was captured unhurt. Four Bf 109s that did come down in the sea were Bf 109E-4 4141 of 6./JG 3, which crashed in the Channel and the pilot was rescued by *Seenotdienst*. Bf 109E-4 5340 of III./JG 3 also crashed in the sea. *Oberleutnant* Rech was wounded and rescued by *Seenotdienst*. Bf 109E-4 5333 of 3./JG 27, which went down in the Channel, was also rescued unhurt by *Seenotdienst*. Bf 109E-1 6162 of 6./JG 52 was shot down by fighters in combat over the Channel. The pilot was wounded and picked up by *Seenotdienst*. Two Bf 109E-4s of II./JG 53 were damaged in combat over the Channel. *The Battle of Britain Then and Now.*

11   Scheidt's Bf 109 was Bf 109E-4 1447.

12   P7423.

13   Bf 109E 1538 of 8./JG 54 flown by *Oberleutnant* Anton Schön who was killed, went down near Tilbury Docks. Schön hit a fence trying to land, somersaulted over the main road and crashed in flames near Brenley House, Boughton, east of Faversham.

14   The four Spitfires of Green Section led by Flight Sergeant 'Bill' Steere DFM began their attack on the main formation over Canterbury when they were attacked from behind. Pilot Officer Eric Burgoyne ('Green 4') was shot down and he was killed. The twenty-five-year-old's Spitfire came down at Coldred at 12.30 pm (*The Battle of Britain Then and Now*). Steere opened fire on a Bf 109 from 300 yards' range but when he saw more Bf 109Es coming in from astern he broke away. His victim crashed in the Deal area to take his score to five. His No. 2, Stanlislav Plzak, saw the fighter go down in flames and he then closed in on another Bf 109E from above and behind. Plzak fired three bursts and his victim – Bf 109E-1 3442 of 4./JG 52 flown by *Gefreiter* Bosch, who was wounded, survived and was taken prisoner – crashed through H/T cables at Northbourne Park near Sandwich. Plzak meanwhile, joined up with 616 Squadron and became involved with them in a fight with fifteen Bf 109s over the Dover area. Plzak was shot down over Southend on 28 November 1940 by Bf 109Es of I./JG 26, surviving unhurt. His final wartime score reached three and three shared destroyed. He damaged a Bf 109E on 27 June 1941. On 6 August he was commissioned pilot officer only to be killed in action over Mardyck the following day.

15   The twenty-one-year-old from Swanage, Dorset, had attended Wellington College during the mid-thirties before joining the RAF and becoming a bomber pilot. In early 1940 he was flying Hampdens on 44 Squadron and he received a DFC for his actions on a bombing raid on Kristiansand Bay on 12 April. In August Homer had volunteered for Fighter Command and joined 1 Squadron at Northolt. Homer crashed in flames at Bluetown, Matching Wood, Milstead, at 1225 hours and he was killed.

16   His Spitfire crashed at Wye Court Farm, Wye.

17   During the early cross-Channel sweeps of June 1941, David Cox claimed a Bf 109 shot down on the 27th but his own aircraft was then badly damaged and he only just managed to get back across the Channel and crash-land at Dungeness. He was commissioned the following month. He survived the war, leaving the RAF in March 1946.

18   In mid-May 1941 Holden became CO of 610 Squadron. He destroyed a Bf

109 on 22 June 1941 and damaged two more on 25 and 26 June. He destroyed a Bf 109 and shared another on 6 July and got a 109 probable on 10 July. The award of a DFC followed five days later. After the war Holden re-joined the RAFVR and in 1946 he took command of 616 Squadron when it reformed.

19   *The Battle of Britain Then and Now.*

20   Riley was posted to 145 Squadron on 30 October. Flying with 145, 252 and 272 Squadrons, he scored a further five victories to take his final score to eight and two shared destroyed, three probables and one damaged. He was killed flying a Beaufighter on 16 July 1942 when Wing Commander Riley DFC was involved in a collision with another Beaufighter over the Mediterranean.

21   Nowakiewicz was shot down by ground fire over the French coast on 23 July 1942. After force-landing his Spitfire he was taken in by the French Resistance and Polish immigrants and he planned to try and steal a Ju 88 with five other escapers and fly to England. The day before the attempt was made they were arrested by the *Gestapo* and he spent the next six months in Fresnes Prison in Paris. Finally, he was moved to *Stalag Luft* III. Post war he settled in Manchester and became a local businessman.

22   Maly died on 5 June 1941.

23   Tom Gleave.

24   *Flying Colours: The Epic Story of Douglas Bader.*

25   After the Battle Woodhall went to Malta as senior controller on the island. Group Captain Vasse, the CO of the AFDU, took over from Woodhall as station commander. Woodhall retired from the RAF on 14 July 1945.

26   *Flying Colours: The Epic Story of Douglas Bader.*

27   Early in 1941 Bader began leading squadrons of Hurricane IIs on offensive sweeps over France from North Weald. In March 1941 he was appointed Wing Commander Flying at Tangmere flying Spitfires on offensive sweeps over the continent. He had been awarded a DFC in January 1941 for ten victories and a Bar to his DSO followed in July for 15 and a Bar to his DFC came in September, for four more. On 9 August Bader was shot down over France on a fighter sweep and he spent the rest of the war in German prison camps until finally being released from Colditz Castle in April 1945.

28   Lawson destroyed a Bf 109 on 27 June 1941 to take his final score to six and one shared destroyed. He was promoted to flight commander early in September 1940 and was awarded a DFC on 26 November. Early in June 1941 he took over 19 Squadron from 'Sandy' Lane but he was killed on an

operation to Rotterdam on 28 August. *Battle of Britain: The Photographic Kaleidoscope: Vol., II.*

29   McKnight was KIA on 12 January 1941.

30   *Memories of a British Veteran* by Wallace Cunningham. Lane was awarded a half share in a Bf 110 victory on 15 November (believed to be Bf 110 4N+DH of I(F)/22, which crashed in Thames Estuary, the crew being lost), which took his score to six and one shared destroyed, two unconfirmed destroyed, one probable and one damaged. He left 19 Squadron early in June 1941 on posting to the Staff of HQ, 12 Group, when be wrote a classic book *Spitfire* under the pseudonym BJ Ellan (John Murray 1942). In November 1941 he was posted to the Middle East, serving at Air HQ, Western Desert, and then with HQ, Middle East, from February 1942. In June he returned to the UK and took command of 61 OTU until early December 1942, when he was given command of 167 Squadron. Four days after his arrival he led three other Spitfires off on a *Rhubarb* operation over the Dutch coast. Here Fw 190s were engaged and he disappeared, being reported missing; he had been shot down in AR612 W-U, west of Schouwen Island by *Oberleutnant* Walter Leonhardt of 6./JG 1.

31   On 29 August 1941 Flight Lieutenant Arthur Vokes, the acting CO, led what was left of the Squadron on an ASR sortie over the North Sea. They ran into a number of Bf 110s of 6./ZG 76 and four of the Spitfires were shot down. Vokes was killed a week later, on 5 September, when he crashed in bad weather near Langham aerodrome, Norfolk, on a ferry flight. *Battle of Britain: The Photographic Kaleidoscope: Vol. II.*

32   Leonard Haines was killed on 30 April 1941.

33   The Typhoon had been designed as an interceptor fighter but ultimately, its greatest achievement was as a fighter-bomber with RAF 2nd Tactical Air Force where it acted as a close-support aircraft armed with a battery of rocket-projectiles. The Typhoon had originated in 1937 to take advantage of the new 2,000-hp engines such as the Rolls-Royce Vulture, a twenty-four-cylinder 'X' engine, and the Napier Sabre twenty-four-cylinder 'H' engine then under development. The prototype Vulture-engined Tornado was the first to fly, in October 1939, with the prototype Typhoon flying on 24 February 1940. With a speed of nearly 400 mph, the Tornado became the first British fighter to encounter compressibility troubles. It was originally hoped that the new fighter would enter squadron service by July 1940 but the first production aircraft did not fly until 27 May 1941 with the first deliveries of the Napier Sabre engined Ia, which was armed with twelve machine-guns, being made in August 1941.

34   In March 1942 the Typhoon IAs at Duxford were supplemented by the

arrival of the Mk IB, which was armed with four 20-mm cannon. In May 1942 56 Squadron's Typhoons began operating from Manston in Kent. They were in action over the French beaches during the ill-fated Dieppe landings of 19 August 1942. By the end of the year, following the example of Hurricanes modified for the bombing role and later known as 'Hurri-bombers' they were tested at the AFDU at Duxford, which also evaluated a Wellington with a 40-mm gun in the tail. The Typhoons began carrying two 250-lb bombs beneath the wings. With Nos 175, 181 (which spent about two months at Duxford, from 1 September to 10 December) and 245 Squadrons, they operated throughout 1943 against enemy shipping as part of the 'Channel Stop' campaign. Meanwhile, other Typhoon squadrons were taking part in offensive sweeps over France, Belgium and Holland, attacking enemy airfields and communications. Before long, Typhoons had become famous for their 'train-busting' activities, and by the middle of 1943 as many as 150 locomotives were being destroyed each month. 609 Squadron destroyed 100 locomotives in its first few months of operations for the loss of only two aircraft.

35   On the south side of the airfield, 74 (Signals) Wing was based. Flying a variety of aircraft, including Blenheim IVs, Hornet Moths and the Cierva C30A autogyro, on coastal radar calibration work, the Wing's flying section became 1448 (Special) Flight in February 1942. *Airfield Focus 1: Duxford* by Andy Height. (GMS 1992).

36   At the outbreak of the war 601 Squadron was at Biggin Hill with Blenheim Ifs. At the end of December 1939 the Squadron had moved to Tangmere, where Hurricane Is replaced the Blenheims during February 1940. By the end of the summer 601 Squadron had claimed over 100 victories. In March 1941 Hurricane IIbs were received but at the end of June the auxiliary unit withdrew to Matlaske, one of two satellite airfields twelve miles north-west of the host station at RAF Coltishall.

37   The Airacobra had flown in November 1939. In April 1940 an order was received for the *Armée de l'Air* but after the fall of France the contract had been taken over in June 1940 by the British Direct Purchase Commission. The Airacobra had a 1,150-hp Allison engine behind the cockpit and an extension shaft that went between the pilot's legs and transmitted power to drive the propeller. It was also one of the first fighters to be fitted with a tricycle undercarriage. In July 1941 the AFDU at Duxford received the first RAF Airacobras but the Bell company had greatly exaggerated the performance figures of the aircraft and the first models were found to be decidedly slower in the climb than the Spitfire Vb and increasingly slower at altitudes over 15,000 feet. In September 601 Squadron converted to the type from the Hurricane IIb.

38   An organisation named the Knight Committee was responsible for recruiting nearly ninety per cent of the Eagle Squadron members. The basic requirements for those interested in joining the Eagles were a high school diploma, to be aged between twenty and thirty-one, eyesight that was 20/40 correctable to 20/20, and 300 hours' of certified flying time. Most Eagle Squadron pilots did not have a college education or prior military experience. Once in England, the new recruits were sent to an operational training unit (OTU) for two to four weeks, where they learned to fly Miles Master trainers, Hurricanes, and Spitfires before being posted to a squadron. After OTU some of the men went straight to one of the Eagle squadrons while others first served with other RAF squadrons before being transferred to an Eagle Squadron.

39   *The Eagle Squadrons: Yanks in the RAF, 1940–42* by Vern Haugland (TAB Books 1992).

40   *The Few; The American 'Knights of the Air' who risked everything to fight in the Battle of Britain*, by Alex Kershaw (Da Capo Press 2006).

41   *The Eagle Squadrons: Yanks in the RAF, 1940–42.*

42   *The Few; The American 'Knights of the Air' who risked everything to fight in the Battle of Britain*, by Alex Kershaw (Da Capo Press 2006).

43   *The Eagle Squadrons: Yanks in the RAF, 1940–42.*

44   *The Few; The American 'Knights of the Air' who risked everything to fight in the Battle of Britain*, by Alex Kershaw (Da Capo Press 2006).

45   A total of 9,535 P-38s were built. Its performance was due mainly to two turbo-supercharged Allison C-type V1710 engines. The first unit to operate the P-38 was the 342nd Composite Group, operating from Icelandic bases. Where the RAF was concerned, in trials at Boscombe Down the Lightning's performance proved a disappointment and the P-38 had suffered the same fate as the Airacobra. A contract for 667 export versions of the P-38 powered by 1,090-hp V-1710-C15s with the superchargers deleted was originally negotiated with the French but with the defeat in May 1940 the contract had been taken over by the British on 5 June. An order for 524 Lightnings was cancelled in August 1942.

46   Ultimately, four American fighter groups – the 20th, 55th, 364th and 479th – equipped with P-38H and J Lightnings flew combat missions from England until replacement by the P-51 Mustang in July/September 1944.

47   The Group had been activated at Bushey Hall, Watford, on 1 October under the command of Major B.F. Klocko, and comprised the 345th, 346th and 347th Fighter Squadrons. Some of the pilots had been transferred to other

Fighter Groups, notably the 31st. Because of all the activity at Duxford, only the Group HQ and the 345th Fighter Squadron stayed, the 346th being detached to Coltishall and the 347th to Snailwell.

48   169 Squadron moved to Barford St John on 1 March 1943 and Mustangs of 4 Squadron in Army Co-Operation Command arrived from Cranfield for a very brief sojourn before moving to Clifton.

49   Other American types such as the North American Mitchell, Martin Marauder and Lockheed Ventura were also tested. The AFDU also trialled the first and highly secret Mosquito. In May 1942 a Lancaster piloted by Squadron Leader John Dering Nettleton VC was evaluated for Bomber Command to help develop evasive tactics for heavy bombers. In February/March 1943 the AFDU and NAFDU moved to Wittering and 1426 (EAC) Flight to Collyweston, 1448 Flight to Halton and 169 Squadron's Mustangs to Barford St John and by mid-March flying activity was at a minimum, but a few more Mustangs involved in army co-operation exercises made use of Duxford for a short time. *Airfield Focus 1: Duxford* by Andy Height (GMS 1992).

50   *Battles with the Luftwaffe*, Theo Boiten and Martin W Bowman (Jane's 2001).

51   Schöpfel, who had scored twenty-two victories in 1940 including four Hurricanes on 18 August, was credited with a B-17 kill to take his score to forty-six. He left the *Geschwader* on 10 January 1943 to become Operations Officer of *Jafü* Brittany, the fighter control unit defending the U-boat bases and survived the war with forty victories. 'Pips' Priller, who at the time had eighty-one victories, replaced Schöpfel as JG 26 *Kommodore*.

52   On 20 December the *Luftwaffe* had made its attacks from dead ahead, or twelve o'clock level. Closing speeds of around 550 mph made it difficult to keep targets in effective firing range for more than a split second and there was always the fear of collision at the back of the German pilots' minds. The *Luftwaffe*, not satisfied with the relatively small numbers of bombers being shot down, revised its tactics on 23 January when the Americans attacked U-boat installations at Lorient and they employed larger attacking formations and simultaneous fighter attacks instead of attacks in trail to good effect. While they would still use the head-on approach, the angle of attack would be from 10 degrees above the horizontal – otherwise known as twelve o'clock high, which in experiments was found to be more effective. As before, the best chance of knocking a bomber out of formation was to kill the pilots in the cockpit.

53   The constant drain on 8th Air Force resources was a direct result of the need to supply the 12th Air Force, destined for the Mediterranean Theatre. Unfortunately, few were aware that the 12th Air Force was destined for Operation *Torch* and therefore had top priority when it came to spares, personnel, aircraft and even training. New groups had to be trained for eventual transfer to the 12th Air Force, a task Eaker could well have done without at such a crucial time in the 8th Air Force's history.

CHAPTER SIX

Wings of Eagles

*The Jug's diving prowess become legendary but inexperienced pilots had
to watch out if they got the nose down, as diving several thousand feet and
pulling out was not for the faint hearted. They did not want to go to
paradise but they wanted their enemies to go to Hell.*

In December 1942 homesick Americans in the 78th Fighter Group at Goxhill, a
remote airfield in the flat Lincolnshire Fenland, were hopelessly looking
forward to a cold, and wet and cheerless first Christmas in the ETO. In England
the 8th Air Force occupied many bases, some of which were either leased or
purpose-built for them but 'Goat Hill', as it was quickly called, was a typical
underdeveloped RAF airfield. It had all seemed so different at Baer Field, Indiana,
on 9 February where Colonel Arman 'Pete' Peterson's outfit had been one of the
first groups selected to fly the Lockheed P-38 Lightning. They had gained a high
level of experience on the aircraft before departing for Hamilton Field, California,
and had then sailed for England on the *Queen Elizabeth*, which sailed from New
York on 24 November. 'Pete' Peterson was twenty-eight years old and he came
from Flagstaff, Arizona. Peterson's boys with their well-cut uniforms, new accents
and money, had arrived at their bleak new home on 1 December. The young
American servicemen arriving in Britain created a culture shock in the parochial
parishes of Eastern England but most of them found England's fog and rain very
hard to get used to. It was often very damp and one seldom saw the sun. Blackouts
made it difficult to navigate at night with no lights. Now the prospect of Christmas
away from loved ones brought the harsh realities of separation in war even closer
to home.

Colonel Peterson arranged for five hundred children from nearby towns to
descend on the base for a Christmas party to lift his troops' morale. He has been
described as:

> ...one of those rare commanders in the Army Air Force who was perfect for
> the task of displaying the fledgling 8th Air Force Fighter Command to

visiting dignitaries. He was very tall, slim, personable, highly intelligent and strongly motivated with an air of openness rare in the officer corps. It helped that he, apparently, had the full confidence of the upper echelon. In addition, Peterson was legendary as a leader of the men in the group; his men, who would have followed him anywhere, loved him.[1]

American airmen played Santa for the English children. The 'Yanks' had things English kids didn't because everything was rationed. They gave them ice cream and peanut butter and the kids asked, 'Any Gum Chum?' As a result, Christmas spirit shone out from the station. From that time on English kids were GI favourites and vice versa. Christmas parties for orphans were held each of the next two years, with soldiers saving up rations for presents, weeks in advance. Seven children who had lost one or both parents during the war were 'adopted' by Duxford units. The $400 for each child paid for school and two meals a day for four years. Some units later added to this fund, for music lessons and other purposes. And whenever these or other kids came to the base, soldiers grabbed them up to entertain them. They knew they would have as much fun as the youngsters.

The New Year, however, brought the men back down to earth with a jolt. In January some of pilots took their Lightnings to Chelveston to practise escorting with the Fortresses of Colonel Curt LeMay's 305th Bomb Group but then the 78th Fighter Group had to begin exchanging their Lightnings for P-47C Thunderbolts. After losing their P-38s only fifteen of the original pilots remained and these included Colonel Peterson, his deputies, the three squadron commanders, operations officers and flight leaders. The situation was a massive blow especially since the air echelon considered the Thunderbolt a poor substitute for the Lightning, although the maintenance was appreciably easier than with the P-38. One officer commented that it was like changing from 'thoroughbreds to plough horses'.[2] Thunderbolt-trained replacement pilots arrived from the States while its flight and squadron leaders who remained after the P-38s were sent to Africa had to retrain locally on the P-47. VIII Fighter Command planned to have the first Thunderbolt Group (the 4th), operational by 1 March, the 56th Fighter Group two weeks later and the 78th before the end of the month.[3] As it turned out, the 78th would not fly their first combat mission until 13 April. Pilot training was one problem but the major headache was the Thunderbolt, which still had a number of irritating teething problems.

The Thunderbolt was the largest and heaviest single-engined single-seat fighter ever built, its bulk and shape soon earning it the nickname 'Seven ton milk bottle'. When started, the mighty air-cooled, turbo-supercharged eighteen-cylinder Double Wasp, which took up most of the frontal section, vibrated the whole aircraft like it was going to destroy itself. Early supercharged engines, besides being complex and prone to failure, increased overall weight dramatically. A turbo-supercharger housed in the rear fuselage of the P-47 needed sixty feet of air ducting alone. To taxi this brute took an act of congress. It climbed like a homesick angel and dived for the deck like a rock; and a heavy rock at that. 'It ought to dive', it was said. 'It certainly won't climb!' On take-off a P-47 pilot might wonder if he was ever going to leave the runway at all, the roll being so much longer than that of other fighters. A whole host of other sobriquets included 'the Repulsive Scatterbolt', 'Thunderjug' and the 'Thundermug'. Most pilots favoured 'Jug', which was short for Juggernaut, a Hindu idol once wheeled through towns on a gigantic chariot. Devotees were supposed to have thrown themselves under the wheels in the hope of going straight to paradise. The Jug's diving prowess become legendary but inexperienced pilots had to watch out if they got the nose down, as diving several thousand feet and pulling out was not for the faint hearted. They did not want to go to paradise but they wanted their enemies to go to Hell.[4]

In the spring of 1943 Goxhill's reluctant American inhabitants received a boost with the news that they were heading south, to Station 357 Duxford, nearer to civilisation with Cambridge the local watering hole. Apparently, Duxford was a permanent pre-war RAF station, which was rumoured to have all the attributes of a 'country-club' atmosphere. Any change from the mud and basic living accommodation at Goxhill just had to be good, especially as the Group had been destined for a 'temporary' base at Halesworth in rural Suffolk. On 18 March orders were given for all RAF units to leave Duxford and on 24 March a convoy of vehicles arrived at the main gate carrying the US advance party. The Group, including HQ staff, comprised 1,700 men. Almost to a man they were very pleased with the quality of the accommodation. Imposing red brick buildings, some of them camouflaged, standard for the RAF, mottled with ubiquitous tans, greens and greys, were everything they had been led to believe. The hangars, too, were conveniently located and the only signs of mud were those left by spring rain showers on the large grass airfield. Two-storey brick barracks that housed non-commissioned officers and enlisted men were still more comfortable than the corrugated metal Quonset huts occupied by their counterparts at other fighter and bomber group bases. The Control Tower was typical of those on RAF airfields, a squat two-storey building that resembled one box stacked on another. There was a wide expanse of windows in front and on the sides and an upper viewing deck, or veranda, with a handrail round it. Controllers directed local aircraft traffic from the upper storey, and dignitaries who later visited the base often reviewed take-off and landings from the viewing deck. Soon, wooden huts would spring up and more buildings and some blister hangars began to appear. Squadron dispersal could be cold and wet, the hours were long, and the men were going to be as comfortable as they could! Many of the brick barracks were fitted with modern casement windows and they were centrally heated. All of them had electric lights and some had tiled shower rooms. The buildings on the airfield and the living site opposite were beautifully landscaped with trees, flowers and shrubs. Lawns were kept close cropped and the flower beds were well tended, partially because of their beauty, but also to aid aerial camouflage, making the entire airfield appear to be another sleepy but picturesque English village. The roads were paved and there were paths to walk on. Many of the buildings were covered with ivy while hedges hid the barbed wire. There were garages and four large hangars to accommodate mobile and air equipment. The two-storeyed mess hall building had four dining bays and two steam tables kept food hot for serving. The kitchen was one of the few in the ETO with steam cooking apparatus. From the start china plates were issued but enlisted personnel had to bring their own utensils and cups. The dispensary housed dental clinics, doctors' examination rooms and offices, a first aid room, and treatment rooms. Thriplow House, a large mansion two miles away, was converted into sick quarters and a rest area for station personnel. Motor ambulances took serious injuries and hospital cases to general hospitals nearby.

Having moved in, the Group quickly settled down and began working up the three squadrons, the 82nd, 83rd and 84th Fighter Squadrons, to operational status. Fighter Command's ambitious plans were in tatters as 30 March came and went and still the Group was nowhere near operational.[5] During the week 1 to 6 April seventy-five P-47C Thunderbolt aircraft were finally flown in. Fighter support was becoming critical. Some of the bomb groups had been wiped out and one of them, the 306th over at Thurleigh in Bedfordshire, had even been withdrawn from the battle order for the time being because of a morale problem caused by heavy losses. On 4 April the *Luftwaffe* wreaked havoc among the formations of ninety-seven B-17s headed for the Renault works in the Billancourt district of Paris. North of the French capital I./JG 2 and the operational *Staffel* of JG 105, both led by Spanish Civil War veteran Major Walter 'Gulle' Oesau, *Kommodore* JG 2,[6] made several head-on passes before the Fortresses reached the Rouen area where fifty to seventy-five Bf 109G-4s and Fw 190A-4s of JG 26 began attacks on the formation. JG 26 made repeated frontal attacks, sometimes by four and six fighters at a time. Four B-17s were shot down. Two of them were claimed by *Hauptmann* Wilhelm-Ferdinand 'Wutz' Galland of II./JG 26, brother of *Generalmajor* Adolf Galland. *Oberleutnant* Karl Borris of 8th *Staffel* and Major Walter Oesau of JG 2 claimed the other two victories. At 1433 hours the Spitfire escort reappeared to provide withdrawal support but six of their number were shot down in a seven-minute battle without loss to the *Luftwaffe*. In all, American gunners claimed forty-seven German fighters destroyed. The actual losses were two JG 26 pilots killed and one wounded. Next day 104 B-17s and B-24s were despatched to Belgium to bomb the Ford and General Motors aircraft and engine repair works at Antwerp. The 306th Bomb Group bore the brunt of head-on attacks by Fw 190A-4 and A-5s of JG 26 and II./JG 1, which continued all the way to the target. Major Josef 'Pips' Priller, a veteran of the French campaign and the Battle of Britain, scored his eighty-fourth victory and *Hauptmann* 'Wutz' Galland got his thirty-eighth victory. To the bomber crews each mission seemed to follow the same pattern with the mismatched gunners trying to fend off incessant fighter attacks from all sides. It got so bad that one gunner remarked that 'It was like a feeding frenzy of sharks'.

During the afternoon of 8 April a four-plane flight in the 56th Fighter Group led by the CO, Colonel Hub Zemke and four pilots in the 78th Fighter Group flew from their base at Horsham St Faith just outside Norwich to the 4th Fighter Group base at Debden. They were to take part in a *Rodeo* set up by the RAF.[7] The combat-experienced Lieutenant Colonel Chesley G Peterson, 4th Fighter Group Executive and Operations Officer, led the combined force of twenty-four P-47Cs that took off from Debden and climbed to 30,000 feet and then swept over Dunkirk at full power. They penetrated twelve miles into enemy territory and returned after ninety minutes without seeing any enemy fighters.

A few days of unsettled weather kept fighters on the ground and it was not until five days later that the 78th flew its first mission from Duxford. Just before noon on 13 April Lieutenant Colonel Arman Peterson led twelve P-47s into the air from Duxford to join two squadrons from the 4th Fighter Group on a *Rodeo* to the Pas de Calais with the aim of luring the 'Abbeville Kids' into combat. The object of a fighter sweep was to draw up and engage *Luftwaffe* fighters but this seldom occurred. Nevertheless, they provided an excellent way to 'break-in' new and green combat pilots. If a dogfight did ensue then it was a mad scramble. The P-47s flew over the French countryside at approximately 30,000 feet and penetrated as far as the *Luftwaffe* base at St Omer but they sighted neither enemy planes nor flak. Lieutenant Colonel Joseph L. Dickman baled out north-east of Calais on the way home and he was picked up by Air-Sea Rescue. Back at Duxford he was awarded his Group's first Purple Heart. Less than four and a half-hours after he landed, Peterson took off again, leading twelve Thunderbolts to the St Omer area once more with more Jugs from the other two Groups but over France no enemy fighters showed. On the evening of 15 April the two new fighter groups met the *Luftwaffe* for the first time during another sweep of the Pas de Calais, when the 78th put up twenty-four Thunderbolts. When a warning was radioed to the P-47s cruising over Belgium the eager American pilots headed for Bruges but the 'enemy' aircraft to the west of them were Jugs. The 4th Fighter Group did get into a fight on this occasion when they tussled with fifteen Fw 190A-4s of II./JG 1 over Ostend, claiming three Fw 190s destroyed. Major Don Blakeslee was credited with the first enemy aircraft shot down by a P-47.[8]

With three missions flown in co-operation with other groups, the 78th Fighter Group struck out by itself for the first time on 17 April when Peterson led two squadrons of sixteen Thunderbolts each on two missions, Both proved uneventful. On 21 April the Group sighted their first flak over Rotterdam but no damage was reported. As the unit's experience increased, so did its striking power and on 29 April it sent out its first formation of three twelve-plane squadrons. There were tense crowds listening to the R/T speaker in the window of the 82nd pilots' room sweating out the first missions. On 3 May Duxford despatched forty-seven Jugs and then, just before five o'clock in the afternoon of the next day the Group settled into what was to become a familiar pattern of operations. 'Colonel Pete' led three squadrons of sixteen planes each and for the first time the Duxford Outfit escorted bombers when seventy-nine B-17s flew a five-hour round trip to the Ford and General Motors' aircraft and engine repair works at Antwerp. In all, twelve Allied fighter squadrons provided fighter escort up to 175 miles while more than thirty B-17s and B-24s that flew diversionary feints towards the French coast succeeded in drawing over 100 German fighters away from the main force. All of the Antwerp force returned without loss after getting their bombs away on the aircraft and engine repair works. The *Luftwaffe* failed to show and the Thunderbolts cruised uneventfully over Dunkirk, Calais and St Omer. During the next two weeks the Group flew two more uneventful missions.

On Monday 14 May the Group chalked up its first victories and suffered its first losses when they escorted the bombers attacking targets at Antwerp. Arman Peterson who had just been promoted to full colonel led three squadrons of sixteen P-47s each. When he saw the enemy in the Antwerp area he said, 'I am making a 90-degree turn and going down. They're Huns lads! Give them hell! Here we go! Tallyho! OK lads. Stay in pairs now.' They had encountered more than twenty Focke-Wulf 190s and Bf 109s at 20,000–24,000 feet and dogfights broke out all over the sky. Major James J Stone, CO of the 83rd Squadron, claimed a Fw 190, which was heading for the bombers.[9] Stone said later:

> Diving away is the ace in the hole for a fighter pilot. Once the Focke-Wulf could break combat and get away in a high-speed dive. But the P-47 can out-dive the Fw and since, like all American planes, it is extremely well built, will hold together while catching him in the dive. What's more, a one-second burst from those eight fifties will down any fighter made. Our '47s have been in combat since April 1943. Since that time we've made a believer out of many a German pilot. We worry them and that alone is a big part of our job.

Captain Robert E Adamina also claimed a Fw 190 while Captain Jack J Oberhansly Jr, a twenty-four-year-old pilot from Spanish Fork, Utah, got a probable. Captain Charles Pershing London, twenty-five-years-old, from Long Beach, California, flying *El Jeepo* also got a probable, ten miles north-west of Antwerp. Colonel Peterson, Lieutenant William H Madole, Lieutenant James E Stokes Jr, Lieutenant William H Julian, a Texan from Dallas, and Flight Officer Harold S Askelson all claimed a Fw 190 damaged. Adamina, Captain Elmer E McTaggart and Flight Officer Samuel R Martinek were shot down.[10] Martinek baled out over the North Sea ten miles north-west of Knocke, Belgium, and was captured. McTaggart worked his way southward across the Pyrenees into Spain, losing twenty-five pounds in weight in the process. Adamina, who ditched his Thunderbolt into the sea, is believed to be the first and perhaps only pilot to ditch a P-47 successfully. The success of the Thunderbolts in protecting bombers strengthened the belief of senior staff officers that the bomber escort theory was sound.

On 15 May 193 B-17s bombed targets at Emden, Heligoland and Wilhelmshaven and the 78th Fighter Group flew an unproductive sweep to Amsterdam from the forward base at Horsham St Faith near Norwich. 2nd

Lieutenant Jack S Sandmeier failed to return when his Thunderbolt suffered a mechanical failure and he was lost in the North Sea, the graveyard of so many Allied pilots. Next day VIIIth Bomber Command was stood down while maintenance was performed on the battle-scarred B-17s, blackened by two days' continuous combat. Bomber crews were glad of a respite, brief though it was. There was no respite for the three Thunderbolt Groups, who flew two sweeps of the Dutch coast and Northern Belgium on 16 May. A fighter sweep by 117 P-47 Thunderbolts of all three groups over Northern Belgium just after midday resulted in combat action. Thirty fighters of II./JG 1 led by the *Geschwaderkommodore*, Major Hans 'Fips' Philipp, had been sent off late from Woensdrecht. The twenty-six-year-old combat veteran had assumed command of JG 1 on 1 April having seen action on the northern sector of the Russian Front, where he was almost venerated by his men. In March 1943 the JG 54 *Experte* had become only the second German to score 200 victories and he now had 204 confirmed *Abschuss* but by the time contact was made in the Vlissingen area, the fifty P-47s of the 78th Fighter Group had the height advantage. They dived on the German fighters and shot down 'Black 1', a Fw 190A-5 flown by *Hauptmann* Dietrich Wickop, *Kommandeur* II./JG 1, who was killed, into the sea. The twenty-eight-year-old *Kommandeur* who was noted for his strong personality, had fought with I./JG 2 from December 1940 and in July 1942 had been posted to the General Staff of Fighters – Holland before joining JG 1. He had thirteen *Abschusse*[11] including three B-17s.

At 1312 hours Major Philipp claimed a P-47 as his 205th *Abschuss*, followed one minute later by another Jug claimed shot down by *Oberleutnant* Harry Koch, *Staffelkapitän* of 6th *Staffel*, as his sixteenth victory.[12] The P-47 pilots were prevented from scoring more victories by the intervention of Major 'Pips' Priller's *Geschwadergruppe* and the Third *Gruppe*. Though short in stature at only 5 feet 4 inches, Priller, who had been promoted to *Kommodore* of JG 26 on 11 January, has been described as a 'giant' in the fighter cockpit. His style of leadership was marked by a quirky sense of humour and he was reputed to be the only fighter leader who could make Hermann Göring laugh when things were going badly. The twenty-seven-year-old JG 26 *Kommandeur* opened fire on one of the Thunderbolts flown by Flight Officer Charles R Brown and Priller saw the P-47 crash into the Scheldt Estuary. Brown was wounded in the foot, leg and head and baled out over the sea. He was picked up by a German destroyer off Walcheren and taken into captivity. The second Thunderbolt claimed shot down was probably the P-47 flown by 1st Lieutenant Andrew M Barba, who despite damage to *Joker*, managed to limp home safely to Duxford. Colonel Arman Peterson claimed a Fw 190 destroyed and Major John D Irvin claimed another Focke-Wulf. *Unteroffizier* Friedrich Kaiser of the 6th *Staffel*, JG 26, was shot down north of Ghent and he died in his Fw 190A-4.[13] The Bf 109 of *Unteroffizier* Hermann Leicht of 4./JG 54 was also lost in this same combat. Leicht was killed attempting an emergency landing in a grain field when he hit an embankment and the gunsight crushed his skull when the fighter impacted. Eleven more missions were flown during the rest of May without making any claims. On 20 May 2nd Lieutenant Richard A Murray baled out in the North Sea forty miles off the English coast. He failed to get into his dinghy and he perished.

A 'parade of notables', including the King and Queen of England, Chief of the USAAF General Hap Arnold, Bob Hope and many others, toured Duxford during the spring and summer of 1943. On 26 May King George VI and Queen Elizabeth visited Duxford. Although censorship forbade mentioning units or places, Duxford began to grab headlines both in the UK and in the USA. Hugh Baillie of the United Press, William Randolph Hearst Jr, Gladwin Hill of the Associated Press and others visited the station and wrote about it. Major Stone and Captain London made broadcasts to America on George Hicks' 'Blue Network' feature and a part of one Army Hour programme originated at Duxford. In addition, the station's dance band, the Thunderbolts, appeared on transatlantic radio programmes. As well as playing for Station dances they also appeared in Cambridge and London and at other 8th Air Force bases. At Duxford on Tuesday 15 June Wing Commander Matthews handed over command to Colonel Peterson in front of the station flag pole. The RAF ensign was lowered and the 'Stars and Stripes' proudly raised, snapping in the breeze for all to see.

In June, the P-47D was introduced to service. It was an improvement over the earlier version though it differed little from previous models except for the standardisation of water injection into the intake manifold to produce more prolonged combat power of 2,300 hp at 27,000 feet.[14] The P-47D's top speed of 433 mph at 30,000 feet and its formidable dive performance made it ideal for top cover of the high-flying B-17 and B-24 bomber formations eventually reaching as far as Berlin from bases in eastern England. On Sunday 13 June 102 heavies attacked Bremen while a smaller force bombed Kiel. Both forces were unescorted, the short-ranged P-47s being used instead, during the morning and afternoon, on two diversionary sweeps off the Belgian coast. In the morning the 56th Fighter Group (which had claimed its first victory the day before) came upon 10./JG 26. Over Dixmuide Colonel Hubert 'Hub' Zemke, the CO, claimed two of the Fw 190s, and Lieutenant Robert Johnson got a third before the German pilots knew what hit them.[15] In the afternoon forty-four Thunderbolts of the 78th Fighter Group flew their sweep over Ypres and St Pol. II./JG 26 shot down two of the P-47s for no loss.

Eaker now decided to send his bombers on the first really deep penetration of Germany on 22 June, to the IG Farben Industrie Chemische Werke at Hüls on the edge of the Ruhr.[16] Most of the route would be flown without escort although the 4th and 78th Fighter Groups were tasked to provide withdrawal support. Three diversionary raids were therefore planned to pull off most of the fighters from the main attacking force, which would still have its work cut out coping with the numerous flak guns, which made Hüls the most heavily defended target in the *Reich* at this time. Throughout East Anglia on the morning of June twenty-two fighter pilots and bomber crews were awakened and ushered into briefing rooms to hear about the part they would play in the Hüls mission. The Hüls force assembled over England and flew a dogleg course over the North Sea to a point off the West Friesian Islands where it turned south-west for the target. An intended diversion by a formation of twenty-one B-17s was delayed because of ground mists and other problems and played no major part in the proceedings. Also, two other Bomb Groups, which were flying their maiden missions, were behind schedule and failed to make contact with the Spitfires and Thunderbolts, which were to escort them to the Ford and General Motors plant at Antwerp. This lapse placed the forty-one B-17s at the mercy of Fw 190s of JG 26, which had refuelled after an earlier raid by RAF medium bombers, and Bf 109s of II./JG 1. Head-on attacks succeeded in shooting down four B-17s while three hardly damaged survivors flew their own formation, hugging the waves all the way back to England. Major 'Pips' Priller, leading his *Geschwader*, led the first JG 26 attack from the front before the Fortresses reached the target. The Fw 190s made one pass through the bomber ranks in flights of six to eight and shot three B-17s of the 381st Bomb Group out of formation. Priller, *Feldwebel* Adolf 'Addi' Glunz, *Oberfeldwebel* Johann Edmann and *Unteroffizier* Niki Mortl claimed victories. *Hauptmann* 'Wutz' Galland and the IInd *Gruppe* reached the Fortresses as they were leaving the target and they attacked from the rear. They made repeated attacks and were out of ammunition when the P-47s of the 4th and 78th Fighter Groups finally arrived, over Walcheren Island, to provide withdrawal support. Captain Charles London in *El Jeepo* claimed his first victory (a Fw 190) and the Group claimed two other enemy fighters, both Groups claiming a total of eight fighters for no loss but JG 26 lost no further Fw 190s, although two pilots were wounded.

Two days later, on 24 June, the 78th Fighter Group was bounced by Bf 109s between Lille and Ostend, Belgium, and the P-47s claimed one victory. On 25 June 275 B-17s were despatched to bomb targets in north-western Germany. Cloud hampered bombing at Hamburg, the main objective, and split up the formations and scattered some of the Groups in the sky – an open invitation to fighter attack. Eighteen Fortresses failed to return and sixty-one B-17s were damaged. Four of the bomber losses were credited to I./JG 26 from Rheine. I./JG 1 from Schiphol; III./JG 1 at Leeuwarden; III./JG 26 from Nordholz; III./JG 11 at Oldenburg, and 12./JG 54, were other units involved in the air battle of 25 June. The American gunners claimed sixty-two enemy fighters shot down though the real score was twelve lost and six damaged. Cloud interfered on the 26 June, when in the early evening, 165 B-17s bombed Triqueville airfield and an aircraft factory at Villacoublay in the Paris area, while eighty-one Fortresses bombed Le Mans airfield. Five B-17s were shot down by Fw 190s, including one Fortress, which fell to the guns of Major 'Pips' Priller, *Kommodore* of JG 26, between Dieppe and Le Treport on the return. JG 26 also intercepted the forty-nine P-47s of the 56th Fighter Group near Forges, France, as the Jugs arrived to provide withdrawal escort for the bombers. Five P-47s were shot down without loss to JG 26, and a sixth came down in the sea off Scratby.

On 28 June 191 B-17s went to St Nazaire and a smaller force of fifty B-17s headed for Beaumont Le Roger airfield further inland. Units of JG 26 at Vendeville and Vitry took off to intercept but soon landed when the bomber formations passed out of range. The German controllers waited until the Spitfire escort had turned back and then sent III./JG 2 into the fray. *Hauptmann* Egon Mayer's *Gruppe* claimed nine Fortresses for the loss of one Fw 190 and its pilot.[17] Next day the 78th Fighter Group took off from Ford on the south coast of England to provide withdrawal support for the 1st Bomb Wing returning from a raid on Villacoublay airfield. The P-47s rendezvoused with the B-17s over Rouen where they found the bombers in heavy flak and under attack by Bf 109Gs. In the vicinity of Gournay Captain Charles London flying *El Jeepo* flew through the B-17 formation and the exploding flak to knock down two of the Messerschmitts for his second and third victories. Only JG 2 and JG 27 were sent off to intercept the B-17s (the 4th Wing attacked targets around Le Mans), the other *Staffeln* spending the day on routine patrols.[18] *Leutnant* Eberhard Burath, a Fw 190 pilot in I./JG 1, recalls:

> The days passed with defensive patrols, sea reconnaissance and repeated alarms without contact with the enemy. But on 1 July there was something new in the sky; in the vicinity of Hoek van Holland we met up for the first time with Thunderbolts. From a distance they looked disconcertingly similar to the Fw 190. What they were able to fire from their eight squirters I frequently came to feel later on.[19]

During the 1 July dog fight with I./JG 1 the Duxford Outfit claimed four Fw 190s destroyed and five damaged. At Duxford the ground crews, other base personnel and Hugh Baillie, President of United Press, listened intently to battles going on high over the continent and waited for their Thunderbolts and their CO to return but 'Pete' was missing. Baillie recalled:

> When Pete did not come back his gang sat around waiting. Plane after plane came in, but no Pete. The softball game fell apart. Minutes seem like hours when you wait like that. What was the last time anybody saw him? Well, he spotted a bunch of bandits below and said, 'There they are. Here we go.' Pete's boys swooped down at ninety degrees. They think they saw Pete vanish into a cloud. But nobody realised he was gone until they began counting noses at home. Finally after waiting as long as they could, Pete's crowd fuelled up their fighters. Nobody gave orders for that dash, the boys just did it spontaneously. They went back over the area where they had fought, looking for Pete – also looking for German or Germans, the more the better. The boys flew around hunting, looking, hunting, looking, until their gas ran low. Then without the whimsical, almost kidding voice of Pete's to tell them to scram, they had to turn back for home base. That night there was a vacancy at the head of the table in the mess – vacancy but no mourning. Pilots aren't like that. Of course there's always a chance that Colonel Peterson parachuted down, that he fell into the 'drink' and was

picked up by Air Sea Rescue craft, or that he descended behind the German lines and was made a prisoner of war. It's a cinch that all the fellows in Pete's fighter base will keep on hoping that someday Pete will show up again and his familiar drawl will be heard instructing his crowd to watch out for bandits. It's a long shot but perhaps he may even read this story some day. I hope so.[20]

But Colonel Arman 'Pete' Peterson, who had called his Thunderbolt *Flagari* so that people would not forget the old home town, was dead, shot down in combat with 1./JG 1 near Ouddorp on Goeree-Overflakkee, Holland. *Feldwebel* Martin Lacha claimed the victory. Peterson had managed to bale out but his parachute was torn and he was killed landing at Oostdijk in the village of Ouddorp on Goederde Island near Rotterdam. Morale sagged and the Duxford diarist noted that 'for some days few smiles were seen'. Lieutenant Colonel Melvin F McNickle took Peterson's place. The Duxford diarist went on. 'Comedian Bob Hope and Singer Frances Langford visited Duxford airfield two days later and even the Hollywood gagster admitted that he had trouble getting laughs out of his audience. The Fourth of July wasn't much of a holiday, either, with an uneventful mission being flown during the noon hour and followed by an outdoor supper on the athletic field.' The weather continued cloudy and VIIIth Bomber Command flew several more missions to France in the hope of spotting its targets.

On 14 July, Bastille Day, groups appropriately attacked targets in the vicinity of Paris. Amiens/Glisy aerodrome force came in for heavy fighter attack, by 3./JG 27, II./JG 2 and JG 26, who took on the Thunderbolts of the 4th, 56th and 78th Fighter Groups. The Thunderbolts had rendezvoused with the B-17s at 0730 hours and at about the same time Major 'Wutz' Galland's formation had caught sight of the escorts. Over the radio Galland gave the rallying cry, 'What are you waiting for' and three formations of German fighters attacked. They tore into the Fortresses for twenty minutes before the Thunderbolts were able to fend them off, inflicting heavy damage to thirty-four of the bombers while one B-17 fell to the guns of a Bf 109 of 3./JG 27. Two more badly damaged Forts limped home to crash-land in England. 3./JG 27 and II./JG 2 had been ordered to land as soon as the P-47s had intervened and they put down at Poix to refuel and rearm. After a record turnaround time of twelve minutes they were airborne again and they headed for the Villacoublay force but without apparent success. Meanwhile, Fw 190s of I./JG 2 and Bf 109s of II./JG 2 took on the 4th Fighter Group P-47s to the west of the Somme near Le Treport while Major 'Wutz' Galland and his pilots battled with the 78th Fighter Group near Hesdin. Major Harry J Dayhuff had led his Group P-47s to Hornoy, where the Jugs had made a rendezvous with B-17s bombing Amiens. Near Montreuil he led his P-47s into a large group of Fw 190s heading for the bombers at Le Touquet and more enemy aircraft joined the fight. 1st Lieutenant Donald 'Dixie' G Jackson was killed when he was struck by gunfire from the B-17s in the chase. Captain Jack C Price, twenty-five years old from Grand

Junction, Colorado, who was flying *Feather Merchant*, scored his first victory when he downed a Fw 190 twenty miles north of Abbeville. Captain Charles London flying *El Jeepo* claimed a Fw 190 and a Bf 109 damaged.

In the ensuing air battle Major 'Wutz' Galland claimed a P-47 over the north bank of the Somme Estuary north-west of Hesdin and he claimed another ten to fifteen kilometres west of Etaples. 2nd Lieutenant August V DeGenaro flew the first of these P-47s. He had the right side of his canopy and instrument panel shot out causing shell splinter wounds in his hands, ankles and right knee. At first he thought he was going to die but he quickly recovered and got 'damned mad', diving to 2,000 feet into a swarm of Focke-Wulfs where he shot one down from 100 yards, probably destroyed another and damaged a third.[21] Then he headed for the Channel, ducking into low clouds to evade three more Focke-Wulfs that followed him almost to the coast. All this time DeGenaro was flying his plane with no instruments and controlling it with his forearms only. The right aileron was gone and the right wing and tail were badly damaged. A crash-landing was out of the question because he had unhooked his safety belt in combat and he could not re-hook it. DeGenaro recalled:

> I headed out to sea again to bale out because I was afraid that if I baled out over land the plane would crash into one of the towns along the coast. I knew I was over England, because I saw the cliffs of Dover. I saw a fishing boat just off shore and decided to bale out near it.[22] The canopy of my plane had jammed and would not open, but since some of the glass had been shot away, I was able to punch and force my way through the canopy, bale out and open my chute. The fishing boat picked me up at once. If it had not, I would have drowned, because I was unable to undo my parachute harness and was getting weak from loss of blood.[23]

At Duxford on 30 July, as the Thunderbolt pilots went into briefing at about 0800 hours they knew it was going to be an unusual mission. The ground crews realised that recently arrived drop tanks denoted a long haul[24] and the big briefing map confirmed it. It was to be withdrawal support for 186 B-17s in the 1st and 4th Wings going to Kassel, a round trip of 600 miles, when Bomber Command brought down the curtain on 'Blitz Week' with take-off at 0854 hours. At Duxford Lieutenant Colonel McNickle led the show. The weather was fine and the new tanks meant that the P-47s could escort the heavies almost to the target and back again. Without the P-47s, losses would have been on an alarming scale because the Fortress formations were hit by a ferocious onslaught of enemy fighters. As the 78th Fighter Group approached the enemy coast, the new belly tanks were dropped fifteen miles offshore of the Hook of Holland. The Group then climbed to penetration altitude as they flew on over Rotterdam and Nijmegen and entered Germany near Kleve before heading for the Rendezvous Point at Haltern. Nearing the rendezvous, the bombers were sighted at eleven o'clock twenty miles north and the Jugs turned left at 28,000 feet, 4,000 feet above their charges, and began to take up station. Shortly after the turn, near Winterswijk, Colonel McNickle's oxygen system failed. He lost consciousness and collided with his wingman, 1st Lieutenant James Byers, who baled out but was killed. When McNickle regained consciousness, he was still strapped in his cockpit in the wreckage of his inverted crashed P-47 with the Dutch Underground trying to extricate him. McNickle had two broken shoulders and other serious wounds.[25]

The intervention by just over 100 P-47s prevented further bomber losses and they claimed twenty-four enemy fighters shot down. The Group claimed seven Bf 109s and nine Fw 190s. Captain Charles London was Red Flight leader. He climbed to 23,000 feet and 180 mph above the English Channel, jettisoning his drop tank fifteen miles off the Dutch Coast and continued across Holland at 27,000 feet. The 83rd sighted the bomber force just beyond Haltern and just as it was about to be attacked by a large mixed group of Bf 109s and Fw 190s. At 1020 hours three Fw 190s were positioning themselves for a frontal attack on the bombers when London's flight appeared on the scene. The Fw 190s took no evasive action, as they did not expect to find American fighters penetrating so far into the occupied territories. As London closed on his first target, a Bf 109 pulled up alongside *El Jeepo* but did nothing, presumably because the German pilot assumed that the P-47 was in fact a Fw 190. Despite his unwanted companion, London continued his firing run on the Fw 190, which began to smoke, and one wheel came down. London looked out to find that the escorting Bf 109 had vanished and he came around to explode the crippled Bf 109 with a short burst. London climbed above the bomber formation so he could dive on the enemy fighters and convert the diving speed back to altitude in a climb. London spotted a Bf 109 below him coming out of a dive and he tore after him. Once on the Bf 109's tail, London fired from seventy-five yards and the fighter exploded into pieces directly in front of him for his second victory of the mission.[26] These two victories made him the first American 'ace' in the European Theatre of War. London said later. 'I still don't know where they came from. The thing that saved us was our system of sending down one flight after the other – for assurance. [James M.] Cooper, my roommate, could hear us yelling that there were a lot of them and he got his flight down fast. The Germans scattered like a school of minnows when you toss a rock into the water.'

Twenty-six-year-old Major Eugene P. Roberts, from Washington State, had been flying *Spokane Chief* on 1 July when he had claimed a Fw 190 probable. He scored the first triple victory in the ETO.[27] Roberts recalled:

When we sighted the bombers off to our left we made a 90° turn and picked them up near Winterswijk. One straggling bomber was observed flying below the main formation in a dive, trailing black smoke and being attacked by about five E/A [enemy aircraft]. I peeled my flight down and to the rear of the straggler. This would be about 1,000 feet below the main formation at about 21,000 feet. All E/A sighted us and took evasive action to the extent that I was unable to close, although I did fire a burst with improper deflection. The E/A was in a diving attack from the rear on this straggler. I initiated my attack from the port side rear of the fighters, swinging in behind them to the right and broke sharply downward to the rear. I followed them in the climb, attempting to get a deflection shot. When he broke downward I found I was directly beneath the bombers and saw a number of ball turret gunners firing at my flight. I broke down and to the rear and pulled up to starboard side of the bombers about 1,000 yards out and at about their level.

Looking up, I observed six E/A flying parallel to the bombers and about 1,000 feet directly above me. They failed to see us and did not take any action, so after they passed I made a climbing turn to the left to come up to their level and behind them. At this point I missed my second element and found myself alone with my wingman. In our pull up we missed the original six E/A sighted but sighted a single E/A ahead on the same level at about 1,500 yards. I dived slightly below, opened full throttle and closed to about 400 yards. I pulled up directly behind the E/A and opened fire. Several strikes were observed on E/A, his wheels dropped and he spun down trailing a large volume of dark smoke and flame.

I continued parallel to the bombers and sighted two more E/A about 2,000 yards ahead. I used the same tactics, closing to 400 yards astern, pulled up and opened fire on port aircraft. I observed strike reports and E/A billowed smoke and flame, rolled over and went down. I was closing so fast that I had to pull up to avoid hitting him. I observed my wingman, Flight Officer Koontz, firing at the second aircraft but did not see the results. Both of these aircraft were Fw 190s. After this second engagement, we were about two miles ahead of the bombers still well out to their starboard side. About this time I observed a Me 109 peeled to starboard to attack the bombers head-on and I followed, closing to 500 yards before opening fire. Two bursts were behind but the third burst caught him and he spun down, trailing smoke and flame, 1,500 yards ahead of the bombers.[28]

For fighting off superior numbers of enemy fighters in getting his triple, Major Eugene P Roberts won the Group's second Distinguished Service Cross within a month.

About 100 enemy aircraft were attacking the B-17s from the front and the rear. The rear attackers were firing their new rockets into the bombers as the 84th Squadron came diving in behind and up sun. Deputy Group CO Lieutenant Colonel James Stone eased in behind a Bf 109 and exploded him, as his wingman, Lieutenant Julius P Maxwell flying *War Eagle*, the Auburn University team name, flew through the debris. Captain Jack Price in *Feather Merchant* scored his second and third victories when he destroyed two Fw 190s near Winterswijk. His Cajun wingman, Lieutenant John R Bertrand, downed a Focke-Wulf. Major John D. Irvin, who had named his P-47 *Unmentionable*, claimed two Bf 109s in formation abreast far behind the bombers. Near Didam Flight Officer Peter E Pompetti, twenty-three years old from Philadelphia, flying *Darkie*, made another attack on three Bf 109s. The right one dived away and the leader took hits and just floated along on his back as Pompetti turned to the left Bf 109, pulling in behind at fifty yards and firing with the few guns he had still working. Smoke poured out of the Messerschmitt and pieces fell off. The pilot was probably dead as Pompetti pulled up to avoid colliding and he lost sight of the disabled aircraft. Pompetti was a pugnacious, pimply, red-faced, short and slightly round pilot. He later re-named his Jug, *Axe The Axis*. *Unmentionable* was later to become *Geronimo*.

Major Harry Dayhuff found a Bf 109 making side attacks on the bombers and destroyed the fighter. 1st Lieutenant Arthur B. Richie dived after a Fw 190 and fired all his ammunition into him, leaving the enemy aircraft belching smoke in a dive. 1st Lieutenant William H Madole caused an enemy aircraft to dive away with his first attack. Climbing back up in a vertical bank, he saw a Fw 190 on a P-47's tail. Rolling, he raked the Fw 190 with hits, nose to tail. Pulling up and going into his second attack on the enemy aircraft Madole witnessed the pilot take to his parachute. Running low on fuel by this time, the Group was forced to break off escort and head for home from near Tiel, Netherlands. Quince L Brown, a twenty-six-year-old slim, freckle-faced, sandy-haired, not-to-be-denied 'Okie' from Hydrock, Oklahoma, was chased to the deck by two Fw 190s. A known red hot, 'hot rod' in his beloved Jug he had named *Okie*, Brown soon out-distanced his pursuers. Following the rail lines near Leiden he saw a freight train and he shot it, probably becoming the first American pilot to strafe a ground target in the ETO in the process. Crossing the coast Brown took *Okie* down so low to the sea to avoid the shore batteries that he hit the water with two of his prop blades, bending their tips, but he still made it home. 1st Lieutenant Paul Lehman was on his way to the Channel when flak struck his engine but it held together long enough for him to get out over the sea and bale out. A Walrus of ASR arrived about an hour and a half later and flew Lehman back to Duxford. 1st Lieutenant Bill Julian was forced to belly-land his damaged P-47 at West Wickham (successfully) and 2nd Lieutenant Warren E Graff was shot down in the air battle.[29] Altogether, twelve Fortresses were lost, including some that were so badly damaged that they never flew again. Six fighters were also lost. When intelligence officers at Duxford pieced together the results of the near three-hour mission, the first Group penetration of Germany was one for the record books.

Next day, 31 July, VIIIth Bomber Command announced a three-day stand down from combat after a week of exhausting raids, which had cost about 100 aircraft and ninety combat crews. This reduced its combat strength to under 200 heavies ready for combat. Crews had flown themselves almost to a standstill and were glad of the rest. At Duxford the statistics for July reflected the increased pace of combat with nineteen missions, twenty-one victories, five pilots missing in action, one wounded in action, two crash-landings and two air-sea rescues.

On 4 August Lieutenant Colonel James J Stone took Colonel McNickle's place as commander. He flew his first Group lead as CO eight days later when 243 heavy bombers were despatched largely unescorted to targets in the Ruhr. Once again the weather was to dog the mission and cause many groups to seek targets of opportunity. The Bomber Groups became strung out and the *Luftwaffe* seized the opportunity to strike at the widely dispersed formations and inflict heavy losses. The Duxford Outfit, using seventy-five-gallon belly tanks, provided withdrawal support for the heavies and rendezvoused with them at Heinsberg in Germany to escort them to the Belgian coast at Flushing–Antwerp where a few enemy fighters showed but the P-47s beat them off. Over 300 bombers were sent to attack targets in Holland and France on 15 August, part of the *Starkey* deception plan. This was created to make the Germans believe that an invasion of the French coast was imminent to relieve some of the pressure on Russia and halt troop movements to Italy. Strikes against enemy airfields in France and the Low Countries continued on 16 August. Early that evening crews knew something special would be in the offing for the anniversary mission next day, but what? The first ever American air raid on Berlin? An attack on Hitler's mountain retreat at Berchetsgaden? In fact Eaker and his planners had conceived a most ambitious and daring plan, to attack, simultaneously, the ball bearing factories at Schweinfurt and aircraft plants at Regensburg. The selection of Regensburg and Schweinfurt as the targets for the anniversary mission of VIIIth Bomber Command came at a time when the *Luftwaffe*'s operational fighter strength on the Western Front was showing a significant increase. Regensburg was the second largest aircraft plant of its kind in Europe – the largest was at Wiener Neustadt near Vienna – and it was estimated that the total destruction of the plant would entail a nine-month delay in production. Immediate results would be felt in operational strength, it was hoped, between one and a half to two months.[30]

The 1st Wing would attack Schweinfurt while the 4th Wing went to Regensburg. To minimise attacks from enemy fighters the 4th Wing B-17s would fly on to North Africa after the target. The 1st Wing, meanwhile, would fly a parallel course to Schweinfurt to confuse further the enemy defences and return to England after the raid. Four P-47 groups were scheduled to escort the Regensburg force but only the two squadrons in the 353rd Fighter Group (later relieved by the 56th Fighter Group) rendezvoused with the bombers as scheduled. But their task was impossible. The overburdened Thunderbolts could not possibly hope to protect all seven groups in the 4th Wing in a long, straggling formation that stretched for fifteen miles. Fortresses in the rear of the formation were left without protection at all. The 4th Wing encountered so many fighters en route because the 1st Wing had been delayed by thick inland mists for three-and-a-half hours after the 4th Wing had taken off and this had effectively prevented a two-pronged assault, which might have split the opposing fighter force. The delay gave the *Luftwaffe* time to refuel and re-arm after dealing with the Regensburg force and deal now with the Schweinfurt force. VIIIth Bomber Command lost thirty-six Fortresses on the

Schweinfurt raid with a further twenty-four being lost on the Regensburg strike, making sixty lost in combat. For their part the 78th Fighter Group shot down two twin-engined fighters after breaking escort south-east of Aachen. Major Gene Roberts scored his fourth victory when he downed a Bf 110 and Flight Officer Pete Pompetti claimed a Messerschmitt 210 for his second victory. Lieutenant (later Captain) Glenn H Koontz collided with Roberts' Bf 110 and lost eighteen inches of his left wing but still managed to make it home.

The heavies were stood down on 18 August but on the 19th the 1st Bomb Wing bombed the airfields at Gilze-Rijen and Flushing and the 4th Bomb Wing bombed the airfield at Woensdrecht. P-47s and Spitfires shot down three of JG 26's fighters while one Fw 190A-4 crashed out of fuel and two Bf 109Gs were shot down by return fire from B-17s attacking Gilze-Rijen and Flushing. One of the Bf 109Gs of JG 26 is thought to have been hit and its pilot wounded by either a 78th or 56th Fighter Group P-47. The Schweinfurt losses were still having a mighty effect on the B-17 groups and for three days no Fortress missions were flown. Then on 24 August 110 B-17s of the 1st Bomb Wing were sent to Villacoublay airfield near Paris, with a dozen more B-17s flying a diversion. The 4th Bomb Wing put up forty-two B-17s for a raid on other airfields. Some 166 P-47s flew escort, the 78th Fighter Group accompanying the Fortresses attacking Villacoublay. Only one bomber was lost on the day's missions and the Jugs claimed six fighters for no loss to themselves. Two of the enemy fighters were shot down during the early evening by Major Gene Roberts who downed a Fw 190 and a Bf 109 between Rouen and Evreux to make him the second 78th Fighter Group ace. The Fortresses were out again on 27 August, when 224 B-17s were sent out on the first of the raids against V-weapon sites, when 187 B-17s got their bombs away on Watten. The heavies were escorted by 173 Thunderbolts; one, of which, was lost while they claimed eight enemy fighters shot down. Four B-17s were lost.

Shallow penetration raids dispatched to bomb airfields in north-western France remained the order of the day throughout September, as VIIIth Bomber Command was not yet strong enough to mount raids deep into the *Reich*. The 78th Fighter Group flew fighter sweeps and escorts for the heavies. On 2 September five forces totalling 319 B-17s were despatched but cloud conditions prevented most of the Fortresses from dropping their bombs. Next morning the Thunderbolts were aloft again when four P-47 groups escorted 233 B-17s who pounded Romilly-sur-Seine and other targets in France. Then on 6 September General Eaker switched his attention to the aircraft component factories at Stuttgart but cloud interfered with assembly over England and it also prevented accurate bombing at the target. Next day enemy airfields in France and the Low Countries were attacked. On 13 September VIIIth Bomber Command was officially divided into three bombardment divisions. Next day over 100 B-17s and B-24s were despatched to attack airfields at Woensdrecht and Lille-Nord but they were forced to abort because of bad weather. On 15 September almost 140 bombers attacked the Renault aero engine works and a ball bearing plant at Paris, while a comparable force attacked airfields at Chartres and Romilly-sur-Seine. On 16 September more than 130 heavies returned to the French Atlantic coast in what was then the longest trip planned by VIIIth Bomber Command, bombing port installations at Nantes and an aircraft plant at Bordeaux at the mouth of the Gironde, a 1,600-mile round trip lasting eleven hours. Thirteen bombers were shot down and bombing results were poor.[31]

A force of 305 bombers went to Emden on 27 September. Forty-five P-47s, each carrying 108-gallon wing tanks for the first time, led by Lieutenant Colonel Harry Dayhuff flew to Hethel airfield in Norfolk as one of six Fighter Groups tasked to provide withdrawal support for the returning bombers. The treated pressed-paper tanks gave 325 miles' range but they were known to cause some problems. The grass field at Duxford for instance was uneven and it was not unusual to punch a hole in the tank on take-off. And sometimes they were difficult to drop in combat, because they occasionally froze at high altitude.[32] The P-47s crossed into Holland and headed for the bomber rendezvous point ten miles west of Emden just in time to take on about thirty enemy fighters firing rockets and making attacks on the bombers at around 25,000 feet, several thousand feet below the Thunderbolts. Pete Pompetti claimed a Bf 109 and a Bf 110 to take his score to four. Quince Brown in *Okie* followed his leader, Major Gene Roberts, who could not get into a firing position on a Bf 109. Brown, however, closed to dead astern on the Messerschmitt and opened fire and it went down spouting flame and black and white smoke for his first victory. Captain Jack Oberhansly in *Iron Ass* scored a Bf 109 probable and destroyed another for definite. The P-47s finally broke off low on fuel forty miles from the Dutch coast having claimed nine enemy fighters shot down and no losses.[33] Flak and fighters of late had deprived the Group of several experienced pilots but replacements were filtering though to Duxford that September.

1   *A Mississippi Fighter Pilot In WWII* by Ernest E Russell (Trafford Publishing (UK) Ltd 2008).

2   *The Mighty Eighth* by Roger A Freeman (MacDonald 1970).

3   Most pilots of the 4th Fighter Group at Debden had some combat experience and a few had extensive experience, having been formed from the RAF Eagle Squadrons on 12 September 1942 when 71, 121 and 133 Squadrons were transferred to the USAAF. The 4th Fighter Group retained its nimble Spitfires until March 1943 when it converted to the P-47C. Forty-year-old Colonel E.W. Edward Anderson, the CO, was given the task of bringing the 4th Fighter Group into line with USAAF procedures but his task proved difficult. His pilots were reluctant to change the lessons learned in the RAF and most pilots were unhappy about converting from the Spitfire to the Thunderbolt. On 8 March three squadrons of RAF Spitfires

escorted the bombers and for the first time the 4th Fighter Group's P-47C Thunderbolts flew interdiction strikes against airfields ahead of the bombers.

4   *See P-47 Thunderbolt vs Messerschmitt Bf 109* by Martin W Bowman (Osprey Publishing 2008).

5   The 56th Fighter Group, which had begun receiving P-47s in June 1942, was, like the 78th Fighter Group, placed on operational status on 13 April 1943.

6   Oesau, who claimed ten aircraft in the Spanish Civil War, was the third German pilot to reach 100 victories, on 16 October 1941. After a short spell on the Eastern Front he returned to the West to lead JG 2, then JG 1. Physically and mentally exhausted, he was shot down and killed in combat with P-51 Mustangs and P-38 Lightnings on 11.5.44. He had 125 victories.

7   Code name for several squadrons carrying out a high-speed sweep over the enemy-occupied territory to entice enemy fighters to combat.

8   In fact the German unit suffered no loss, although *Oberfeldwebel* Hutter of 5./JG 1 force-landed with battle damage at Woensdrecht. Lieutenant Colonel Chesley Peterson had to bale out over the Channel due to engine failure. ASR picked him up, wet but well. Two 4th Fighter Group P-47s and their pilots fell victim to *Oberfeldwebel* Ernst Heesen of 5./JG 1, his twenty-sixth/twenty-seventh victories. On 17 April another Rodeo aimed at diverting enemy fighters away from a B-17 mission was unsuccessful and for the 56th Fighter Group uneventful when a sweep along the Dutch coast a week later was similarly devoid of any contact with the enemy. Hub Zemke tried out a new formation staggering the squadrons and flights so that the group formation was like a giant V when viewed in plan. There was no edict on how formations should be flown and the P-47 groups experimented to find the most desirable for control and deployment against the elusive enemy. In France meanwhile it was announced in *Luftwaffe* circles that JG 26 was to transfer to the Russian Front where it would trade places with the Green Hearts *Geschwader*, JG 54. However, the transfer was only partially complete when in the spring of 1943 the growing strength of VIIIth Bomber Command increased pressure on the *Jagdgeschwaders* in the west and the transfer of the remaining *Gruppen* and *Staffeln* was first postponed and then cancelled by *Generalmajor* Adolf Galland.

9   Possibly *Oberfeldwebel* Siegfried Beyer of JG 26 who was WIA (wounded in action). *The JG 26 War Diary Vol.2* by Donald Caldwell (Grub Street, London, 1998).

10   *Oberleutnant* (later *Hauptmann*) Rudolf 'Rudi' Leuschel, *Staffelkapitän* of
      10./JG 26, claimed a P-47 six kilometres North of Ath. *The JG 26 War
      Diary Vol.2.*

11   *Luftwaffe* pilots were on a points system, which converted to various
      awards. An *Abschuss* or shoot down of a *Viermot*, or 4-*mot* (four-engined
      bomber) earned three points, while a *Herausschuss*, or separation, was
      worth two. A pilot, who finished off an already shot-up four-engine bomber
      was awarded one point for *endgültige Vernichtung*, or final destruction.
      Decorations were awarded after points' totals were reached. For instance,
      one point earned the recipient the Iron Cross 2nd Class and three, the Iron
      Cross 1st Class. Four points were needed for the *RitterKreuz* (RK or
      Knight's Cross) although this varied in practice.

12   *Hauptmann* Harry Koch was KIA during combat with B-17s in the region
      of Badbergen on 22 December 1943 when he collided with his wingman
      who baled out to safety. Koch had twenty-eight victories. Also On 16 May
      Feldwebel Martin Lacha of JG 1 claimed a 'probable'. Hans Philipp was
      KIA on 8 October 1943 during air combat with B-17s and escorting
      fighters over Nordhorn, Germany, after having claimed a B-17 for his 206th
      and final victory. *Defending the Reich; The History of Jagdgeschwader 1
      'Oesau'* by Eric Mombeek.

13   *The JG 26 War Diary Vol.2.*

14   Other changes included additional armour protection for the pilot, further
      fuel and oxygen system changes and the exhaust ducting was again
      modified for improved reliability and performance. Paddle-bladed
      airscrews of increased diameter were fitted to absorb the full war
      emergency power of the R-2800-59 engine. The P-47D-15 was the first
      Thunderbolt built with underwing pylons and fuel system plumbing within
      the wings to use underwing droppable fuel tanks. The internal fuel capacity
      was also increased to 375 gallons and the bomb load increased to 2,500 lb.
      The canopy was completely jettisonable. The 'blown' Perspex canopy,
      known as the Malcolm Hood, as used on RAF Mustangs, was also adapted
      for the Thunderbolt and the 'Bubble' canopy P-47Ds began reaching the
      squadrons in England in early June 1944 though 8th Fighter Command
      could never get enough of them. Altogether, 12,602 examples of the P-47D
      were built – surely the largest production quantity of one sub-type of any
      fighter ever produced.

15   Only one Fw 190 was lost. *Obergefreiter* Heinrich Zenker was killed in the
      P-47 attack and *Oberfeldwebel* Karl-Heinz Bocher was wounded.

16   The chemical and synthetic rubber plant near Recklinghausen, which had
      been almost untouched by war since 1942 when it was last bombed by the

RAF, was essential to the German war effort since their rubber supply in the Far East had been cut off by the Allied blockade. Hüls accounted for approximately twenty-nine per cent of Germany's synthetic rubber and eighteen per cent of its total rubber supply. Every month it was turning out 3,900 tons of synthetic rubber, much of it going to the Buna tyre factory nearby.

17 In an attempt to bring more firepower to bear on the B-24 and B-17 formations, both the Fw 190A and Bf 109G had their armament increased substantially. The Bf 109G-6/R6 now carried three MG 151 cannon in addition to its two MG 151 13-mm machine-guns and the Fw 190 now carried two Rheinmetall MG FF-M-20 cannon in addition to its two MG 151s. During July also, the Fw 190A-6, equipped with two MG 151 20-mm cannon in place of the MG-FF-M, became operational in the *Jagdgruppen*.

18 *The JG 26 War Diary Vol.2* and *Eagles of Duxford: The 78th Fighter Group in World War II* by Garry L Fry (Phalanx Publishing 1991).

19 *Battles with the Luftwaffe* by Theo Boiten and Martin W Bowman (Jane's 2001).

20 *WHEN 'PETE' DIDN'T COME BACK* by Hugh Baillie.

21 *Unteroffizier* Harry Kubon of the 5th *Staffel* JG 26 was WIA. He baled out of his Fw 190A-4 into the Somme Estuary and was rescued.

22 *The Little Old Lady*.

23 Later in hospital DeGenaro was awarded the Distinguished Service Cross, the second highest American award for valour, and he was sent home to recover from his wounds. Major 'Wutz' Galland's second P-47 that he claimed also made it back to England where the pilot baled out into the Channel and was also rescued. Major Wilhelm-Ferdinand 'Wutz' Galland, *Kommandeur* II./JG 26, was killed in a surprise attack by 56th Fighter Group Thunderbolts west of Maastricht on 17 August 1943. At the time of his death, 'Wutz' had flown 186 combat sorties, during which he had accumulated fifty-five victories, including eight American *Viermots* and thirty-seven Spitfires. Two months prior to his death, Major Galland had been awarded the *Ritterkreuz*.

24 Early P-47 missions without belly tanks averaged 1 hour and 45 minutes to the maximum of 2 hours and 5 minutes. With the 75-gallon pressurised tanks, missions were from 2 hours 30 minutes to 2 hours and 50 minutes. The 165-gallon tanks gave another 45–50 minutes' range and with two 108-gallon treated pressed-paper tanks the P-47 Groups flew shows up to 5 hours and 30 minutes but the metal tanks were in short supply.

25   After radioing England for directions the resistance turned him over to the Germans for medical treatment and he was made PoW near Ravestein in Holland. Byers' P-47 was probably claimed by *Hauptmann* Hermichen of I./JG 26, who destroyed a P-47 at 1015 hours in the Dordrecht area. At least twenty-four *Luftwaffe* fighters were lost over Holland. JG 1 lost eight Fw 190A-4s and A-5s destroyed with another three severely damaged when their pilots crash-landed their Bf 109G-6s after being damaged in air combat. JG 2 lost seven destroyed; JG 11 lost one Bf 109G-6 destroyed with another five G-1s and G-6s between fifteen and eighty per cent damaged. JG 26 had four write-offs and JG 54 lost another four. In all eight Bf 109s and sixteen Fw 190s were destroyed. Ten *Jagdflieger* were killed and two were MIA. Another nine fighter pilots were injured. Spitfires escorting the B-26s in the early morning attack on Woensdrecht airfield shot down two of these fighters, both of JG 26. The remaining twenty-two *Luftwaffe* fighters lost were all victims of the fierce dogfights with P-47s and in attacks with the B-17s.

26   See *Victory Roll! The American Fighter Pilots and Aircraft in WWII* by Dr William Wolf (Schiffer 2001). No JG 26 fighters were lost so the victories probably were at the expense of JG 1 and JG 11.

27   Flying P-47C-2-RE 41-6240 WZ-E. The rest of his victories were all scored while flying P-47C-5-RE 41-6330 WZ-Z *Spokane Chief*.

28   As Roberts was dispatching his target's wingman, Flight Officer Glenn Koontz set fire to another, which went into a death dive.

29   Graff evaded capture and he returned in September. (*Hauptmann* Rolf Hermichen of I./JG 26 claimed a P-47 destroyed at 1015 hours in the Dordrecht area.) Major William H Julian finished the war with five victories. See *Stars & Bars: A Tribute to the American Fighter Ace 1920–1973* by Frank Olynyk (Grub Street 1995).

30   Over 300 fighters drawn from JG 1, JG 2, JG 3, JG 11, JGr 25, JG 26, 11./JG 27, 11./JG 51, III./JG 54, JG 300 and ZG 26 were ranged against the B-17 formations.

31   At the end of September 1943, apart from the single-engined Bf 109 and Fw 190 day fighters, B-17 and B-24 crews now faced over 150 Bf 110Gs and Me 410A-1/B-1s in five *Zerstörergruppen*.

32   One of the tricks used to jettison a recalcitrant tank was to have a wingman slip his wingtip between the tank and the wing and knock it off the pylon. Late in 1943 P-47 Groups were using up to 480 tanks a month and tried to keep a six to eight mission back stock on hand. Fighter units were assigned their escort relay points by the size of the tanks they carried on the show, which dictated their range.

33   Lieutenant Colonel Harry Dayhuff took command of the 4th Fighter Group
      on 7 December 1944 and remained in command of the Eagles until 21
      February 1945.

CHAPTER SEVEN

Rite of Passage

*I had never been where I could be shot at – at least to my knowledge, and
I was about to do just that; fly deliberately into harm's way, where
someone sought to kill me. I had no idea what was going to happen and
did not have the questions to pose. Not surprisingly, none of the old hands
felt compelled to enlighten us. They knew that any flight into enemy
territory had the potential for turning deadly, but seldom did. And that was
the secret.*

Ernest 'Ernie' E Russell[1]

Over the Atlantic at no more than 10,000 feet an Air Transport Command Douglas C-54 Skymaster, the Air Corps' biggest transport aircraft, headed for Britain, its twenty rows of eighty seats filled with its precious cargo of seventy-four highly trained, combat-ready fighter pilots. None of them had a clue as to which theatre they were going too and surprisingly not much was said about it. Their wooden footlockers had been shipped on ahead and only the senior officer in charge of the group, who carried their sealed orders, had the answer to that question. After a leave of seven days in July the contingent of replacements had departed from Tallahassee rail station in a long drab green and plain vanilla troop train. One by one, they climbed up the high steel steps, onto their car to find a seat. Ernest 'Ernie' Russell, a Mississippian from Carpenter, had never been out of Mississippi and Louisiana until he joined the service. He could not believe what was before his eyes. 'A posh 1890s passenger car: red velour, or plush, seats; gas, or kerosene, chandeliers hanging from the ceilings above the aisles; spittoons; Victorian décor and on and on. The cars on this train must have been retired during WWI, and brought out of storage for WWII to relieve the wartime transportation shortage.' Like all troop trains it had compartmentalised coach cars, each one of them crammed with multiple stacks of bunks. Russell soon found an open bunk in a stack. He threw his duffel bag on the bunk and settled down for what he

141

suspected was going to be a long, jerky, bumpy, hot and dusty trip. He was not disappointed. 'There was no air conditioning and with the summer heat, the windows had to be open or we would have suffocated. As a result cinders from the steam engine were continually flying back into our car, often in our eyes. It was either shut the windows and burn up or live with the cinders. So we just wiped the cinders out of our eyes.' The train rumbled on though Atlanta before heading north. Russell had to think European Theatre of Operations 'but we could be going anywhere from here'.[2]

Georgia came and went: then South Carolina, then North Carolina, and then Virginia and, the next day, they pulled into the train station in Washington DC. Their stop in the capital was short, only long enough to get off and stretch their legs. Russell was impressed at the large number of civilians in the crowds, many of whom were draft age.

Even so, there were a lot of uniforms around, too but, what really caught my eye were the attractive girls. There were loads of them, but they weren't for us – later, maybe. Even so I managed to meet a very pretty girl and got her address – for future reference. After a short respite we were herded back onto the train and on our way north once more. We passed Camp Kilmer, New Jersey, which was a known Port of Embarkation, during the night unbeknownst to us, and we awakened next morning to a rolling, lurching train with a bright summer sunlight pouring through the small window, which served for ventilation. The scenery had changed from pines and hardwoods to spruce and fir, and the station signs told me that we had slept through New England. I saw a small station on which the word 'MAINE' jumped out at me – we were in Maine! Wherever we were headed, we weren't going by boat, for sure.

We were 'served' our breakfast rations and it wasn't long before the train began to shake and clatter and the brakes began to squeal. We were slowing for a stop. Looking out the window I saw a large train station come into view. A sign read 'BANGOR, MAINE'. An enlisted man, the conductor, passing in the aisle called out, 'Grab your bags, you're getting off here!' My first thought was where do you go from Bangor, Maine? My question was answered after we had taken another ride on the hard seats in the back of one of those ubiquitous camouflaged '6-bys'; after a while the truck pulled into a petite station. Waiting there in the cool morning air was a miniature steam engine resting on narrow gauge rails; the cars looked like versions of the 'Toonerville Trolley', smaller versions of the New Orleans streetcars that I knew so well. The several carriages were open and airy, and the shiny, hard, wooden benches were spotlessly clean; only the necessities were to be provided – transportation. In the afternoon we pulled into a small station to be greeted by a sign, 'PRESQUE ISLE, MAINE'. There, another convoy of '6-bys' stood waiting, and, after another ride through the country side, we found ourselves at an Army Air Force base that I didn't know existed – it was the 'jumping-off' place for transatlantic flights across the Atlantic.

Many had been expecting to finally alight at one of the East Coast ports such as New York, Jersey City or Boston for a sea journey to England on one of the Queen-size luxury liners turned troopship. Most of the pilots had had no sleep since Florida and by the time they had passed Boston and several other large cities along the New England coast they were looking forward to the prospect of a five-day ocean voyage aboard the *Queen Mary* or the *Queen Elizabeth*. Presque Isle, however, was a welcome sight after forty-eight hours in the stifling heat of the troop train and it offered good mess hall food, which was what their stomachs yearned for most right then. To 2nd Lieutenant Richard Dick Hewitt, a twenty-four-year-old New Yorker from Lewiston, Presque Isle 'sounded French and probably was, as Canada had to be getting close'. He and the others had thought, 'Now for those showers and a quiet, rock n' roll free night in a good old GI sack'. But back on the busses again, instead of a short drive to the BOQs (Bachelor Officers' Quarters) they stopped near base operations and at the flight line the seventy-four pilots and six back-up crewmembers boarded the Skymaster for take-off to who knew where. 'Normally we were a raucous bunch,' recalls Ernie Russell, 'but for a change no one said a word'.

Prior to 1942 troop movements to overseas theatres were usually made by sea but replacement pilots were sorely needed in the ETO and with the prowling U-boat Wolfpacks hunting the shipping lanes, air transport was the only way to reduce the risk and speed up demand. Though it was unpressurised and normally used for cargo, the Skymaster was the only aircraft capable of ferrying all seventy-four pilots to Britain in one hop.[3]

Ernie Russell continues:

When we were all aboard and strapped in a sergeant closed and locked the two large cargo doors at the rear of the airplane. The quietness was broken by the whine of a flywheel in an inertial starter. The door to the pilot's cabin was open and from my vantage point I could see what the pilots were doing. The pilot engaged the starter and a propeller began to turn, slowly; the engine coughed, the propeller jerked into motion, smoke poured out of the exhausts and an engine began to run. Before long all four engines were running smoothly, and the pilot finished his checklist; he then unlocked the brakes, gunned the outboard engines, and the big transport plane began to move forward on its tricycle landing gear. I could feel the big airplane lurch to the right as the pilot turned onto the taxiway. Within minutes we were at the end of the take-off runway. The pilots did a thorough check. I heartily approved as it was logical to think that we going to cross the Atlantic Ocean, and there is a lot of cold, dark, deep water to fly over before we would see land again. Lined up on the runway, I could feel the C-54 begin to shake and shudder as the four big engines were slowly throttled up to full power. Suddenly, the brakes were released and we were on our way. Slowly at first the fully loaded plane gathered momentum down the take-off runway and after a brief roll lifted off the runway. The wheels came up, clunked into the wheel wells, and, when the C-54 reached a safe airspeed, the pilot began to 'milk up' the flaps. We were on our way to wherever we were going.[4]

The transport's four 1,450-hp Twin Wasps easily pulled the huge machine with its tricycle undercarriage into the air and the C-54 turned on its north-easterly course to head out towards Gander, Newfoundland, to top off the fuel for the 2,000-mile great circle flight to Prestwick. Less than an hour later, in the darkness of evening, they were out over the North Atlantic, on instruments. The C-54 was not a speed merchant, but it did have endurance and it was not long before the drone of the huge Pratt & Whitney radials put most of the passengers to sleep. Dick Hewitt was one of the exceptions. Glancing around the Skymaster his thoughts went back to over sixteen months earlier when he left the family farm home in western New York. When the Japanese bombed Pearl Harbor on 7 December 1941 Hewitt was in his junior year in college, headed toward a degree in chemistry at Niagara University. Rather than wait to be drafted he had enlisted in the Air Cadets, a decision he did not regret for a single moment.

'What a cross-section of American young men,' Hewitt thought as he glanced around the transport's interior. In the seat beside him sat Arthur S Granger or 'Johnny' as he was known to most of them, of Richmond, Virginia, a salesman for the Phillip Morris Tobacco Company. Seated directly across the aisle were Vernon Y Jones and Grant M Turley, a gangly twenty-three-year-old cowboy from Snowflake, Arizona, who would name his P-47D *Kitty/Sundown Ranch*, in part for his wife Kathleen. 'Jonesy' was from a small town, Pattison, Mississippi. In front of them were twenty-one-year-old Alvin 'Max' Juchheim, who was from Grenada, Massachusetts, and Paul Keller, who was from Pittsburgh, Pennsylvania. In front of them were Franklin Resseguie of South Gibson, Pennsylvania, and Ernie Russell. Across from them sat Herrick and Randal Hathaway, who was from Thomaston, Connecticut. Then Donald Whinnem and Kenneth Williams, both from the north-east, Connecticut and Massachusetts, as far as Hewitt could recall. Faintly he could make out Dave Zimms and Edward Zellner, the two 'Z' boys, as they called them. Others who he knew fairly well were obscured in the dimly lit cabin, seated further forward in the transport. Most of them had been together throughout their pilot training. Hewitt recalls that 'the military had a personnel system that "followed the alphabet" and most of us would develop a close relationship or buddy from this last-name first-letter proximity. Some of us, I knew, would not come back. Would I be one of those? Time alone would tell'.

Theatre induction and the shock of the new was experienced at Atcham replacement depot near Shrewsbury – a 'cruddy place' where in August the new contingent got their first UK flight. Orders for Fighter Group assignments finally came on 9 September and Dick Hewitt and Ernie Russell were two of the seventeen pilots 'almost ecstatic to see their names on the listing for the 78th Fighter Group at Duxford'. The others in the contingent went to four other bases. Ernie Russell recalls:

The train ride from Atcham to a foggy London train station made for a long day but the beautiful green and gold of the English countryside through which we passed more than made up for it. Soon we were in agricultural East Anglia, a beautiful rolling and fertile area that greatly resembled the rich Black Prairies back home in Northeast Mississippi. We began to see clusters of brick and stone houses built around ancient stone churches with tall, slender, steeples in the little villages; all appeared to be grimy, or was it the weather? The villages became more frequent and larger the further south we travelled. Finally, there were continuous blocks of 'row houses', stacked like dominoes, side by side. Only when we were pulling into the station did I grasp that the row houses were in London. The great cavernous station wreathed in a steamy mist from the numerous steam engines, impressed me but the acrid smoke made my eyes smart and insulted my nostrils. Nonetheless, the long concrete platforms were bustling with people hurrying hither and thither. Uniforms were everywhere. The good looking blue uniforms of the Royal Air Force. The slightly baggy, almost shoddy, but serviceable wool khaki uniforms and hob nailed boots of the British Army. The neat looking uniforms of the Women's Auxiliary, and a few kilts; servicemen in Polish and Free French uniforms with their strange looking hats were scattered through the crowd. The civilians, men and women, had on warm clothes, but most were seedy – after all, the British had been at war for four years and clothing was rationed. Everyone was scurrying about, head down, rushing like they were about to miss a train. We had a short stop in London and then boarded another train to the north, which, on the big board, said 'Cambridge'. The ride was shorter this time, again through beautiful countryside that was dotted with little villages. The time passed slowly, but, finally, the train squealed to a stop, without a single bump or bang, at a typical, small, railway station marked 'WHITTLESFORD' – where was Duxford? Time would tell that it was the next little village to the west, on the east side of the 'aerodrome'.

Minutes after we passed through Whittlesford large red brick buildings began to appear through a row of hedges on our right. The '6-by', slowed, and turned right through a gate in the hedge. Another right turn brought us to a circle, and we stopped in front of a beautiful, redbrick building with fan glass windows framing the entrance above the door – the Duxford Officers' Club. And this was war? At the time, we didn't know how lucky we were; most of our classmates were assigned to temporary bases; living for the most part, in Quonset huts and the perpetual mud of recently constructed airfields that dotted the East Anglia countryside. As soon as the truck came to a stop in front of that magnificent building, we jumped down and followed an enlisted man into the club. The foyer met my expectations, airy, open with high ceilings, and comfortable chairs scattered around. After a short walk down a hallway we lined up in front of an office to receive our room assignments and, as it turned out, bed linens. Our bags were waiting for us when we returned to the truck, in front of the Officers' Club. I grabbed my baggage and, with help, got them to my new room. That night I unpacked my baggage, what there was of it, and got everything sorted out for what I hoped would be a long stay.

The room assignments were alphabetic and Ernie Lang and my good friend, Macie V Marlowe an old classmate from RTU, were assigned to rooms near to me. 'Marlowe', as we called him, was a tall, lanky, somewhat bleary-eyed tousled haired Virginian, who was just short of being handsome. He had been married to a strikingly beautiful girl only a short time before we embarked for overseas. Finding our new 'digs' is when I discovered that most of our friends in the earlier part of the alphabet had been assigned choice rooms in the main, steam-heated, two-storey BOQ (Bachelor Officers' Quarters) attached to the Officers' Club. The billeting officer had run out of spaces in the main building and had assigned us to rooms in a detached, temporary, wooden, barracks building just west of the main Officers' Club, which some thought were the least desirable quarters, as they were unheated and not in the mess. However, we had the advantage of our own private room and they beat the open barracks at Atcham, or the huge, corrugated metal, half culverts called 'Quonset huts', or the tents in which many of our classmates were living. The wooden barracks had some distinct advantages. First, I had the privacy of my own room – no roommate. Then, I was out of the heavy traffic in the Officers' Club. Wandering drunks looking for someone to spill their woes seldom bothered me. And I didn't have a roommate who might not come home from a mission, as did 'Dick' Hewitt who had to adjust to the loss of several.[5]

Ernie Russell was assigned to the 84th Squadron, which was commanded by Eugene Roberts, one of the early aces in the Group.

He was a soft-spoken man, about average size for our generation, with a large round head from which the hair was beginning to show signs of early retirement. [He had] bright, intelligent eyes, a 'pixyish' but warm smile and the ability to put everyone at ease. I was impressed. He was a perfect leader. Like the other new recruits I didn't know what to expect but when Colonel Roberts finished I knew I was welcome. Still, he gave us no idea as to when we would go on that first combat mission. Fortunately, the service had been a good teacher; I had learned how to wait; all would be done in due time.

Assignment to the various squadrons had been strictly military – alphabetical. With a few exceptions, my friends whose names started with A to about G were assigned to the 82nd Squadron. Those from about H to N were assigned to the 83rd Squadron and those whose surnames began with letters in the last part of the alphabet, Lang, Marlowe, Russell, etc, were assigned to the 84th Squadron. Richard Hewitt, et al[6] were assigned to the 82nd and V.Y. Jones, Alvin Juchheim, etc were assigned to the 83rd. There were exceptions; Grant Turley didn't get assigned to the 84th. I paid no attention to the paper work, but took what I got; it made little difference where I was assigned; bitching just focused the spotlight on you.[7]

To Hewitt's dismay his buddy, Johnny Granger, was assigned to the 83rd. New replacements were not allowed to pick their own roommate so Hewitt and Granger were bunked in a small, first floor room located in the south-west corner of the officers' quarters, just across from the PX (Post Exchange). The beds were typical military cots. By now they had got used to them and as tired as one got after a hard day's flying, they found that they could sleep on anything.

Ernie Russell's first days in the 84th were both 'busy and lazy'.

The 82nd facilities were on the west end of the flight line; the 83rd in the middle and, the 84th had the last buildings on the east end of the flight line. Our squadron ready room was in a long, low, single-storey, camouflaged, brick building whose casement windows faced out to the runway; entrances were on all sides. The Operations and the CO's office were on the west end. The ready room on the east end of the building was the pilots' 'domain'. Two dozen of us used up our days in that very plain, anything but cavernous, room. There were numerous nondescript folding metal chairs, plain oak chairs, a table or two on which to play cards, a cheap wood book rack in which there were a few 'secret' intelligence reports in red covers, an occasional newspaper, and little else. It was a mystery to me how we got all those pilots and staff, and their equipment, into that one small building. A large permanent hangar, which was assigned to the 84th, stood north of our ready room. A nondescript, two-storey, brick building housing group headquarters was about midway between the squadrons. Looking south, from the ready room, one could see the control tower, and beyond that a very wide east–west grass runway; it reminded me of Carlstrom Field, in Florida. The thought passed through my mind, 'How can the earth support a 7½ ton fighter?' That question was soon to be answered – beautifully.

Dick Hewitt continues:

There was no waiting around to fly, the 78th had plenty of operational planes. After an orientation flight to get familiar with Duxford from the air, we began an intense period of training for our first combat mission. It was close formation take-offs, camera gunnery and then high altitude combat (battle) formation. A tour of combat for a fighter pilot was initially set at 200 hours. Once fighter pilots had started a tour, the hour total did not increase, only for those just beginning.

The first four fighter missions of October were flown routinely as bomber missions grew in intensity. On 8 October, after what seemed time without end, Ernie Russell learned that, finally, he was scheduled to fly on a fighter sweep into northern France in an area that had, until recently, been a hornet's nest. Ernie Russell recalls:

Shortly after daybreak on 9 October a soft knock on the door of my room roused me from a sound sleep. I recognised the knock; it was our Batman, a wizened, little, old man who rattled round in his clothes who had been long in the service of the RAF.[8] It was the same knock at the same time every morning, seven days a week; After a minute or two, I galvanised myself, 'bit the bullet' and jumped out of my warm bed, hitting the bleak, splintery, wooden floor with a yell. It was chilly. This was one of those few times when I envied my friends and squadron mates who lived in the steam-heated comfort of the main Officers' Club dormitory next door. At least the chill energised me to wash, shave and dress in a hurry. Within a few minutes I had put on my 'long johns', khaki Ods, tie, wool sweater, my wool-lined khaki jacket and heavy wool socks and my RAF flying boots, issued when I joined the squadron. I loved my RAF boots. They were snazzy, ox-blood coloured, lined with trimmed sheep fur and very warm. One boot had a small pocket that contained a beautiful little pearl handled, single-bladed knife with which to cut off the tops. Still, some wore the heavy, GI issue high-topped shoes but the Gestapo could see them a mile away. I thought they were clodhoppers. Sunglasses were a must. Lastly, I picked up my cap, put it on my head at a slightly rakish angle and headed for the door. I stepped out in the hall, pausing only a second on the way down to knock on the door of Macie Marlowe my next-door neighbour. No doubt he missed his strikingly beautiful wife terribly and his routine after supper seldom varied; he would step across the hall to the Officers' Club bar and drink a Martini, order two more and take them back to his room next to mine. He would sit down at his desk, put the Martinis down in front of him, open his letter writing kit, and start a letter to his new wife. As he wrote his far-off wife, he sipped on the Martinis, until, before long, he was in the land of 'nod'. I never disturbed him. Till now. Marlowe opened the door with his 'ratty' flight cap in his hand, ready to go.

We made our way outside and quickly across a grassy area on a narrow walk. We entered a transverse hallway through the west wing, or dormitory, of the Officers' Club. There others joined us. Passing the billiards room and then into the big main entry hall and reception room with its large arched entryway, we entered another hall and slipped by the bar that smelled of stale, sour beer and whiskey, mingled with cigarette smoke from the night before. We turned left, through double doors and stepped left into the Dining Hall. The dining area was the brightest spot of any dreary morning, warm and inviting, and alive with the commotion of those preparing, those serving, and those eating breakfast. The dining hall, mess hall, was not the most sumptuous room in the club, but it was functional, a large open hall with high ceilings filled with three rows of long, serviceable tables and benches. White cotton tablecloths covered each table and utilitarian salt and peppershakers; a bowl of sugar, a can of Pet evaporated milk with two holes punched in the top and condiments were centred on each table. Individual places were provided with a GI issue knife, fork and spoon and a heavy stoneware coffee cup. The smell of toasting bread and hot coffee were enough to awaken anyone's senses. One or two large pots of steaming hot coffee were already on the table and hungry twenty-year-olds were already groping for their first cup of coffee when we got there. The coffee got few compliments, but my father's observation regards strong coffee applied. 'You didn't need a cup to hold the coffee because it could stand by itself.' One thing for sure, the raw, super strong, black coffee shocked you to life instantly.

Breakfasts were nourishing, though not elegant. In wartime England meals seldom were. Typically the breakfast menu, like those for other meals, rotated. One morning the main course might be chipped beef in thick white gravy on a slice of toast made from heavy brown English bread, commonly known as SOS [Shit On a Shingle], marmalade and coffee. The next, it might be powdered eggs and fried spam or, rarely, fresh eggs for the combat pilots. Oatmeal that resembled mucilage was a constant and Corn Flakes, or Grape Nut cereal, were always there. Once in a blue moon we had an orange, but forget fresh milk. English cows were not tuberculin tested and, further, we were cautioned not to drink milk. Following breakfast we left the mess hall and walked through the Officers' Club to the front door, past the circular garden in front and down the drive towards the flight line. The privileged few who owned bicycles rode them. Those of us who were not so privileged had to brave the morning air on foot.

October 9 was a day I had waited and trained for; all of a sudden, it was here. For nearly a month most of the other replacements and me had been on hold and I was impatient to get on with it. My name was on the operations board, which listed me as number two-man in a flight, on the inside of the formation – the beginner's slot. I was scheduled to go off on an expedition into the great unknown. I had never been where I could be shot at – at least to my knowledge, and I was about to do just that; fly deliberately into harm's way, where someone sought to kill me. I had no

149

idea what was going to happen and did not have the questions to pose. Not surprisingly, none of the old hands felt compelled to enlighten us. They knew that any flight into enemy territory had the potential for turning deadly, but seldom did. And that was the secret. At least I had heard and understood all the explicit instructions on baling out, dinghy drills and escape procedures that had highlighted the possibilities and problems. I was ready and 'rarin' to go'.

Captain John D Irvin, the Operations Officer, broke into the noisy ready room with, 'Briefing at Group in twenty minutes.' The clamour died down and a stream of pilots headed for the door. I followed the 'old hands' out to the Macadam road in front of our ready room and into the sunshine of a Fall day and headed towards the Briefing Room about a block down the road near the middle of the flight line. We entered the simple front door, turned left and passed through another set of double doors into a large open room with a low platform in front. To the left, there were double windows, behind drawn blinds, that opened onto the airfield. A speaker's stand stood on the low platform and behind it a large bed sheet was pinned to the wall; obviously, it covered something. A mix of wooden and metal folding chairs filled the large open room. As in church, everyone vied for the chairs about half way back in the room. Only those who were late, or bucking for a promotion, sat on the front rows. We took our seats near the middle of the room and, seated, discussed where the mission might be going. The room droned like a beehive. Everyone was talking until there was a loud, 'Ten-shun!' from the back of the room. Chairs rattled, as we all jumped to attention. You could have heard a pin drop. Footsteps echoed on the floor and then, 'At ease men'. We all dropped into our seats. Colonel Stone, a nice-looking, blonde-headed man with watery blue, humourless eyes strode to the stage followed by our Operations Officer. The weatherman and the Group Intelligence Officer, who had been putting last minute data on the black board, sat down as Colonel Stone ascended the low platform and began the briefing.

Colonel Stone quickly outlined our mission. There were no rendezvous, or escort duties; it would be a Type 16, radar controlled, fighter sweep over northern France. Then he outlined the order of battle; which squadron would lead, which would follow, call signs, start engine and take-off time, ETAs and what he thought we might anticipate in the way of enemy action. He hoped that the Abbeville Kids or any other Luftwaffe units would challenge us. It was a short briefing and he sat down. The Group Intelligence Officer rose and briefed us on anticipated flak, areas to avoid and the potential for seeing German fighters – low. The weatherman's briefing was short. The weather en route would be good and the weather at home base would remain CAVU.[9] With that the Colonel stood up, looked at his watch and said, in a low voice, 'Hack watches! In 45 seconds the time will be fourteen hundred hours.' I set the fluorescent hand on my military issue watch at 2:00, left the stem out and listened to the count-down, 'Ten, eight, seven, six, five, four, three, two, one, Hack!' I snapped the stem in and watched the second hand begin to track on the black face of my watch. Then the 'Exec' shouted; 'Ten-shun!' and we all stood. Colonel Stone said, 'Dismissed!' There was a rush for the door; we had to fight our way through the crowd. My first briefing for a combat mission was impressive.

I followed, or dragged, through the doors of the Briefing Room into the fresh air. Catching up with my crowd, I headed down the road to the 84th Ready Room. A few minutes later I was standing in front of my locker, where several pilots were slipping into their flying gear. But, before I did anything else, I checked with my flight leader to confirm the number of the ship he was flying and asked if there were any final instructions. He said, 'No, just stay in formation, keep your head turning and don't run over me in the crossovers.' As his number-two man on the inside of the flight, I wanted to be damn sure not to screw up. Some pilots were taking a last smoke, some were joking, others were quietly going about their business – those types always did. I had watched the same procedures unfold so many times during the last month that I didn't need to be told what to do. I just did it. The ritual began. I took all identification out of my pockets, including my wallet and put them on the top shelf. Then I took my soft leather leather flight helmet with built-in receptacles for headphones off the hook and checked my goggles, all US Army Air Corps issue. The British issue chamois-lined leather helmet and goggles were more comfortable and most pilots preferred them. British flying goggles had two-piece glass lens elements that were planar and did not distort. Lenses in USAAF issue goggles were plastic, curved and could distort distant objects. Also, they restricted peripheral vision. On very cold days I would wear a woollen olive drab GI sweater under my twill jacket. Four hours is a long time to be cold. Another critical item of clothing was my long gauntlet-like leather gloves with silk liners, another RAF innovation, which not only kept my hands warm, but also protected against flash fires. Our USAAF demand type oxygen system automatically metered oxygen, depending on the altitude and most of us considered it superior to the British mask. It was constructed of soft smooth rubber that fitted the contours of your face comfortably, sealed easily, was efficient, and almost never failed.

Next I reached for my Mae West, checked the cords to the oxygen cylinders that inflated the dinghy and the harness – OK. I slipped the flat yellow life jacket over my head on top of my leather A-2 flying jacket, drew one line under my crotch, put the waist cord through the loop in it, and tightened it around my waist. I was ready to go to the counter, check out my escape kit and get my seat parachute and dinghy. The dinghy was bulky, uncomfortable and heavy, but the few who had to resort to it, thanked God it was there. The dinghy sat on top of the parachute and an opening in it allowed the parachute straps to come through it. It was not comfortable to sit on, so I put a flat leather covered pneumatic seat cushion on top of it. I signed for my equipment, grabbed the leg harnesses of the parachute, and picked up the whole thing – it seemed to weigh a ton. I was loaded down with paraphernalia, as I struggled out the door. But I had time to do what most pilots did before going on a mission – take a leak in the long, porcelain, trough-like urinal in the latrine next to the hangar. That became almost a ritual.

Several vehicles, including a weapons carrier and a couple of 'Jeeps', were waiting; I threw my load up on the hood of the nearest. When all the seats and the fenders were full, the Sergeant cranked up and headed off to the hardstands. When I reached my assigned Jug, I said, 'This is mine'. The Jeep stopped and I jumped to the ground, grabbed my chute and dinghy and headed to the Jug. The crew chief, a highly intelligent, hard-working and conscientious South Carolinian named Tolleson, wasn't any older than I was; barely twenty. He grabbed my chute, welcomed me to the plane, walked around and threw the whole mass onto the trailing edge of the wing. My next question was to ask how the plane had been running.

'OK.'

'Any problems?'

'None!'

It was my turn to ground check, and you can believe that I checked every detail of that Jug, including the guns. No leaks, struts up, every thing in order, I was ready to go. I grabbed my chute off the wing, put my arms through the shoulder harness and fastened the chest lock, pulled the chute and dinghy up behind me and proceeded to mount the wing. The first step onto the wing, with all the paraphernalia, was a big one. Then I stepped into the seat, then onto the floor and sat, parachute and all, in the shiny aluminium bucket. I reached down between my legs to grab the two parachute leg harnesses, pulled them up, and snapped them shut. I reached for the two ends of the seat belt and Tolleson handed me the straps to the two Sutton harnesses; the two metal loops slid into the tongue of the seat belt and locked them together. I then adjusted the straps so that they were comfortably tight. Strapped in, I pulled out the Form 1A to check for any 'write-ups' by previous pilots; none were important. I handed the notebook to Tolleson, they were not carried into combat, and began the cockpit check. It took several minutes. My watch said that 'start engine' time was still minutes away, so I looked for something else to check. Nothing. The pilot in the next hardstand appeared unconcerned, alternately adjusting something in the cockpit, leaning back against the headrest, bored to tears. Not me. Finally, I saw my flight leader hold his hand above his head, index finger up, and turn it round and round; engine start – my watch was seconds short. Tolleson, standing by with the fire extinguisher, had seen the signal and was waiting. Within seconds my engine was running and, as I looked up from my final chores in the cockpit, Jugs began to roll out onto the steel mats on the taxiways. I motioned for my chocks to be removed and waited for my turn to get in the line. My flight leader passed and, when he did, I pulled out and followed him. For the next two and a-half-hours I would devote my entire attention to following and covering him, the flight and squadron. In turn, I hoped that they were covering me.

Three squadrons, 48 camouflaged, 'razor-back' P-47s with white rings around the front of their cowlings, were all rolling toward the east end of the grass runway, our marshalling and take-off area. The lumbering procession of fighters brought to mind a circus parade of elephants following, one after another. For sure they weren't holding each other's tails. I followed my leader to the end of the runway and watched as the squadrons lined up on the runway in flights of four, four flights to a squadron. Engines had been checked before the flights moved into take-off position. Our squadron commander moved into take-off position behind the squadron in the lead. By now, I didn't need to look at my watch. I just followed my flight leader onto the runway. Soon, all forty-eight airplanes were lined-up, waiting for the signal to takeoff. The wait just before takeoff on a mission was always the most anxious time for me. Exactly on the dot, the Group lead's flight of four Jugs began to roll; halfway down the runway their tails left the ground; when they did, the next flight began to roll; just like clockwork. Our flight's turn came and I fastened my attention on my flight leader. As he began to move I poured the coal to my engine, determined to maintain my position. We gathered speed and I stayed socked in on his wing. I was so intent that I was almost unaware of pulling my wheels up after leaving the ground and of reducing power settings. My flight leader began a climbing left turn to cut off the flight ahead in the turn and, when safe, I slid under him to his left wing. One circle around the field, and the squadrons and flights were in trail, and on course towards northern France. Me, I was making damn sure that I didn't waver in my position on the wing of my flight leader. The four flights in a squadron were spread to the corners of a rectangle with the number two men, the least experienced, on the inside of the rectangle. This was my position. Squadrons followed line astern. It soon became apparent that station keeping several hundred feet out was not easy due to the difficulty of recognising small changes in position but our

153

training in the US had been superb, so it was no problem. I was hanging in there, 'glued' into my position. All I could think was, 'I'm on my way'.

Except for a little static and a few terse comments, all was quiet – radio silence was enforced. I was driving a $150,000 dollar airplane, paid for by my country – all those folks at home, my group and my friends, not to mention my own hide. For most of the flight, I was so busy keeping position that I saw little of the land we were flying over. The basic combat unit was the element made up of two ships, the element leader and his wingman; two elements made up a flight, with the lead element being the flight leader. When we reached the English Channel, the group spread-out almost line abreast so that each person could cover the other's tail. The Channel was a known combat zone. Much of the Battle of Britain had been fought over the cold waters. I soon discovered that once out of position, you had to play catch-up. That required large power changes in the thin air at high altitude, as planes do not slow down or gain speed quickly. Fuel was no problem. We weren't on a maximum endurance mission but in a potentially hostile environment, where fuel can be a problem, the manner in which one kept station could be very important.

A cyclic buzz began to sound on my VHF radio that I would learn was radar 'painting' us. We had climbed above the haze level, so common in Europe and were more than three miles above the earth when a few desultory puffs of dark black 'smoke' – flak – blossomed in the sky nearby – for the first time, I was crossing into France. But I wasn't on a sight seeing trip. Slowly, I was beginning to get the hang of station keeping to the point where I could begin doing what I was there for – look for enemy airplanes in the brilliant, icy blue sky over France. Fifteen minutes later, still heading south, I was startled to hear a detached British accent say, 'So and so Leader, there are bogeys at 11 o'clock, thirty miles from you, at Angels 27.' We were at Angels 22. Our leader answered, 'Roger' and began a gentle turn to 11 o'clock and to climb to intercept the bogeys. I had to increase my throttle. The next thing I heard was, 'Red Leader, bogeys at 10 o'clock high.' I strained to see the bogeys in that section of the sky. Suddenly they came into focus. I was fascinated. There were about twelve of the most strikingly beautiful, but lethal, Fw 190s I could imagine. Painted robin egg blue, they were flying parallel to and several thousand feet above us. They must have determined not to engage us as they hung there for a minute or two, then split-essed and dove vertically towards the deck, flashing briefly in the sun light on their way down. Well beyond our reach, accelerating at a tremendous rate, they were out of sight and range before we could engage them. They, and the German radar, probably had been watching us all along, and, apparently, not liking the odds, they thumbed their noses at us and went home. I had been very fortunate. I had seen twelve enemy fighters on my first combat mission. (I would go on nine more missions before I saw another enemy airplane.) The trip home was anticlimactic – flak, let down, landing and debriefing. I didn't have a chance to tell my story to the Intelligence Officer; it had been told many times over, by more experienced hands. Also, I was not introduced to the customary shot of whiskey after the mission. That was more movie garbage. I had been on a combat mission, had seen flak and enemy fighters, and returned whole; I was a combat pilot and was now eligible to wear that blue patch behind my wings. Combat missions weren't too bad, after all.[10]

Dick Hewitt flew his first mission with the Group on 10 October, when in the mid-afternoon forty-eight Thunderbolts provided withdrawal support for the B-17s near Ochtrup-Rheine. Hewitt recalls:[11]

We had just crossed the English coastline at 16,000 feet and were headed southeast toward German occupied Belgium. Our mission was a fighter sweep in the Ghent/St Nicholas area, scheduled for an altitude of 32,000 feet. My position was 'tail-end Charlie', a spot frequently filled by many first mission pilots. I was anticipating a vicious air battle with the Luftwaffe. Belgium, for some reason, did not seem like it should be enemy territory. The Germans had occupied it since late 1940, about the same time period in which they had overrun most of the rest of Western Europe. The Germans had set up numerous airfields all long the coastal area from France to the northern tip of the Netherlands. These were positioned on routes so as intercept Allied aircraft on their way to and from targets in Germany or any of the occupied countries. A fighter sweep was designed to search out these enemy aircraft, entice them into battle, and knock 'em out of the skies, thus hopefully reducing their numbers and attack capability against the RAF and 8th Air Force bombers. It all looked and sounded good on field orders, but the plan did not quite work out that way. This was their 'home field' and they would control the degree of engagement. My throat was dry and my hands inside my heavy sheepskin lined gloves were already damp from perspiration most certainly not from the heat, as the temperature inside the Jug's cockpit was barely above freezing. Outside it had to be far below zero. Oh, for something to relieve my dryness; even a sip of warm British beer or ale would have tasted great. Breathing pure oxygen had a tendency to make you dry, but never in all my training flights had I felt this parched. I'd heard of first mission jitters but I didn't think it would he anything like this. Needless to say I was scared.

Our flying time told us we had to be getting close to the enemy coast. Yet how was one to know? The cloud cover was 10/10 below which did give us one distinct advantage. The dark silhouette of any enemy aircraft against the billowy cloudbank below would stand out like a sore thumb. But then we

155

weren't exactly obscured either. At 32,000 feet, the P-47 pulled a very persistent contrail. Forty-eight planes left a mark that would be erased only by high winds or a significant change in atmospheric conditions. The one thing I had not anticipated was that being in the 'enemies' court', they would call the shots. The sudden dozen or so bursts of flak that appeared slightly right of our course left no doubt that we had made landfall and this was definitely enemy territory. We were right on time, probably a little off course. Heavy flak was a pretty good indicator that we had passed almost directly over a well-fortified coastal city not in accord with our flight plan. Immediately our group leader called a ten-degree left turn. No sooner had we straightened out on our new course than more bursts appeared, only this time they were about exactly where we would been had we not made that slight alteration in course. Now I really began to sweat. They had a dead bead on our altitude and had we not taken that evasive course change, who knows what might have happened? In our briefing, Intelligence had told us where the heavier flak spots might be and had plotted our course to avoid them. As fighters, we were more fortunate than the bombers in that we could at least take some evasive action. The Heavies could make slight changes but not near as fast as we could. Once locked in on a bomb run, they could do little except to hope and pray. Those black puffs were 88 mm and one hit in a vital spot would have been 'all she wrote'. Again we changed heading, only this time we lost a couple hundred feet in addition. The flak appeared once more. This time it was well above and behind us. I had learned enough about evading flak in those few seconds that would ultimately save my life on several subsequent encounters.

By now the Germans knew exactly what we were doing, right down to our altitude, general direction, approximate numbers and type of aircraft. Their radar could lock in on us almost from the time we left the English coast. They pretty much knew our intent and could govern their response accordingly. Since fighters alone at high altitude posed no real threat, they could sit on the ground and observe as we burned up our fuel. The speed and size of the radar blips told them that no heavy bombers were coming and our altitude told them we little guys were not strafing or dive bombing. And unless we dropped a lot lower, we were probably on one of our main, high altitude sweeps, hoping that they would come up and challenge us. But with the odds mostly in our favour, they had very little, or nothing, to gain and a bit more to lose. It would have been about as one-sided as walking into the batters' box with a two strike and no ball count. They could choose to wait for a future day when the battlefield would be a bit more in their favour.[12]

Our sweep turned out to be totally uneventful, except for the flak. We had spent a total of close to one hour inside enemy territory, at or near 32,000 feet. With a Thunderbolt's indicated airspeed of roughly 240 mph, at 32,000 feet, our ground speed was well over 350 mph. We had covered a lot of miles. Not one enemy aircraft was sighted except at one point, far inland and slightly lower than our flight path, two contrails did appear. If they were enemy aircraft, they had no intent of engaging any of our 48 P-47s. They were probably only scouting our mission or acting as decoys to lure us into a trap, for almost as soon as they were spotted and called out, they had high-tailed it down through the clouds below. It was not to be a day of engaging the enemy. On our course for home, we began a very gradual descent, made a couple of slight course changes but did not see one more puff of flak. The clouds had partially cleared below and I got my first hook at the North Sea. It looked cold and bleak. Little did I realise at the time that I, as well as many of my closest flying buddies, would have numerous close encounters over it in the next year and a half. It would become the final resting-place for many thousands of allied troops during WWII. Once back inside the United Kingdom, Duxford was usually a fairly easy airfield to find. We were on the main rail line from London to points north. Normally we used this means of dead reckoning and navigation to locate our base. There was a homing device that, if weather made it unfindable you could get a fix and a heading direct to the base. With the haze, fog and other foul weather conditions that prevailed on many returns, it was not unusual to take advantage of this more certain course for home.

My first mission would have been called a 'milk run' by many but to a combat greenhorn, it was anything but that. Besides, what milkman ever got shot at, by 88-mm cannon at 3.00 am, by a Jerry ack-ack gunner and at an altitude of 32,000 feet? Of the total number of combat hours I would eventually amass, none would be any easier than the two hours and 19 minutes I had logged on this one. How I managed to survive it all, you can call it luck, skill, the grace of God, parental prayers, or whatever. For certain, all would play an equally important rôle. I would be far luckier than the thousands who would end up in some Stalag prison camp or perish in the skies over Europe.

No bomber missions were flown from 11 to 13 October. When on 14 October the heavies attacked the ball bearing plant at Schweinfurt for the second time in three months the 78th Fighter Group was grounded by bad weather. The mission, which was designed to deliver a single, decisive blow against the German aircraft industry and stem the flow of fighters to the *Luftwaffe*, was a disaster with sixty bomber losses. A further five B-17s, including one that force-landed at Duxford with shot up landing gear and a dead bombardier aboard, crashed in England as a result of their battle-damaged condition and twelve more were destroyed in crash-landings or so badly damaged that they had to be written-off. The enemy fighters used a new tactic whereby they engaged the escort fighters at the coast forcing them to jettison their drop tanks early and thereby restrict their effective range.

October 1943 had seen nine missions flown from Duxford with seven victories claimed for the loss of two pilots, one in action and one to other causes. Fortunately, non-combat losses involving mechanical, oxygen or oil and fuel problems were few. A fuel leak had resulted in the loss of 2nd Lieutenant Quentin Charlton over the North Sea on 22 September for that month's only operational loss. On 18 October 2nd Lieutenant Franklin B Resseguie, who was on his second combat mission, suffered a prop failure near Lens and St Omer and he was last seen 10,000 feet below the Group gliding inland. Resseguie was taken in by the French Underground and he had to make a forced night walk across the Pyrenees into Spain where he had to race to a telephone booth in a small town just across the border. He just had time to call the American Consulate in Madrid before being thrown into a roach-infested jail by Spanish police.[13] Many downed airmen made their way through France and into Spain while others escaped across the English Channel by PT boat. RAF high-winged Lysanders picked up some downed fliers at lonely improvised French airstrips at night. Major Gene Roberts meanwhile had been promoted to Lieutenant Colonel and had recently become Deputy Group CO. On 20 October he scored his ninth and final victory of the war when he downed a Bf 109 at Dinant. Having flown eighty-nine missions he was transferred to VIIIth Fighter Command and in 1945 he flew a second tour as CO of the 364th Fighter Group.

Time and missions moved slowly after Ernie Russell's first mission.

It was nearly two weeks, 21 October, before my 2nd mission. Two days later I was assigned another mission. It was a bomber escort and the start of three missions on which my aircraft would experience mechanical problems with the belly-tank. We had taken off, climbed out and were over Holland on the continent on the way to rendezvous with the bombers. When my belly tank ran dry, I reached down and pulled up on the 'T' shaped release handle to release the empty tank. Nothing happened. The release was as if set in concrete. Nothing I could do would budge it. I struggled for several minutes before it became obvious that the belly tank was not going to release. The ironclad rule was that I must return to base. Disappointed, but hoping that my flight leader would let me continue on the mission, I called him and reported my problem. Unhesitatingly, he motioned me to go home and for my element leader to go home with me. It was a long way home, especially since I had to abort the mission. I continued to struggle with the release to no avail. Finally, we saw the English coast and within fifteen minutes were letting down into Duxford.

On the ground I wrote up the belly tank release in the Form 5 and told Tolleson what had happened. After I had climbed down out of the cockpit, he got in, pulled the release and the stuck belly tank fell off. I could not believe my eyes and he probably thought that I was mistaken. But that was not the end of the mystery. On my next mission twelve days later, I flew the same plane on another escort mission; and, yet again, when it came time to release my belly tank over eastern Holland, the same thing happened, my tank would not release. Now I was really unhappy, I would have to abort the mission for the second time in the same plane. When I got home this time, it was my crew chief's time to shake his head in dismay when the tank fell off when he pulled the release. I had him replace the tank, and I took the plane to altitude to see if it would happen again. Sure enough, at 25,000 feet over the North Sea, I reached down and pulled the tank release; it was rock solid, no matter how hard I struggled, it would not budge. What in the world was going on? I landed and the same thing happened, again; the crew chief pulled the release handle, and the tank dropped to the ground. I wrote my flight up and left him shaking his head.

Early next morning my crew chief came in and told me that he had located the problem, which was simple; rain water had run down into a low place in the loop of the conduit holding the release cable, where it was trapped. When I reached altitude where the temperature was in the order of minus 40° Fahrenheit, the water in the conduit froze solid, like concrete. On returning to a lower altitude the warm air melted the ice and freed the cable. Needless to say, the mechanic removed the water and I never had any more trouble and combat missions settled down into a routine, more or less. The group's main assignments became bomber escort missions. By November I was no longer a rookie, so I was scheduled on a regular basis. I flew seven missions in November, all bomber escorts and, except for the ever-present flak, they were uneventful. At the end of November I had ten combat missions under my belt. Like most fighter pilots, I loved my airplane and, in my opinion, it was the single best fighter plane flying. My second Jug, the one that took me through most of my combat tour, was an old Jug, one of the first assigned to the squadron. It had a plain vanilla, super-dependable, turbo-charged Pratt-Whitney R-2800 engine that yielded a dependable 2,000 horsepower, which was absorbed by a Curtiss Electric 'tooth-pick' prop. It never baulked, was always there when I reached down to get it, and I never had to abort a mission due to mechanical difficulty. No way would I have traded WZ-C, not for anything. In WZ-C I knew that I could whip any 'Spam Can' (the tag Jug pilots put on the P-51) and on all occasions that I met one, did; I had 500 feet of gun camera film to prove it and gun camera film came in fifty foot rolls. The Jug could also outfight a Me 109G on the deck and I had gun camera film to prove that too. However, I must admit that you had to get the drop on a Spitfire; make one pass at him and go home. Never, never turn with a 'Spit'. And, turning with top Me 109 or Fw 190 pilots at low altitudes was not habit forming, either. Most average Jug and 'Spam Can' pilots who tried it, whether due to circumstances beyond their control or not, didn't spend that night in their own bed. If you weren't a believer you didn't need to be flying Jugs, or for that matter any fighter.

In November news was received that fighter pilots would no longer complete a tour once they reached 200 flying hours but would have to carry on flying combat. Another talking point was fighter bombing and the new tactic was employed for the first time on 25 November when the 78th Fighter Group provided close and high cover for the 353rd Fighter Group bombing St Omer airfield in northern France.[14] Then on Friday 26 November 633 bombers, the largest formation of American bombers assembled to date, were directed against targets as far apart as Bremen and Paris. The Jugs took off from Duxford at 0927 hours and headed for mid-Channel where they made rendezvous with 128 Fortresses of the 3rd Bomb Division. After taking up escort above the bomber stream, the force flew the route of Dieppe-Montford-Evreux to the target, a bearing industry at Montdidier near Paris. As the Forts made their turn for the target east of Paris, about thirty German fighters went into attacks on the bomber's front and rear ranks. The fighter pilots quickly positioned themselves to meet the attack and went after the enemy. Jack Price, who was flying *Feather Merchant II*, had been promoted to major on 13 November. He started firing at a Fw 190 from 550 yards to prevent it making a head-on pass at the bombers and got good strikes all over the German. The major closed to 100 yards but he had to break off to avoid running into the bombers. The Fw 190 stalled and went down trailing smoke. Next, Price caught a climbing Bf 109, came in astern at 300 yards and exploded it in flames for his fifth victory. He had also damaged a Bf 109 on 20 October over Belgium. Captain Howard S Askelson closed to 200 yards with an out-of-the-sun astern run at three Bf 109s near bomber level and sent one straight down in fire and lots of black smoke. The battle went on in a running fight until the force reached the Beauvais area. 2nd Lieutenant John Herrick, who went down ten miles north-east of Beauvais and 2nd Lieutenant Wayne M Dougherty who was downed north of Paris, survived to be taken prisoner. Flight Officer Ralph E Cormier was shot down and killed.[15] 1st Lieutenant Warren M Wesson, twenty-four years old, from Brooklyn, who was flying *Jeanie*, took a long 600-yard shot at the line of flight of a Fw 190 and held his trigger down as one of the Germans passed through his fire. Another pilot who saw his victim crash confirmed the victory, Wesson's first. The Group left the continent at Cayeux at 1120 hours and headed for England, where three P-47s crash-landed at south-east coastal airfields.

Four days later, on 30 November, Major Jack Oberhansly in *Iron Ass* led the Duxford Outfit on a mission to provide withdrawal support for the bombers near Aachen. The P-47s finally rendezvoused with the 'Big Friends' at Eupen, Belgium, where Oberhansly singled out a Fw 190, which was trying to finish off a straggling Fortress. The Major, who had two fighters probably destroyed and one confirmed destroyed, on 27 September, got on the enemy fighter's tail but he had to break off his attack when a radio call said that the fighter was a P-47. Oberhansly correctly identified the aircraft as a Focke-Wulf and went into the attack once more, shooting it down with a burst of fire from 200 yards to claim his second victory.[16] The Group returned to England in a heavy overcast and broke out of the murk over London but all made the fifty miles to Duxford safely. 30 November ended a rather fruitless weather plagued month of eleven missions, six victories and three combat losses.

Ernie Russell recalls:

There weren't many real gung-ho fighter pilots in the 84th as I saw them in November 1943. Quince Brown, Peter Pompetti and the past Squadron Commander, Lieutenant Colonel Eugene Roberts, who had recently left for VIIIth Fighter Command with a chest full of medals. All I wanted for Christmas was the chance to get into a position where I could fire my guns, but that was only a remote possibility, seeing that I was just a wingman. I had yet to recognise that it paid to have rank to have that chance. Unless, of course, you were someone like Pompetti who was known for leaving the squadron on the way home from a mission and hunting on his own, a practice highly frowned upon by the squadron and group staff as well as the VIIIth Fighter Command.

December 1st dawned as usual with a cold, damp morning fog draped over the buildings like a wet blanket. East Anglia did not escape this curse. At least the coal smoke was not as bad as it is in London but this was not a day for seeing the ground in England. On good fine days, about twenty-five minutes after take-off, at about 15,000 feet, you could make out the outlines of the wide Thames Estuary shining through the ubiquitous London haze, far below. To the west, barrage balloons floated serenely in the smog. I could visualize them, tethered to the ground by steel cables, and beneath the sausage-like balloon hung an array of shorter steel cables like tentacles of giant jellyfish, whose purpose was to ensnare anyone unfortunate enough to hit them. Seeing the balloons always brought to mind an irreverent remark I had heard an irate and slightly smashed 'Yank' soldier make to a 'Limey' bartender who he felt had mistreated him: 'They ought to cut the cables on those damned balloons and let this damned island sink into the ocean.' (I'm sure that he was not the originator of that sentiment.) But we were 'kids' and after an early breakfast a gaggle of us oblivious to the fog were laughing and joking with each other on our way to the flight line. It would burn off. The schedule read, 'Lieutenant Russell, Blue 2.' I was flying the wing of one of the 'old' hands in the squadron, the flight leader. He wasn't a hot-rod or a ball of fire. One might call him a plodder. Briefing went as scheduled and we learned that our group was to rendezvous with the bombers in Germany. Their mission was to bomb an industrial complex in

Ligaaten, a small town on the east side of the Rhine, near Cologne. For about thirty minutes, we were to prevent German fighters from attacking our Big Friends; then, it was home, sweet home. Colonel Stone and the group intelligence officer pointed out during the briefing what I already knew, that the last few missions had been rather uneventful and in Stone's opinion, we didn't have much hope of seeing Jerries. So what was different? I had not seen a single enemy fighter up close since my first mission, when I saw about a dozen Focke-Wulf 190s near Lille – briefly. Colonel Stone had not shown me that he was a 'Tiger'. He had been flying combat since April and it was my immature judgement that he would undertake to keep us out of harm's way. No thrills here today and it looked like another milk run.

When the briefing ended I headed out to the nearest weapons carrier, piled on and waited for the driver to take me to my Jug, WZ-C. I was anxious to have time for another chat with my Crew Chief, Staff Sergeant Tolleson, about my factory new D-12RE Jug's abnormally high fuel consumption. I had consumed an anomalous amount of fuel on the preceding two missions and my fuel warning light had come on long before it should have. Tolleson told me that he had changed out the carburettor but I was still uneasy about the excessive fuel consumption of WZ-C when I hauled my chute onto the wing.

Start-engine, take-off, and the climb out went off without a hitch, so we made our rendezvous as expected. Within minutes we were in our tactical positions, guarding the Big Friends. For thirty minutes, or so, we weaved back and forth over the big birds looking and hoping that the Jerries would give us a chance. When our relief arrived, on time, the 78th turned and headed for the barn. The weather was fairly good and slightly hazy. There was a gauzy high overcast and far below a thin layer of broken clouds. A hundred yards or so out and nearly abreast of my flight leader, in a modified line abreast formation, I scanned the sky looking for E/A. My woollen uniform shirt was rubbing the back of my neck raw. We were north of Aachen at about 27,000 feet when I spotted a lone B-17 five or six miles ahead at about 2 o'clock and several thousand feet below us. A thin wisp of smoke was trailing one engine. Obviously crippled he was headed home – a sitting duck. I called the cripple out to my flight leader, but got no reply. As I was to discover in a few seconds, I was not the only one who saw him. Our cruising speed was 60 mph faster than a B-17, especially a cripple, so we were overtaking him rapidly. Then I spotted a single mottled grey Me 109 at about 3 o'clock high on our Big Friend, but below us. Obviously he was in the process of setting-up for a firing pass. It was what the Luftwaffe did to perfection – cripple a bomber so that it can't keep up with the formation and then finish him off at leisure. However, the 109 pilot was so intent on finishing off our Big Friend that he had not seen the flight of four Jugs high above him and up-sun.

When I saw the Me 109 I called my flight leader. 'Blue Leader from Blue 2. A Me 109 is bouncing our Big Friend from 3 o'clock high!' Again, there was no answer, so I called again; again, no answer. Then I tried to get my flight leader's attention by 'skidding' my Jug to within a few feet of his right wing tip. He was looking straight ahead; seemingly unaware of what was going on below. Frantic, I tried again, this time sticking my wing tip behind the trailing edge of his wing nearly into his cockpit, and called him again with the same message. His response to my intrusion was to show considerable irritation at my behaviour for he looked around at me as if to say, 'What the hell's the matter with you?' What was the matter with him? Was he asleep? I motioned frantically towards the B-17 then in the process of being attacked by the Me 109. Surely he saw what was going on. And here was an opportunity for him to shoot down a Me 109 and save a Big Friend. To my alarm he ignored my gesturing and radio, looked straight ahead and continued on his way home. The crippled bomber was 'dog meat', a set-up for the 20 mm cannon of the Jerry. Unable to get my flight leader's attention, I knew that I had to do something, even if it hair-lipped him. I called him yet again and told him that I was going to get the Jerry. Again, no reply!

Just then the Jerry pilot began to roll downward from his position above the crippled bomber into a firing pass. Time was up. It was now or never. I couldn't stand idly by and watch a preventable slaughter and do nothing. Despite the consequences of leaving my flight without permission, I slammed my throttle and prop to the firewall, flipped my gun switches to 'ON' and rolled downwards, towards the Me 109. I hoped that my flight leader would cover me. The Jerry pilot must have seen me coming, for instead of continuing his pass at the bomber, he rolled to the left underneath the bomber and straight down. Outnumbered, he had taken the only other way out: he was going to try to out dive the Jug. Although not the best choice that's about the only one he had as I was in the 'cat bird' seat. I fell in behind him, quickly. He was perhaps a mile below me, and well out of firing range. But, I was diving vertically, too, at 22–23,000 feet, and accelerating rapidly. I didn't look at the air speed indicator, but knew that I had to be pushing 500 mph. There was no sensation of speed, only the exhilaration of the chase. I pushed forward in my seat, trying to go faster and overtake the drab little Me 109, the first one that I had ever seen this close. I forgot everything, my flight leader, instruments, the B-17; everything but closing the space in front of me. The only measure in my mind now was the distance between the Jerry and me. I determined to give him a short burst when he was within maximum range of the eight fifty calibre machine guns – about 600 yards. Ideal range was 250–300 yards, I knew, but I would give him a 'squirt' at max range to see whether my lead was correct. Slowly the gap between us closed, and I began to calculate my range with the ring in my reflex gunsight.

Soon his wing span in the glowing ring on the glass plate of the gunsight told me that he was within 600 yards. I calculated the correct lead for an angle of about 15 degrees and a speed of about 500 mph. That was easy, about one-third of a ring. Subconsciously I checked the needle and ball to prevent skidding, and, simultaneously, eased the glowing dot on the reflex gunsight through the length of the fuselage of the Me 109 and in front of his nose. When it reached one-third of a ring I squeezed off about a two second burst – about 160 rounds. It was the first time I had fired all eight guns at once. It felt good, but I was a little surprised at how much the wings shook under the impact of the recoil; I could feel the vibration of the guns and hear their rumbling above the sound of the engine. I don't know what I expected, but many spark-like flashes of my incendiaries exploded on the left side of the engine, almost to the cockpit and on the wing roots of the grey Me 109. I had hit his engine hard with my first burst. I knew that for every flash I saw there were four other armour-piercing bullets, which I couldn't see, probably impacting the engine and wings of the Me 109. I would get closer and finish him off.

Shortly, to my surprise, the canopy of the Me 109 flew off into the slipstream. He was preparing to bale out! I was elated, convinced that he was done for and that I had my first victory. In my eagerness, I overlooked something important; I had not confirmed the kill with the camera. All that would show were the hits. I had made a first timer's error; not following through and validating my kill. When I considered that the Me 109 was destroyed I was nearly three miles below where I had left my flight, below 14,000 feet and travelling at more than 500 mph. I yanked back on the stick, hard; the elevators took hold almost instantly. My Jug bottomed out of its dive and shot straight up; the 'g' forces jammed me into the seat. I cleared myself, instinctively and took stock of my situation. My flight was nowhere to be seen. At the same time, I noticed that everything on the instrument panel was in the green except for the oil temperature gauge. The dial was blank! When I had slammed the throttle forward the gauntlet sleeves on my flying gloves had inadvertently toggled the oil cooler door switch to 'Closed'. Quickly, I pulled the toggle switch back to 'Open' and heart in throat, waited for the needle to do something before the engine bellied-up on me. By that time I had reached the top of my zoom climb, about 24,000 feet, and had levelled off, the needle had crept back into the green. I remembered the magnetic course home, turned to it and headed back to the barn.

The sky over Germany and Belgium was empty. Nothing but a few washed out contrails showed in the distance. The only noise came from my steady pulse of my engine and the ever-present hum from the German radar in my headset. For a while I searched for my flight leader and the rest of the flight, but they were nowhere to be seen. I just had to get home, by my lonely, some 300 miles. I was uneasy but I was as busy as a one-armed paper hangar, making sure that some Jerry didn't do to me what I had just done to one of theirs. I didn't have anybody watching my backside. Once I had reached my cruise altitude and set course I checked my fuel levels. What I saw was not encouraging and being all too familiar with the fuel guzzling character of my Jug, it didn't take a PhD to figure out that my real problem was fuel. During the encounter with the Me 109 I had been at War Emergency Power for perhaps ten minutes. At WEP settings an average Jug burns more than 300 gallons of fuel per hour – or more than five gallons per minute. I had probably burned more than 50 gallons of fuel in the encounter. The question – did I have enough left to reach England? I estimated that that it would be close. I set my manifold pressure and rpm as low as I dared and hung in the air knowing that even then my engine was burning more than 100 gallons of fuel per hour. It was some relief when, through breaks in the clouds, the North Sea finally came into view. When the yellow Fuel Warning light flickered on then glowed steadily it meant that it had reached the 40-gallon mark. I had about 20 minutes of flying time remaining and I was over Belgium. I had no maps so I could only guess that I was about 200 miles from 'home' and about 150 miles from the English coast. If I averaged a little better than 300 mph, about five miles per minute, I probably had fuel for 120 miles, maybe more. I bored on. Near the Belgian coast I delayed my letdown because of the flak and after some random bursts, I was over the North Sea. I dropped my nose and began to pick up speed and began to eat up the 100 plus miles to the welcome coast of England. After what seemed an eternity, it began to materialise out of the haze and clouds. No flak greeted me when I crossed the coast near Clacton-on-Sea headed toward Colchester. By now I was about 2,000 feet but suddenly, I was jarred by the fluctuation of the needle on my Fuel Pressure gauge. I was not going to make it to Duxford.

Ernie Russell selected a marshy field and bellied his Thunderbolt in. WZ-C hit the soft ground just above stall speed, about 105 mph in a slightly nose high attitude and slid straight ahead for several hundred feet before coming to rest. Russell continues:

'Slid' may be a misnomer. To me, strapped into the cockpit, it was more like a big dog shaking a small cat. Never had I experienced the severity of the shaking that the Jug gave me when it made contact with the ground. The time between the first contact and the time the Jug jolted to a stop was a blur. The simple fact is that the Sutton Harness and seat belt saved me from injury. In one piece and stopped, finally, I sat for a moment, dazed; unbelieving that so much could have happened today. Any fleeting thought that I may have had must have lasted but a second, and then my senses told me – get out of this plane. I hastily loosened my harness, released my chute harness, and jumped out onto the left wing. It was unreal. WZ-C did not appear to be excessively damaged. The propeller was bent and there were some belly scratches. One consolation – that gas-guzzling engine had met its end. I wasn't going to sweat out fuel another time in that plane. The sadness was that I had lost my new Jug. I looked up and saw several ruddy, stalwart English workers running through the marshes to assist me. I was still a little shaken but I thanked them and asked them to get me to a telephone so that I could report my belly landing. A short while later I was on my way to Duxford.[17]

Back at base Russell discovered that two other Thunderbolt pilots that ran out of fuel had crash-landed at airfields on the south coast of England. Three pilots claimed 'probables'. Russell could claim only a 'Damaged'. 1st Lieutenant Charles N Keppler got a Fw 190 for sure and 1st Lieutenant James Wilkinson scored his first victory since joining the 82nd Squadron in November, being credited with the destruction of a Bf 109. Wilkinson, twenty-eight years old from Swathmore, Pennsylvania, had been at Debden with the 4th Fighter Group from January to April 1943 when he had broken his back in a flying accident. He had since wooed and then married his English sweetheart. After this mission the weather worsened and missions were scrubbed. On 21 December the Group flew area support for a raid on targets in France by B-26 Marauders but they shot down four RAF Typhoons in a bounce near Doullens. To make matters worse RAF Spitfires shot down a fifth Typhoon. A three-day investigation resulted in the four P-47 pilots concerned being transferred out of the Group along with others who were suffering fatigue and nervous problems.[18] Only nine combat missions were flown from Duxford during December and the Group claimed eleven enemy aircraft destroyed.[19]

By late December 1943 Ernie Russell had melded into the squadron, had fired his guns in 'anger' and knew how to go to a pub and order 'mild and bitters'.

The 78th eased into the first English winter most of us had ever seen and suddenly, winter was here. First, a little more fog and mist, then more cold fronts, with damp, cold, miserable, drizzly rain for which England is noted. We flew a mission on Christmas Eve but Christmas day dawned with miserable weather and we were cleared for a big Christmas dinner. The Christmas dinner that was served in the Officers' Mess was one of the best meals I can remember in England: turkey with all the trimmings, including cranberries. A big Christmas tree, lights and all, had been erected in the lobby of the club and that helped give us the Christmas spirit. I can't remember anyone giving gifts, but the Xmas spirit was present, even in the midst of a war. On Christmas night, I invited my crew chief and armament chief and some other friends to my room for a drink and shared with them a very rare quart bottle of White Horse scotch given me as my share of the Officers' Club 'loot'. My guests were hungry for a taste of real whisky and the lone bottle of scotch didn't go far. The evening was still young when the bottle ran dry. Nobody got drunk, or even high, but we did have a good time. We enjoyed the Xmas respite, but on December 27th we were back in the middle of the daylight bombing campaign.

1   *A Mississippi Fighter Pilot In WWII* by Ernest E Russell.

2   *A Mississippi Fighter Pilot In WWII* by Ernest E Russell.

3   *Target of Opportunity: Tales & Contrails of the Second World War* by Lieutenant Colonel RA Dick Hewitt (Privately Published November 2000).

4   *A Mississippi Fighter Pilot In WWII* by Ernest E Russell.

5   *A Mississippi Fighter Pilot In WWII* by Ernest E Russell.

6   Keller, Herrick and Grant Turley were also assigned to the 82nd Squadron.

7   *A Mississippi Fighter Pilot In WWII* by Ernest E Russell.

8   Traditionally, the RAF officer had the services of a personal 'man', his batman.

9   Ceiling and visibility unlimited.

10 *A Mississippi Fighter Pilot In WWII* by Ernest E Russell.

11 *Target of Opportunity: Tales & Contrails of the Second World War.*

12 When the Thunderbolts arrived they found thirty-plus single and twin-engined fighters attacking the straggling Fortresses and they went into the attack immediately. Captain Philip R 'Swede' Larson claimed a Bf 110 and Captain Charles W Silsby got two twin-engined fighters before the group had to break off low on fuel and return to Duxford. Captain Silsby was KIA on 15 April 1944 and he left a widow at home in Dothan, Alabama. West of Enschede Major Gene Roberts destroyed a Bf 110 and a Me 210 to take his score to eight making him the top scoring 8th Air Force fighter pilot.

13 The account of his escape is told in his book *Feathers In The Wind* (1995).

14 Colonel Loren G McCollom, the 353rd Fighter Group CO, was shot down by a direct flak hit. He baled out and was taken prisoner.

15 At Chantilly at 1040 hours *Oberfeldwebel* Adolf 'Addi' Glunz of 5./JG 26

claimed a 78th Fighter Group P-47. *Unteroffizier* Franz Vandeveerd of the 3rd *Staffel* JG 26 also claimed a 78th Fighter Group P-47 NW of Paris at 1100 hours. See *The JG 26 War Diary Vol.2.*

16   On 30 November JG 26 lost four Bf 109G-6s in combat, two of which were credited to the 78th Fighter Group. It is therefore possible that Oberhansly's victim was *Feldwebel* Ludwig Pötter of 10./JG 26 who was one of three pilots in the *Gruppe* who died in combat that day. *Unteroffizier* Hans-Gerhard Fieguth was WIA after a fight with a 78th Fighter Group P-47 and he landed safely at Rheine. See *The JG 26 War Diary Vol.2.*

17   *A Mississippi Fighter Pilot In WWIII* by Ernest E Russell.

18   *Eagles of Duxford: The 78th Fighter Group in World War II.*

19   On 30 December part of the Group provided penetration support from near Amiens in France to Traben/Trarbach during the mission to Ludwigshafen by more than 700 bombers. Over France another force of P-47s from Duxford shepherded the returning bombers home. 1st Lieutenant Warren M Wesson claimed a Bf 109 in the Reims area. 1st Lieutenants Manuel S 'Manny' Martinez and William T Hegman also claimed victories over the attacking Bf 109s. Flight Officer James C.P. Eastwood was forced to abandon *Skonk Hunter* over the Channel thirty miles south of Beachy Head. He baled out and was seen to get in his dinghy but he was never seen again.

CHAPTER EIGHT

The Burning Blue

The poor weather continued unabated after Regensburg with intense cold and solid overcasts – or should I say high undercasts – the rule. Seldom did we see any evidence that Europe existed, only clouds and, once we got above the overcast we were looking at a dazzling blue sky over a glaring white cloud deck. How intense was the glare above the clouds? One day I forgot to wear my sunglasses – a no-no – and burned my eyes so bad that I spent the night in agony. Never again!

Ernest 'Ernie' E Russell[1]

January and the New Year brought not only more bad weather but sad news for Ernie Russell who received a yellow Western Union telegram from his mother telling him that his father was dead in Louisiana, after a long illness. There was no going home to comfort his mother, younger brother and sister; the war precluded that. Nearly a year would pass before he would get home. He recalls 'January was a slow month for me as well as the Group. I flew only five missions during the month. On 4 January the Group flew an escort mission to Münster and the Jerries came out for a change.' The Group provided withdrawal support for the bombers of the Third Bomb Division attacking Münster. After arrival at Ahaus the P-47s bounced five Fw 190s and 1st Lieutenants Harry C. Roff and James E. Stokes destroyed two of them. Quince Brown in *Okie* destroyed two more to take his score to three overall. 1st Lieutenant Pete Pompetti, flying *Darkie*, became an ace when he destroyed a Bf 109 in the Coesfeld area and he also damaged a Fw 190 at the same time. En route home James Wilkinson scored the Duxford Outfit's first locomotive victory when he destroyed one near Dorsten. Manny Martinez downed a Bf 109, which wheels down, was approaching an airfield. The exploding Messerschmitt drenched Martinez's P-47 in oil and when it cleared he spotted an airfield with Bf 110s on it. He strafed the airfield and claimed the Group's first ground victory of the war.

2nd Lieutenant Richard Dick Hewitt, who now flew his first mission of the war, recalls:

The target on 5 January was the sub pens at Bordeaux, which had been the target on 31 December 1943. When the sub pens at Bordeaux appeared again, as our mission on 5 January, it told us that the bombers had either not gotten desired results or they were going back to hopefully catch the subs in for refuelling and supplies; probably both. This also meant the Jerry fighters would be waiting and ready for us. The Field Orders had come in about 8:00 pm on the 4th. As pilots, all we knew from a Field Order was there would be an early briefing. Details were withheld. The Group and Squadron Ops people, along with Intelligence and Base Weather personnel, were the only ones who knew the target. Preparation started for them in the wee hours of the morning, plotting courses to and from the target, rendezvous time, leave bomber time, start engines, and every other minute detail one could imagine. Setting up the briefing room's large wall maps showing the bombers' courses from enemy lines, diversionary target, alternate target, IP and each fighter groups pick up point and leave bomber point, all in colour-coded lines, was an involved process. Few details were ever missing. The one thing never known for certain was what the weather would be like to and from the target, as well as when we were to land. From our 31 December mission we did know that Bordeaux was close to our maximum endurance time. Any extensive enemy encounter or weather variance could jeopardise our ability to make it back to Duxford.

Our first indication that all was not right came when our bomber rendezvous was late. We were to have made contact with the lead group of B-17s about 45 minutes before target; stay with them for approximately 25 minutes, then head back. Instead, we did not meet the first group until after they had bombed and were on their return. Stragglers with an engine smoking or feathered meant heavy target area flak and/or enemy aircraft had been encountered. Meeting them, as we had, told us we must have had a strong tail wind to make our rendezvous practically at the target area. After a shorter escort time than scheduled, and since there were no enemy aircraft in or around this lead group of '17s, we had little choice but to break off and head north. It was immediately apparent that our head winds at 28,000 feet were far greater than we first thought. (As it turned out, we had encountered a 100-mph wind out of the north. Weather forecasters had missed it completely. It also once again pointed out that the Germans knew exactly where we were and could easily prey on us in any similar circumstance. That one-sided part of the war would haunt us many times in the next year and a half.) Our ground speed was a very slow, less than 150 mph. Our group leader called for us to descend to 15,000 feet, hoping for some improvement. We had leaned our mixtures to the minimum, throttled back for maximum fuel economy, and were chugging along at much reduced power settings. Everyone was concentrating on the immediate problem and forgot about the other possibility: enemy aircraft. Then, 'break left', 'I'm hit', 'bale out' – all in a matter of a few seconds. The Jerries had bounced us from behind and were gone, almost before many of us knew what happened. Some of those hit probably never knew what had hit them. They had attacked from high and out of the sun, no doubt vectored onto us by their ground radar, who had detected our precarious plight; one of the distinct advantages they had over us throughout the war.

As Major Oberhansly our CO, called out a 'break left', we saw the 109s go through and past the 83rd and 84th. Our initial reaction was to go after them. Had we done so, [I] am sure it would have been an even worse disaster for the Group. We had no idea at the time, but Granger, Leach and Putnam and Hartman would be KIAs and Hindersinn a PoW. The 84th and 83rd Squadrons had been hit probably because they were up-sun and a little behind the 82nd – exactly where they were supposed to be, protecting the lower, down-sun squadrons. At our much reduced power they may have even climbed up from our rears and caught us that way. There was no way of ever knowing for certain. In the 'break' action V.Y. Jones and I had become separated from the rest of the squadron. Radio silence was the best mode to assume at the moment so I did not call to see where others may have been. The attack had not only cost us valuable fuel with full throttle during the break but in turning back south for those few minutes, we were now even farther from the coast. I quickly checked 'Jonesy' for his fuel status. He was in a little better shape than I was. All '47s, like cars, did not consume the same. My best guess was I had a little more than an hour with the French coast still a long way off. Any further interruption or diversion meant a sure bale out or ditching before reaching the English coast. My mixture control was now at super lean. The engine had sputtered, as I adjusted it to as low as it could go. Though it seemed like an eternity, the French coastline could not have come any sooner. I had been pondering over taking my chances at heading back inland and baling out, hoping the French underground would be better odds than an ice-cold Channel ditching. We were crossing out near Le Havre and I knew the distance to the English coast from here was a little less than 90 miles. My main fuel tank was down to about two needle widths above the low-level warning light, which meant barely 30 minutes' flying time. Not much to spare but now the worst appeared to be a bale out inside the coast of England, should I not find a close-in base to set down on.

At 6,000 feet the White Cliffs of Dover could not have looked any brighter than here near Brighton, where I guessed we were crossing in. I had flipped on my IFF, a radio signal that identified us as friend and not foe. This hopefully identified us as friendly to any British gunners who could not visually tell a P-47 from a '109 or '190. All we did not need now was some trigger-happy 'limey' ack-ack gunner taking a pot shot at us. What a sight! I had hoped there was a base close in and this one turned out to be British – Tangmere. I flipped to our common radio transmission channel and called for a straight-in, emergency, low fuel approach. 'Pick your own runway, mate,' was the reply that came back. I almost laughed into the mike, as there was only one. I dropped my wheels and flaps and almost simultaneously the red, low fuel, warning light came on. This P-47 razorback Jug was gonna make it even if the engine conked now. No way was I about to miss this landing or risk a go-around. There was plenty of runway. Jonesy followed me in and we taxied to a stop at their mobile tower. Our props had barely stopped turning as their petrol truck was pulling along side; no doubt they were used to refuelling Spitfires and Hurricanes during the diehard days of the Battle of Britain. There was no wasted time on the ground for them but we were not quite in that much of a hurry to get back in the air. It had taken him less than ten minutes to top off our main tanks. Before we knew it, he was done and pulling away. I threw him a quick salute and he called back, 'Good luck, Yank.' Little did I realise that this would be one of the easiest of my low fuel returns.

We arrived back at Duxford after a brief episode with London's numerous barrage balloons. These were anchored in place with large steel cables, designed to cut the wings off or chew up the prop of any low flying German aircraft. Their tops were around 5,000–6,000 feet and on a cloudless day pretty easy to spot. Our intelligence had warned us to stay away from London at any altitude, much less under 6,000 feet. What a sad way that would have been to end any mission. One such encounter with those 'babies' was all it took to make that point. In our mission debriefing, our intelligence told us several 83rd pilots were yet to report in. It was then that I learned that Johnny Granger, my roomie, was one of them. All the 82nd had made it okay. As darkness settled in, it became apparent that our Group's losses of five pilots would be the heaviest of any single day thus far.[2]

I slept very little that night. Granger's loss was almost like losing my brother Harold, who had died very suddenly, after less than a 36-hour illness, when he was thirteen years old. There was a slim chance Johnny might have baled out but reports from other 83rd pilots were that he was one of three seen going down in flames and no apparent chute. I kept my hopes up for several days. The chance he was a PoW or with the French underground faded. The reality of his not coming back came after about three weeks when the personnel officer came around for his personal effects. Going through his belongings and deciding what should and should not be sent home brought tears. I knew Granger was one heck of a pilot and I would sorely miss him. Ken Hindersinn had also trained and gone over with us. He was now a PoW but a far better fate than Granger's was. Since Johnny was a Phillip Morris salesman, he had several cartons of cigarettes stowed in his footlocker. The Supply Officer did not want to send these back to his home in Virginia so suggested I just keep them. Well that was a bum decision on my part as it got me started smoking. Phillip Morris were not the best tasting 'fags' and probably fortunate for me as I never really became an addict. I eventually gave most of them to the guys on the flight line who were big smokers. With rations of only three to four packs a week, they were thrilled to get them.

My first 15 missions were certainly not my most memorable. Everything from bomber aborts, due to inclement weather over the target area, to zero sightings of enemy aircraft. Not that the Jerries were not coming up to intercept the big friends, just that it did not occur on our 'leg' of the escort. Other fighter groups, at this time, were having better luck, I'd call it, than the 78th. The two or three Groups located further east had a greater mission range by almost 100 miles. This allowed them to reach further into the Reich or to stay with the bombers for longer periods, an advantage we did not have.

Ernie Russell's next escort mission was to the major ball-bearing plants in Regensburg.

It was to be one of those that the 8th Air Force bigwigs probably would have rather brushed under the carpet. We had been warned that a mission was scheduled, and, just after daybreak on the drizzly morning of 11 January I awakened to the distant throbbing of hundreds of four-engined bombers forming up for a mission. We, the 'Indians', still didn't know the destination. I rolled out of bed and began to dress for a long cold mission. It was not a pleasant morning. Low clouds scudded across the field and there was an occasional flurry of mist and drizzle. Instead of improving, the weather seemed to promise worse. At briefing the Intelligence Officer pulled away the sheet covering the mission map. The bomber route laid out in coloured cord stretched out over the North Sea to Holland and into central Germany, a feint, where it turned to the south-east into the heart of Germany, Regensburg, far beyond our range in view of our 108-gallon belly tanks. The red cord stretched from Duxford to the point in Germany where it joined the bomber line and followed the route of the bomber penetration for about a hundred miles. Then, abruptly, on the head of a pin that was short of the target, it headed straight back to Duxford. Obviously, we couldn't escort the bombers all the way to the target, only the 'Spam cans' and P-38s could do that. Even so, our mission was a deep-penetration into

Germany. The Intelligence Officer told us where we could anticipate flak and that we could be expecting the Luftwaffe to go after the bombers in force, once they figured out that Regensburg was the target. The weatherman had few encouraging words as he described the predicted bad weather all the way into Germany. How right he was. Colonel Stone told us which boxes of bombers we were to be escorting and assigned squadrons to high or low cover, order of take-off, and then told us start engine time; take-off time, rendezvous time, magnetic heading out and back and call signs. The weather was just as lousy when we headed back to the ready room to suit up.

On the dot, the Group Lead gave his signal and the show began. Joining up in good weather is hazardous enough, but for forty-eight loaded fighters, crossing over near the ground can be downright hairy but we all made it. Having some idea of what was ahead, I snuggled up to my Flight Leader. We were loaded to the gills with fuel and ammunition so we climbed slowly at three to 400 feet per minute with minimum power settings at about 180 mph IAS for the most economic fuel consumption. At these settings it took a long time to get to 28,000 feet. Our airspeed of about three miles per minute put us over the North Sea in about twenty minutes and near the Belgian Coast in about forty minutes. Sure enough, at about forty-five minutes into the mission we were caught in a flood of flak. Greasy black puffs blossomed in the clouds next to us – the Jerries' coastal flak batteries. None of the bursts were near enough to hear or to rock our 'boats' but the uncertainty of where the next burst would be had a tendency to raise one's anxiety level. We were at 15–17,000 feet, well within range of the flak batteries for longer than I wanted to be. Luckily, they only fired one barrage that I saw. My Flight Leader dropped his belly tank, and, then, my fuel pressure gauge needle began to fluctuate; 'fuel starvation' my belly tank was empty. We knew why the Jerries stayed out of our range, and we knew what would solve the problem – bigger belly tanks. We weren't getting our share of the big new 207-gallon steel tanks. We were getting the 108-gallon tanks. Ninety-nine gallons is nearly an hour more, 150 miles further inland. The big tanks were in short supply and we were inland from the coast. It made sense to give Groups like the 56th whose turn around point on escort missions was further inland priority on the larger tanks, as they could escort the bombers further than we could. I reached down automatically and switched my fuel selector lever from belly tank to auxiliary fuel tank; my engine didn't even cough. Next, I got rid of my belly tank. I could feel the click when the tank shackle released. 'Tanks away!'

We continued to climb slowly and tediously into Germany and, finally, after what seemed forever, my flight broke out into valleys between cloud tops. We were in a large open space in the frontal system; not a contrail was in sight, except for ours. I began to see sun glisten off canopies as flight after flight of the Jugs started 'popping-up' out of clouds in all directions. We were all alone – no bombers, no Jerries, and, except for us, just empty space! The Group joined up quickly and Colonel Stone had a decision to make. Either we could continue on to our rendezvous with the Big Friends, or abort. In fact, there was little choice. We were near the limit of our range with almost no chance to meet the bombers in the overcast, so it had to be abort. Reluctantly, we turned and headed for home; it was the only time in my combat tour that the Group was unable to rendezvous with the bombers as planned. We headed home and popped right back into the same overcast we had popped out of and onto instruments, again. But, a few minutes later we flew into bright sunlight and passed over the clouds we had just climbed up through, on instruments. The trip back and landing at Duxford was uneventful, but back in the Ready Room we heard that we were not the only Group to abort. None of the other Jugs and only one of the Spam Can groups were able to rendezvous with the bombers, so the Jerries had a field day until they arrived. Without fighter escort the bombers were at the mercy of the German fighters, who took full advantage of the situation. The 'grape vine' was that VIIIth Bomber Command had had an opportunity to recall the mission early due to the weather, but had declined to do so. It was our feeling that heads should have rolled but that did not happen. Instead the 'grape vine' was that some of the generals received Silver Stars. It looked like a cover-up to us. It was a tragedy.[3]

After Regensburg the poor weather continued unabated with intense cold and solid overcasts. Fighter pilots seldom saw any evidence that Europe existed, only clouds. Once they got above the overcast, they were looking at a dazzling blue sky over a glaring white cloud deck. One day Ernie Russell forgot to wear his sunglasses and 'burned' his eyes so badly that he spent the night in agony. He flew four more escort missions in January, to Lille, to Frankfurt, and to German airfields in Holland twice. On 24 January 857 bomber crews were intending to attack aviation industry plants and marshalling yards at Frankfurt but bad weather during forming up played havoc with assembly procedures. Dick Hewitt recalled:

It was the typical early morning briefing, with the bombers scheduled to strike a heavily used German fighter airfield on the outskirts of St Vith. Weather was forecast to clear sufficiently by take-off time to allow us to climb up through a low cloud layer. As we scrambled out through the windows and door of the briefing room, as we usually did to get out in far less time, we could not see halfway across the field. Typical English pea soup fog. Surely the mission would be scrubbed but with the bombers off well ahead of the fog settling in, it meant one thing. The mission was 'on'.

On a corner of the airfield Sergeant Earl Payne watched the 'Big fleets' of bombers taking off for Germany. He saw a B-17 flying near the field, which happened to blow up in mid-air before crashing into the hills beyond.[4] Payne counted six parachutes and they seemed to take a long time to get down. Four landed out of sight but two landed near the roundabout out of Whittlesford. One of the chutes failed to open because it was burned. 'The poor fellow landed on his feet, which were driven clear up to his stomach and burst his lungs. His entrails coming out of either side of his body beneath his armpits.'[5]

Dick Hewitt continues:

Taking off was no big deal, but what if one had to abort and return instantly due to mechanical problems? That's one I hoped I would never encounter. This was never given a second thought as we lined up in our two-flight, eight-abreast, take-off formation. The two flight leaders would go on instruments the second their wheels left the ground. Each element and their wingmen slid into tight formation the instant they were airborne. Really 'no sweat' as we did the same on many subsequent foul weather take-offs. It was just that first time and your quick prayer that you'd not have to abort for any reason. Radio failures, however were fairly common and this mission would turn out to be fatal for two of the 82nd pilots for this very reason.

Weather in the St Vith area was cloud layered, as it was on many missions. This would sometimes keep the German fighters on the ground but meant that flak would be thick enough to walk on. Needless to say the bombers got this on almost every mission but it was unusual for us to be faced with this, especially when you were in and out of the layered clouds on most of the mission. Our evasive action to the flak and cloud conditions resulted in the group and squadron getting pretty well split up.[6]

1st Lieutenants Cliff Hahn and Willie Neel, unknown to anyone at the time, became separated from the Squadron. Both, it turned out, were experiencing radio malfunctions. They were transmitting brokenly but apparently not receiving. British radar subsequently picked them up off the coast of Dieppe, headed on a course that would take them out the Channel, toward the Atlantic Ocean. Their visual or spotty contact with the water below had apparently led them to think they were further north, over the North Sea, and would hit the English coast on a westerly heading. Both presumably ran out of fuel and either ditched or parachuted into the sea.[7]

On 25 January the Duxford Outfit was briefed for its first fighter-bomber mission and took off to hit an airfield in France, but weather caused the planes to bring their bombs back. Four days later the Group provided penetration support for the bombers and north-east of Koblenz. Three Fw 190s that were attacking the heavies were claimed destroyed. When the P-47s were finally forced to withdraw they were bounced by up to twenty Fw 190s and Bf 109s, which hit two of the

Thunderbolts and 2nd Lieutenant Milton H Ramsey was forced to bale out and he became an evader. A second Thunderbolt struggled back to England where 1st Lieutenant Claude B Godard, who was wounded by 20-mm shell fragments in the knee, put down safely at Bottisham. On 30 January 1st Lieutenant Quince Brown in *Okie* downed a Bf 109 near Rheine for his fifth victory. Next day the Group flew its first dive-bombing mission when eighty-seven P-47s including those led by Major Jack Oberhansly and forty-seven P-38s dropped 500-pounders on Gilze-Rijen airfield in Holland. More fighters up above provided top cover. They encountered eighty-four enemy fighters and in a fierce battle six P-38s were lost. The US fighters claimed thirteen enemy fighters destroyed.

All in all January was a slow month but the tempo began to pick up and in February the war got 'hotter'. On 4 January 433 bombers in fifteen combat wings of B-17s and B-24s were dispatched to Frankfurt on the Main River.[8] The *Luftwaffe* was limited in its operations by the weather though JG 26 claimed seven of the total of ten bombers shot down by the German fighters. During combat with escorting P-47 Thunderbolts of the 352nd and 56th Fighter Groups JG 26 lost one of its pilots and three others were wounded in action. On 5 January 450 B-17s and B-24s attacked airfields at Châteauroux, Avord, Tours, Châteaudun, Orleans and Villacoublay. The bombers were given good fighter-protection and kept the losses down. Next day 206 bombers bombed more airfields in France and rocket-launching installations at Eclimeux, although bad weather prevented more than 400 bombers completing their missions. It was a day of mixed fortunes for the American and German fighter pilots. Two flights made the first organised strafing attacks undertaken by Duxford aircraft when they attacked four airfields at Orleans-Bricy, Beaumont, Chartres and Evreux. The P-47s hit the deck when they were bounced by German fighters and two Fw 190s were claimed destroyed in the air. One of them fell to the guns of 1st Lieutenant James W. Wilkinson. He and Pete Pompetti destroyed two aircraft on the ground and six other aircraft were damaged. Three freight locomotives and a tugboat were also damaged.

Ernie Russell, who flew twelve missions, almost one mission every other day, recalls:

> February was a short but busy month. Practically all of the missions were long and the weather was wretched and extremely cold. I'm sure that the German fighter pilots didn't like the weather any more than we did. Anyway, they knew where we were and they avoided us like the plague. We were lucky when we chanced up on them. But they had to make instrument let downs through the soup many times and then land. That took courage and, to survive, skill. We seldom saw the ground and as a result we often flew unknowingly into barrages of flak, which was now being radar controlled. Frequently the first burst would be highly accurate and right up among us. What made it so disturbing was that this happened when we weren't with the bombers and when we were least expecting to be 'painted'.

We felt that if the crews saw us first they weren't nearly so deadly as they would resort to their judgement and tend to fudge on the radar.[9]

Dick Hewitt recalls:

Targets in the Ruhr Valley, the heartland of Germany's major steel manufacturing facilities, had been blasted by the heavies, almost around the clock for the better part of a week; the RAF by night and the USAF by day. The belief by the RAF that successful bombing could only be done at night was being dispelled by the Americans thanks to the increased protection of our long-range fighter escort. We were now equipped with 16½ gallon external fuel tanks. The 78th's escort mission for the B-17s to the Brunswick area on 10 February was one of our deepest penetrations of the war. Rendezvous was to be on the bombers' leg, just before the bomb run. Flak would be the heaviest imaginable and 109s and 190s were almost certain to be up in full force. With this increased fuel, our staying time was upped by approximately 30 minutes. It would be one of the first missions wherein the bombers would have fighter escort all the way to the target and return. All that was needed for a textbook mission was a break in the clouds in the target area. We got our wish. It was almost cloudless and the B-17s looked ominous at 28,000 feet. Their contrails were persistent, which made them not only easy for us to spot but for the Jerries as well. The heavy presence of flak told us we were nearing the target area. This also meant that the enemy fighters would not be attacking at that instant. Not that they did not attack before the bomb runs, but this gave them an ideal time to refuel and be back up. Bombers would take their heaviest toll from the flak during the bomb run, then the enemy fighters would show up to continue their attacks. It seldom failed to happen in this sequence and today would be no exception.

The 82nd had just set up an 'essing' pattern, slightly below and off to one side of the bombers. The 83rd and 84th were similarly positioned, one off to the opposite side, slightly higher, and the other squadron well above and on the same course as the '17s. Our zig-zag or essing, as we called it, kept us even with the heavies who had a much slower airspeed than ours. Then the Jerries hit. Their tactic of coming in from high and head-on to the bombers was one of the most difficult to defend against. Diving through and between the tightened bomber formation, firing as they went made it extremely difficult for the '17s' gunners to get off good shots and at the same time not risk hitting one of their own. It was a 'cardinal rule' for a friendly fighter to not follow the enemy fighter through the bomber formations. Anything that penetrated their airspace was fair game. More than one little friend got shot down this way and one could certainly not blame the B-17 gunners.

Our 82nd was low and left and our planned tactic was to dive and pick up the enemy aircraft as they came out below the bombers and before they could queue up for another attack. Our other two higher-up squadrons tried to intercept before they could attack. After a pass or two, and if we had not beat them off they would head for the deck, in trail, hopefully protecting the guys' rear in front of them. The 'fly in their ointment?' The Jug could outdive either the Me 109 or the Fw 190. White Flight leader with Chuck Clark and V.Y. Jones as his wingman, took off after the first two 109s. I was in Yellow Flight on Doug Munson's wing and we tailed after the next pair. It did not take long to close, as I saw Munson getting numerous hits on the 109 in front of him. My instinct to go after the other 109 was soon forgotten. I first saw the tracers go whizzing by, then glancing quickly to the rear, I saw the 20-mm gun flashes from what turned out to be a pursuing 109. Probably seeing he was not gaining he had fired from a little out of range. Damn fortunate for me. I called out 'break' and broke hard left, pulling up into a tight chandelle. Two 109s went by and with almost no effort I had shaken them. Instinct again said, 'go after them', but knowing for sure there were more, I continued in a tight level left turn, checking to see if I had a wingman with me. No one! Swanson and Harold Ludwig who were # 3 and 4 in our flight, had apparently continued after one of the other 109s. Then I heard Jonesy's voice. He sounded frantic as he called for someone to get down here! 'I've got a 109 on my tail and I can't shake him!' The Jug was about an even match for the 109 or 190 at high altitude, with its dive and zoom advantage, but not at lower altitudes and especially at treetop level. At slower speeds, either enemy aircraft could outturn the '47. It was just not a good place to get caught. I called for V.Y. but got no answer. Apparently alone at 15,000 feet, I was not about to go searching blindly. Munson, Clark, Swanson or Ludwig had to be closer than I and perhaps had heard his plea for help. Not sure who the #3 or 4 were in Clark and Jonesy's flight, but they should also be in the area and have heard him.

My job was now one of survival and I started a gradual climb on a 280 degree westerly course, one I knew was close to the heading for home. A lone fighter in enemy territory was a prime target for a sneak attack, one like they had pulled on that Bordeaux raid. Their radar, no doubt, could have me pegged and vectoring one of the 109s in the area onto my butt would be pretty easy. Then I spotted it. A lone P-47, below and slightly to the right of my course; he would have been a dead duck if it had been an enemy aircraft. I made a quick call and identified myself as 'a friend coming up on your tail, slightly higher and to your left'. He had no idea I was there. By his squadron letters, MX and white nose cowling I knew it was 82nd. He turned out to be Swanson's wingman, 2nd Lieutenant Harold Ludwig, in MX-H. He acknowledged and I could tell he was elated. It was only his second or third mission as I recall. We climbed back up and levelled off at 20,000 feet. I told him to put his 'little old neck' on a continuous swivel. If attacked at this altitude, we had ample fuel to stay and fight or dive for the deck and make a run for it. We also had the Jug's 'ace in the hole': water injection. I had tried it twice on a test flight. A mixture of water and alcohol was injected directly into the cylinders, giving a cooling effect that boosted the Jug's speed by about 15%. It had an effect similar to the afterburner on a jet fighter of the post-war era. Its only drawback, if you could call it that, was it had a duration of only about 15 minutes, but it provided a quick 'fix' if you had to make a run for it.

Not sure at that time where my flight leader, Doug Munson, had ended up. Probably too intent on the Me 109 or maybe my 'break' call was not heard. Our flying time back to the Dutch coast and the Walcheren Island area had to be close to an hour. As soon as I got some kind of a coastline identity, I'd refigure our course heading home. Then I saw the lone bogey, slightly lower and off to my right. Could be another 82nd Jug but why was his heading not close to the one we were on? 'Better check him out,' I thought, so I called Ludwig to follow me, boosted my power, and headed in his direction. We closed fast and immediately saw that it looked like a P-47 but so did a Fw 190, at least from my angle. It took less than a few seconds and I was certain it was not friendly. No elliptical wing like the Jug and for sure no white-collared nose. I was several hundred yards back and still slightly above when I saw the swastika. Now dead astern and so excited, I almost forgot to flip on my gun switch. Yardage looked a lot closer but I was at least 300 or so back when I squeezed off a quick burst. Pieces flew off the tail and right wing tip, with a few hits on the fuselage near the cockpit area. Then off came the canopy and what had to be the pilot baling out. My first kill. I had an eyewitness and, hopefully good film, both a 'requirement for a 'kill' in the 78th. I made a quick orbit and there he was, oscillating in his parachute, probably a thousand feet below me. That's one for Granger, I thought, but even a dozen would not have made up for his loss. The same way they had snuck up on him; only difference was this Hun would be back up again. Johnny was dead. Wished I'd closed to about a 100 yards and perhaps he'd have met a similar fate. Sounds gruesome but war made you feel that way. I glanced in my mirror and saw Ludwig. 'Close it up,' I called and he pulled alongside. 'Long way home, spread out and keep your eyes open.'

Now to find some landmark. We should be getting close to the Zuider Zee so decided to drop down a bit and at the same time pick up a little more ground speed. The clouds were more broken now so we levelled off just above their tops at about 8,500 feet. Not a good spot to be caught at, normally, but now we could use them to our advantage, if necessary. The Zuider Zee came into view and we appeared to be hitting it, close to dead centre. 'Where the hell did that come from?' I thought, as several bursts of 40-mm flak appeared just in front of us. I racked it hard right, turning away from Ludwig knowing he'd follow me. Up on one wing I hooked down and saw that damned flak boat, always parked about in the middle of the Zuider Zee, to take pot shots at anyone who got close enough. 'Follow me,' I called to Ludwig and headed back east. We'd drop down and give them a little of their own medicine. They were about to find out what eight .50-calibres on the front end of two Jugs looked like. At about three miles out we did a 180 and headed back west on the treetops, a tactic we often used to surprise-attack any ground target we knew would shoot back.

We crossed the coastline and were chewing the wave tops as we lined up on the flak boat. Ludwig was to my left and out a couple hundred feet. A quick burst showed I was hitting low At 350+ mph, the Jug was a bit 'tail high' so I pulled the gun sight up a hair and squeezed off a good five-second burst, walking the rudders slightly to spray the superstructure from the centre to the right end. I saw Harold's results and he too had blasted them, but good. Staying on the wave tops, as we exited their range, I felt they could not fire much below horizontal. And, at our speed we were out of range in no more than a few seconds. Those gunners were also probably in a state of shock after ducking from those sixteen .50-calibre armour-piercing incendiaries rattling off their superstructure. In either case, they did not fire another shot. A quick glance back showed some smoldering and even though we did not sink it, I'm certain we had inflicted sufficient damage to require a lengthy 'port of call' for repairs.

Now to get for the Dutch coast and home. We had one more potential obstacle and that was the sandbagged gun emplacements, spaced intermittently along and on top of the coastal dike. We'd stay 'glued' to the deck, for sure. Knowing we'd be there in a few minutes, I again called Harold to get lower as I noted he was at least 20–30 feet higher than I was. Dead ahead I spotted one of the gun emplacements. As we skimmed across it, I saw the gunners scrambling to man their guns. 'Get down,' I again called to Ludwig. His depth perception may have told him he was lower but I was literally chewing the North Sea wave tops. As he pulled abreast, I noticed it. A streak of black, probably oil or hydraulic fluid, coming from the underside of his plane. He said nothing but almost immediately started to fall behind me. No radio call or any indication he had been hit. Again I called to see if he was OK as he now was visible, only in my rear view mirror, gradually falling way back. No response, so I made a quick 180 to check him out. I could not believe what I saw. His prop was dead still. 'My God, he's ditching!' I knew the P-47 with about a zero tolerance for a successful ditching, would sink like a tank. With the high, white-capped waves, he must have gone under immediately on impact. I looked frantically for his yellow Mae West or dinghy. Either should have been visible, even in the choppy seas. Nothing, so I quickly flipped to our Air/Sea Rescue B-channel. 'Mayday-Mayday-Mayday.'

We had to be no more than five miles off the Dutch coast. I started a spiralling climb, trying to stay immediately overhead and hopefully get a 'fix on his ditch' for Air/Sea Rescue. The cloud cover was now solid at about 2,000 feet. On instruments, I climbed on up to around 8,000 feet, repeating my Mayday. Even a German ASR would have been OK. Any hope from ours, this far away I knew was a long longshot. I kept calling in hopes someone would hear me. Only dead silence. My fuel now became my second major concern. I had no more than 45 minutes left with over 100 miles to reach the English coast. I turned to 270 degrees and started a descent to get under the clouds, or at least I hoped to. What if the ceiling had dropped down to the wave tops? I'd level off regardless at 2,000 feet and fly instruments if necessary. I made several more Mayday calls, but not one response from ASR. I was just too far from the English coast for my radio to transmit. I said a quick prayer that somehow Harold would survive, but I knew deep down inside, that his chances were very slim. There was nothing more I could do, or could have done. His fate was now in God's hands.

At about 2,000 feet, through the breaks in the clouds, I could see the white caps below. I was half on instruments and half Visual Flight Rules (VFR) as my altimeter could easily have been off. Changes in barometric pressure and the resultant altimeter error has killed many a trusting pilot by running into the ground. I also had one eye glued on my gas gauge. It could not be far now and I was sure to hit the coast somewhere close to Felixstowe. My IFF was on. I knew I was below the preferred minimum crossing in elevation and trusting those 'Limey' shore gunners' recognition was never a sure bet. Not that they would intentionally try to hit you, but it was more of a harassment to tell you they could if they really wanted to. And, that you should be above 8,000 feet. As I concentrated on my instruments, the shoreline almost flashed by without my realising it. No 'pot shots' today. I needed some good luck, as so far it had all been bad. The gunners could have all been out to tea. It was close to that hour for most British. Now for a close-in base. A lot of bomber bases were in the area. I no sooner had the thought than a B-17 loomed in front of me. I saw immediately that he was on three engines; his right inboard was feathered. There were two other bombers behind that first Flying Fortress. Then their runway appeared dead ahead and was it ever a beautiful sight. On 'Charlie' channel I called for landing instructions. Their tower said, 'You are #4 in the pattern and it will be at least 15 minutes. One of the three has wounded on board, and one other also is shot up and has an engine out,' they advised. My plea that I was getting low on gas went to deaf ears as they said only 'You're #4, little friend.' My low-fuel red warning light had still not come on but had to be darned close. 'There's a fighter base dead west about eight minutes,' the tower came back.

'Roger, thanks, I'm outta here,' I responded.

They pegged it perfectly. I wasn't sure of the base identity but it had P-51s dispersed and looked beautiful to me. My call was responded to PDQ. This time I told them my fuel was critical with no more than a few minutes. I fibbed a little but as I did my final turn, that 'glowing red' fuel light came on again. My second low fuel encounter in less than two weeks. I hoped it would be my last. Probably wishful thinking – time alone would tell. My mood was sombre as I waited for the fuel truck. They weren't as speedy as the RAF but then I was in no hurry. I called the tower to see if they had any way to check Air/Sea Rescue. Nothing they said. My thoughts were 100 miles east in that frigid North Sea. If Ludwig survived, it would have to be a miracle. Then I remembered Jonesy. With Ludwig's plight, I had almost forgotten him his plea to 'get that '109 off my tail'. I'd never forget. He, Paul Keller Grant Turley[10] and I had 'roomied' since Granger's loss. Was I gonna lose another roommate? And how many other 78th pilots would be lost today?[11]

Jonesy's loss hit Ernie Russell, his Mississippi friend, with whom he had gone through flight school, especially hard.

It would have been V.Y.'s fifth victory over Fw 190s. I was told that he turned the wrong way with the Focke-Wulf and lost. There was one direction you didn't turn with a Focke-Wulf if you could help it because their four cannon were deadly. V.Y. was one of the finest and nicest, most unassuming of friends. His loss saddened all of us. We knew that the game we were playing was for 'keeps' and some had to lose, which was sobering if you dwelled on it, but we didn't. Perhaps the fact that you didn't see your friends' bodies, as did ground troops and bomber crews, cushioned the shock. Maybe it was because of our youth, or maybe it was because their death was so removed. Death happened miles away, high in the air during the rush of combat; perhaps that is what made it seem so impersonal. The only visible sign was the empty chair in the Ready Room next day, or in the mess or bar that night. The missions went on, so the sadness passed quickly. We weren't callous, we just weren't next to death. Most of the time it was not where we could see it. You can't get up and fly the next mission if you allow yourself to dwell on the loss of a friend for long. If youth is one thing it is resilient.[12]

On Friday 11 February when the first P-51s joined VIIIth Fighter Command, the B-17s attacked industrial targets at Frankfurt-Main and a V-weapon site at St Pol-Siracourt again while 130 heavies bombed Ludwigshafen and other targets of opportunity and targets in the Pas de Calais. The heavies were protected by fifteen groups of escorting fighters and they helped keep bomber losses to five. Duxford's Thunderbolts flew withdrawal support for the Fortresses returning from Frankfurt, as Grant M Turley, the gangly young cowboy from Arizona, recalled.

> We escorted them out from North Central France. Just after rendezvousing with the bombers we ran into about 20 Me 109s. I was No. 3 in Lieutenant John J Hockery's flight when we went into the middle of them. My wingman lost me (a bad habit my wingmen have had lately) but I bounced a 109, followed him through a cloud and got in a good burst. Saw strikes all over the cockpit and wing roots and a lot of smoke. He went straight down out of control. I am sure that the pilot was dead. I pulled back up through a cloud layer and went around and around with another one. This Jerry had one yellow stripe on his fuselage indicating that he was a squadron leader. He was plenty good. I only got a couple of 90° deflection shots at him. Came home on the deck. Shot down a Focke-Wulf 190 that was taking off. The flak and tracers were really buzzing around. I got lost and was sweating out my gas when I found that I had flown way out over the Brest Peninsula. I didn't know where I was until they started shooting flak at me over the Channel Islands. I really prayed to God coming across the water. I was at 2,500 feet. They shot flak all around me. I could hear it go 'whump' about ten different times. That's getting pretty close. I really kissed the ground at Warmwell, the base I landed at. I had only 17 and a half gallons of gas left. The weather was bad and my radio was dead but I started on to Duxford. I was forced down by the weather at Chettingford. Spent a bad night under wool blankets in a Quonset hut. It was rough and cold.[13]

On 13 February the Chiefs of Staff accepted a revision of the CBO Plan when targets were reduced to a number that could be decisively attacked and target lists were revised to keep up with the effort of the enemy to relocate vital industrial plants. Disruption of lines of communication and a reduction of the *Luftwaffe* fighter strength were now given high priority.[14] Early in 1944 the *Luftwaffe* was still a force to be reckoned with, especially when one considers its day fighter *Geschwaders* of conventional fighters could and did, shoot down dozens of B-17s and B-24s on a single mission. Operation *Argument* was the first battle involving the mass use of bomb groups of the US Strategic Air Forces (USSTAF). General Carl 'Tooey' Spaatz and his subordinate commanders, Major General Jimmy Doolittle (8th Air Force) and Major General Nathan F Twining (15th Air Force), planned to make a series of co-ordinated raids on the German aircraft industry, supported by RAF night bombing, at the earliest possible date. Good weather finally permitted Operation *Argument* to take place during the week 20–25 February, which quickly became known as 'Big Week'. On Sunday 20 February 1,028 B-17s and B-24s and 832 fighters were assembled to attack twelve aircraft plants in Germany as the anticipated cloud scudded across eastern England, bringing with it snow squalls that threatened to disrupt the mission. The 1st and 2nd Divisions hit the Messerschmitt plants at Leipzig, bombed only a few hours earlier by RAF Bomber Command, and the 3rd Division flew an equally long and arduous route to Posen in Poland. Meeting a formation of B-17s the 78th Fighter Group claimed three victories, one of which was credited to Grant Turley, his fifth victory, which made him an ace. There was no let-up in the campaign against the German aircraft industry and the next day, 21 February, 924 bombers and 679 fighters fought their way through dense contrails and biting cold to their targets at Diepholz, Brunswick, Hanover and Achmer.

On 22 February the elements were responsible for bomber collisions during assembly and the 3rd Division was forced to abandon the mission completely. Overcast hampered the 2nd Bomb Division assembly over East Anglia and eventually conditions became so bad that the Division had to be recalled while flying a scattered formation over the Low Countries. The 78th Fighter Group nevertheless completed their rendezvous with the bombers near Cologne where they helped the 4th Fighter Group in beating off attacks by upwards of forty enemy fighters in fighting from 22,000 feet down to the deck. 2nd Lieutenant John H Johnson was shot down flying *El Jeepo*, made famous by Charles London, and he baled out to be taken prisoner. Both sides made several victory claims. Lieutenant 'Max' Juchheim celebrated reaching twenty-two years of age by destroying a Bf 109 and damaging a Fw 190. *Oberfeldwebel* Adolf 'Addi' Glunz, commanding 5./JG 26, claimed a P-47 of the 78th Fighter Group shot down fifteen kilometres north-west of Geilenkirchen. He also put in claims for two B-17s destroyed and two more shot out of formation.[15] *Feldwebel* Peter Crump of the 6th *Staffel*, JG 26, managed to outrun his pursuers in the 335th Squadron, 4th Fighter Group, and they were forced to break off the attack. Three of the 83rd Squadron pilots took up the chase. Crump decided that his best means of escape was to out-climb the P-47s, which were heavier than his Fw 190A-7, but it allowed two of the Thunderbolts to close the range and the three aircraft entered a Lufbery circle.[16] The third P-47, which was flown by 1st Lieutenant William M 'Mac' McDermott, arrived above the circle seconds later and cut across it, firing a high-deflection burst of machine-gun fire, which hit the Focke-Wulf in the canopy and wing roots. Crump got rid of his canopy, drew up his legs and climbed out. He was at 700 feet so pulled his ripcord immediately. After one swing he hit the frozen ground hard. His only injuries were damaged ligaments in one knee.[17] It was McDermott's first victory.

On 23 February bad weather kept the 8th Air Force heavies on the ground but 102 bombers in the 15th Air Force destroyed twenty per cent of the ball-bearing works at Steyr, Austria. Next day 238 Fortresses attacked Schweinfurt, losing eleven B-17s, while 295 B-17s struck at targets on the Baltic coast with the loss of five Fortresses. The target for eight Liberator Groups was the Messerschmitt 110 aircraft works at Gotha, 420 miles due east of the White Cliffs of Dover.[18] Twenty miles off Dummer Lake, at Furstenau, the 78th Fighter Group bounced twenty to twenty-five enemy aircraft making head-on passes from above the bombers and chased them down to the deck. Near Dummer Lake, 1st Lieutenant Grant M Turley saw a 359th Fighter Group P-47 600 yards above a Bf 109 firing at it but not getting any closer or getting any hits on it. As the P-47 finished firing, Turley closed to 150 yards and lit up the Bf 109's wing, canopy and engine with hits. Pouring smoke, the Bf 109 rolled over and the pilot baled out. It was the Arizona cowboy's sixth victory. 'Max' Juchheim took his score to three in two days when he followed two Bf 109s to the deck, hitting one steadily with a pair of two-second bursts at 200 yards. The Bf 109's canopy came off and the fighter crashed in a field. Pulling up on the second one, Juchheim chased him over a little town where he streamed black smoke and rolling inverted, crashed in a small wood. Lieutenant Robert E Wise closed up astern of a Fw 190 to fifty yards and exploded him with fuselage hits. Lieutenant Charles M Peal, who was from Nashville, Tennessee, and was piloting *Miss Norma II*, hit another fighter in the fuselage and wing roots. His victim flattened out on the treetops with his prop windmilling and crashed and disintegrated into the ground.[19] 1st Lieutenant Walter Tonkin fired a long burst at a Fw 190 at fifty feet and the fighter, flashed, smoked and hit the ground in flames. Tonkin's wingman, 1st Lieutenant Randal B Hathaway, saw three P-47s chasing a Bf 109G around a church steeple and he joined in the chase. Closing to 10° deflection, fifty feet off the ground, Hathaway got heavy strikes in the Bf 109's fuselage and wing roots, causing the fighter to hit hedges along the street and blow up into flames as it hit the ground.[20]

Cloudbanks over the Continent brought a premature end to 'Big Week' and enabled higher command time to weigh up the results and implications of their actions over the past five days. Total losses were 226 bombers. Some 6,000 tons of bombs had been dropped, depriving *Luftwaffe Gruppen* of many replacement aircraft and halving fighter production the following month but the small size high-explosive destroyed only the factories, leaving machine tools, lathes and jigs virtually untouched beneath the wreckage. It was only a matter of time before this equipment was recovered from the wrecked plants and put into full production again. However, Doolittle and his staff officers believed the 8th had dealt the German aircraft industry a severe blow. He and his staff officers now felt confident to strike at Berlin, the biggest prize in the Third *Reich*.

After a few false starts caused by bad weather, on Monday 6 March 730 B-17s and B-24s and 801 P-38, P-47 and P-51 escort fighters were despatched to targets in the suburbs of 'Big-B'. Crews were well aware that the defences in and around the German capital had now been fully alerted and a rough reception could be expected. The column of bombers stretched for sixty miles and attracted so many *Luftwaffe* fighters that one bomber pilot who surveyed the scene said he saw what 'appeared to be a swarm of bees – actually German fighters. Guesses ran to as much as 200'. The first American air raid on Berlin certainly flushed out the *Luftwaffe*, just as Doolittle had hoped it would. The Fortress gunners and the fighter pilots claimed over 170 German fighters destroyed[21] but the Americans had suffered record losses of sixty-nine bombers and 347 damaged.

(*Left*) Major Eugene Roberts, 84th FS CO indicating the two kills that made him an ace on 24.8.43. On 30.7.43 Roberts scored the first 'hat trick' of 'kills' to become the first US pilot to notch a triple victory in Europe. (*via Andy Height*)

(*Right*) 1st Lt William S. Swanson of the 82nd FS, pilot of P-47D-6-RE 42-74733. Swanson was KIA flying this aircraft on 11.2.44. (*USAF*)

Captain Ben I. Mayo, acting 82nd FS CO in the cockpit of P-47D 42-26671 *No Guts – No Glory!* (*USAF*)

P-47Cs of the 82nd FS at Bassingbourn in late 1944. Below the cockpit of P-47D 42-27339 (the first fighter to shoot down a jet) are eight victory swastikas denoting kills by Major (later Brig Gen) Joe E. Myers. Behind is 42-26387 *Miss Behave*. (*USAF*)

Lt (later Lt Col) Richard 'Dick' Hewitt (24), a New Yorker from Lewiston, who on 20.3.44 became 82nd FS CO. (*Hewitt*)

P-47D of the 78th FG at Duxford. (*Russell*)

1st Lt William DeGain in his P-51D 44-63632 *LEE D* with armourer Cpl Nick Vale on wing. (*USAF*)

Richard 'Dick' Hewitt aloft in P-47MX-E 42-26635. (*Hewitt*)

Duxford on 6.7.44 following the crash of B-17 *Ready Freddie,* which crashed upside down in the 83rd Barracks area killing all thirteen men on board. (*USAF*)

1st Lt Quince Brown (kneeling, second from left) on 16.3.44 just after had shot down two Fw 190s and a Bf 109 near St Dizier and destroyed a Bf 110 and a Ju 88 on the ground. The other 84th FS pilots in front of *Okie* are (from left): Harold Stump (KIA 10.6.44); Captain George J. Hays; 1st Lt Ernie Russell; 1st Lt Ernest 'Ernie' Lang. Kneeling (l–r): Captain Gray H. Doyle; Brown and Captains Edward R. Fleming and Dorian Ledington (KIA 21.4.45). (*USAF*)

P-47C-5R-RE 41-6330 *Spokane Chief* flown by Major Gene Roberts. All except two of his nine victories were achieved flying the *Chief*. In 1945 Roberts flew a second tour as commander of the 364th FG, which was equipped with P-51Ds. (*USAF*)

Major Quince L. Brown a 'not-to-be-denied Okie' from Hydrock, Oklahoma, who scored his 12th victory on 1.9.44 on his 135th combat sortie. On 6.9.44 Brown's P-47 was hit by flak. He baled out 2km west of Schleiden only to be apprehended by an SS officer who murdered him in cold blood with a pistol shot to the back of his head. (*USAF*)

1st Lt (later Lt Col) Ernest E. Russell just prior to his first combat mission in late September 1943. The 'mustache' is mostly dark mustache wax because after three weeks growth Ernie still did not have a visible 'mustache'! (*Russell*)

Colonel Frederic C. Gray, 78th FG CO 22.5.43–1.2.45. (*USAF*)

Twenty-year old 2nd Lt Lawrence 'Larry' W. Nelson from Warren, Ohio in his P-51D *Heavenly Body*. (*USAF*)

P-47D HL-G *The Spirit of Sycamore Hill Oyster Bay Long Island* flown by Lt Harry C. Ruff, 83rd FS, near one of the WWI hangars at Duxford. (*via Andy Height*)

Colonel Fred Gray presents the 78th FG's 400 victory silver beer mug to Captain J. Patrick Maxwell as 82nd FS pilots look on. Third from right is Dick Hewitt. (*USAF*)

Captain Alwin 'Max' Juchheim's P-47D HL-J 42-26020 *Lady Jane* with two 108-gallon tanks. Distinctive black-and-white chequerboard squares were first applied to the engine cowling shutters of the 78th FG P-47s in April 1944. (*via Andy Height*)

78th FG Thunderbolts taking off at Duxford. (*via Andy Height*)

Duxford was grass rather than concrete so the 78th FG took off eight abreast instead of two and they lined up in rows of eight – a total of forty-eight Thunderbolts. (*via Andy Height*)

P-47 42-25871 *Nigger II* flown by Captain Richard M. Holly, 84th FS CO. The Thunderbolt was named after Holly's always-suntanned wife. (*via Andy Height*)

P-47 WZ-G 42-74694 *Joker* with 100+ mission symbols and armed with 5-inch rocket tubes. (*via Andy Height*)

Colonel Arman 'Pete' Peterson came from Flagstaff, Arizona and he called his P-47 "*Flagari*" so that people would not forget the old home town. Peterson was shot down in combat with 1./JG 1 over Holland on 1.7.43 and baled out but his parachute was torn and he was killed landing near Rotterdam. Morale sagged and 'for some days few smiles were seen'.

1st Lieutenant (later Captain) Huie Lamb who survived 40 minutes in the North Sea on 29/12.44. (*via Andy Height*)

P-47 42-74742/O being overhauled at Duxford. (*USAF*)

Duxford flight line and control tower (with B-17 nose bubble atop) in 1944. (*USAF*)

At Bottisham on 31.8.44. 20th FG P-5ID *Gentle Annie,* 352nd FG *Straw Boss 2*; 56th FG P-47D *Hairless Joe*; 55th FG P-51D *Da Quake*; 356th FG P-47 *Judy,* 353rd FG P-47D and 479th FG P-38J. (*USAF*)

78th FG P-47s strafing ground targets on the continent. (*USAF*)

P-51D Mustangs of the 84th FS in one of the WWI hangars at Duxford. (*via Ian McLachlan*)

P-51D *Gruesome Twosome*, one of two unarmed two-seaters at Duxford.

Colonel John Landers, 78th FG CO, 22.2.45-1.7.45. (*USAF*)

P-51Ds of the 78th FG at Duxford on 7 June 1945. *(via Andy Height)*

P-51D 44-72218 *Big Beautiful Doll* flown by Colonel John D. Landers. (*USAF*)

Flight Officer Edward J Downey was killed when Fw 190s attacked him in the Barenburg area. Grant M Turley chased three Fw 190s down to the deck and got on the tail of one before turning into a Lufbery circle with another on his tail. The six-victory ace was seen to hit the Focke-Wulf but by the third turn, the Fw 190 on his tail pulled off a deflection shot on the P-47 and shot the Arizona cowboy down in flames. Turley died in the cockpit of *Kitty/Sundown Ranch*.

1   *A Mississippi Fighter Pilot In WWII* by Ernest E Russell.

2   After rendezvousing with the heavies, who were attacking airfields in western France, at Pougeres, a Section in the 84th Squadron was bounced by about six Bf 109s behind the bombers. Captain 'Swede' Larson and Quince Brown claimed one each although Brown's claim was not upheld. The P-47s outstayed their welcome and soon ran very low on fuel. While they concentrated on eking out their fuel enemy fighters approached in dead astern out of the sun near Nantes and shot down four Thunderbolts. Three Fw 190s bounced another element and raked the P-47s with machine-gun and cannon fire, destroying one of the P-47s and causing another to limp away for home. 1st Lieutenant George T Hartman of the 84th was killed north of La Rochelle. Major C Leach and 1st Lieutenant Melvin D Putnam of the 83rd were killed after probably being jumped in the same area as Hartman. 2nd Lieutenant Kenneth Hinderssin of the 83rd baled out in the same area and was taken prisoner.

3   *A Mississippi Fighter Pilot In WWII* by Ernest E Russell.

4   B-17 42-40009 in the 324th Bomb Squadron, 91st Bomb Group, flown by Lieutenant Marco DeMara.

5   Only fifty-eight bombers completed the mission. The 2nd Bomb Division was recalled before being despatched and at 1020 hours all Groups were recalled due to worsening weather en route. All except the leading combat wing in the 3rd Bomb Division, which were at the German border and decided to select a target of opportunity, turned for home as instructed.

6   In the Malmedy-St Vith, Belgium area. South-west of Brussels the P-47s were bounced by Fw 190s of the IIIrd *Gruppe*, JG 26, who claimed two P-47s shot down. (One was subsequently changed to a 'damaged'.) 1st Lieutenant Robert H Knapp claimed one of the Fw 190s, which was blindly following his wingman, Flight Officer Edward J Downey, but JG 26 suffered no losses and neither did the 78th Fighter Group.

7   'Hahn's body would eventually be found, no details, but Neel's would not be and is today MIA. His name is listed on the wall at the Cambridge Madingley Cemetery – 1st Lieutenant William F. Neel, Americus, Georgia;

his body 'sleeps in an unknown grave'. The names of over 4,000 other US servicemen, all MIAs from the WWII era, are similarly engraved on that marble wall. Their losses, along with Franklin Ressigue's forced bale out due to mechanical difficulties [on 18 October 1943] and John Herrick's having to bale out [on 26 November 1943] due to what was believed to be mechanical, increased the 78th's non-combative losses to four in fewer than thirty days. None were attributed directly to enemy action. Both Ressigue and Herrick would escape with the superlative aid of the Belgium/French undergrounds. They would not, however, return to combat in the ETO, as any subsequent capture by the Germans could have possibly resulted in 'forced' revelation of those in the underground. Firing squads for those patriots involved, if caught, was a certain fate from the SS. Franklin and John both returned to the ZOI for reassignment. Neither were PoWs, as listed in some books. Ressigue's book, *Feathers In The Wind*, attests to his fate. Since Herrick was in the 82nd, I personally knew of his escape and return.'

8   Fifteen fighter groups escorted the bombers. Frankfurt was almost within P-47 range, although target support could only be carried out by the few long-range P-38 Lightning and Mustang groups while eight Spitfire squadrons covered the final stages of the return flight.

9   *A Mississippi Fighter Pilot In WWII* by Ernest E Russell.

10   1st Lieutenant Grant Turley claimed two Bf 109s on 10 February for his first victories. In all, the 82nd and 83rd Squadrons claimed nine.

11   'It would turn out that 2nd Lieutenant Vernon Y Jones would be KIA. Ludwig's name is now also engraved on that marble wall, along with William Neel's, in Madingley Military Cemetery. His "final resting place may be unknown", since his remains were never recovered, but unlike many others who they think may rest at the bottom of the North Sea or English Channel, I know exactly where Harold's remains are located. Probably still strapped in the seat of his P-47 MX-H, less than ten miles off Egmond aan Zee, Netherlands.'

12   *A Mississippi Fighter Pilot In WWII* by Ernest E Russell.

13   Two 78th Fighter Group pilots FTR. 2nd Lieutenant Donald R Morsch and 1st Lieutenant William S Swanson of the 82nd Squadron might have been killed in a mid-air collision. What is certain is that the claims of *Feldwebel* Gerhard Wiegand of 4./JG 26 for two 78th Fighter Group P-47s south of Arras was upheld. JG 26 also claimed four P-38 Lightnings in the 20th Fighter Group, three of which were confirmed. On 29 March 1944 *Fähnenjunker-Feldwebel* Gerhard Wiegand, who had twenty-one victories was awarded the *Deutsche Kreuz im Gol* (DKG or German Cross in Gold).

14   Over 1,000 *Jagdwaffe* fighter pilots, many of them irreplaceable veterans, were lost in the first four months of 1944 and several were victims of P-47 action. On 1 January Horst-Gunther von Fassong (136 victories) was shot down and killed by P-47s. Egon Meyer, the first to score 100 victories entirely in the West, fell to Thunderbolts at Montmedy on 2 March and Kurt Übben (110) fell victim to P-47s on 27 April.

15   The Duxford Group's only loss on this mission was at the Dutch Coast where Fw 190s bounced 2nd Lieutenant John H. Johnson. He was shot down and survived to be taken prisoner.

16   A Lufbery (or 'Luftberry' as it was sometimes known in its corrupted form by American fighter pilots) was named for the WWI American fighter ace Major Gervais Raoul Lufbery of *Escadrille* SPA. 124 – the *Escadrille Lafayette*. The Lufbery Circle was a defensive tactic, in which a group of aircraft flew in a tight circle, making it difficult for enemy aircraft to break into and attack without themselves being attacked. Lufbery, born in France of French parents who later emigrated to America, was third in the roll of American aces with seventeen confirmed victories. When WWI began Lufbery joined the French Foreign Legion and obtained a quick transfer to the *Service Aéronautique*. In December 1914 Lufbery successfully applied for pilot training and he was posted to *Escadrille* VB.106. In May 1916 he was transferred to the *Escadrille Lafayette* and he had scored five victories by early October. His subsequent career brought him promotion and many decorations, including the first award of the British Military Cross to an American. With America's entry into the war Lufbery was transferred, with the rank of major to the US Air Service and he was subsequently given command of the famous 94th Aero Squadron. He was killed on 19 May 1918 while attacking an Albatros two-seater reconnaissance aircraft over the 95th Squadron's base at Tool when his Nieuport 28 burst into flames. Lufbery fell from the burning aircraft at an altitude of 6,000 feet, whether deliberately or accidentally, will never be known.

17   See *The JG 26 War Diary Vol.2* and *Eagles of Duxford: The 78th Fighter Group in World War II*.

18   A ninth, the newly operational 458th, flew a diversionary sweep over the North Sea.

19   Peal was KIA by flak near Noyon on 14 August 1944. He was on his second tour and had flown forty missions. *Eagles of Duxford: The 78th Fighter Group in World War II*.

20   At least four of the Bf 109Gs were from JG 26. *Obergefreiter* Helmut Greim, *Fähnenjunker-Feldwebel* Kurt-Heinz Dylewski, *Führer Burghardt* Wölke and *Oberleutnant* Karl Wunschelmeyer were all KIA.

Wunschelmeyer had earlier destroyed a 92nd or 306th Bomb Group B-17 at Hasselünne. Two other JG 26 Fw 190A-4/6 pilots were shot down by P-47s in the 56th Fighter Group. Unteroffizier Gerhard Mohr was KIA and *Feldwebel* Franz Vanderveerd was WIA. *Hauptmann* Karl Borris, *Staffelkapitän* 1st Gruppe JG 26, claimed a 56th Fighter Group P-47 north of Rheine. See *The JG 26 War Diary Vol.2*.

21   US fighters claimed eighty-one enemy fighters shot down and the bomber gunners claimed ninety-seven destroyed; the *Luftwaffe* actually lost sixty-four fighters destroyed and two damaged beyond repair. This was a loss rate of 12.5% of those committed to action.

CHAPTER NINE

Aces and Strafers

A Me 110 on a taxiway to the right with its engines turning over presented me with a head-on shot. Nose down, I centred my needle and ball, put the glowing dot in my reflector gunsight on the target and waited until I reached less than 400 yards range before squeezing the black Bakelite trigger on the control column. My Jug's wings shuddered from the recoil of a three-second burst – 240 rounds – from the eight Browning machine-guns. I heard their deep muttering over the roar of my engine at full throttle. Almost instantly, the front of the 110 was lit-up by the flashes of armour-piercing incendiary rounds igniting on impact...I fired until I was somewhat less than two hundred yards from him; at which point it seemed judicious to pull up.

Ernest 'Ernie' E Russell[1]

Fighter pilots pitied the poor bomber crews who had to drive straight into and through the flak bursts that sometimes were so numerous they formed peculiar-looking clouds in the sky. On 8 March 623 bombers in ten combat wings returned for the third raid on 'Big-B' that week. Some 539 heavies got their bombs away over the German capital, which once again was heavily defended. Thirty-seven bombers were lost to fighter attacks and flak and eighteen fighters were lost. At briefings Intelligence Officers continually filled in the details on expected *Luftwaffe* response, which was difficult to predict but information for flak briefings was mostly good, coming as it did from a number of sources. Fighter pilots could depend on getting flak at the coast, especially near major production centres like the Ruhr, larger German cities and transportation centre. The entire coast was dangerous, but some sections were worse than others. It was always like running a gauntlet and if possible, groups were routed around major flak centres. Flak had become particularly accurate and hazardous and it made fighter pilots' lives more and more miserable at altitudes below 15,000 feet when the Germans began to site new radar-controlled batteries. Isolated batteries rarely caused much damage and if a fighter pilot saw the first burst he could take evasive action. Ernie Russell noted:

> However, when escorting bombers the defence threw everything but the kitchen sink. By this stage of the war I had been in combat for six long months, mostly in that miserable winter of 1943–44 and it was my 'turn' to go to the 'Flak House'. These retreats in the country away from the war were where combat personnel would go for a week and hopefully 'patch-up frayed nerves' but as a general rule, fighter pilots didn't need to have their nerves patched-up. For them R&R was just a longer, paid-for, forty-eight hour pass; a lark. It was the bomber crews who needed R&R. They were the ones who waded straight and level through jungles of flak, dodged enemy fighters, watched their friends' planes blow-up and their own crewmembers being blown to pieces. They had to nurse crippled planes for hundreds of miles and then maybe have to crash land when they got home. If they did.[2]

Back at Duxford on 16 March one short month before his twenty-first birthday, a knock on Ernie Russell's door aroused him from a deep sleep.

> Groggily, I half mumbled, half-shouted: 'OK!' Rolling over, I blinked at the hands on my watch hands that were pointing to 5 o'clock. Beyond the blackout curtains of my small cold room I knew that it was pitch black dark. Today there was no hesitation, cold floor or not; we were scheduled for an escort mission, and I was anxious to learn where we were going. We finished breakfast in short order and were out of the mess hall across the cold damp grass on our way to the flight line. In the glow of the gathering dawn we made our way to the Squadron Ready Room. Major Stump and Bertrand were already there and had posted the mission assignments on the Schedule Board. I was assigned as element leader with Quince Brown as flight leader. My wingman would be 2nd Lieutenant Ross Orr, who was a relatively 'new' man in the squadron. I was pleased to be flying with Quince who was a veteran and an Ace with six victories [the day before he had destroyed a Bf 109 west of Münster for his sixth kill] – all the hard way – in the air. When all the formalities had been done, I looked at the status board for my 'Jug'. WZ-C was ready and assigned to me, so I went to my flight equipment locker to check my flight gear.

Dick Hewitt had just been promoted to the rank of 1st Lieutenant. With the loss of several more senior pilots in his squadron and this being a maximum effort, six-flight mission, his first opportunity to fly as flight leader had come early. At the briefing he and Ernie Russell and fellow pilots discovered that the Group would be escorting the 679 bombers who were attacking Augsburg. Another 740 other B-17s and B-24s were going to factory and airfield targets at Ülm, Gessertshausen and Friedrichshafen in southern Germany. Russell recalls:

A bright red cord stretched across the mission map like a broken arrow connected Duxford to invisible names in France, Belgium and Germany where it intersected a blue cord, the bombers' route, that led to Augsburg. Colonel Stone and his staff gave another of their dull, dry briefings. They told us which bomber boxes we were assigned to protect, our place in the escort process, including which fighter group we were to relieve, when and where, who was to relieve us and when and where and our routes, times and altitudes out and back.

Dick Hewitt adds:

Weather for the entire mission was forecast to be the best most of us would experience to date. I hoped they were right this time. This meant the Jerries would be out in force; they could not rely on the factor of weather to obscure the target. It meant too that they would be out to clobber the bombers before they made their bomb runs. Our escort leg would be on the return leg, about halfway to the target area. We were to stay with the 'big guys' all the way back to the Dutch coast. (To reach that far into Germany and give the bombers maximum protection, our Thunderbolts would be equipped with the new pressed-fibre, pressurised, external 108-gallon wing tanks. They were cheaper than metal tanks, but cheaper was about the only advantage, as many times they leaked, would not feed and would hang up as we tried to jettison when empty. Regardless, no target inside the Third Reich was any longer beyond fighter range. What a plus for the 'big friends'!) There was sure to be enemy action. Stragglers from the heavy flak would no doubt be scattered all along the return route. Knowing all of the above factors, the bombers were to be at or near 25,000 feet.[3]

Continuing climbing to Angels 28 over Belgium and Germany, towards the rendezvous point, Russell observed that they were above the inversion level in the crystal clear sky where he could see for hundreds of miles.

The outside air temperature frequently hovered at –40°F or lower at this time of the year. Sadly, it was virtually impossible for the hot-air heater in the Jug to keep the cockpit warm. The Group bored onward and upward. We climbed into the 'contrail level' and a fine tail of gauzy ice crystals began to appear behind Quince's and other Jugs' super charger buckets. It spewed from the turbine bucket in a long, spiralling trail of white ice crystals. I had learned not to look at it. It could mesmerise you. Suddenly, out of the corner of my eye, I saw the needle on my fuel pressure gauge do a little dance telling me that my engine was sucking up the last fuel from the bottom of my belly tank. I was not surprised. Subconsciously, I had been waiting for the tank to run dry, as I didn't want my engine to cut out from fuel starvation. I quickly switched the fuel valve to Auxiliary and watched the fluctuating fuel pressure needle flicker a time or two and then stabilise.

Now I had to drop my belly tank. Discarding tanks was critical not only because they created drag, but also because they were filled with a highly explosive mixture of gasoline fumes and air, easily exploded by a cannon shell. Hopefully the tank would release. I didn't want to turn around at this late date and take my wingman home. Aborting a mission was frustrating, and I didn't want to go home now. I did my housekeeping and, checking to see that all was clear, reached down beside the seat, grabbed the little 'T-shaped' release handle, and pulled up on it. With relief, I felt the tank drop away; looking around belly tanks began falling from other fighters. One distasteful thought always went through my mind when I dropped my belly tank. Would it land in somebody's yard or even hit someone? I would hope, initially, that it did not, but then I would remember that some of my fellow airmen on today's mission would not get home and think: 'So what, we didn't start this war; it's pay-back time!'

Dick Hewitt continues:

My altimeter read 25,500 feet as we approached rendezvous. The Thunderbolt could 'breeze' at this altitude. 'Little friends coming up on your right,' our group leader called out. Radio contact was always made in advance. The bombers never knew for certain if we were friend or foe. A special coded call sign was also used to prevent the Jerries from sneaking in on them. Identifying the group of bombers we were to be escorting was never easy. With as many as 1,000 planes, strung out halfway to and from the target, it was never a simple task. Today it was the 3rd Bomb Division, with its triangular tail marking and squadron alphabetical letter inside. They were in broken, scattered formations, if you could call them formations. This was a sure indication that flak and enemy aircraft had hit them hard.

On station in the 'catbird seat' above the bombers Ernie Russell was scanning the sky, straining his eyes for any sign of a 'bogey'.

Our True Airspeed was about 330 mph, nearly 100 mph faster than the bombers; so in order not to over-run them we set up a 'weave pattern' back and forth across the bomber stream. The crossovers that took place within each flight and the squadron at each turn were complicated and required considerable co-ordination but in time they had become routine. From our vantage point high above the bombers, we had an overview of the string of bomber boxes stretched out below us for miles. It was an impressive sight. If only I had time to watch it. However I knew how rapidly the view could change and it did. Without warning there were hundreds of greasy black, 'bow-tie'-shaped bursts of flak in the boxes of bombers; intelligence would call this 'heavy and accurate'. Suddenly, one of the B-17s began to trail smoke from an engine, but he held in formation. It brought to mind a similar event that had transpired a few missions earlier when I had watched a 'Big Friend' hit by flak lose power and fall out of the protective box. Evidently, his controls had been severely damaged and like a yo-yo, he began a series of near vertical climbs and stalls. Finally, the pilot lost complete control and, at the top of an almost vertical climb, the Fortress stalled out and began to spin slowly downward. Chutes began to blossom behind it. I counted them as they opened. Not all the crew made it. In a very short time, the Fortress, still spinning and, by now, burning fiercely, disappeared from sight. I had to disengage myself from what I had seen.[4]

Hewitt continues:

We had just eased on up to near 26,000 feet when I noted a dark blotch off in the distance, approaching the '17s from the rear. It was at least 1,000 feet or so above our altitude. It had to be enemy fighters. They had to be intercepted or the bombers would get massacred, especially the cripples and stragglers. Radar had undoubtedly picked up the bombers but had not figured on us being there. There were at least sixty or more enemy aircraft. Being below them, they had not yet detected our presence. Our only offensive tactic appeared to be a climbing firing pass, almost head-on and from slightly below. A quick one-second burst at the lead plane and I saw no flashes, indicating I had hit 'zilch'. I could now tell they were 190s and not 109s. Never having made a gunnery pass at a head-on target, plus our combined closing speed of nearly 700 mph, my deflection, or 'lead', was a pure guess. I squeezed another longer burst and pulled my nose higher as I was still in a climb. 'Hits' this time and I knew they had seen us. A couple broke off and headed down, perhaps the ones hit, or others pulling their 'follow me' tactic as they had on the Brunswick raid. 'Not this time guys', and I racked the Jug in as tight a turn as I could. A quick glance told me my flight was close behind, so I was not worried about my tail, at least for that instant. Trying to overtake them from the rear was now my immediate challenge. The nearest 190 was now well out of range. Then I saw the bombers; one was straggling lower than the rest and with what appeared to be one engine feathered. Fw 190s were queuing for an attack. I called 'Yellow 3' to take the one on the right and I'd get the other. The 190 saw me and broke right as I fired. Then he committed a fatal mistake. 'You can't outrun a Jug in a dive, but be my guest and try it.' My rate of closure was so fast that I almost overran him. One burst was all it took and he was smoking; flames then appeared along the engine. No canopy eject or chute. Maybe this was the payback for Granger. Not about to follow him down, I headed back toward where the bombers should be. Number 3 had followed his 190 down and I did not know his fate until we got back. His claim, like mine, was one Fw 190 destroyed. I also claimed a damaged 190, as I know I had hit at least one on my second head-on burst. My gun camera would confirm both my claims.[5]

Ernie Russell continues:

After escorting the bombers for about thirty minutes I spied contrails approaching from the northwest – our relief. When they arrived, we exchanged positions with them with hardly a sound on the R/T. My squadron made a big sweeping turn away from the bombers and joined up with the Group, leaving our 'Big Friends' to continue on with their new 'Little Friends'. Then it was us our turn to speed home to Duxford. Our Squadron Leader pulled his four flights into position behind the lead squadron and the Group Leader set course for home with three squadrons in tow. We had not gone far when I noted Quince motion to our leader and then roll down and away. I knew at once where Quince was going, down to look for targets of opportunity. Within minutes we had left the squadron and group behind, at nearly 28,000 feet and were on a steep roller coaster ride to the deck where dark patches of woods and lighter patches of field with spider-like roads were more than five miles below us. We plummeted downward and as we did I moved my element in closer in order to anticipate sudden changes in direction. Rudder pressure and back pressure on the control stick began to build in a hurry. Automatically, I reached down on the left side of the cockpit and adjusted my rudder and elevator trim tabs to counter the forces. My altimeter was unwinding at an awesome rate and the needle on the airspeed indicator quickly passed the 450 mph mark. Quince throttled back so as not to run the risk of compressibility. Speed didn't make me unhappy. To a fighter pilot in enemy territory speed and altitude, especially speed, are like money in the bank. I checked my reflecting gunsight and all my instruments and fuel levels. On a heading of about 250 degrees we were on our way towards a German airbase near St Dizier, nearly 100 miles east of Paris. Below 10,000 feet we began to shallow our dive towards a dark patch of earth that I could see in the distance. Trees and woods began to flesh out as we got nearer the dark patch and I could recognise a camouflaged north-south runway, a taxi strip and a few buildings to the northwest of the runway.

We had throttled back again and I spread my element out to get manoeuvring room. We were not diving as steeply now, nevertheless, my airspeed indicator needle was still indicating well over 400 mph. Several miles east of the airfield and at about 3,000 feet, Quince began a slight left turn to the south, positioning us for a south to north pass along the runway. Apparently Quince saw something in the traffic pattern and he depressed his nose and headed for the southeast side of the airfield. At about the same time I saw a mottled blue and grey Me 109 ahead of me, apparently in the traffic pattern; there may have been more, but my eyes were set on the one that was straight ahead of me. Still several hundred feet higher than the 109 and a mile or so east of the runway, Quince, with my element on his right side, continued a shallow diving left turn, obviously to get into firing position. Our airspeed had bled off to just under 400 mph but we were rapidly overtaking the Jerry who was directly in my flight path, from his 4 o'clock position. I estimated his speed at about 150 mph. Rapidly closing on the Me 109, Quince, who was several hundred feet to my left, reversed his left turn rolling to the right. His sudden turn into my element, which was nearly abreast of his element, caused me to chop my throttle and roll to the right. The turn placed me on a curve of pursuit that positioned me for a perfect firing pass on the Jerry, now less than 250 yards away. I was not going to pass up this opportunity. As the Me 109 filled my gunsight, I pulled the bright dot in the middle of the glowing ring along his line of flight for a deflection shot of about thirty degrees, about three-quarters of a ring and squeezed off a burst. Immediately, APIs from my eight .50 calibre machine-guns lit up the right side of the grey engine cowling from the canopy to the prop. My closure rate was so great that I passed over the 109 a fraction of a second later. I had no time to see what happened to the Me 109 that I had plastered because Quince lowered his nose and headed for the south end of the runway.

Though they did not know it, the enemy fighters were from JG 26 and St Dizier airfield was their home base. JG 26 had attacked a Liberator wing in the 2nd Bomb Division and stirred up a real hornet's nest. As Captain Julius P 'Pat' Maxwell's flight passed under the B-24 formation the Bf 109s split essed down onto the P-47s from eleven o'clock high just as the Thunderbolts jettisoned their 108-gallon wing tanks and climbed in a head-on firing pass. Maxwell fired at one of the 109s, which flew through his gunnery pattern and it exploded. JG 26 had begun returning to St Dizier just as Quince Brown's flight had spotted the Bf 109s and Fw 190s in their landing pattern. They were easy prey but 1st Lieutenant Walter Tonkin was killed when his wing hit the ground as he chased a Fw 190 down to the deck. Chopping throttle and skidding to slow down, Brown got behind a Bf 109 and at fifty yards he fired, scoring hits until the 109 flamed and crashed to the left of the runway. He and his wingman made a sharp 180° diving right turn and lined up about half a mile south of the south end of the runway.

Ernie Russell continues:

My element was several hundred feet east of Quince who was lined up on the runway. I was lined up on the taxiway serving the take-off runway. A Ju 88 was preparing to take off to the north [Brown set the Ju 88 on fire with a short burst]. A Me 110 on a taxiway to the right with its engines turning over presented me with a head-on shot. Nose down, I centred my needle and ball, put the glowing dot in my reflector gunsight on the target and waited until I reached less than 400 yards range before squeezing the black Bakelite trigger on the control column. My Jug's wings shuddered from the recoil of a three-second burst – 240 rounds – from the eight Browning machine-guns. I heard their deep muttering over the roar of my engine at full throttle. Almost instantly, the front of the 110 was lit-up by the flashes of armour-piercing incendiary[6] rounds igniting on impact. My guns were bore sighted to converge at 300 yards so most of the rounds I fired were concentrated in a small area, probably less than ten feet in diameter, and I was not 'kicking' the rudder to spray the shots. I fired until I was somewhat less than two hundred yards from him; at which point it seemed judicious to pull up.

Skimming over the battered 110 Ross and I dropped to the 'deck', parallel to Quince and his wingman who were on our left. Quince turned slightly to the left towards a built up area, and I turned my element to join him. Just a few feet above the grass, our four 'Jugs', line abreast, thundered across the airfield at full power. It didn't take long to leave the untidy heaps we had created on the end of the runway at 350 mph plus, more than 500 feet per second. I saw no other planes on the runway or taxi strip on which I could bring my guns to bear. Even if I had, I was so low it would have been difficult to depress my guns enough to hit anything without first pulling up, not to mention the problems it would have presented to Ross who was on my right side. A building that looked like a control tower to the left of my flight path loomed into view; but, too low, too fast, and not in the right flight path. There was no way I could bring my guns to bear on it without running over Quince. Apparently, we had taken the Luftwaffe base by surprise for we saw no anti-aircraft fire. However, we strongly suspected that we had stirred up a hornet's nest and lacking any obvious targets, Quince decided not to replay that hand. He wasn't anybody's fool. I didn't object. So far we had shot down at least one Me 109, perhaps two or three in the traffic pattern and had destroyed a Me 110 and Ju 88 on the ground. It had been great. What we didn't know was that the Jerries were about to provide us with a lot more entertainment a few miles northwest of the air base. Hugging the deck and dodging treetops, our speed began to bleed off even at high power settings. Most importantly we were at a distinct disadvantage on the deck. Undoubtedly, we had been reported, and good judgement dictated that we climb to a safer altitude. Accordingly, at a comfortable distance from St Dizier Quince began a steep high-speed climb to get some fighting room before any 'hornets' caught up with us. It didn't take long.

Climbing to 7,000 feet, Quince Brown encountered two Fw 190A-6s coming at him from nine o'clock. *Leutnant* Klaus Kunze of 1st *Staffel* was piloting one of the Focke-Wulfs. As Brown got into a left-hand Lufbery circle with the two Fw 190s, the wingman deserted his leader, who kept trying to out climb and outturn the P-47 but Brown used water-injection and he caught up with Kunze who dived through the clouds followed by the Thunderbolt. Keeping Kunze in his sights and firing at 350 yards, Brown watched the Fw 190 roll on its back smoking and crash into a small creek. The German pilot was killed.[7]

Russell continues:

> Climbing in a spread formation we throttled back to climb power settings and had gained several thousand feet when I spotted a mixed gaggle of maybe eight to ten Me 109s and Fw 190s right on us, 'bouncing' us out of the haze from about 3 o'clock high. I didn't have the time or the disposition to count them. There was just a bunch of them. They were above us, less than a mile away. Here was our entertainment committee, and they had us 'dead-to-rights'. I don't know how Quince or the rest of the flight had missed seeing them, but they didn't. As is the case more often than not, it happened so suddenly that the sequence of events that followed is not altogether clear. I called, 'Break right!' and broke into the gaggle of Jerries – head-on. No time to think but instinctively, I knew that I wanted to get my guns on them as soon as possible. That was the only way to even the odds. I slammed the throttle and prop into War Emergency Power settings, pulled the stick all the way back into my right leg and jammed in the right rudder. My Jug clawed the air as it skewed around trying to meet the lead Me 109 head-on, but that was impossible given his position. He had the advantage of speed, altitude, and position. My luck was that he wasn't behind me. My only advantage was the fact that he had to make a head-on pass from the side and from above, which would present him with a tricky firing angle. I trusted that he would miscalculate the lead and miss me on this firing pass; if so, I would get a free pass. After that I had to manoeuvre him into a position where I had the advantage – all in head-on passes. Given his attack angle and my position I could only try to cut the angle between us. I had to get my guns on him. I knew from experience that the Jug had a good climb rate at full power and I was confident that the Jug could out climb and out turn him in a climbing turn. But more important, I could turn on a dime at the top of a near vertical climb and give back change; a manoeuvre we called a 'Stall Turn'.[8]

In a dogfight you never let your opponent out of your sight and I could see my opponent all too well. After the violent break we were looking down his gun barrels at a slight angle. Although he had a slight deflection shot at us during the near head-on pass I do not remember seeing those telltale flashes from his 20-mm cannon and machine-guns, even though I had my eyes locked on him. My intent was to get my guns on him and I'm sure that our eight 'fifties' must have caused him some concern too. I knew what my next move would be. The instant I passed him I pulled up vertically, preparing for a stall turn. Straight up I climbed, looking over my shoulder to see that the Jerry was doing the same thing opposite and parallel to me. There he was and as expected I was above him. I waited for him to be forced into a stall turn. He did and committed to a right turn just as I had hoped. My Jug was right at the stall point now and I rolled into a left turn in order to meet him head-on. WZ-C rolled beautifully and headed down. I looked opposite and he was just completing his turn. I had gained on him in the turn. Now he was committed to another head-on pass, only this time he wouldn't be able to get his guns on me. Neither would I be able to get my guns on him but I had made the first cut. Now to force him into another stall turn and improve my advantage.

We passed again and I yanked my Jug straight up. Swivelling my head, never letting him out of my sight, I turned; keeping the Me 109 in sight, over my shoulder, I held WZ-C in a vertical climb at full throttle, and waiting for him to commit himself. The 109 pilot was forced to match my climb or run, but he must have known that running from the Jug wasn't much of a choice for, behind me, he had pulled up into a vertical climb as I did. Going straight up, I waited patiently for him to reach the top of his climb and commit himself again. Once more, my object was to force him to commit himself. Up we went. I waited and watched him directly opposite me and significantly lower. Finally, nearly stalled, he committed himself to a left turn. At the top of my climb I rolled my Jug into a stall turn in the opposite direction, into him. Yet again, I beat him out of the turn. Now it was my turn. I had gained so much on him that I was able to manoeuvre into a firing position about 45° astern. As I did, he rolled into a steep tight left turn trying to out turn me, but that was futile. I was less than 150 yards behind him. Instinctively, like aiming at a quail, I pulled the glowing dot in my gunsight through him, sensed my lead, and squeezed the trigger. In the first burst the eight guns fired for about two seconds. More than 150 fifty-calibre API projectiles were on their way. Numerous flashes appeared on his engine cowling marking where the bullets impacted. But during my next burst, still in a very tight high G turn, the din of my guns dwindled to a 'pop-pop-pop' and my wings stopped shuddering as seven of my eight guns jammed. All of a sudden he was less than 50 yards away and going under my nose. To prevent over-running him I pulled up into a steep climbing turn and rolled downward to take another pop at him, if I had to. Fortunately, he was out of the fight, but it would have been unwise to follow him down to get a confirmation since there were at least eight or ten other Jerries in the neighbourhood. Later my camera film appeared to show fire coming out of his engine, but I didn't notice fire, only the flashes where the APIs impacted.[9]

I pulled up to engage the next set of Jerries, the skies were empty in our area and no Jerries were in sight. Oddly, but typically, we were alone. When we were certain there were no more Jerries, I pulled up and Ross and I began climbing to a safer altitude. Within minutes we spotted two Jugs off at 10 o'clock – Quince and Smith. Minutes later we joined them and set course again for home, climbing at 42 inches of hg and 2,550 rpm. As it worked out he had had his hands full nearby and had gotten a 109 and a 190. His victories made him one of the first double 'aces' in our group.[10]

Dick Hewitt summed up the mission thus: 'We could chalk this one up as 'one helluva mission accomplished.'[11]

On 17 March bad weather prevented bomber missions being flown and so as the Duxford Outfit was needed for escort duties they carried out strafing missions against airfields in France instead. One of the P-47s was shot down by flak over Reims airfield and the pilot survived to be taken prisoner. At Beauvais airfield Pete Pompetti set a Heinkel 111 on fire before he too was set on fire by flak. He pulled straight up and baled out, coming down in a marshalling yard. The Resistance sheltered Pompetti for a short time but that same evening he was captured by the Germans and later sent to a PoW camp in Germany. A few days later, on 23 March, Quince Brown scored his tenth kill when he met a Fw 190 head-on in the area of Goch in Germany and shot it down after getting on his tail. The Focke-Wulf exploded and showered pieces of aircraft all around *Okie* and Brown had to put the Thunderbolt into a violent wingover to 500 feet to avoid the flying debris. Returning home he shepherded two B-17 stragglers with their wheels and bomb-bay doors down, one after the other towards the English coast. Other Group P-47s circled for forty-five minutes over a B-17 of the 94th Bomb Group down in the sea.[12] Colonel Stone and his wingman dropped their dinghies to 2nd Lieutenant Fletcher H Johnson's crew in the water and they were all later picked up. Next day, 1st Lieutenant John J Hockery was credited with the destruction of a Ju 188 flying very low near Paris for his fourth victory. It crashed and exploded in a field in a 300-foot ball of flame as Hockery's wingman, 1st Lieutenant Karl R Wagner, went through the blaze.[13] Enemy airfields in the Low Countries were strafed on 30 March. Quince Brown was awarded a third share in a Dornier Do 217 victory at Twente-Enschede airfield. In April Quince Brown was promoted to captain and further promotion to major soon followed.

During this period General Doolittle decided that American fighters should seek out targets of opportunity after they finished escorting the 'Big Friends'. Ernie Russell recalls:

Missions were planned so that we had barely enough fuel to get home, let alone go down looking for targets. Doolittle broke that vase. Staying with the Big Friends had become so much a policy that by early 1944, if you wanted to bug some of the commanding officers and get in heaps of trouble, take off on your own to hunt Jerries or trains. Peter Pompetti in our squadron stayed in trouble because of his penchant for going off by himself and looking for Jerries – alone. Doolittle's decision now meant that if, after we completed our mission, we chose to seek out locomotives and rolling stock on the continent or to beard the Jerries on their own airfields we were free to do so. The General also knew something that we didn't; the invasion was set for May or early June and one of the highest priorities set for the invasion was that, when the landings were made, the Allies must have complete control of the air over France. So, for the first time we were turned loose, and it didn't take long for word to get down to the squadrons. However, not all flight leaders nor squadron commanders were anxious to go out looking for 'targets of opportunity', as it was known to be hazardous. But, it was right up the alley of pilots like Pompetti and my Flight Leader, Quince Brown, an 'Okie' with a chip on his shoulder who had multiple confirmed victories. It seemed to be a personal war with Quince and he wanted to prosecute it to his limits. He was a true hunter with superb vision, and he was able to spot a bogey long before most other pilots in the squadron, including me, and I had hunted all my life and had 20/10 vision. Luck is a factor.

I had my first experience at ground strafing around this time. It was a beautiful sunny day for a change, the farmlands in north Germany spread out below us. We had finished our escort mission and were on our way home when something on the ground caught Quince's eye, so he heeled over and headed down to check it out. Cutting through the brown farm fields, I saw a railroad that passed through a small village with rail switching yard. Quince had seen the village, the rail yard and other infrastructure, so we cleared ourselves, rolled over and headed down toward it. Ground strafing was not new to Quince. In mid-1943 he had been one of the first to shoot up a train. He must have been proud of it because he painted a train on his Jug alongside the swastikas for aerial victories. I didn't need an invitation either but I began looking for additional targets. My wingman and I followed Quince and his wingman down in trail. I checked my instruments and circuit breakers, my fuel, my gunsight and flipped my gun switches on. As we began to level off out of the dive I spread my element out from Quince's element to give myself room to manoeuvre. No trains or cars were in the station but several large transformers and numerous power lines feeding them on the east side of the railway station caught my attention and I rolled into position to make a firing pass at them. I trimmed my plane on the descent for about 350 mph so everything was centred. My pass was planned at a slight angle so that I could rake all the transformers. There would be only one pass, as Quince didn't like to make second passes and I didn't 'cotton' to the idea as the second time around gave the gunners time to set up. Anyway I knew that eight fifty-calibre machine guns could do all the damage necessary on the first pass. I picked my aim point, trimmed my plane again, put the reflective bead in the centre of my gunsight and at 500–600 yards I squeezed the big black Bakelite trigger on my control column. The Jug shuddered under the recoil and instantly, hundreds of armour piercing incendiary (API) rounds began flashing as they slammed into the transformers. Blue electrical sparks began to fly in all directions as each of the armour piercing shells went through the casing and cores of the transformers. I held the trigger down, firing as long as I could hold the target in my sights, which was not long. I had to begin my pull up at about 200 yards from the target – flying into the target was non-habit forming – which gave me about three seconds to fire 200 plus rounds with airspeed in the order of 360 mph. I cleared the transformers, flew over the end of the rail yard on the deck and continued to the east, following the railroad track, hugging the ground to avoid any possible antiaircraft batteries that might have been there. I saw none. Beyond the town I pulled up to look for other targets and as I did I noted a puff of smoke or steam on the tracks ahead. It was all I needed to see.

I rolled out to the right to set up a firing pass at the engine, checked my gun switches again and rolled onto the target. I held my sight on the barrel of the engine in front of the cab and at about 600 yards, squeezed the trigger again. My Jug shook again and a multitude of flashes appeared on the engine in front of the cab as hundreds of armour piercing incendiary rounds slammed through the steam coils buried inside the engine, punching holes through the boiler tubes. My impression was that the engine 'blew-up', as it was enveloped immediately in a spectacular cloud of white steam. I was satisfied that the engine was destroyed and would probably never run again. I pulled up after 'destroying' the first locomotive, checked my tail and my wingman and lo and behold there was another locomotive nearby. Quickly, I set up another approach on the second locomotive. It was a repeat. The locomotive seemed to explode in a cloud of steam under the impact of the heavy fifty calibre slugs. When I got home I claimed two locomotives destroyed and a power station heavily damaged but I didn't paint them on my plane as many did, nor did I ever see them on my records. Maybe locomotives don't count, except when you reminiscence.[14]

Dick Hewitt recalls:

Up until the Friedrichshafen raid on 16 March we had never made scheduled low-level attacks against ground targets. At least they were not a Field Order scheduled mission. Now with our increased fuel, longer airtime capability and once our escort was complete and uneventful, we were clear to search out and destroy any suspected military targets. Since rail was the primary mode of movement for all military supplies throughout Germany and the occupied countries, steam locomotives became one of our prime targets. They were easy to spot, with their plume of steam and smoke, standing out like a 'sore thumb' from almost any altitude. Few missions were flown from here on without firing our guns. In addition to its eight .50 calibre machine guns, the Jug was outfitted to carry armament of one bomb, up to a 1000 pounder, under the fuselage, or two bombs, one under each wing, either 250 or 500-pound. With one bomb of either size, we would carry our usual 108-gallon wing tanks. Similarly, with the two wing-slung lighter bombs, we'd carry a 165-gallon belly tank. This gave us the capability of searching out and destroying almost any target that presented itself.[15]

Though the Jug could outdive any other fighter at low and medium altitudes it could not match the rate of climb or manoeuvrability of the Bf 109 or Fw 190. It was the Thunderbolt's low-level performance that prolonged its service in the ETO and brought about a change of role to that of fighter-bomber. The aircraft's 'universal' wing and underbelly mountings permitted various combinations of up to 2,500 lb of bombs, two 150-gallon tanks and one 75-gallon tank to be carried. A full bombload meant that ammunition for each of the six or eight 0.5-in machine-guns was reduced from 425 to 267 rounds, but the firepower remained undiminished. During strafing attacks the weight of the bombload and drop-tanks added to that of the aircraft resulted in a terrific increase in speed. It could cause a surge or vapour lock in the fuel lines and the fuel pump was unable to meet the g loads imposed and a number of P-47s suffered engine failure over enemy territory.

On 1 April Dick Hewitt was among those who were 'missioned' to dive-bomb and strafe targets in the Ludwigshafen area. He recalls:

Our payload was a 500-pound bomb, centre slung, a full load of .50 calibres and two 108-gallon wing tanks. We'd drop the wing tanks as soon as they emptied. I was element leader in white flight. Cloud bottoms were well above our traffic pattern altitude of 1,000 feet so it was going to be no sweat on take-off or so I hoped. Turned out the take-off was normal, tucked in on the right wing of my flight leader. Once airborne, I moved out a little and then took a quick check of my instruments and flight gauges. 'What the hell goes on?' I thought. My airspeed says 'zero' and my altimeter shows I am going down and below ground level. 'White 3 here. No airspeed or altimeter I'm breaking off and returning.' I eased out of formation and called the tower 'Surtax White 3 here. No airspeed or altimeter. Am staying in pattern for emergency landing.'

'Hold for instructions; four more flights waiting take-off' they responded. I guessed my altitude at or near 1,000 feet and made a wide, level circle of the base, keeping it well in sight. I watched as the last mission flight got airborne and again called the tower to tell them, 'I'm coming in.'

'Surtax White 3, you cannot land here with that bomb. 'You'll have to dump it and your fuel tanks before landing. Suggest the dive bombing range off Felixstowe.'

That's 120 miles round trip, and I've no airspeed or altimeter? I'm gonna fly there and back, hoping the ceiling doesn't drop or that something else doesn't fail? 'Sorry tower I'm calling this one,' I quickly thought. I could jettison them in the nearby boondocks but even with the bomb still armed, I felt I had a 50-50 chance of making it down OK. The wing tanks should be fine providing I didn't set down too hard. Fires could easily result, and the bomb could explode on contact if I dropped it – these would be even more devastating. I had seen this once earlier when I was Officer of the Day. An A-20 had crashed close by killing a couple of GIs and a nurse who had gone to their rescue. I had driven the Officer of the Day jeep to within a dozen yards from it when the bombs and ammo started going off. A sergeant who was with me and I scrambled through a hedgerow that was so thick, I'm not sure how we ever made it. I knew from that harrowing episode I had no intention of baling out or dumping this load on or even close to anyone below. 'I'm calling this one tower,' I called. 'Alert the crash truck and ambulance. I'm coming in.'

I had one big concern. There were over 2,000 pounds more weight than I ever landed with before, to say nothing of the underslung bomb, or the zero airspeed. I'd carry extra throttle over the fence and set down two-point, not stalling out but flying the Jug onto the metal airstrip. Altitude did not bother me as I could guess it close from regular landings. The speed was not so easy, but it should work; now to do it. At half throttle and a steeper than normal glide, I had no idea what speed I was going The fence at the end of the field went under me so fast, I knew I was 'hot'. Forward stick, the wheels screeched, and I cut off all power. There was no going around. About opposite the tower I was a third of the way down the strip and still moving way too fast. Full rear stick, into three-point, then I started pumping the brakes. Now I could see the hedgerow and tree line at the end of the field and it was coming up too darn fast. Full brakes. I had left the metal tarmac and was now on the grass. Then hard left rudder and brake as I started an arc to the left. With the Jug's wide landing gear I'd ground loop, if necessary. I was confident the gear wouldn't collapse – at least that was in my favour. Dirt and grass flew everywhere as I skidded along the hedge line at the east end of the field. I had made it. Glancing out, there was the 'meat wagon' and fire truck. I had the canopy open, gave them the OK sign and eased on a little power to taxi back to my parking spot. They followed, but not very close. Couldn't blame them, as I still had that 500-pounder slung underneath. Hopefully it was still safely armed. Phil Doloway my crew chief was already out and came up to the wing. I cut the throttle and crawled out. 'Now what, Lieutenant?' he asked. I had my hunches as to the source of the problem. I said nothing but knew the altimeter and airspeed had close proximity connections near the left wing tip.

'Open the cover plate,' was all I said, as I pointed to the spot on the wing tip. It took him only a few seconds and there, plain as the colours yellow and blue, were the two connections. Why Republic Aircraft had not 'opposite threaded' these two or something other than rely on some colour-blind person to correctly match these colours, will always remain a mystery. The airspeed, being connected to the altimeter line, registered no pressure as the plane ascended, thus causing it to peg at zero. The altimeter registered positive pressure through the pitot tube, instead of negative from the barometric instrument in the wing tip, causing it to go down instead of up. Phil could have easily blamed it on his assistants, Trantham or Montgomery, but the buck stopped with him. It was about the only 'mar' against a near-perfect, no-abort record, as crew chief on my Jug.

I had one other take-off abort in the Jug but I was not flying Doloway's aircraft that day. It happened on a subsequent flight. Several others experienced that same malfunction, but never lived to tell about it. It was called a 'runaway prop' and resulted in an almost complete loss of power and the ability to stay airborne. The electrical motor controlling the propeller's pitch failed and sent the prop to 'flat pitch'. Resseguies' baleout over France was the result of a similar prop failure. Mine was on take-off, the worst possible time. At about 300 feet, my first indication was I could not gain in flying speed. I had two full wing tanks and knowing I'd 'prang' for sure, I jettisoned both, then staggered at full throttle around the pattern. I'm sure the tower knew I was in extreme difficulty as the tanks had hit the ground just west of them. The 'gods' were with me on this one. All mission flights were airborne and I was immediately cleared to land. Baling out was not even a consideration with the minimum altitude I was able to attain. No traffic pattern or peel off – I came straight in and was extremely fortunate to have been that close to the field. Dozens, I know had to bale out or were killed trying to crash land. Failures of this nature were partially solved by Republic, converting to a hydraulically controlled prop pitch. I say partially, as any loss of hydraulic fluid usually meant a similar fate for the Jugs.

Combat time built up fast after early April. During a stretch of less than 20 days, like many others, I had accumulated an additional 40 hours of combat. Nazi ground transportation facilities and airdromes were our first-line targets during this period. We knew the day of invasion of the continent of Europe had to be getting close. Troop and equipment buildup in southern England was humungous. Ninth Air Force groups, based in close proximity to the Channel, were pounding targets all along the French and Belgian coasts. Their mission, strictly tactical, meant they would ultimately be in close support of ground forces once they were on enemy soil. Preparing for the invasion, like the 8th Air Force, they hit everything that was military stationary or moving, every day, from dawn to dusk. Our targets were rural rail lines close to the German border. I had what was probably my most satisfying 300-pound bomb strike, on a rail line leading from Volkel to Wesel. One very successful tactic was to pick a spot, very rural and remote and 'cut it' from service. We would approach from about 16,000 feet, flying just off centre and parallel to the rail line, do a wing over, head down in a near vertical dive, putting our gun or bomb site on the centreline of the tracks. At about 6,000 feet we would start pullout and at the same instant release our bomb; our pullout was parallel and on the centreline of the rails. The bottom of our pullout arc was well under 2,000 feet so we could easily glance back to see our results. This one hit smack in the centre of the two rails and I could see ties and rails go flying in all directions. Their first indication of the resulting damage was most likely not until the next locomotive came through, screeching to a halt at the bomb crater. If not discovered until after dark, the results could have been far more devastating Cutting the main line track was far better than one of their switching tracks in a major marshalling area. Here there was one hell of a lot less 'flak' – a big plus for us.

On 5 April and again on 8 April, we bombed and strafed airdromes in the Paris and adjoining areas. My claims were a shared air destruction of an Arado 96, ground destruction of a Go-242, a DFS 30, a Ju-52 and three Me 110s. Water towers, hangars, buildings of all sizes and services, gun emplacements and flak towers were blasted with our bombs and eight .50s. On our way home on the 8th, we caught and destroyed four locomotives. Some had to be carrying ammo and other explosives, as in the aftermath of their destruction; multiple explosions and fires were set off by our machine guns.

On 12 April the 3rd Division was badly mauled by fighters and ten Fortresses were forced to head for Switzerland with many others either shot down or badly damaged. The B-24s, which did not turn back until they had reached the German border also came in for some rough treatment from three *Staffeln* of JG 26 and two of JG 2 which were assembled over Juvincourt by their ground controller. One of the B-24s in the 453rd Bomb Group carried the 2nd Combat Wing Leader, Major James M Stewart, the Hollywood actor, who on 31 March had joined the Group as Operations Officer. Once the Liberators' route had been determined the German fighters were directed towards Luxembourg to meet them and they were intercepted near Liège. The Liberators were being escorted by Thunderbolts of the 366th and 78th Fighter Groups, the latter now sporting black and white checkerboard nose cowlings following the 56th Fighter Group's varied success in fooling the Germans with coloured nose paint. The distinctive markings also provided an easier form of recognition for trigger-happy bomber gunners and other escort fighters alike. Despite foul weather conditions the 78th Fighter Group stuck with the 2nd Bomb Division until south-east of Aachen where the B-24s aborted, the last division to do so. The 445th Bomb Group B-24s lost sight of their P-47s when they entered a thin layer of stratus cloud and *Oberleutnant* Walter Matoni who was leading the JG 26 formation saw the opportunity to attack from underneath. They were joined in the fight by JG 2. The Focke-Wulfs fired 20-mm cannon shells into the B-24s with devastating effect. JG 26 claimed two of the Liberators and JG 2 three more before the P-47 pilots could see what was happening. The Thunderbolts pitched into the fray and chased the Focke-Wulfs in and out of the cloud layer claiming six shot down. Four of the enemy pilots were killed and the two others baled out safely.[16]

Captain Quince Brown was leading his Squadron near Duren when thirty plus Fw 190s and Bf 109s emerged from above heavy clouds, flying in the opposite direction. The Oklahoman's formation turned and pursued the enemy fighters in a steep-climbing turn that overtook the German fighters, which scattered and dived for the deck. Brown picked out a Fw 190 with a belly tank and at 5,000 feet raked the fighter from left wingtip to cockpit. The Fw 190 exploded and Quince flew safely through the flames and debris. It was his eleventh victory and any more would have to wait because he now went on well-earned leave to the ZOI. Later near Malmedy, Belgium, Major Leonard P Marshall along with 1st Lieutenants Karl R Wagner and Robert L Baker and Captain George J Lundigan, chased several Fw 190s to the deck. Marshall overshot his quarry, allowing Wagner to get in two long, wide angle deflection bursts, which caught the Focke-Wulf as it was belly-landing. The Focke-Wulf's left wing broke off and it flipped on its back and exploded. As Wagner passed the Focke-Wulf's remains he saw the pilot lying off to the side where the explosion had thrown him.[17] Near Sedan, France, at about the same time a section of four pilots stumbled upon six Ju 87s beneath them milling around Ensheim airfield with another fifty plus parked on the field. The Thunderbolt pilots had difficulty trying to hang behind the *Stuka* dive-bombers long enough to take aim but the outcome was never in doubt as each man destroyed one before giving the aerodrome a quick squirt. One of them fell to the guns of Captain John Hockery to give the pilot from Independence, Missouri, well-earned ace status.

On 15 April wide ranging operations in central and western Germany resulted in the destruction of fifty-eight enemy aircraft on the ground but at a cost of thirty-three fighter pilots including two in the 78th Fighter Group, which then returned to escorting the heavies again as Dick Hewitt recalls.

> The first B-24s that my log show 'escort' were on the last two missions of tour #1. On 22 April we picked them up in the target area of Frankfurt. The big difference between escorting the Liberators and the 'Forts' was the 'Libs' operated at a slightly lower altitude. This made them more vulnerable to flak and enemy aircraft attacks. Watching a huge bomber get a direct flak hit and blow up less than a few hundred feet away was about as defenceless a position as one could be in. If it was from an enemy fighter, you could at

least give them a dose of the same. Then watching, as we did this day, and seeing only two or three chutes when you knew there were ten men on board, gave one an even worse, sick feeling.

Our 24 April mission was to the Stuttgart/Schweinfurt areas, again with the B-24s. Aircraft parts and related manufacturing facilities were the prime targets, Stuttgart being the primary and Schweinfurt the alternate. I needed only 2 hours and 35 minutes to reach the required total of 200 hours. Since this was easily a four-hour mission, it was to be my last. The escort would turn out to be uneventful. Not only did we not encounter any enemy aircraft, but also even the flak was very minimal. The only logical explanation – our escort leg was well before the target area. For certain, there was flak down there and the Germans were far from beaten. The 'leave bomber' time came and we headed for the deck. Our noble leader that day decided to pick on a large railyard on the outskirts of Cologne – a poor target selection, to say the least, as every flak gun within 100 miles must have been marshalled there. Anything in the Ruhr valley Germany's prime industrial and manufacturing area, was noted for its flak defenses. Ask any RAF pilot, as this was one of the heavier hit areas by their night bombers. Our first pass told us we had 'bitten off a huge chunk,' more than most of us had bargained for. That was true for me, it being my last mission.

My wingman, 2nd Lieutenant Harvey Eakes, on my right, took a direct hit and went straight in. 'My last mission and I am about to be blown out of the sky,' I thought. I continued my firing pass and raked a long section of rail boxcars, to a point where I knew my ammo was low. Tracers employed to show a dwindling ammo supply were placed near the end of each gun's 'magazine rack'. One gun in my right wing had also stopped firing – another indicator of low ammo or a possible jam. This irregular firing also caused an aiming error, making a moving aerial target almost impossible to hit. As I pulled up, a 20-mm burst went off just under my tail section. It flipped me almost on my back. There was no 'clunk' sound so I hoped it was only from the percussion of the explosion. Rolling out and almost on the rooftops I headed, full throttle, on the deck. My controls seemed OK and a quick glance showed my gauges to be normal. Inspection later showed I had received a couple of small flak holes in the horizontal stabiliser. Luck was again on my side. Now to get out of here, as I was all alone, one 'hell' of a long way from home and completing my final first tour mission. Never fly a straight-line course, I'd long since learned, so I zigged and zagged in a westerly climbing heading. Just ahead and above at around 8,000 feet I could see a light cloud layer, my haven and hope for escape. Alone, I needed all the help I could get. As I entered the clouds a few puffs of flak appeared. Remembering that first mission, I made a slight change in course, then a minor gain in altitude. No more flak, at least from that gunner.

I began to break in and out of the clouds. Far ahead, I could see almost blue sky so I knew my cover was about to disappear. I'd keep my altitude and use it to fight or run, if I had to. With a low ammo supply it could be the latter. Keeping one eye half-glued to the Jug's rear-view mirror and the other in an arc around me, all seemed to be going well. No problem with fuel so I maintained a hefty throttle setting. Probably would take an hour to the Belgian coast, my cross-out point. Time to ponder the past eight months and the future, now that I was about to complete my tour of combat. But I'd best not count my chickens yet. Several pilots had finished ahead of me. Some had taken assignments in Fighter Command. A few had gone stateside for R&R with plans to return for a second tour. I could do the same, or did I want permanent Zone of Interior assignment, with Training Command, or even the South Pacific Theatre of Operations? The latter for some reason failed to excite me, but I knew it would not be a choice if I went back to the United States. I did have a choice of the 30-day R&R and return to the ETO and the 78th Fighter Group. With D-Day the allied invasion of Europe, looming just around the corner, our job here was really just beginning. It would seem better to use my experience here to fight on in any way I could, and help complete the routing of Hitler's forces from the European continent. Then I thought of all the Killed in Action, Missing in Action, Killed in Friendly Action and Prisoner of War guys who had started out with me. There was little doubt of my decision now. I could not desert them. I could be home and back in less than 60 days, maybe not even miss the big invasion, or so I hoped. Reassignment to anywhere else was just not 'in the cards' for me. Another 100 hours would not be any easier than the first 200, but at least it would go a lot faster with missions now almost double the time of the first ones. But, I was still a long way from home. I'd better concentrate on finishing this one.

Were those two tiny specks in my rear mirror dirt? I sure hadn't noticed them before but there they were, getting larger by the minute. They were reflections of something. Banking slightly left; I could make them out more clearly. Someone was definitely on my tail. Had I been certain of my ammo supply, I'd have met 'em head on. Then flashes! Firing from extreme range, no doubt and fortunate for me. Single-engine enemy aircraft and more than likely they were Fw 190s, as the Me 109 flashed its nose with its 20-mm nose-mounted cannon. I firewalled MX-T, pushed the nose down, but they were still closing on me. 'Water Injection,' I thought, and hit the button on my throttle. A split-second hesitation and then that surge of power. Wow! The blobs in my mirror gradually got smaller and they had quit firing. 'Better save some water, just in case,' I thought again to myself so after five or six minutes I flipped the switch to off. I had left those two suspected 190s far to the rear. They were no longer even tiny specks in my rear mirror.

Hopefully they had given up and turned back. Bet they wondered what the hell I had under the cowling of my Jug.

The coastline could not have come into view any sooner or looked any more beautiful than it did today. At 3,000 feet the old North Sea looked even better than it did anytime since way back in October '43. Probably just as cold and bleak, but with the sun shining the white caps glistened. My crossout appeared near Ostend, Belgium, just us south of the Walcheren Islands. Not wanting to encourage any flak, I veered well to the south of the city, then to a 280-degree heading which should put me about dead on Manston, on the Thames estuary. I had landed there once earlier on another of my low fuel returns. My recollection was clear as a bell as my Jug had quit dead near the end of the landing roll. 'Get that bucket of bolts off the airstrip,' their 'limey' control tower radioed! 'Sorry mate, I'm plumb out of petrol,' I called back. 'You'll have to come and tow me.' It was near dark and I ended up spending the night. Even more memorable was that British cot. I'd not have to spend the night on one of those as I had plenty of fuel this time. With Ceiling & Visibility Unlimited (CAVU) conditions, it could not have worked out any better. I even flirted with the idea of giving the 'limey' gunners a cheap thrill – a buzz job at cliff-top level to shake 'em up a bit. But what if they were 'cocked and ready' and were to get a lucky hit? Second thoughts, and on went my Identification – Friend or Foe. Some other time, perhaps, but not today.

Once well inside the United Kingdom, I called for a heading home. Not that I needed the 'fix', but just to let them know that olde MX-T my ship that day was on the way in. I couldn't have cared less who might hear me. As the landmarks around Duxford came into sight, I had a plan I was about to execute. Any other time it might have gotten me into a tiff with the CO but I was prepped to handle it this one time. The tower cleared me east to west. After a slight change in course, the field came into view. It was not uncommon to 'rake' the field at grass top level after returning from a mission. 'Just stay away from the buildings and control tower,' was the rule. This one was going to be special, with a couple of extra 'yahoos' on the peel-off to celebrate. I firewalled old MX-T and headed straight down the runway; a few feet lower and I'd have made sparks fly from the metal tarmac. If I had practised, it could not have gone any better. Peel oft cut the throttle, up to 500 feet, wheels down and locked, half flaps, then a tight 270, touching down almost on the spot, directly above my peel-off spot. Mission #84 and 201.25 hours were 'in the book'. There'd be some celebrating in 'Ye Olde Duxford Officer's Club' tonight.[18]

On 30 April the Duxford Outfit took on twenty-five plus Fw 190s at 20,000 feet during an escort mission for the heavies. Captain 'Max' Juchheim downed two for his sixth and seventh victories and he also got a Fw 190 probable and damaged another.[19] A Focke-Wulf that was being chased at low level by 1st Lieutenants Fred White and 'Mac' McDermott clipped a hilltop and crashed in a fiery explosion. It brought the monthly total to seventeen aerial victories, twenty-nine ground victories and twenty-eight locomotives destroyed for the loss of seven pilots in action and flying accidents.[20]

Early in May combat tour time for fighter pilots was increased from 200 hours to 300 hours. On the morning of the 8th 378 B-17s set out to bomb Berlin and 287 B-24s and forty-nine B-17s hit factories near Brunswick. The 78th Fighter Group rendezvoused with the first box of Liberators just west of Hanover and tried to protect the stragglers. More than ten enemy fighters bounced the Thunderbolts and one who was too far from the formation was picked off. Two Liberators also went down in the same pass. For the next few days the heavies made repeated bombing raids on targets in France and the Low Countries. On 12 May when 800 bombers attacked oil targets they were confronted by an estimated 430 enemy fighters and forty-six bombers were shot down despite the efforts of the fighter escorts. South-west of Koblenz Captain James Wilkinson and his four flights of P-47s were flying 1,000 yards ahead and above the lead bomber box when 100 plus Fw 190s appeared closing on the lead bombers at twelve o'clock level. The first two flights turned into the enemy fighters and split their formation in half before diving down and chasing after them at low level. Wilkinson opened fire on a Fw 190 at 200 yards range and scored hits on the wingroots and cockpit, setting it on fire. It went down with its pilot. 1st Lieutenant Robert L Baker fired at another enemy fighter at 400 yards range and the fighter's canopy flew off with flames in the cockpit. The pilot baled out and hit the ground before his parachute could fully open. 1st Lieutenant Daniel D Hagarty lost the rest of the formation but he set a Fw 190 on fire and it crashed into hills south of Koblenz. He chased another Fw 190 to the deck and fired the last of his ammunition, which blew the enemy fighter's wing off and he crashed into trees below and exploded. Out of ammunition and alone, Hagarty was shot down and he baled out and was taken prisoner. 1st Lieutenant Merle R Capp and Captain Benjamin M Watkins each downed a Fw 190. Watkins' victim baled out and hit his left wing and the Thunderbolt pilot returned to Duxford with part of his parachute caught on his wingtip.

On 19 May the 78th Fighter Group escorted some of the B-24 boxes of the Third Air Task Force which hit industrial areas at Brunswick. The P-47s were at eleven o'clock level with the lead box of Liberators when a large gaggle of sixty plus enemy fighters in two waves approached the bombers head on in line abreast to spread their firepower. The Thunderbolts broke up the first wave and as more P-47s came in above and together the P-47s broke up the second wave. James Wilkinson hit one of the enemy fighters from 200 yards astern. It split-essed and the pilot baled out. In all the 78th Fighter Group claimed twelve enemy fighters shot down without loss. Even so 1st Lieutenant Harold F Beck only just managed to make it home after three Bf 109s scored several hits with their 20-mm cannon near the Dummer Lake, which disabled the supercharger and air ducting. Beck lost manifold and hydraulic pressure, his gyro compass and airspeed indicator were put out of action and oil covered his windscreen. The fighters pumped more shells into the foundering Thunderbolt and smoke poured out of the engine, which caught fire. Beck lost power and the oil pressure dropped to ten pounds while the oil temperature increased to maximum but Beck tried to shake off his pursuers by diving to 2,000 feet, which blew out the engine fire. He was helpless but two of the Bf 109s and then the third fighter ran out of ammunition and they left the scene as Beck limped towards the enemy coast. Over the sea he let down from 12,000 to 4,000 feet in solid haze and overcast and headed for home. Nearing the coast of England he headed for an emergency airfield but his engine seized at 2,000 feet in poor visibility. Beck spotted an airfield and he shook his wheels down and managed to put down and without brakes he made S-turns until the P-47 came to a stop. Close inspection revealed that the P-47 had ten 20-mm hits and many smaller calibre holes, the propeller was holed and the tops had been shot off two of the engine cylinders.

Two days later thirty-three-year old Colonel Frederic C Gray took over command from Colonel James J Stone who returned to the ZOI. On 24 May VIIIth Fighter Command tried out a new form of attack when Major Harold Stump flew the Group's first 'Droopsnoot' bombing mission, to a railway bridge over the Oise River south of Creil in France. The specially modified P-38 Lightning was fitted with a Plexiglas nose area containing a bombsight and the bombardier's job was to tell the P-47 pilots by radio when to drop their bombs on the target. The first bomb run was aborted but the Thunderbolts carried out a 360-degree turn and aimed their bombs from 18,000 feet and claimed to have demolished part of the bridge. On 28 May when almost 900 bombers attacked aircraft and oil targets in Germany an estimated 450 enemy fighters opposed the missions with about 350 of them concentrating in the Magdeburg area. Captain 'Max' Juchheim was at 22,000 feet near Gardelegen manoeuvring to attack an enemy fighter when a 363rd Fighter Group Mustang suddenly converged and collided with his Thunderbolt. The P-51 exploded and killed the pilot. Juchheim managed to get out of his spinning fighter and he baled out to become a PoW.[21] 1st Lieutenants 'Mac' McDermott and Fred White covered his descent and chased off an enemy fighter, which dived past 2,000 yards away. White got several hits on the fighter, which overshot with glycol streaming from the engine. McDermott finished it off with a burst of fire that sent the enemy plane down in flames.

By now Ernie Russell, who had been in combat for eight months, was near the end of his combat tour having miraculously survived thus far without a scratch or an 'emotional blemish' as he put it.

My final missions were to Rheims, Osnabrück, Berlin, Aachen, and targets southeast of Paris. All turned into 'milk runs'. My 64th and last mission completed my tour of combat of 201 hours and 21 minutes. May is a beautiful time in England, the grass is greening, the trees are putting on new growth and the flowers are in full bloom. But as a 'brand-new' twenty-one year old I took that for granted. What I didn't see was the imminent invasion of Hitler's Europe and neither did my friends. It was too carefully camouflaged and hidden. But the signs were there for the seeing. Troops were pouring into southwest Britain, an allied invasion fleet was forming on the coast and East Anglia had to be sagging under the weight of fighter and bomber bases! Doolittle had relaxed the rules of engagement and more and more of the bombing strikes were aimed at the infrastructure in northern France. While we knew that we were part of the monumental undertaking, flying our missions, doing our job and looking forward to our next 'Forty-eight hour pass', it just didn't register with us. How could we have missed something so huge? We couldn't see the forest for the trees. This could go on forever but the juggernaut was coming.

1   *A Mississippi Fighter Pilot In WWII* by Ernest E Russell.

2   *A Mississippi Fighter Pilot In WWII* by Ernest E Russell.

3   *Target of Opportunity: Tales & Contrails of the Second World War.*

4   *A Mississippi Fighter Pilot In WWII* by Ernest E Russell.

5   *Target of Opportunity: Tales & Contrails of the Second World War.*

6   'Prior to 1944 we fired either armour-piercing or incendiary rounds; but someone had the bright idea of combining them in order to increase the chance of fire. They were very successful, but in short supply and we were allowed only fifty rounds per gun – the first fifty.'

7   See *The JG 26 War Diary Vol.2.*

8   'My friend Max Juchheim and some others call this manoeuvre a "Hammer-head stall". My chief advantage was that the Jug happened to have the fastest aileron roll of any fighter, even at low speeds, which made the stall turn my favourite manoeuvre in a dogfight. The manoeuvre is relatively simple. In a vertical climb at full power, just before the Jug stalled, I would roll my wings with my ailerons and smoothly apply rudder in the direction I wanted to go, gently nurse the stick back to get the nose down, and, once headed down, the Jug would accelerate rapidly. I could almost fly back down the air corridor I had ascended in. I had used this manoeuvre many times in dogfights with P-51s and it had never failed to secure me an advantage, so I had faith that it would work on a Me 109 as well.'

9   'I did not see the 109 pilot bale out or crash, but did see the strikes. So, following the rules, I claimed a Damaged. When Fighter Command reviewed the films they awarded me a "Probably Destroyed" probably due

to the fire but in all likelihood it was a "Destroyed". Was the gaggle that bounced us from another Group?'

10 Brown had discovered two Bf 109s trying to tag them from behind. All the Messerschmitts went into a Lufbery turning battle and again the German wingman split from his leader. The leader then tried to outrun the P-47s on top of the clouds but the Thunderbolts stayed with him without resorting to water-injection. Brown cut him off from a hole in the clouds and scored hits. The leader was last seen going vertical into the clouds with heavy smoke streaming from his engine and wing roots. Three Bf 109s of the 10th *Staffel* JG 26 were shot down and their pilots suffered various degrees of injury. Quince Brown's three victories on 16 March took his overall score to nine and he was awarded a well-deserved Silver Star for leading the mission. In all, the P-47s of the 56th and 78th Fighter Groups shot down and killed five pilots of JG 26 and the latter Group wounded three more. Ernie Russell was awarded one destroyed and one probably destroyed and Ross Orr, one 'damaged'. Russell did not claim the Me 109 in the traffic pattern.

11 *Target of Opportunity: Tales & Contrails of the Second World War.*

12 42-31120.

13 *Eagles of Duxford: The 78th Fighter Group in World War II.*

14 *A Mississippi Fighter Pilot In WWII* by Ernest E Russell.

15 *Target of Opportunity: Tales & Contrails of the Second World War.*

16 Two of JG 26's Fw 190s were destroyed by the 352nd Fighter Group and three more were shot down either by the 78th or 366th Fighter Group pilots.

17 *Unteroffizier* Karl Gathof of 6th *Staffel*, JG 26, was KIA 5 km south of Malmedy in his Fw 190A-7. *Leutnant* Wolfgang Grimm was also KIA in his Fw 190A-6 at Malmedy. *Unteroffizier* Karl Willand of 8th *Staffel*, JG 26, who was flying a Fw 190A-5 was KIA north of Dinant by a P-47 pilot in the 78th Fighter Group. See *The JG 26 War Diary Vol.2.*

18 *Target of Opportunity: Tales & Contrails of the Second World War.* Dick Hewitt was promoted to captain on 28 April. He volunteered for a second tour and departed on his thirty-day R&R leave.

19 Juchheim's eighth and ninth and final victories were scored on 25 and 27 May respectively. On 28 May he was involved in a mid-air collision with a 363rd Fighter Group Mustang whose pilot was killed in the explosion. Juchheim survived and he was taken prisoner.

20 *Eagles of Duxford: The 78th Fighter Group in World War II.*

21 Juchheim's score was nine confirmed victories in the air. On the same day 1st Lieutenant Phillip H Hazelett was KIA in the Osnabrück area by flak while strafing an airfield.

CHAPTER TEN

Battle for the Sky

When the briefing was over, we climbed into the trucks that would drop us off at our planes. I now had a shiny new Thunderbolt. I was ready for that racehorse start! We taxied out and took our position among the group of forty-eight planes. On signal we poured on the power and were off into the 'Wild Blue Yonder!'...Unfortunately, the wild blue yonder wasn't always so blue since many missions were flown over complete cloud cover. It was rather tense flying through dense clouds in close formation. If you lost your leader, there were a lot of planes to collide with – forty-eight to be exact.

2nd Lieutenant Lawrence 'Larry' W. Nelson[1]

England at this time was gripped with 'Invasion Fever' as the long awaited 'Second Front' approached and Duxford lost most of its 'country-club casualness'. Before all passes were cancelled and travel was restricted, airmen returning from a '48' in London were full of vivid accounts of trucks, jeeps, transports and staff cars jamming the English roads and narrow winding English country lanes and causing vast traffic snarl-ups. In Andover, Hampshire, office workers were given fifteen minutes' extra at lunchtime to cross the street! Passenger trains were being withdrawn and trains out of the capital were crammed. For some weeks the headlines in the London press and *Stars and Stripes* had proclaimed that Operation *Overlord*, the invasion of the continent, was imminent. But where and when? Planning the final date for the invasion involved a certain amount of guesswork and it had kept the planners at SHAEF[2] awake for several nights too. Only a select few knew that a stretch of the Normandy coastline from Quineville to just south of Caen had been selected for the long-awaited Second Front. The invasion had been due to take place in May 1944 but General Dwight D Eisenhower, Supreme Commander at SHAEF, then postponed the date by a month to enable extra landing craft to be built. On 8 May he selected 5 June as D-Day but the weather conditions had to be right.

Security was tightened and when passes at Duxford were cancelled even the Newmarket to Royston road, which separated the airfield from the domestic site, was closed and all civilians were barred from the area. Blackout restrictions were tighter than ever and special wardens patrolled the base to see that they were enforced. Airfield personnel worked flat out to prepare the Thunderbolts for 'the big one' as guards were posted and a permanent alert force of forty-nine men and one officer was maintained around the clock. Pilots were ordered to carry their .45s at all times and ground crews were issued carbines, gas masks and helmets to have at the ready, in case German paratroops attempted to sabotage any suspected plans. With double summer time in effect, darkness came very late and the nights were much shorter. All the P-47s were removed from the far perimeter area at night and some of the enlisted men had to sleep in the dispersal areas. The Thunderbolt's low-level performance made it ideal for the ground attack role and thirty-four Jugs were transferred to the 9th Air Force, which was tasked with tactical missions in France before and after the invasion came, cutting each squadron back to twenty-eight aircraft, or sixteen per mission. During all of these precautions on 30 May Duxford airfield was rocked by the concussion of exploding bombs when an ammunition dump near Great Chesterford exploded. The explosions lasted until mid-afternoon and personnel had to keep all the windows opened in case of a new and bigger blast. At 1613 hours Major Harold Stump led a second 'Droopsnoot' mission to the railway bridge at Beaumont-sur-Oise. The Thunderbolts dropped fifty 500-lb bombs from twenty to fifty feet altitude and good hits were claimed on both ends of the bridge. During take-off from Duxford a 500-pounder with an eight-second-fuse dropped from one of the P-47s blew a four-foot crater in the grass runway. When the mission returned, another bomb that had failed to release over target, fell from a landing Thunderbolt, but failed to explode. A RAF bomb disposal team later safely defused the UXB. By the end of the month the 78th Fighter Group had flown twenty-five missions, suffered the loss of nine P-47s and had claimed twenty-five aerial victories, four ground victories and twenty locomotives destroyed.

On the first five days in June the field sent out six missions, all uneventful bomber escort jobs. On 4 June Captain James W Wilkinson, the acting CO of the 82nd Squadron, who had recently been quite successful in strafing locomotives on the continent, was invited by the RAF to demonstrate his strafing technique against a locomotive in Wales. Tests on locomotives disproved that they were put out of commission permanently after strafing attacks even though penetrated by numerous bullets. The effects might have been spectacular but it was demonstrated that the holed engines could be repaired fairly rapidly and back in service within short order.[3] The thirty-one-year-old airman pilot was of the opinion that strikes in the right place could put a locomotive out of action for months rather than days. Bad weather *en route* held up his flight clearance so in order to get airborne, Wilkinson said that he was going up for a local test flight and then he headed for South Wales. On arrival the landscape was covered in mist and Wilkinson hit the mountainside near Llandovery, Carmarthenshire, and he was killed. A few weeks later his attractive English widow was presented with his Distinguished Service Cross and Silver Star, which had been awarded for the two occasions when, single-handedly, he had fought off and broken up entire formations of enemy fighters attacking the bombers. A model Thunderbolt containing the chronometer from the P-47 was made by Wilkinson's crew chief, Staff Sergeant Ismal W Boase, and this was also presented to Mrs Wilkinson. The distraught widow was found dead in London a month or so after the presentation. A photograph of her husband was near her body. Captain Benjamin I Mayo, twenty-five years old from Little Rock, Arkansas, later took permanent command of Wilkinson's squadron.

On Monday 5 June – D-Day minus one – there were all sorts of rumours about an imminent invasion of the enemy coast. At 1545 hours top secret orders were flown into Duxford for Brigadier-General Murray C Woodbury, commanding 66th Fighter Wing at Sawston Hall. From early May onwards meteorological flights had been gathering intelligence and weather data. A local storm front, forming suddenly east of Iceland, forced Eisenhower to postpone the invasion for twenty-four hours. General Bernard L Montgomery, C-in-C Land Forces, was prepared to go despite the weather but ACM Sir Trafford Leigh-Mallory C-in-C AEAF Allied Expeditionary Air Forces, was not in favour, as so much depended upon air superiority. All convoys at sea had to reverse their courses but two British midget submarines continued to their positions off the beaches to act as markers for the invasion army when it arrived. Group Captain JM Stagg, the Met Officer, predicted thirty-six hours of relatively clear weather with moderate winds and on 5 June Eisenhower turned to Montgomery and asked whether he could see any reason for not going on the morrow. Monty replied, I would say 'Go!' The other commanders agreed. 'OK' said Eisenhower. 'We'll go.'

On 5/6 June the sky was overcast and an occasional mist made it even darker. At Sawston Hall the 66th Fighter Wing HQ night staff watched the plotting table and knew that something big was in the offing. The betting was 'Dollars to doughnuts, this is it'. At some airfields towards midnight the sky above the low clouds was filled with the continual throbbing drone of aircraft. It was too steady and lasted too long to be RAF Bomber Command going out on another night operation. Personnel saw and heard RAF aircraft carrying paratroops or towing gliders filled with more of the same going over, 'wave after wave' and many knew that they would be going in the morning. The constant sound of aircraft flying overhead made sleep impossible for many. Betty's tearoom was closed that evening for the only time during the war. (It was re-opened next morning.) Enlisted men in their huts listened alternately to the BBC and the enemy propaganda station. Finally, mechanics, armourers, radiomen, pilots, ground officers and enlisted men who had not been on night duty were roused from their sacks. Hours before daylight they completed the long preparation for the first of three D-Day missions. Admin staff were given paintbrushes and told to help ground-crew paint black and white invasion stripes under and over the wings of the aircraft and around the rear fuselage. A South African RAF squadron leader who was visiting Duxford to make arrangements for the 'Thunderbolt All-American Swing Band' to play a dance at his airfield discovered next morning that his Spitfire had also received the black and white stripes![4] Other personnel were pressed into service as truck drivers and ammunition linkers. Red Cross workers made piles of sandwiches and gallons of coffee, which were taken around to the men as they worked or walked their guard posts. Because of the sentries, it became an accomplishment to drive around the perimeter track. D-Day had arrived![5]

By 0330 hours the 83rd and 84th Squadrons, with pilots who had slept only an hour or two that night, were ready and the first of the three 8th Air Force missions of the day took off. VIIIth Fighter Command code-named the three fighter missions, *Full House*, *Stud* and *Royal Flush*, which either by design or coincidence were in keeping with the giant gamble the Allies were taking. It could also be said that the Allies held all the aces for they had surprise and superiority in numbers.[6] The first mission flown by the 8th Air Force was primarily concerned with neutralising enemy coastal defences and front-line troops. Subsequent missions would be directed against lines of communication leading to the bridgehead. The bombers would be in good company with no fewer than thirty-six squadrons of Mustangs and Thunderbolts patrolling the area. Initially, they would protect the 'Big Friends' but would later break off and strafe ground targets. It was evident that there could be no delay and that any stragglers would be left to their fate. Any aborts were to drop out of formation before leaving the English coast and then fly back to base at below 14,000 feet. It was a one-way aerial corridor and the traffic flow intense. Aircraft would fly to and fro over the length of England dropping various coloured flares to denote the aerial corridors. If an aircraft had to be ditched, only those ships returning to England from the bridgehead would stop to pick up airmen. They were told that if they were shot down they were to wait in uniform until they could join their own troops in France. The Thunderbolts' task was to provide cover for the Normandy landings.

Over the landing beaches the P-47 pilots reported seeing flashes over the coastal area and ground rockets being fired in the distance. After the first mission was completed the P-47s returned to Duxford where they were re-armed and refuelled, ready to go again. The 82nd Squadron, which had remained behind, went out on the second mission to relieve the earlier aircraft and bombed and strafed railway lines in the area near the invasion area. Single squadron fighter-bomber sorties were flown from midday from 0945 hours to 1430 hours with eight P-47s bombing and eight more providing top cover before the roles were reversed. A railroad bridge forty miles north-west of Paris was bombed and the P-47s also glide-bombed the marshalling yards at Alençon with fourteen 250-lb bombs, which damaged two locomotives, thirty to forty-five box cars, eight to ten coal cars and ten flat cars loaded with motor vehicles. One truckload of soldiers was reportedly left burning and three others damaged. Two locomotives were destroyed by bombing and the P-47s machine-gunned five freight cars. A large explosion was also caused in a nearby ammunition dump. This frenetic activity lasted all day. The only contact with the *Luftwaffe* came on the third mission, a fighter bomber effort to St Valery aerodrome and the marshalling yards at Mayenne, which was led by Colonel Fred Gray. Near Mayenne the Thunderbolts bounced eight Fw 190s and shot down two of them. The P-47s also bombed and strafed two locomotives and shot up a few other rail targets.

Duxford's last mission of D-Day took off at 1822 hours when thirty-two P-47s plus spares were despatched to patrol the northern and southern sectors in the area of Chaillone Coulonche. The Jug pilots looked in vain for enemy aircraft reported by the controller but they failed to find them in the dusk and they departed for Duxford at 2130 hours. Some others had better luck. They strafed a twelve-car petrol train, which exploded sending debris into the air and pieces hit three of the low-flying Thunderbolts. 2nd Lieutenant Wallace R Hailey had to abandon his damaged Thunderbolt over the Channel and ASR picked him up unhurt. The two other damaged P-47s landed safely at Ford on the south coast. The rest began arriving back at Duxford at around 2300 hours. Altogether 2,362 American bomber sorties and 1,880 VIIIth Fighter Command sorties were flown with claims for twenty-eight enemy fighters shot down. An indication of the success of the operation was contained in a message from Lieutenant General Doolittle. 'Today the greatest effective strength in the history of the 8th Air Force was reached; an overall effectiveness of approximately 75 per cent of all crews and airplanes assigned. Please extend my congratulations to all members...for their untiring effort in achieving this impressive strength.'

There was no respite even though the weather, which had not been good since the invasion, got worse and the Thunderbolts were over France again during the next two days as everyone worked flat out to keep the momentum going. Regular news broadcasts plus a mimeographed sheet of station news kept everyone informed about the progress of the landings they were working. The weather prevented any flying on 9 June but next day the weather abated to allow four missions to be flown. The first, a fighter-bomber strike along the rail system in the vicinity of Le Touquet-Evereux-Conches, was an indication of the high losses to come on what was to become the worst day in 78th Fighter Group history. They arrived in the area at around 0720 hours and skip dive-bombed and strafed bridges, marshalling yards, rail cars, trucks, tanks and flak towers. 1st Lieutenant Robert L Baker was lost when his P-47 exploded after flak hit his underwing bombs while he was strafing at low level. 2nd Lieutenant Richard S Kuehner's Thunderbolt hit a pole on his bomb run and he crashed at Beaumont Le Roger and his full bombload exploded.

The second strike comprising about forty P-47s took off at 1245 hours led by Major Harold E Stump, 84th Squadron CO, who was flying the first mission of his second combat tour after returning from leave in the US. The Thunderbolts arrived in the area south of the Normandy beachhead bomb line at Bernay-Lisieux-Argentan-La Ferte Mace, shortly before 1400 hours, eight of the 82nd Squadron continuing along the railway lines toward Rennes looking for targets. Stump led the P-47s in a dive-bombing attack on a railroad bridge south-west of Argentan. The first five aircraft had released their bombs and were pulling up when they were bounced by twenty Bf 109s reportedly painted in Allied markings. Major Stump, Captain William F Hunt, and 2nd Lieutenant Daniel T Loyd, who had belly-landed his flak damaged P-47 near Duxford returning from the first mission of the day, were shot down. The CO and Hunt were killed. Upon crashing Loyd was taken captive by two SS soldiers who murdered him in cold blood.[7] The rest of the Thunderbolts jettisoned their bombs and climbed back up to intercept the enemy fighters and five were claimed as destroyed. 1st Lieutenant Robert J McIntosh, who claimed one of the enemy fighters, and 1st Lieutenant James F Casey were shot down. They survived to be taken prisoner. 1st Lieutenant Vincent J Massa was shot down and killed and Major Donald W McLeod, who claimed two fighters destroyed, was shot down though he was able to evade capture and he was later taken in by the French Resistance. Heading for home 1st Lieutenant Herbert L Boyle was forced to crash-land his damaged Thunderbolt at Manston.

At 1730 hours thirty P-47s took off from Duxford for the third and final mission of the day to bomb an ammunition dump south of Falaise. During the outbound climb through overcast toward the south coast, two P-47s collided near Southminster, south of London. 2nd Lieutenant Francis J Kochanek was able to bale out and he suffered a broken ankle when he hit the ground. 1st Lieutenant William M McDermott died trapped in his Thunderbolt as it hit the ground. The remaining P-47s flew on to France and bombed the railway bridge north of Falaise and some canal barges at Montfort. News of the losses caused morale at Duxford to sag temporarily.

Despite the weather, forty-five missions were flown during June and as July beckoned travel restrictions were lifted to a distance of twenty-five miles from Duxford though London was out of bounds. July got off to a bad start with the loss of two pilots on the first day of the month when their P-47 fighter-bombers collided on take-off in a crosswind. 1st Lieutenant Edward T Kitley and 2nd Lieutenant Cleon W Raese had just lifted off when their P-47s, which were carrying two 250-lb bombs on each wing and a full belly tank, crashed about a quarter of a mile from the end of the runway. Both men died instantly. Four days later 1st Lieutenant Jack B Miller had to abort the mission when his Thunderbolt developed failing oil pressure. Over the Seine Bay he was shot down by RAF Spitfires and he was forced to bale out over the Channel where he was picked up by an Allied beach patrol and later flown back to Duxford from a beachhead airstrip.

On 6 July the Group set off for an early morning attack on trains on the railway line from Orleans, south of Paris. Led by Captain Richard Holly the P-47s made their usual landfall at Le Treport on the coast at 0600 hours and flew south between Rouen and the west of Paris. At 0615 hours at 15,000 feet the P-47s spotted a formation of twenty-five Fw 190s at seven o'clock high and turned into them head-on. The enemy fighters split-essed for the deck near Rambouillet, south-west of Paris and the Thunderbolts chased after them. Captain Foy C Higginbottom downed one of the Fw 190s and the German pilot abandoned his doomed fighter. 1st Lieutenant Franklin R Pursell dived vertically down at 450 mph on another Fw 190 and shot it down before pulling up out of the dive at 8,000 feet. Other P-47s pilots chased the fleeing Fw 190s to near the Paris suburbs where the enemy tried to lure their pursuers between two flak towers while ten to fifteen more 190s circled at 9,000 feet waiting to bounce the P-47s. Captain Harry T Lay, who had flown a first combat tour on B-17s with the 91st Bomb Group at Bassingbourn, climbed his flight to 7,000 feet and the three Thunderbolt pilots attacked. Lay shot one Fw 190 down at 800 feet. 2nd Lieutenant Charles E Parmelee downed another with a burst of fire from 150 yards and 1st Lieutenant John B Putnam downed another after scoring thirty hits in the cockpit area. The Focke-Wulf crashed into a block of houses. The rest of the Fw 190s latched onto Putnam's tail but he out-ran them in a five-minute chase. Eleven days later Harry Lay was lost after strafing a German troop train near Liffel-le-Grand when AA hit his P-47 fire. Lay baled out safely and he was seen running into a wood pursued by German troops who jumped from the train. As they went after the American other P-47s circled and machine-gunned the troops until they ran low on ammunition and had to head home. Lay was never seen again.

On 19 July more than 1,100 bombers operating in five forces attacked targets in Germany. Over 730 fighters operating in nineteen separate units supported them. At 0705 hours Major Ben I Mayo, the 84th Squadron CO, took off and led three squadrons comprising forty-eight P-47s plus spares on the escort for the bomber stream headed for targets in west and south-west Germany. Turning above some Liberators, the Thunderbolts flew past the mass formation of bombers and took up their assigned position at the lead box of Fortresses. Ten minutes later they were relieved by a P-51 group and the Jugs broke away to seek ground targets at Eutingen airfield near Koblenz-Limburg, which had been spotted earlier and was full of parked aircraft. The Jugs let down in a wide circle to the north of Eutingen and flew on at low level to the west of the target where the leading flights flew in across the airfield four abreast. Each pilot picked out a target and there was very little flak so after pulling up two miles to the east they returned for another pass from north-east to south-west. Ben Mayo almost ran head-on into a flight of P-47s coming in from the west. Still there was little flak and he called for a third pass. By this time the airfield was almost hidden by thick smoke from seventeen burning Ju 188s, Do 217s, *Stukas* and Me 410s and the attack had to be aborted. On the way home a locomotive was destroyed and other P-47 pilots found and attacked an airfield at Freudenstadt near Stuttgart. On his first pass Major Norman 'Doug' Munson, who was flying his fourth mission of his second tour, destroyed a Ju 52 transport and 1st Lieutenant James E Kinsolving got another. Munson made a second pass, approaching west to east across the grass airfield and got good hits on another Ju 52, which caught fire. His Thunderbolt then appeared to take a flak hit and it nosed down and struck the ground at a slight angle and caught fire before sliding along the airfield and into an adjoining field. Munson was a popular squadron commander and his pilots took their frustrations out on a locomotive on the way home.

As usual after a big day, nearly everyone on the base who was feeling pretty good made for the clubs and bars on base. Officers retired to the Officers' Club, the sergeants, the Sergeants' Club, others, the Aeroclub or Duffy's Tavern, the mixing pot of the base. Over glasses of beer (specially brewed for Duxford) many a mission was retold many a ball game was replayed; many a TS [Tough Shit] problem was aired; commented on and the accompanying 'TS slip' dutifully punched. Captain W.L. 'Duffy' Owen, who doubled as station athletic officer, was a frequent host and bull-shooter. The Officers' Club housed mess and kitchens, a comfortable lounge, card rooms, recreational rooms and a bar. The dining room had become a dance floor for parties. When the sun did shine the front terrace and lawns were popular for lounging and sun bathing. The Aeroclub was everybody's meeting place. Coffee hour in the morning found everyone gathered together over rolls and coffee, swapping rumours, trading news and gripes. Downstairs was a large snack bar and lounge, used for dances three nights each month; kitchens and staff quarters; and a small lounge named the State Room, used by officers during the day and for small social functions each evening. A stage opened into the snack bar and the second floor was devoted to a library, reading and writing rooms, lounge, barber shop and offices. The Sergeants' Club had a modern, half-circular bar, lounge; card room and billiard room. A ballroom was used for the monthly dances; for ping-pong games; as additional lounge space and for private parties. On cool nights groups of men gathered around the several fireplaces in the club to sip beer and swap tales and experiences.

At least two of the P-47 pilots passed on the clubs and bar. Their recreation would come later on that warm July evening. For now, John Putnam and Martin Smith waited expectantly for the arrival of their buddy, Lieutenant James A Sasser, a B-17 pilot at Horham, Suffolk. Sasser had been a member of the 84th Squadron before joining the 95th Bomb Group. He appeared over the field in his B-17, *Ready Freddie*, with three other crewmembers on board. They landed and picked up Putnam and eight other members of his Squadron. Sasser then took off and proceeded to buzz the control tower. *Ready Freddie* headed towards the tower and the technical site from the east only a few feet above the flying field. Sasser judged his pull up over the tower accurately but evidently did not see the warning blinker light mast on top of the 84th Squadron's hangar behind the tower. *Ready Freddie* clipped the mast and the impact sheered off part of the left wing, which folded back and tore off the left horizontal stabiliser and part of the rudder. The B-17 rolled inverted to the left over the top of the Officers' Club, dropping the stabiliser on the lawn outside and the wing section on its roof while a fuel tank landed on an empty hut. *Ready Freddie* passed over a corner of the ball fields at the back of the Club, causing the ballplayers to scatter and crashed into the main barrack block of the 83rd Squadron. All thirteen men on board were killed. Smith, who died in the crash, had just eight hours remaining to finish his tour. Sergeant Ernest Taylor, who was in the barracks, also died. Two others were badly burned. The Fortress was fully loaded with fuel and the barrack block burned for three hours and was destroyed. With the help of the Cambridge Fire Department, base firefighters finally managed to extinguish the flames. Captain William J Zink the Chaplain made two unsuccessful attempts to rescue the man in the barracks. At first unable to reach him because of fumes and smoke, Zink dashed out, grabbed a gas mask and helmet and re-entered the building but falling beams and fire stopped him. Then he gave last rites for the victims and helped medical personnel extricate bodies from the wreckage of the bomber. He was presented with the Soldier's Medal for his actions and thus became the first 8th Air Force chaplain to receive the award. Flames gutted most of one Squadron building while pieces, which hit the officers' barracks and a barracks, caused lesser damage. After the crash, squadrons held formations and checked rolls carefully for men missing in the accident. Had the accident occurred thirty minutes or so later, at least a hundred men would have been in the building because by then the crewmen would have been in off the line.

During July the Group had flown twenty-eight missions with eleven Thunderbolts lost and had claimed nine aerial victories and another twenty ground strafing victories as well as a big haul of locomotives and other transportation targets. 1st Lieutenant Dick Hewitt arrived back in England on 27 July following his thirty-day R&R in the States.

> The 78th had lost over 30 pilots during our leave. Major Norman D Munson, our 82nd acting CO, who also returned just ahead of me, was killed strafing an aerodrome in Germany on 19 July. Then my fifth roommate, Captain Jim Wilkinson, had also perished while I was away. Al Juchheim had crashed, head-on, with a P-51 over Germany shortly after I finished tour #1. He was fortunate to have baled out and was now a PoW. Al had 76 missions at the time and it had to be close, if not his last, mission of his tour. Having also lost Grant Turley, roommate #4 way back on 6 March, my anxiety became even greater.[8]

On 2 August the month got off to a bad start when Captain Charles Clark, the 82nd Squadron CO, was shot down during a bombing and strafing attack in the Beauvais-Compiègne area when his Thunderbolt was hit by flak. Clark at first tried to nurse his badly damaged fighter home but it was no use and he baled out and was taken prisoner. Major Joseph Myers, a pilot of twenty-six years from Canton, Ohio, who had been born in Hazard, Kentucky, and who had five kills to his name flying P-38s in the 55th Fighter Group, took command of the 82nd Squadron. On 24 August Captain Dick Hewitt flew his first mission of his second tour of combat.

It was back to escorting the Forts and it could not have possibly felt any better. There was plenty of flak but no enemy fighters. With the target in the Hannover/Brunswick area, the latter was somewhat of a surprise. But then, with the advancing armies from the invasion now getting close to the liberation of France, this should have been expected. The German fighters were viciously supporting their ground troops, who were now losing ground to Allied forces, especially General Patton's tank battalions at a fast pace. Between 26 August and 10 September the 78th would revert back to attacking enemy ground targets. We dive bombed and strafed on an almost round-the-clock basis, hitting airdromes; locomotives, tanks, troops and literally everything that moved that appeared to be an enemy. Cutting off and destroying strategic military materials and supplies to their front line troops was our number one goal. The Ninth Air Force, which had now moved to France, was similarly engaged and combined; this would be the start of a major turning point in the war. But there were to be some long, hard months of conflict ahead.[9]

On 28 August the Duxford Outfit flew two missions, which would turn out to be quite a day for the 82nd Squadron pilots. But it did not get off to a good start for twenty-year-old 2nd Lieutenant Lawrence 'Larry' W Nelson from Warren, Ohio, whose first combat mission this was. As a youngster living near Akron it had been easy to visit the giant dirigible hangar on weekends with his father to watch the construction of the *Akron* and *Macon* dirigibles for the US Navy. One of Nelson's early flying experiences was when his dad took him for a ride in a Ford Tri-Motor, a great thrill. Charles Lindbergh, who was the first to fly solo across the Atlantic Ocean, was one of his early idols. In 1927 he became the first person to be awarded the Distinguished Flying Cross. Little did Nelson realise that one day he would receive the DFC. Another of his heroes was Colonel Roscoe Turner, an extrovert racing pilot who he saw at the Cleveland Air Races each Labor Day weekend. The one-time 'barnstormer' had taken up air racing in 1929, winning both the Thompson and Bendix Trophy races. Nelson recalls:

Barnstorm pilots did loops at low level in Ford Tri-Motors, flew in close formation and performed many death-defying tricks. The Army, Navy and Marines always put on special group displays [but the big event] was the Thompson Trophy Race, a closed course race around pylons. Roscoe Turner competed in and won that race three times. The final time he won was in 1939. I took a picture of him walking behind his plane[10] on the way to a 'race horse start' where they lined up abreast and started with the drop of a flag.

Larry Nelson carried the photo of the flamboyant showman in his wallet at Duxford, where on that warm August day in 1944 he and seven other Thunderbolts lined up on the hallowed grass airfield for their own line abreast take-off.

It was a real eye-opener. Since our field was grass rather than concrete, our

Group took off eight abreast instead of two. We lined up in rows of eight – a total of 48 Thunderbolts – with me amongst them. I must admit I was a bit taken aback since I had never taken off in such a large group before. The sound was deafening. To make matters worse, the worn-out plane assigned to me was a 'klunker' (an old plane whose next stop would he the scrap pile). The 'klunker' came equipped with two 500 pound bombs hanging off the wings and a 250 gallon belly tank for extra fuel. Being a bit timid and inexperienced, my take-off lagged behind the other seven planes in my row. As a result, the prop wash from the other planes caused my plane to lose altitude and ripped through a row of trees on the edge of the field. The tree limbs bent my prop, damaged the engine cowling, took off a large part of my left wing, and dented one of my bombs (which, fortunately, was unarmed). Somehow I managed to guide my 'klunker' to a safe landing. As a result of this rather bad beginning, the 'klunker' was consigned to the scrap pile where it belonged. Second, I received a brand new P-47D Thunderbolt. Third, no plane ever got ahead of me during take-off in any of my 66 missions. Fourth, I got the rest of the day off!

On their second mission of the day the 82nd Squadron became the first Allied squadron to shoot down a Me 262 *Sturmvogel* ('Storm Bird') jet aircraft. The P-47s were flying at 11,000 feet in the vicinity of Termonde, west of Brussels, when Major Joseph Myers noticed an unusual aircraft flying 'extremely fast' and 'low to the ground'. Leaving four of his flight to give top cover, Myers led the other three of his aircraft down to investigate in a 45-degree dive. His P-47 was indicating 450 mph when he overhauled the enemy aircraft, which he identified as a Me 262. *Oberfeldwebel* Hieronymous 'Ronny' Lauer of I./KG(J)51 *Kommando Schenk*, who was in the process of transferring from Juvincourt near Reims to a base at Chievres, Belgium, was piloting the jet.[11] Lauer must have seen the P-47s closing in on him because at the last moment the German took evasive action in the way of flat turns. Myers was about to fire at the jet from above as it flew along at 500 feet when the Me 262's wing hit the ground and he crash-landed in a ploughed field, 'skidding to a halt after some distance'. Lauer scrambled from the cockpit and ran for cover in nearby trees where he watched as the Jugs strafed the wrecked aircraft. Lieutenant Manford O Croy Jr, Myers' wingman, fired on Lauer and claimed to have hit him as he was running from the wrecked aircraft but he was not injured and subsequently flew many more jet sorties and survived the war.[12] Myers and Croy were given half shares in the Me 262 victory. Major Jack Oberhansly the Group Deputy CO was credited with downing a Ju 88 near Charleroi, Belgium, which he blew up after diving down from 11,000 feet and firing from 200 to 50 yards' range. It was Oberhansly's sixth and final aerial victory of the war. The Thunderbolt flown by Lieutenant Colonel Olin E Gilbert was hit by flak while strafing Charleroi airfield and he had to belly-land his ailing aircraft. Gilbert clambered out and successfully evaded capture and with the help of the Resistance he was back at Duxford on 12 September.[13] 2nd Lieutenant John F Lacy's Thunderbolt was hit by debris during an attack on a train near Beaumont, Belgium, and he also had to belly-land. He was led away to become a prisoner as the rest of his Squadron strafed his wrecked Thunderbolt.

It took time for new pilots like Lieutenant Larry Nelson to get into the 'Routine of War'.

Every day was a learning experience, as I discovered with my first take-off. Fighter pilots were pilot, navigator, bombardier, gunner and radioman. I would generally be told in advance if I were scheduled to fly a mission the following day. However, from time to time, we were aroused from our sleep to put on a 'maximum' effort or to respond to an emergency. Since we could get forty-eight planes in the air in a relatively short time, our group was called on often. Normally, the wake up officer would call us at four or five am. Often we were already awake because we could hear bomber planes from surrounding bases taking off and forming up. They had to get a head start on us because they were slower. We would rendezvous at a predetermined point before we entered enemy territory. One good thing about mission day was that each pilot got a fresh egg prepared just the way he liked it! That was a real treat.

After breakfast, we were briefed on our flight plan by the CO. Walking to a briefing from the officers' club in the early morning darkness, the sentries on guard would salute us as we entered the flight area. One sentry in particular enjoyed saluting me with the greeting 'Good Morning, "Shorty" Sir.' I was probably the shortest and youngest pilot in the group. When I sent my mother a picture of my single-seat plane, she asked if I were the only one in it. I think she was worried! During the briefing, we were shown the target of the day, told where to expect flak, and alerted as to the kind and number of enemy aircraft we might encounter. Flight and element leaders were given a 3 x 5 mission card on which was written, or typed, call signs, headings, times and distances. We also synchronised our watches. Since we never flew a direct course to the target, we also were given directions back to the base if we had to abort for any reason. During our briefing, the crew chief and armourer warmed up the planes, added ammunition and topped off the gas tanks. When the briefing was over, we climbed into the trucks that would drop us off at our planes. I now had a shiny new Thunderbolt. I was ready for that racehorse start! We taxied out and took our position among the group of forty-eight planes. On signal we poured on the power and were off into the 'Wild Blue Yonder'!

Unfortunately, the wild blue yonder wasn't always so blue since many missions were flown over complete cloud cover. It was rather tense flying through dense clouds in close formation. If you lost your leader, there were a lot of planes to collide with – forty-eight to be exact. You had to trust your instruments because your brain could not discern up from down. Once I accompanied a friend with engine trouble from Poznan, Poland, to England over complete cloud cover. We had to fly what seemed like hours for the base to hear our radio and give us a vector home. Eventually we found we were nearly where we were supposed to be. However, due to a shortage of gas, we landed on an English airfield, which was located right on the English Channel. That was scary – I was only 20 years old. But I was lucky and I was very well trained. We called our Commanding Officer 'the old man' although he was only 24-years old. The rest of us were just a bunch of kids straight out of high school. Our youth worked against us at times. On one mission, we were preparing to strafe and dive bomb an airfield. I armed my bombs and headed for a hangar full of planes. In order to do maximum damage to the airfield I released my bombs and belly tank, with its remaining fuel, directly on the target. But the one thing I forgot was that I was using gas from that tank to fly the plane! When I pulled up to return, my engine began to sputter. My first thought was that I had been hit by flak. We were taught to change tanks when the engine stopped. When I switched tanks my engine regained power. Once again luck and training carried me through another tough situation.

On one of my early missions we were sent out to protect a group of bombers from enemy fighters. We divided into three squadrons. One squadron flew above the bombers ('top cover'), one group flew with them, and the third flew 'on the deck' to strafe and dive bomb flak positions and targets of opportunity. Eight of us were flying top cover when we spotted a group of forty Me 109s at 20,000 feet preparing an attack on the bomber group. Our squadron leader called the rest of our group to tell them we had the forty Me 109s 'cornered'! When the group leader asked how many of us there were, he replied, 'eight'! That was the laugh of the day when we returned to base. But we dove into them fearlessly, diverting them from their plan and knocking three from the sky. How did we do it? We were young and carefree and had very good airplanes. We felt invincible.

On 1 September VIIIth Fighter Command announced that the combat tour had been shortened from 300 hours to 285 hours, which was especially good news for pilots who did not know that they had completed their tour until after they had landed. Major Quince L Brown, who had returned to the 84th Squadron on 28 August after leave in the US after his first tour, scored his twelfth victory on 1 September when he destroyed a Bf 109 between Liege and Trier. It was his 135th combat sortie. The Oklahoman seemed destined to increase his score with the squadron he had joined in April 1943.

There was a light drizzle the next day when Bing Crosby's USO Troupe performed a show at one of the single-bay Belfast hangar entrances, which had been converted into a theatre by the RAF and used for dances and shows. Special Service personnel had soon updated the building and installed foldaway seats in rising rows and a stage, complete with curtains and stage lighting, which filled one side. The walls were enclosed in panelling removed from crates and boxes; the seating space enlarged; a new motion-picture projection booth built, paint added, more lights and stoves were fitted and soon they had a first-class theatre. Many travelling shows requested Duxford as one of their stops because of the theatre's fine dressing rooms and stage, and large seating capacity. Apart from Bing Crosby the theatre was to host several well-known stars of the cinema and radio such as James Cagney, Bob Hope, Frances Langford, and Tommy Farr. Refinements like this made Duxford one of the most comfortable AAF bases overseas but then two tragedies that struck during the first week of September 1944 shook the very foundations of the 'Country Club' atmosphere that pervaded Duxford.

The first occurred during the late afternoon of 3 September when a RAF Halifax bomber crashed near Pampisford and an engineering platoon from Duxford arrived on the scene to help. Unfortunately while trying to locate survivors the bombload exploded, killing the Fire-Fighting Platoon Commander and three other personnel from the base. Three other men were struck by a flying tree trunk but escaped serious injury. All five members of the Halifax perished in the fire. Three days later, while scouting Vogelsland airfield near Weimühle in Germany Major Quince Brown's P-47 was hit by flak. He succeeded in baling out two kilometres west of Schleiden only to be apprehended by an SS officer who murdered him in cold blood with a pistol shot to the back of his head.[14]

On 9 September the 78th Fighter Group flew an escort to Aachen. Captain Peter T Keillor, who had just been assigned to the 84th Squadron, flew his first combat mission this day. Keillor had flown a combat tour on P-39s in the South Pacific in 1943 before transitioning to P-47s and being sent to England in the late summer of 1944. He had not been enamoured with the old P-47C models during his stint as a pilot instructor at Baton Rouge. There they had only 80 octane gasoline so they could only use about 42 inches of mercury for manifold pressure, just enough power to drag off the ground and climb about 800 feet a minute. He was used to climbing 3,500 feet a minute in formation in a P-39. During a formation and orientation flight at Duxford on 8 September his opinion of the Thunderbolt changed. Another squadron bounced the formation and a mock dogfight ensued during which Keillor pushed the throttle up to war emergency power (72 inches of mercury and 2,700 rpm) and the P-47 became 'another kind of beast'. The escort mission to Aachen proved uneventful for Keillor until they were on their way back.

I was flying wingman on the flight leader, cruising along straight and level at 10,000 feet when I heard a low wump, wump. I looked around and right behind us there was a bunch of big black puffballs and catching up fast. I hollered BREAK and did so immediately and I guess everyone else did too. We formed up again and came on home. I had a little shrapnel in my wing and the fellow whose plane I was flying complained bitterly because that was the first time his plane had been hit.[15]

Some of the pilots shot up locomotives in the Giessen-Frankfurt-Fulda area. Major Ben Mayo and his Flight were very low on ammunition when they spotted eight Fw 190s flying low twenty miles north of Frankfurt heading east. Mayo, who knew that he had only about seventy-five rounds remaining in all four guns, was determined to close to point blank range to make his few rounds count. He latched onto a Fw 190 and gave it two short bursts. The Fw 190 nosed over and went straight in from just 75 feet. Mayo then attacked and shot down a second Fw 190, the German pilot baling out from 1,000 feet before his stricken fighter half rolled and exploded in a wood. The enemy pilot's parachute failed to open. Another Fw 190 was attacked by Lieutenant Wilbur K Grimes and was finished off by 1st Lieutenant Richard N Dunham who hit the pilot as he was baling out. The fighter hit a hill and exploded. Other pilots attacked a dozen Fw 190s taking off from an airfield near Giessen and 1st Lieutenant Howard S Scholz caused two to crash. Captain Wayne L Coleman got three others, the third after a long chase. Captain Herbert K Shope dropped his two 250-lb bombs on the airfield and destroyed three fighters before shooting up and destroying a Ju 88 at another airfield to the south-west.

Next day, 10 September, the Group claimed forty German bombers strafed and destroyed at Mainbullau and Gernsheim airfields in the Aschaffenburg-Mannheim area of Germany. Captain Raymond E Smith was the top scorer, claiming five Heinkel He 111s and three shared ground victories. 2nd Lieutenant Charles E Parmelee's P-47 was hit by flak and he attempted a belly-landing near Wiesbaden only for his Thunderbolt to hit a stone wall and he died in the explosion. 2nd Lieutenant William O Lacey's P-47 was hit by intense flak at Mainbullau and rolled over on its back. Lacey was trapped inside and he was killed when the Thunderbolt crashed and burst into flames. Strafing a marshalling yard at Heilbronn in *Thoroughbred*, 2nd Lieutenant Lawton E Clark hit the top of a train and he too was killed. Only the day before Clark had had problems pulling out in time and he had hit a tree. This was not the first time either, because the forward fuselage of his P-47 now had two tree symbols added to his scoreboard of five locomotive and five truck kills. The other pilots guessed that Clark had trouble with his depth perception and had kidded him about his bad eyesight. 2nd Lieutenant Paul H McKenney failed to return after being hit heavily by flak at Gernsheim airfield. He survived and was taken prisoner. Robert Clague was also downed by flak but he bellied in south-west of Darmstadt and he was also captured. Altogether, the Group claimed thirteen aerial victories, forty-seven ground victories and eighty locomotives during twenty momentous missions in September but eighteen P-47s were lost. Losses were high mainly because of the strafing missions on 10 September and six flak-suppression and air support missions the Group flew during Operation *Market Garden*, 17–26 September.

One of the biggest operations of the war, *Market Garden* went ahead using American and British airborne divisions to take the Eindhoven, Nijmegen and Arnhem bridges on the Rhine with support provided by the Allied air forces. The operation has been described in an official report as 'by far the biggest and most ambitious airborne operation ever carried out by any nation or nations'. The aim was to cut the German-occupied Netherlands almost in half and to prepare the way for the invasion of Germany that would bypass the northern flank of Germany's Westwall fortifications (The Siegfried Line).[16]

On Sunday 17 September fifty P-47s took off from Duxford and flew to Holland. In all, 1,113 medium and heavy bombers escorted by 330 fighter aircraft carried out bombing attacks to eliminate the opposition before the airborne forces of *Market Garden* went in later that day.[17] Paving the way for the parachute drop in their assigned area the 78th Fighter Group sent a flight down to between 2,000 and 2,500 feet to draw enemy flak while others strafed and dropped 260-lb fragmentation bombs on the well-fortified German flak and 88-mm gun emplacements. After this the P-47s would return to the Dutch coast to escort the first glider towing transports to their landing zones.[18] Captain Dick Hewitt recalls:

We came in around 8,000 feet, armed with two 250 pound frag bombs and a full load of .50 calibre ammo. Our plan, which sounded like we were to be the flak gunners' 'clay pigeons', was to 'tool' along at 8,000 feet, getting them to fire first. Once we spotted their gun flashes or the flak bursts, we'd go after them, firing as we dove, and then drop our fragmentary bombs right up their gun barrels as we pulled out. After expending our two bombs, we would continue to rake them until our ammo was gone. If successful in knocking out their flak emplacements, a lot of paratrooper lives would be saved. Well it sure did not work out as planned. Those flak gunners must have been experts at playing possum.[19] The C-47s and C-46s came in with gliders in tow, all loaded with paratroops. Several were hit and knocked down with their gliders still in tow. It was another one of those totally helpless feelings, to watch the gliders cut loose and then see men and planes go crashing to the ground. We did try to retaliate but with paratroopers, equipment planes and gliders all over the sky and ground, it was hopeless cause. We lost five 78th pilots in two days of this 'hide and seek' tactic. A total of 18 men and planes were lost in 20 day period during Market Garden. 2nd Lieutenant Don C Hart of the 82nd came within a 'gnat's eyebrow' of being one of the casualties.[20]

Hart recalled:

I was flying #2 on Major Conner, the CO's wing. I came in low on my bomb run, hoping to skip bomb the flak emplacement and knock it out. I released my bombs and almost instantly knew I had been hit, either by their flak or the flying bomb fragments. Since the explosion was immediate and right under my wings, I figured I had been hit by my own bombs. The metal on the top of the wing had protruding holes, indicating it had come upward from below. It didn't look too bad. I called Major Conner, who came abreast and agreed it looked to be just in the wing. We decided to head back for England, but about three miles off the Dutch coast, my prop 'ran away'. Controlled by hydraulics, the line servicing its engine-driven pump had evidently been severed by the flying shrapnel. The engine froze up almost immediately and quit dead. I figured I'd ride it down to 1,000 feet and then bale out. Canopy open, harness and seat belt released, I dived for the trailing edge of the wing on the right side, just like the book said. Hand on my D-ring one hard pull, and my chute opened. Then one short swing and I was in the water. I had almost figured it too close. I did not see my plane hit but it must have 'sank like a tank.' It was nowhere in sight. I was wearing a seat pack chute so the dinghy was slung underneath my butt. 'Now how do you inflate this?' I thought as I pulled it from its pack. My Mae West was barely keeping me afloat and I was swallowing a lot of seawater. We had an earlier training class on the procedure for doing this but 'smart-ass me', I thought it was a waste of time and had played hooky. Here I was, six months later, splashing around in the North Sea, about to drown, and I didn't know how to inflate a dinghy.

With a picture filling my mind of my mother back in Walla Walla, Washington, getting a War Department telegram saying I had drowned at sea, I grabbed the CO_2 bottle, and with the strength of desperation, I sheered off the cotter pin holding the valve closed. The rescue crew verified this later. The dinghy only partially inflated. I was now so fatigued, I could barely pull myself up and into the dinghy. At least I was now on top of the water. Looking up, I heard a plane and saw it was Conner, circling high above me. He had called ASR, giving a good fix, as I found out later an RAF Wellington [sic][21] showed up in about 15 minutes, dropping some rations and a 'mummy bag' from the bomb bay. On days and missions like this one, they were almost in a 'waiting pattern', to respond quickly to to emergency situations like mine. I was supposed to crawl into the bag for warmth, but I was too exhausted to do anything now.

I could see Major Conner still circling, and with my bright yellow dinghy I hoped he'd be able to keep me in sight. There was no choice but to lay in the dinghy and wait. But how long could he stay and would his gas hold out? I think I prayed a little as the Lord was my sole help at the moment. After what seemed like an eternity (Conner later told me it was about an hour), a big British air rescue launch pulled alongside of me. Conner said he almost 'shot the dammed thing' – it had taken so long. I could hardly blame him, as his fuel had to be getting darned low. Thank God he didn't, though. They hauled me aboard, gave me a big shot of rum, which was supposed to warm me. It did nothing as I 'upchucked' it along with about a quart of seawater I had swallowed. Rescuing me seemed almost secondary as they were more interested in my gear and were a bit put out that I was not wearing the high, fleece-lined, flying boots we often wore. Being a lower altitude mission, I had chosen not to wear them that day. They kept my flight suit, flying jacket and even the packet of survival food. Why they took that seemed so trivial. I was now safe, wrapped in a couple of rough wool blankets and starting to warm up a bit. I recall little after that except I recuperated in an R&R facility for three days and won $28 playing poker with some GIs. Gambling with enlisted men was a 'no-no' but I couldn't have cared less.

On 18 September, when the Germans counter-attacked and forestalled an American attempt to capture the bridge at Nijmegen, 252 Liberators, each loaded with about 6,000 lb of perishables and fuel supplies, set off to drop their loads over LZ.N Knapheide-*Klein Amerika* (Little America) near Groesbeek. Late in the afternoon Lieutenant Colonel Jack Oberhansly led the Group to Holland again and the P-47s succeeded in destroying twelve light flak guns and a twenty to thirty truck convoy. Overcast down to 500 feet in some places hampered operations and flak was heavy and accurate. The 56th Fighter Group lost sixteen Thunderbolts shot down and the Duxford Outfit lost five. 2nd Lieutenant Eugene W Wood, who had reported to Duxford at the same time as Pete Keillor, was hit and set on fire by flak in the Nijmegen area. Keillor described the fellow wingman as a 'real eager beaver' who 'couldn't wait to get into combat but he hadn't learned that you had to dodge bullets. First off he made a pass at one of the emplacements and went right on into the ground. We lost Lieutenant Fee too'. 1st Lieutenant John R Fee was hit by flak at the north end of Nijmegen Bridge and was seen to spin into a lake from 2–3,000 feet. Remarkably, Fee survived and he was taken prisoner. 1st Lieutenant Russell C MacDuffee was hit by heavy flak near Turnhout and he baled out to be taken prisoner also. 1st Lieutenant Richard C Snyder was also captured after he was shot down by flak south-west of Rotterdam. 1st Lieutenant John R Logering was hit by flak south-west of Goch and belly-landed inside the Allied lines at Brussels.

On 19 and 20 September poor weather largely grounded the Allied and German air forces although on 20 September the 78th Fighter Group was despatched to Holland. The Group patrolled the Hertogenbosch area but could find no suitable targets so Major Richard E Conner led the P-47s north of Arnhem where they bombed five light flak positions and six more west of Nijmegen. Along the route they strafed a German troop convoy. Flak claimed several RAF Stirling glider tugs and many C-47s but all the Thunderbolts returned safely. On 21 September only ninety P-47s of the 56th and 353rd Fighter Groups were able to provide escort and patrol support for the airborne forces.[22] The 56th Fighter Group claimed twelve enemy fighters destroyed for the loss of one Thunderbolt but they could not prevent JG 26 from claiming seventeen to twenty RAF C-47 Dakotas in 38 and 46 Groups. The P-47s of the 353rd Fighter Group reached the Nijmegen area in time to take on some of the attacking fighters of the IInd and IIIrd *Gruppen* JG 26 and the Wolfpack claimed fifteen fighters shot down and one damaged. But the Fw 190s nevertheless shot down three transports. The 353rd Fighter Group claimed three Fw 190s destroyed and one probable and one damaged for the loss of one Thunderbolt.

On 22 September the bad weather grounded all except a handful of essential reconnaissance missions over the Arnhem Bridge. At 1421 hours on 23 September Colonel Fred Gray led his P-47s off from Duxford to Holland to carry out flak suppression in the RAF resupply drop zone although unbeknown to the Allied Commander, the British troops had withdrawn some time previously. Circling Arnhem, the Thunderbolts approached from the south and turned 90 degrees west to Kasteel where they were enveloped by 20—40-mm light flak from along nearby hedgerows and woods north of the town. Colonel Gray took a squadron and temporarily silenced these guns while enemy guns in a church south of the woods were put out of action by other P-47s. Just west of Heteren, 2nd Lieutenant Dunstan D Hartley, Gray's wingman, received a direct hit and he went straight into the ground. Another formation of C-47s approached the drop zone from the south at extremely low altitude to drop their supplies. Three were shot down by some of the guns, which were soon silenced again by the Thunderbolts. The enemy flak emplacements were very well hidden and the Germans held their fire until the P-47s had passed and were banking away. It was only when they began firing again that the Thunderbolt pilots knew where they were and could attack them again. More and more C-47s and Stirlings appeared at very low level and in areas that had been flak suppressed they were able to drop their supplies without drawing fire but in an area where there was no flak suppression, four Stirlings were shot down in flames. Thirteen of the Thunderbolts returned to Duxford showing signs of battle damage.[23]

No missions were flown on 25 September because of the weather. Next day Major Leonard Marshall and the new 84th Squadron CO vice Ben Mayo, who having finished his tour returned to the States, led the Group on their final Arnhem support mission. The P-47s patrolled the area at 2,500 feet for almost an hour but the only activity they saw were a few bursts of flak at Arnhem and Hertogenbosch and some C-47s landing and taking off from a strip in the area. The 237 sorties the Group flew in support of the operations at Arnhem and Nijmegen earned the Duxford Outfit its first AAF Distinguished Unit Citation. In October they flew mostly escort missions for the bombers. Ground strafing had largely become the main responsibility of the US 9th Air Force Thunderbolt groups.[24] At Duxford the return to escort missions for the bombers was a welcome relief after the heavy losses that had been incurred on ground strafing and flak suppression missions in September. The Duxford Outfit lost just two pilots in October and, ominously, both were shot down during strafing attacks on ground targets. The first of the two pilots lost was on 7 October when 2nd Lieutenant Robert D Smith was killed making a second firing pass at a locomotive north-west of Neustadt. 1st Lieutenant Jack LaGrange Jnr was hit by flak during a strafing pass at Fassberg airfield on 15 October. He baled out and was taken prisoner. During the month the Duxford Outfit claimed twelve victories in the air to take the Group total to date to 239 aerial victories. The first of the month's victories occurred on 7 October when 1,300 B-17s and B-24s bombed five synthetic oil refineries in Czechoslovakia and central and north-eastern Germany.[25] Despite mounting losses there was increasing evidence that the 8th's bombing offensive, against oil targets in particular, was reaping rewards. The *Luftwaffe* was therefore forced to live off stocks accumulated during the winter and spring and began to feel the bite as the fuel crisis grew. The 78th Fighter Group was tasked with penetration and target support for the bombers attacking Leipzig. The Duxford Group claimed its second jet aircraft shot down when Major Richard E Conner intercepted and destroyed a Me 262 of I./KG(J)51, which had its wheels down and was making its final approach to one of the airfields near Osnabrück at 1220 hours. The German pilot baled out and was unhurt.[26] Lieutenant Colonel Joe Myers, who had been the first to shoot down a Me 262, on 28 August, also destroyed a Bf 109 in the Leipzig area. He closed from 300 to 150 yards and opened fire but found that his K-14 gunsight was not functioning properly so he closed to fifty yards dead astern and gave the enemy fighter a burst using his fixed sight.[27] The Bf 109 began burning and went down with the pilot baling out before it crashed. It was Myers' fourth and final victory. A third 78th Fighter Group victory went to 1st Lieutenant Robert R Bosworth. The Leipzig mission was the longest to date with some of the pilots returning to Duxford after five hours and twenty minutes' flying time in the air.

On 15 October the P-47 pilots claimed seven more enemy aircraft. Captain Robert T Green claimed four Fw 190s and 1st Lieutenant Julian S Reems and 2nd Lieutenant Lloyd L Eadline[28] one apiece while Captain Huie H Lamb in the 82nd Squadron claimed a Me 262 near Osnabrück. He spotted the jet while flying at 15,000 feet and he immediately dived down to the Me 262's level at 4,000 feet. Closing to within 1,000 yards in a steep dive at 475 mph Lamb saw the jet begin to pull away but he was able to close very slowly but surely using his water-injection. Once in range Lamb fired a burst and the jet, which was being flown by *Fähnenjunker-Feldwebel* Edgar Junghans of I./KG(J)51, turned left allowing the Thunderbolt pilot to easily turn inside him and score many strikes. Junghans carried out a 180-degree turn and led the American back over an airfield and through an intense light flak barrage. Junghans finally had enough and he jettisoned his canopy. The jet caught fire as it flipped over on its back and exploded. Junghans was severely injured and he died of his wounds in hospital six days later.[29]

Larry Nelson also had a brush with a Me 262 as he recalls:

After a successful raid we were on our way home when I noticed a lot of activity on an airfield we were passing over. I alerted our group and got permission to go down and take a look. I said to my wingman, 'Let's go!' We were at 15,000 feet. I put my nose down and headed for a 'bogey' (our term for the enemy aircraft) dead ahead. The last time I looked I was doing 500 mph. I saw that I was on to a Me 262. I had never seen a German jet before. I had been briefed that it was very fast (over 500 mph on the straight and level), so it was good that I had lots of speed. German airfields had many guns around their perimeter. They opened fire when they saw us. My wingman broke off in the face of all the gunfire coming at us. I latched on to the 'bogey' very close. I started firing bursts. He dropped down to grass-top level. He went right across the airfield so his friends could get a good shot at me. Their tracer bullets were going over my canopy. We were so low they couldn't risk hitting other gunners or their own plane. I kept firing until he bellied in on his airfield. Then, since he was out of the way and I had cleared the field, all guns were focused on me. I don't know how they missed, but I escaped unscathed. As for my wingman, I didn't see him again until we got back to our base. I had used most of my gas. I was all alone with no idea where I was. I knew we had an advanced base at Laon, France, in reoccupied territory. I found the base (don't ask me how), landed, refuelled and headed home alone. Thinking about this now, I don't know how a 20-year old was able to do this. When I returned, I learned I had shot down one of the Germans' newest fighters. This was confirmed by gun cameras in my wing that took pictures when I fired my guns.

Many years later after telling this story to my fellow workers at The Upjohn Company, one of our scientists went on a trip to Germany to exchange scientific ideas. He talked to a German scientist who told him a remarkably similar story of how he was shot down while flying a Me 262. He was burned badly, but survived. If I was the one who shot him down, I'm glad that both of us survived.

1   *Historic Tales of the Wild Blue Yonder* by Larry Nelson (Privately Published 2006).

2   Supreme Headquarters Allied Expeditionary Forces, whose HQ since 28 May 1944 was at Southwick House near Portsmouth.

3   *A Mississippi Fighter Pilot In WWII.*

4   *Eagles of Duxford: The 78th Fighter Group in World War II.*

5   *Duxford Diary 1942–45.* 1945, 1975.

6   The aircraft available in the ETO for Operation *Overlord* totalled over 9,900 operational and non-operational aircraft including 4,709 fighters and

fighter-bombers. 8th Air Force Fighter Command had an effective strength of 961 fighters and the 9th Air Force, 1,123 fighters. On D-Day, 6 June, the Allied air forces numbered over 4,100 fighters of which 2,300 were USAAF day fighters and 1,890 fighters of all types by the RAF. In response the *Luftwaffe* had only 425 fighters of all types in Normandy of which only 250–280 were serviceable on any one day.

7   Shortly after the war a French war Crimes Tribunal found them guilty and they were both executed.

8   *Target of Opportunity: Tales & Contrails of the Second World War*. Captain Hewitt was surprised to learn that he had in fact been transferred to the 55th Fighter Group at Wormingford during his absence but he fought the move all the way and remained in the 82nd Squadron at Duxford for the remainder of the war.

9   *Target of Opportunity: Tales & Contrails of the Second World War*.

10   After recircling a missed pylon Turner overtook the field in his 1,050-hp Laird-Turner LTR, then retired from racing. In the 1934 Melbourne Centenary Air Race between Mildenhall and Melbourne the Boeing 247D crewed by Colonel Roscoe Turner and Clyde Pangborn came third. See *Bombers, 'Blackbirds' & the 'Boom Years' RAF Mildenhall* by Martin W Bowman (Tempus 2007).

11   *The Messerschmitt Me 262 Combat Diary* by John Foreman and SE Harvey (ARP 1990).

12   While attacking 9th Air Force P-47s of the 386th Squadron, 365th Fighter Group, in the Dusseldorf area on 2 October 1944 his Me 262 ran out of fuel. Too low to bale out, his wing hit the ground and the aircraft cartwheeled, coming to a dead stop and exploding. Lauer, although seriously injured, survived. *The Messerschmitt Me 262 Combat Diary*.

13   In the interim, Jack Oberhansly Jnr, who was promoted to lieutenant colonel, took over as Gilbert's replacement. Oberhansly joined the 4th Fighter Group on 4 December 1944 as Deputy CO, serving until 26 February 1945.

14   *See Stars & Bars: A Tribute to the American Fighter Ace 1920–1973* by Frank Olynyk (Grub Street 1995). In 1946 the War Crimes Trial executed the officer for his crime.

15   *Wandering Through World War II* by Pete Keillor (Privately Published 2003).

16   The Allied plan was to capture bridges on the Rhine in Holland at Veghel, Grave, Nijmegen and Arnhem. The 1st British and American 82nd and

101st Airborne Divisions, cut off the Germany Army in the Belgian sector and saved the bridges and the port of Antwerp for the American army units and British XXX Corps advancing north from the Dutch border.

17   The first airlift alone involved 360 British and 1,174 American transport aircraft and 491 gliders, accompanied by 910 fighter escorts. During the course of the operation 20,190 parachutists, 13,781 glider-borne troops, 5,230 tons of equipment and stores, 1,927 vehicles and 568 pieces of artillery were landed behind the German lines.

18   On the way home, Captain Herbert K Shope destroyed a Bf 109 on the ground at Gilze-Rijen airfield.

19   Ten or fifteen minutes after the attack began all but one unlocated 88-mm flak battery had stopped firing. Sixteen multi-gun sites were claimed destroyed and thirty-seven more damaged.

20   *Target of Opportunity: Tales & Contrails of the Second World War.*

21   Actually a Vickers Warwick rescue aircraft of 280 Squadron from Beccles (Ellough) in Suffolk.

22   The situation of the British 1st Airborne Division in Arnhem was now desperate and despite poor weather the Polish 1st Parachute Brigade was at last dropped in the area to the south of Arnhem. Sixteen Stirling glider tugs and thirteen Dakotas crashed in the Arnhem-Nijmegen area out of 114 transports despatched. JG 26 claimed twenty C-47s. The Polish Airborne Brigade failed to break through and the survivors mainly covered the return of the remnants of the 1st Airborne Division across the Rhine on the night of 24/25 September.

23   Of over 10,200 British airborne troops landed in the Arnhem area, 1,440 were killed or died of their wounds. 3,000 were wounded and taken prisoner and 400 medical personnel and chaplains remained behind with the wounded and about 2,500 uninjured troops also became PoWs. There were also 225 prisoners from the 4th Battalion, the Dorsetshire Regiment. About 450 Dutch civilians were killed. The operation also cost 160 RAF and Dominions aircrew, twenty-seven USAAF aircrew and seventy-nine Royal Army Service Corps despatchers were killed and 127 taken prisoner. A total of fifty-five Albemarle, Stirling, Halifax and Dakota aircraft from Nos 38 and 46 Groups failed to return and a further 320 damaged by flak and seven by fighters while 105 Allied fighter aircraft were lost.

24   By June 1944 thirteen P-47 groups of the IXth and XIX Tactical Air Commands in southern England were equipped with the P-47D Thunderbolt to support the coming cross-Channel invasion and once bases had been established, move to the continent as soon as airstrips had been

built by IX Engineer Command. For the first seven weeks after D-Day, IX TAC maintained its intensive campaign against German forces in co-operation with ground forces. XIX TAC moved to France with the 100th and 303rd Fighter Wings in July 1944, its task from 1 August to co-operate with the US Third Army. In September XXIX TAC was activated to co-operate with the newly formed US 9th Army and became operational on 2 October with the 84th and 303rd Fighter Wings under its control. In March 1945 XIX TAC fighter-bombers concentrated on destroying columns of retreating Germans and leading the Third Army toward final victory. XXIX TAC ceased offensive operations at the end of April 1945.

25   By this time the *Luftwaffe* had only 360 fighters and pilots available for combat duty in I./*Jagdkorps*, ninety of which were in action against the US air forces, 7 October. Fifty-two bombers and fifteen fighters were destroyed for the loss of twenty pilots KIA and four injured.

26   *The Messerschmitt Me 262 Combat Diary.*

27   The Mk VIII reflector gunsight and the simple ring and post were the two gunsights fitted to the majority of P-47C (and D) models before the K-14 gyroscopic gunsight was factory-installed in late 1944. Prior to this many Thunderbolts in the ETO had been base- or depot-modified to receive the K-14. Introduced in the spring of 1944, the K-14 gunsight was fairly advanced for its time. It consisted principally of a piece of slanted, clear glass centred above the instrument panel directly in the pilot's line of sight. Onto the glass was projected a centre dot of yellow light, known as a 'pipper', which was surrounded by a circle formed of eight diamond shaped dots. Once the pilot set the known wingspan of an enemy plane using a knob on the sight itself, he then centred the pipper on his target and, using the control knob mounted on the throttle handle, expanded or contracted the diamonds so that they continually 'bracketed' the target. The K-14 automatically calculated the amount of lead needed for the range of the target, and so long as the pilot kept the pipper centred on the enemy aircraft, and enclosed it tightly within the diamonds, he had an excellent chance of scoring hits.

28   KIA 24 February 1945.

29   *The Messerschmitt Me 262 Combat Diary.*

CHAPTER ELEVEN

A Change of Horse Power

*By this time you could really tell who the pilots were because they all
looked like a bunch of racoons. The sun seldom got to the ground in
England, but it shone very brightly at 28,000 feet. The only part of a man's
skin that was exposed was around his eyes, from his oxygen mask to his
helmet. That area was a dark tan and everything else was dead white. It
was hard on the wing men because the sun was always low and you had to
keep your eyes on the leader even though it usually meant looking right
into that bright sun.*

Captain Pete Keillor[1]

At Duxford on 1 November Colonel Fred Gray called the entire Group to the
base theatre and announced that they were being re-equipped with the
P-51D Mustang. To begin the transition to the Mustang the Group were
issued with several old war-weary P-51B and C models for pilot training, although
they were still expected to fly P-47 missions during the changeover. The P-51D had
replaced the B model in March 1944 when Mustangs escorted the bombers to
Berlin and back again for the first time. The D model became the most successful
variant of all Mustangs. It was built in greater quantity than any other variant. It
excelled in high-altitude escort and combat, being superior in speed and
manoeuvrability to all *Luftwaffe* piston-engined fighters above 20,000 feet.
Ironically, the P-47 had been sent to England as a high-altitude escort fighter and
the Mustang was used as a tactical fighter-bomber. When long-range fighters were
needed in quantity the roles were gradually reversed although the progressive use
of bigger and better droppable fuel tanks on underwing pylons and an increase in
internal fuel capacity prolonged the Thunderbolt's escort role. In fact the range
difference between the two types was not significant though the Mustang's range
of 2,080 miles was achieved by the internal fuel it carried.[2] In all other respects too
the Mustang was an entirely different machine to the P-47 and at Duxford the

240

ground crews had to learn new servicing and maintenance routines to cope with the changes, not least liquid-cooled in-line Packard-Merlins instead of air-cooled radials.

Though the Mustang was certainly more manoeuvrable than the much heavier Thunderbolt, most Jug pilots considered that the P-51 was nowhere near as resilient to flak damage as the P-47. The Thunderbolt could always be counted on to get its pilot home and many were reluctant to change. Even German pilots considered the Mustang to be more vulnerable to cannon fire. Larry Nelson thought that it was 'Merry Christmas' when they each got a 'nice new plane'.

We were given a Pilot's Information File (PIF) to read over and be ready to fly the new plane. There was only room for one in the cockpit, so an instructor was out of the question. Being a young pilot, it seemed like a big order. My first take-off must have been something to behold. The PIF said the Mustang was very touchy. It was much lighter and very noisy in the cockpit compared to the Thunderbolt. I over-controlled greatly. It reacted instantly to rudder and stick movement. We had to learn fast because we would be flying close formation soon. After a few take-offs and landings, I had my Mustang 'corralled'.

Captain Pete Keillor recalls:[3]

We were told that we would be changing from the good old P-47s that would stand almost any punishment to P-51s, which were an unknown quantity, and no one wanted to change. One story on the P-47 concerned a pilot in the 84th before the invasion. He was strafing in France when he ran into a cable. It cut off the bottom four cylinders of the front row on his engine and he made it back across the Channel and crash-landed in England. Try that with any other plane. One of our planes that I saw came back with a hole a couple of feet in diameter right at the left wing root. The pilot could have got out of the cockpit and jumped through the hole.

On the second of November we were rousted out by the intelligence officer as usual. We could hear the bombers circling around to get formed up. They took off real early and took a couple of hours to get into formation. We ate breakfast and went to the briefing and on to the ready room and put on our gear. Then we went to the planes, cranked up and taxied out to take off. We lined up, usually in six rows, eight abreast and took off eight at a time. That was an advantage over the normal runways where they took off two at a time. The disadvantage was that, with the rain and heavy traffic, the field got pretty muddy. This morning we were to catch the bombers over the Netherlands and escort them to Dortmund. As we crossed the coast of Holland my engine gave a cough and then another. The coughs became more frequent till there was nothing but coughs and I had to make a choice. I was at 20,000 feet over a country occupied by the Germans and I could take my chances there, or I could head back toward England over about a hundred miles of icy water and hope the air sea rescue would find me. I decided to risk the cold bath and switched to the emergency channel and started hollering 'Mayday'. At the same time I was trying to get the engine to run. I would shut it off completely and restart it and it still backfired. I never heard any response from the rescue people. Finally, when I got down to about ten thousand feet the engine would run a little with the throttle almost closed. Then it took a little more power and by the time I got back to base it was running normally. It had gotten something in the carburettor that had choked off the gas flow, probably ice and when the ice melted it was okay, but it gave me quite a scare.

November was slow, I flew only four more missions by the sixteenth, all escorts. I had a chance to take a week off at a rest home and since we weren't doing much I took it. Spooner and I went down to Aylsfield House for a week. We played golf (my first), rode horses (I nearly bounced off the rough old nag), played tennis (we were both absolute novices) and had a pretty good vacation. After we got back to base I flew one more escort on the thirtieth to Leipzig. We lost one pilot, William Kelly, to a flying accident on 11 November. By this time you could really tell who the pilots were because they all looked like a bunch of racoons. The sun seldom got to the ground in England, but it shone very brightly at 28,000 feet. The only part of a man's skin that was exposed was around his eyes, from his oxygen mask to his helmet. That area was a dark tan and everything else was dead white. It was hard on the wing men because the sun was always low and you had to keep your eyes on the leader even though it usually meant looking right into that bright sun.

When the 84th Squadron got an old B model Mustang to check out in Pete Keillor flew it first, probably because he 'had flown a lot more different planes than anyone else'. Captain Dick Hewitt in the 82nd Squadron, meanwhile, had checked out on the Mustang on 13 November.[4] His log note reads, 'Not half bad.'

Webster describes a Mustang as 'a small, hardy, horse of the western plains.' I'd say it was more like a 'pinto pony with the power of a Clydesdale.' I was often asked which of the two, Jug or Mustang, I thought was the best. Each did the job they were designed to do. There were times I wished I had been in the other's seat but I'd never, ever downplay either. Unless you have been there and done both, best to keep a 'zipped lip'. I'll just say: Thank you, Republic Aircraft and North American Aviation. Both were [the] main reasons I lived to tell the tale.

Hewitt's Thunderbolt had been named *Miss Tibble* but when his P-51D MX-U arrived three days after his twenty-fourth birthday ('What a great, late present!') a new name – *Big Dick* – was conceived.

Crew chiefs often helped pilots name their planes and Phil Doloway was not to he outdone. The two dice, showing a crapshooter's roll of a 'ten', depict the roll called 'Big Dick'. Just like two 'twos' or a 'four' are called 'Little Joe', 'two sixes' or a 'twelve' are called 'Box Cars', and two 'ones' are called 'Snake Eyes'. Being only 5 feet 8 inches and 130 pounds, I'd have preferred 'Little Richard', but Phil being an avid crapshooter and one helluva crew chief, guess who won out? An excellent choice, Phillip!

As if coming to terms with all the aircraft changes was not enough, prolonged winter rains had turned Duxford airfield (which appropriately was nicknamed 'The Duckpond' while Fowlmere was known as 'Hen Puddle') into a mud patch completely unsuitable for fighter operations. On 17 November the aircraft and many personnel were moved to Bassingbourn airfield fourteen miles west. The move was made to allow US Army Engineers to put down a 3,500 feet long by 150 feet wide Pierced Steel Planking (PSP) main runway in between two steel mattings laid down at each end of the field in 1943. (This had helped while the aircraft were stationary but trying to take off or land in water was no joke.) When added to the mats at either end the total length would be 4,100 feet. Work was held up for a time because the majority of PSP matting had been sent to France for the construction of advanced airfields there and in any case everyone thought that it was no longer needed in England.[5] Bassingbourn was a pre-war airfield built for the RAF and the B-17s of the 91st Bomb Group had a tarmac runway for landing and taking off but the dispersal areas were just as muddy as Duxford's. They became badly congested with bombers and fighters when they flew missions from the same airfield, although there were no delays during the fighters' sojourn at the bomber base. Before each mission take-off the ground crews and armourers who still lived at Duxford had to be brought over in trucks. It was very cold on the remote dispersals at Bassingbourn and permanent accommodation was at a premium. Each fighter squadron's engineering and supply section was housed in a single pyramid tent on the airfield with a direct telephone line to Duxford so parts could be sent for quickly.[6]

The first mission from Bassingbourn was flown on 21 November when the Group were part of the escort for 366 B-24s of the 2nd Bomb Division attacking oil refineries at Hamburg. The P-47s rendezvoused with the Liberators at Nordholz and escorted their 'Big Friends' as far as Itzehoe. In the area of Hannover a section was bounced by fifteen plus Bf 109s who approached out of the sun at ten to twelve o'clock high. Captain Richard A Dick Hewitt destroyed a Bf 109 with a five-second burst. The young New Yorker who was flying *Miss Tibble* saw the enemy fighter go straight in from 4,000 feet. 1st Lieutenant Allen A Rosenblum duelled with another Bf 109 for ten minutes before he sent it spinning to the ground. Robert Holmes spotted a Bf 109 on Major Richard Conner's tail. He climbed at full power to intercept the attacker before cutting inside and closing rapidly he fired into the Messerschmitt's wing roots and cockpit area. The Bf 109 rolled over and dived into the ground. Conner fired at a Bf 109 that made the mistake of crossing in front of him and the pilot baled out after taking hits in his engine. Conner then went after a gaggle of Bf 109s and sent one of them down with hits in the fuselage and wings. The enemy fighter lost its canopy in the dive to the ground but the pilot failed to bale out before it crashed. 2nd Lieutenant Harry A Thompson belly-landed his P-47 south-east of Münster and he set it on fire before being taken prisoner. *Leutnant* Herbert Neuner, 2nd *Staffel*/JG 1, recalls:

On 21 November combats began again in dreadful weather: rain and fog. Our formation was directed due south towards a formation of Viermots. Suddenly, voices crackled over the intercom: 'Attention, Indianer behind us!' Our Gruppe was split up. I dived but was hit several times. Having noticed that I was not being followed, I gained altitude and saw a large circle of aircraft. In the circle, aircraft, one behind the other, were weaving. I picked up speed, got behind a P-47 and shot it down. I broke away immediately and set course for home. By chance, the direction was good and I landed at Greifswald. If my memory is correct, only two or three of my companions joined me. We waited for further news. It was very bad: the absentees were posted missing and hour by hour their deaths were confirmed.[7]

On the homeward leg the Thunderbolts strafed Guterslöh airfield for good measure.

Four days later at Koblenz the Thunderbolt pilots saw contrails left by V-2 rockets fired at southern England. On 26 November the Group flew the penetration-target-withdrawal leg for the B-17s of the First Bombardment Division attacking Osnabrück. At 1100 hours the 82nd Squadron was vectored by control toward a forty plus formation of enemy fighters approaching the Fortresses in the Rheine area. Captain Donald C Hart picked out one of the enemy fighters at 25,000 feet and his first burst started coolant coming out of its engine. Hart fought him down to the deck and across an airfield. As he straightened out he hit his engine and the enemy pilot pulled straight up and baled out. Flight Officer Harold R Liebenrood destroyed another of the attackers, which smoking badly, fell off on one wing through the clouds on fire. Captain Manford O Croy took on two Bf 109s, hitting the first one with numerous strikes in the cockpit and wing roots before it caught fire and the pilot baled out. He chased the second Bf 109 down to low level and around a small town where he was greeted with intense light flak. Croy fired a short burst from dead astern and he saw pieces fly off before the enemy fighter burst into flame. As he drew up alongside the Bf 109, he could see the pilot slumped down in the cockpit just before it nosed over and crashed into a field. Captain John J Hockery destroyed two Bf 109s and got a probable Fw 190 for his sixth and seventh victories before his water-injection ran out and he was unable to outrun the Fw 190s who blew part of his wing off. Hockery crashed in a field and clambered out, running for a nearby ditch where he took cover as the Fw

190s strafed his wrecked P-47. Hockery was captured shortly after.[8] 2nd Lieutenant Troy L Eggleston was shot down and killed.

In the 83rd Squadron, Captain Robert R Bonebrake downed a Fw 190 south of the Dummer Lake and the enemy fighter spun into the ground and exploded with its pilot still aboard. Captain Herbert K Shope, who was flying one of the war-weary P-51 training aircraft, was forced to bale out and he was taken prisoner. The victories brought the Group's total for November to thirteen for the loss of four fighters.

On 4 December Captain Dick Hewitt flew his last Jug mission, an escort of B-17s to the Bielefeld area, which turned out to be uneventful although three V-2 rockets were being launched, one so close that Hewitt 'could feel the vibrations'. Observed in the daytime they appeared as a smoking contrail. At night the first indication was an eerie screech, just split seconds before the thunderous explosion of the multi-ton warhead. Hewitt was in London a couple of times and heard them coming and exploding.

> On our way home one of these suddenly appeared just ahead and slightly below me, probably no more than fifty yards away. It was huge, resembling a brownish or rusted cylindrical tube, about four inches in diameter, 40–50 feet long, with a conical shaped nose. Slowly gaining in velocity, it was now almost directly level with me and just slightly off my heading. Why I did not flip on my gun-camera-only switch and get a few frames can only be attributed to my utter state of disbelief at what I was seeing and it was there for only a few seconds. Now looking up almost straight up and above me I had a direct shot up its blazing tailpipe. If it had blown up at that instant my flight of four and maybe more, would have been blown to 'kingdom come'. Wouldn't that have been a 'Grande finale' for MX-R, my Jug, on that 4th December flight! It continued in its upward arc. Now I could feel its thunderous vibrations. Then gradually it bent off to the west and in a direction I felt certain was toward southern England and London. It would come down in mid-afternoon, levelling a city block and taking a toll of death along with it. There was absolutely no defence against it except a few minutes of air raid sirens, sounded by spotting wardens. No doubt, Hitler's intended retaliation for the Allied raids on the city of Berlin.

Captain Pete Keillor recalls:

> Life at Duxford wasn't all flying by any means. We all had bicycles, and there were plenty of roads to ride on. You could head out in any direction and find a village within five miles and then you could turn, go to another village and come back on a different road. Duxford was the name of the airfield and also the nearby village. There was an old church that was only used occasionally. It had been replaced by the new church, which was three hundred years old. The closest town was Whittlesford, which we referred to

as the bottleneck of the ETO. Trains came through frequently and two old men would come out and close the gates several minutes before the train was scheduled. After the train passed, but not real soon after, the old men would come slowly out and open the gates. That's where we caught the train to London, which we did pretty frequently. There were houses run by the Red Cross or somebody where we could always get a room. We could eat at the Grosvenor House Hotel. The ballroom was converted to a huge cafeteria, which always fed hundreds of American officers. There were plenty of places to see, Westminster Abbey, St Paul's, Madame Tussaud's and countless other places. My favourite theatre was the 'Windmill', guess why.[9] London was blacked out so the light was dim with practically no traffic or noise. Once I climbed up to the whispering gallery in St Paul's and while the attendant was whispering, a V-2 hit close outside. The attendant said, 'That was close, wasn't it?' It was…[10]

Life in England had become almost as familiar as it had been at home. Brussels sprouts and tea, spam and powered eggs, fish and chips and rare fresh eggs secured from unquestioned sources were part of it, as were intensive poker playing and crap shooting early every month, the NAAFI (later replaced by the Red Cross), the Church Army, Betty's and Bunty's. Cambridge, which had soon acquired the nickname 'The 49th State', and the surrounding area were well endowed with historic old inns. GIs liked the public houses and there were frequent bicycle 'sweeps' to Duxford's John Barleycorn and other pubs and dances in Hinxton and Sawston, Whittlesford and Harston, Shelford and Thriplow, Fowlmere and Great Chesterford, Foxton and Melbourn, Abington and Ickleton. Peacetime beer was strong and cheap and most preferred it to spirits or hard liquor as the GIs knew it. Cocktails were almost unknown and iced drinks were regarded with horror. All pubs closed by law at 10.30 pm. In Cambridge The Eagle in Benet Street with its smoked ceiling revealing names and numbers of RAF and USAAF squadron numbers and nicknames beckoned. Drummer Street and the Bull Hotel, the Rex Ballroom and the Dorothy, the Cam and Cambridge parks, the smell of mild and bitter and the odour from the fishmongers.

Larry Nelson recalls:

The war wasn't all work and no play. Many celebrities visited our base under the direction of the United Service Organization (USO). These included the famous Bob Hope, Frances Langford, Bing Crosby and Marlene Dietrich who came at various times to Duxford. This was a huge occasion for all of us. After performing for us some would come down into the crowd. On one occasion Marlene Dietrich came down right in front of me. She was as beautiful in person as she was in the movies. I said to her that I would like her autograph, but I didn't have anything to write on or a pen to write with. She sat down on a chair, took off my cap, crossed her shapely legs and gently pulled her dress above her knee to use it as a resting place. Turning my cap over, she bent the soft bill back, took a pen from someone in the crowd and wrote 'Marlene' on it. Needless to say I was the centre of envy among my friends. I wore that cap through the remainder of the war.

From time to time, we would go into town. Our two social cities were Cambridge and London. In London I was not successful getting a BELT (Bacon, fried egg, lettuce and tomato sandwich) but I did find a girl. Her name was Pat Messenger. Little did I know at the time that she was dating a RCAF flyer on alternate weekends from me. (Later I learned from her mother how careful Pat was to keep our identities separate from each other and she married her RCAF flyer.) Cambridge is known for its colleges and for punting on the Cam but what most of us GIs remember was the very popular Dorothy Dance Hall. There were plenty of girls to dance with at the Dorothy. The place was always jumping, especially on a Saturday night. I guess the English girls needed to have a little fun and they sure did love to dance. We had a number of weddings as the result of these get-togethers at the Dorothy. Before going to the dance hall, I usually met up with Don Freer, a hometown friend who flew B-17s from Bassingbourn nearby. We met to talk about what was happening back home and our week of flying missions, many of which we flew together. Then one day in December, Don didn't come back from his mission. I found out later that he had been shot down and taken prisoner. It was great that he survived. Too many of my friends did not make it back from their missions.[11]

On 11 December the new runway at Duxford was ready for operational missions and the Group returned home. Five days later about thirty P-51D Mustangs were flown in from the air depot and parked on the grass around the control tower. All of the Mustangs of course had to be fitted out and inspected and painted in the Group markings with the nose of each P-51 having the familiar white and black chequers added to the sleek natural-metal skin. The 82nd Squadron became the first to undergo pilot training on the Mustangs and their P-47s were handed over to the 83rd and 84th Squadrons for combat missions. Practising on the gleaming new machines, however, was curtailed by the weather. Dick Hewitt recalls:

Our weather turned rotten about mid-December as a low pressure system shrouded the British Isles and most of northwestern Europe in 'pea soup' fog. Things moved at a snail's pace and we were mission-less for what seemed an eternity. Many days we could not see the control tower, which was only 200 yards from our 82nd pilot's Ready Room. With only our link trainer to maintain our IFR proficiency we kept it busy from dawn until long after dark, knowing full well we'd have to fly in this 'soup' if it didn't break up soon. About the only other weather's blessing, if you can call it that, were the hours we got of just sitting in the 51's cockpit, 'doing it blindfolded'. There were a couple of days, not really clear enough to fly, that we 'finagled' a traffic pattern flight. We flew once around at barely 500', just able to keep the field in view. With our move into the 51s, everyone was anxious to get any kind of airtime they could. I managed to get two such flights and just to get the feel of landing this new 'bird' was worth every second. It had torque that would literally screw you into the ground if you failed to fully compensate with left rudder trim before you hit the throttle. Rich Roe, a 'hotshot' 82nd pilot during my tenure as CO 'pranged' three times on take-off from the Mustang's violent torque.[12]

The appalling weather conditions during this changeover period at Duxford enabled Field Marshal Karl von Rundstedt and his *panzer* formations on 16 December, to attack American positions in the forests of the Ardennes on the French–Belgian border. They soon opened up a salient or 'bulge' in the Allied lines supported by an estimated 1,400 fighters in twelve *Geschwader*. The Allied air forces were grounded by fog and the weather was foul for three days. On 19 December the 78th Fighter Group was the only outfit in VIIIth Fighter Command that was able to get airborne. Forty-one Thunderbolts took off although one crashed on take-off. Later on the P-47s rendezvoused with the small numbers of bombers near Trier. No enemy fighters were seen. There was solid overcast from 10,000 feet to the ground with fog 300 feet thick and the attack on Bahen-Heusen aerodrome had to be aborted. The Thunderbolts strafed the railway from Siegen to Giessen and destroyed fifteen tracks from Bonn to Duren.

Later that same afternoon north of Koblenz the 83rd Squadron saw thirty plus Bf 109s that appeared out of the thick cloud at 7,500 feet. The Messerschmitts split and ran for cover in the clouds when the P-47s attacked but about twenty Fw 190s that appeared from the east soon replaced them. 1st Lieutenant John A Kirk III, a twenty-year-old Flight Leader, downed a Bf 109 and then he saw a Fw 190 that crossed his nose level out at 300 feet and the pilot bale out. Francis Harrington got many hits on a Bf 109, which trailed white smoke and rolled over with its undercarriage hanging down. It hit the ground inverted. Harrington then climbed and chased three Fw 190s, firing at two of them and claiming one, which burst into flames, flipped over and crashed into a wood. Robert Bonebrake claimed a Bf 109 after scoring several strikes in the enemy's cockpit and it went straight in from 6,000 feet. Bonebrake then chased a Fw 190 and shot it down for his second victory of the afternoon. The weather was so bad that twenty of the P-47 pilots put down at airstrips on the continent while nine re-crossed the Channel and landed at Castle Camps in Essex. Only eleven Thunderbolts landed back at Duxford. General Doolittle commended the Group for flying the mission and General William Kepner endorsed the commendation. It was not until 23 December that the fog lifted sufficiently to allow 400 B-17s and B-24s to strike communication lines behind the Ardennes area and offer some hope to the hard-pressed infantry divisions in 'The Bulge'. The dozen 8th Air Force fighter groups that could safely get airborne supported the bombers. The *Luftwaffe* was up in force to support the *Wehrmacht* offensive and nearly eighty enemy fighters were shot down. The 56th Fighter Group claimed the lion's share with thirty-seven destroyed (later reduced to thirty-two on the evidence of gun camera film), one probably destroyed and sixteen damaged.

By Christmas Day both the 83rd and 84th Squadrons had each received their complement of thirty-one new Mustangs. The Group was expected to take part in the maximum effort in support of the Ardennes fighting but bad weather prevented any flying from Duxford and many other airfields too were socked in by a heavy fog over eastern England. At all bases ground crews worked right around the clock but it was all in vain. Christmas Day was shrouded in white fog. Pete Keillor said that he had 'three white Christmases in a row – the coral sand of Canton island in 1942, the whitecaps on the Pacific on the ship from Oahu to San Francisco in 1943, and now the fog in England'. He wandered out onto the airfield where the fog was so thick that he 'could have been lost except for airplane tracks in the grass'. Suddenly there was a 'whoosh and a thunk close by' and he found a stick about five feet long and nearly an inch in diameter stuck in the ground. It was from a rocket that the control tower or weather people had shot up through the fog.[13] On 26 December only 150 8th Air Force aircraft were dispatched and the following day the wintry conditions were responsible for a succession of crashes during early morning take-offs.

The 78th Fighter Group finally got airborne again on 28 December when the mist and fog cleared enough to allow thirty-six P-47s led by Colonel Fred Gray to patrol the Koblenz area but the mission was quite uneventful. Next day thirty-two P-47s supported 9th Air Force bombers over Belgium and thirty P-51Ds escorted the 'Big Friends' who attacked the Frankfurt and Aschaffenburg railway marshalling yards. Among those making their way home were Captain Huie Lamb, an element leader in Surtax Yellow Flight, and his wingman, Flight Officer John C Childs. Huie Lamb had flown forty-five missions on P-47s and this was his first mission in a P-51, which he had named *Etta Jeanne*, for his younger sister. Huie Lamb recalls the drama that unfolded off Orfordness on the Suffolk coast.

In the target area we had just made rendezvous when Childs pulled in close and pointed to his headset – a signal that his radio was acting up. I got on his wing and after calling our leader we headed for home. No radio called for an immediate abort. All went well until we were about three miles from the English coast. Then my coolant valve let go and dumped my engine coolant. It immediately 'showed' an engine overheat and was on fire. It quit dead. With the fire and dead stick, I knew I had to get out fast. I tried to open the canopy and then to jettison it. It was jammed. I had already unsnapped my seat belt and pulled off my shoulder harness, expecting to get out PDQ. 'Trapped in a burning plane and I can't bale out?!' Maybe I could make it to shore as I could see it quite plainly. At least I would not die of drowning, trapped in the cockpit of my plane but I was falling too fast and could see I was going to hit way short and in the water. What happened next, I cannot exactly remember.

I came to, thrashing about in the water. I was free of the cockpit, as the canopy had apparently jarred loose when I hit the water. Dazed from the impact and hitting the gunsight with my face, the cold seawater must have revived me enough to kick free of the plane. It sank in no more than .5–6 seconds. Had I not loosened my belt and harness, I'd have gone down with the plane. Normally I'd have left everything fastened, had I intended to ditch. Talk about a miracle. I grabbed for my dinghy and inflated it. By now I was numb from the cold and could not crawl in. I felt my face and knew I had a bad cut on my upper lip. The seawater stung but I was lucky to still be alive. Then I looked up for Childs but he was gone. He had transmitted for a 'fix', but not knowing if he was getting through, he had headed inland for a nearby ASR base. (At the time I had no way of knowing any of this or that Bill Crump in the 356th Fighter Group, who was on a test hop and saw me hit the water, sent a Mayday call to ASR.) Being a good swimmer, I thought maybe I could swim for shore. But which way was the shore? The swells were not too high but I could not see land in any direction. Then a boat of some kind passed within a very short distance but they kept right on going. I waved and yelled but it did no good. Unknown to John, his signals and call for help had 'flickered through'. As he approached the ASR base, he saw a Walrus flying boat used widely by ASR for its ability to set down in very choppy seas, on the runway about to take off. Landing quickly, he taxied up, climbed out and signalled for them to 'follow me'. Once airborne, John in his '51 and the ASR team in the Walrus headed back to sea. With only a speed of a little over 85 mph, John had to constantly circle, gradually leading them back to where I was bobbing like a cork and clutching my dinghy. I didn't have the strength to climb inside.

A biplane with a boat-like fuselage, the Walrus easily set down on the 10 foot swells, in near perfect weather conditions – a rare day on the North Sea. They manoeuvred alongside and their swarthy radio operator reached out and literally plucked me from the water. I hung to my dinghy, so tight that at first he could not lift me out of the water. Then realising I could not help any, I let go of the dinghy. Once inside the rear hatch doorway, they offered me no medication or first aid of any kind. It would be only 10–15 minutes and we'd be back to their base, which was also a US fighter base [Martlesham Heath], shared with the British ASR. Then the Walrus refused to start. Finally after the sixth attempt it started and we were airborne and headed inland. A US ambulance met us and I was rushed to the base hospital where it took numerous stitches to close my lip gash. [He was also stripped and wrapped in blankets and hot water bottles.] An overnight stay and I was flown back to Duxford the next day. Four days later I was OK'd to fly by our Squadron Flight Surgeon. I was not quite that ready to get back in the air, despite what old Doc Pinchbottle our Flight Surgeon thought. Luck played the main part in my survival. At that time there was only one other fighter pilot known to have survived a sea ditching and he had both legs broken. He never flew combat again. I would be back in the air in less than ten days. I praise the men who saved me, especially John Childs. Next come the men on that Walrus and, far from least, the good Lord. He surely had to be watching over me on that fateful day. When things look the bleakest, never ever give up.[14]

On 30 December when more than 1,000 heavies bombed lines of communication, twenty-five P-47s led by Major Leonard Marshall supported the bombers attacking Duren and thirty-five P-51Ds led by Lieutenant Colonel Joe Myers escorted more 'Big Friends' attacking Rheims. On 31 December the B-17s of the 1st Bomb Division kept up the attacks while 3rd Division bomber crews returned to oil production centres. Fourteen P-47s led by Captain Julius P Maxwell flew freelance bomber support in the Hamburg area but nothing was seen of the *Luftwaffe* and at 1230 hours the Thunderbolts turned for home. Maxwell saw a train headed west and with his wingman proceeded to shoot it up but they were going too fast and could only damage it. When he was at 2,500 feet Maxwell spotted a Fw 190 at 1,000 feet below going south and he peeled off to go after him. Maxwell closed very fast from dead-astern and opened fire from 800 yards to 400 yards' range getting strikes in the enemy's engine, cockpit and wings before his belly tank exploded and a long stream of fire shot out of the engine. The Fw 190 flipped on its back and hurtled down from 400 feet leaving a long stream of smoke and fire in its wake before hitting the ground with a terrific explosion. The pilot tried to bale out at 200 feet but his parachute opened just as he hit the ground and he was killed. It was Captain Maxwell's last mission of his tour and the 78th's last P-47 Thunderbolt mission.[15] Back at Duxford Colonel Fred Gray presented Maxwell with a silver tankard in honour of the Group's four hundreth victory of the war.

The USSTAF was clearly winning the battle of attrition in the war against the *Luftwaffe*, as trained fighter pilots at this stage of the war were impossible to replace.[16] January 1945 marked the 8th's third year of operations and it seemed as if the end of the war was in sight. On New Year's Day 1945 two squadrons in the 78th Fighter Group flew deep penetration support for the B-17s of the Third Air Division (this day the prefix 'Bomb' was officially changed to 'Air') raiding Bonn and Frankfurt. Enemy fighters were up in some strength during raids on the tank factory at Kassel, an oil refinery at Magdeburg and marshalling yards at Dillenburg and the Magdeburg force came under heavy fighter attack. The *Luftwaffe* was still far from defeated and it could still be relied upon to make a major effort against the heavies. *Unternehmen Bodenplatte*, a desperate gamble to diminish the overwhelming Allied air superiority, was mounted at about 0900 hours on New Year's Day 1945. The aim was to deliver a single, decisive, blow against RAF and American aircraft on the ground in Holland, Belgium and Northern France using 875 single-engined fighter aircraft, primarily in support of von Rundstedt's Ardennes offensive. The outcome though was far different. Though total Allied aircraft losses during *Bodenplatte* amounted to 424 destroyed or heavily damaged the *Luftwaffe* losses were catastrophic.[17] The big gamble had turned into a disastrous defeat. The *Wehrmacht* advance in the Ardennes came to a halt and ultimately petered out. In the east the Red Army prepared for the great winter offensive, which would see the capture of Warsaw and Krakow and take the Soviets across the German border. Germany had no reserves left. Hitler's last chance now lay in his so-called 'wonder weapons' – the V-1 pilotless flying bomb and the V-2 sub-orbital rocket.[18]

Early in January the Group finally completed the changeover from Thunderbolts to Mustangs though the new aircraft certainly had their share of teething troubles and engine problems. 1st Lieutenant Hubert 'Bill' Davis, a twenty-five-year-old who had been an instructor in the US until his incessant badgering to join a combat unit finally paid off, was assigned to the 83rd Squadron. Within days of his arrival, he had been allocated a newly delivered P-5ID, which appropriately he named *Twilight Tear* after a legendary bay filly racehorse. Foaled in 1941 at the famous Calumet Farm in Lexington, Kentucky, in the heart of America's horse racing industry, the *Twilight Tear* was named Horse of the Year in 1944. Calumet Farm's horses dominated racing in the 1940s and '50s and, over the years, amassed an incredible 524-piece trophy collection. Bill was born in Atlantic City, New Jersey, but grew up in Manhattan with lazy summers on Long Island. His family travelled extensively throughout Europe and he attended boarding school in Switzerland and spoke many languages, including fluent French. Whilst still a young man, Davis continued to travel throughout Europe, returning to Shoreham, Long Island, where he had many friends. He loved to play tennis, run on the beach with his Great Dane, swim and ride his Harley Davidson. He also learned to fly and it became a daily occurrence to see him cruising over the sand dunes in his own aeroplane. He had enlisted in 1942 but his extensive flying experience kept him out of the front line for two years training other pilots.

Pete Keillor flew his first Mustang mission in a P-51K on 5 January and others on the 6th, 7th and 8th – all high altitude escort missions to Kreuznach, Mannheim, Cologne and Koblenz and on 13 January to Koblenz again.

> During that time my cockpit heater didn't work or worked very little. The outside air temperature at 28,000 feet was about 80 degrees below zero. It was cold. I wore wool long handles, wool pants and shirt and an intermediate flying suit (jacket and pants). I had silk gloves under wool gloves under leather gloves and sheepskin boots over my shoes and wool socks. It was still cold.[19]

There were eight Mustang engine failures in January that resulted in crashes, the first two on 5 January when the first all P-51D mission, to Speyer in Germany, went ahead in severe wintry weather with snow flurries swirling around the runways at many bases. At Duxford 2nd Lieutenant Thomas M Reeves lost power on take-off and he crashed at the end of the runway. Another P-51D flown by Captain Raymond E Smith had to be put down a few miles from the airfield after the engine seized but apart from a few cuts and bruises the pilot was unhurt. At the target on 6 January Captain Wilbur Grimes' Mustang suffered a flak hit in the engine, which seized after all the oil was lost. Grimes baled out at 1,200 feet over Belgium and he landed in enemy territory with injuries to his leg and face. He made contact with the Belgian Underground and eventually he was able to return to the Group. Returning to base in fog the Mustang piloted by Flight Officer Gordon L Weston clipped a chimneystack twenty miles from Duxford and crashed. Weston was killed.

Bad weather and snowstorms restricted operations during the month and only nineteen missions were flown with nine aircraft being lost. Fourteen air-to-air victories were claimed and twenty-one locomotives were reported destroyed by ground strafing. On Sunday 14 January over 650 bombers supported by fifteen fighter groups were despatched to mainly oil and other targets in central and north-western Germany again. A smaller force of 187 Fortresses escorted by forty-two Mustangs and preceded by a sweep of the area by sixty-two Thunderbolts attacked the Rhine bridges at Cologne. The 78th Fighter Group claimed six Fw 190D-9s and half a dozen Bf 109G/Ks during a combat with II *Gruppe* JG 26. Major Anton 'Toni' Hackl was leading the formation to their assigned patrol zone in the Cologne area when about half way there they were bounced by seven P-47s in the alert flight in the 366th Fighter Group who had taken off from Asch in Belgium. Despite having an initial advantage the 366th came off worse. East of Liège Hackl claimed a P-47 and west of Koblenz *Führer* Johann Spahn of 8th *Staffel* claimed another of the Group's Thunderbolts.[20] Hackl's formation continued across Aachen and west of Cologne he led them in a shallow left turn. Unbeknown to Hackl his fighters were being tracked by American radar on the continent and the twenty-five P-51Ds of the 78th Fighter Group were ordered to break off their bomber escort and make for the Cologne area.

Three miles south-west of Cologne 1st Lieutenant Willard Warren, who was at 26,000 feet, sighted fifteen plus bogeys down on the deck. Receiving permission to attack he dropped tanks and took his wingman, 1st Lieutenant William J DeGain down on a bounce. They barrelled right through another fifteen enemy aircraft they had failed to see and jumped the original formation. The Germans who were in the process of assembling for an attack on the bombers were taken completely by surprise. Pursuing three of the enemy fighters, Warren opened fire on a Fw 190D with hits in the cockpit that killed its pilot and caused the *Dora* to flick into the ground. DeGain, travelling at 450 mph and seeing that his leader was clear, moved up behind a Bf 109 and opened up with several short bursts, which caused the canopy to fly off and its right gear to drop. As he was passing DeGain saw the pilot

253

standing on his seat just before the Messerschmitt pulled up and its engine exploded, spinning it into the ground. Warren meanwhile caught a *Dora* positioning on DeGain and he rolled over onto it firing a deflection shot. His shells hit the Fw 190D's cockpit canopy, causing the fighter to crash and explode. When the bogeys were called out at 1210 hours 1st Lieutenant Robert E Smith bounced a single Fw 190D going north over Cologne. The two pilots played hide-and-seek from fog bank to fog bank, hopping over churches and tall buildings until Smith eventually got hits in the *Dora's* fuselage. At fifty feet over northern Cologne the Fw 190D's left wing went down and it crashed and exploded in a three-gun heavy flak position.

Major Leonard P Marshall chased three fighters he thought were enemy aircraft but he soon saw that one was a P-51 (flown by 2nd Lieutenant Louis R Hereford) pursuing two Bf 109s. One of the Messerschmitt pilots spotted Marshall behind him and he broke left and tried to belly in. Hitting the ground at 300 mph, the Bf 109 disappeared in a huge cloud of snow and smoke. A wing came off and pieces flew in all directions. Turning his attention to the other Bf 109, Marshall saw that Hereford was having trouble trying to get a bead on it. Marshall approached and the Bf 109 turned and fired a burst head-on. Both P-51s got in position behind the German and fired, Hereford from 400 yards and Marshall from 800 yards. Marshall did not get any hits but Hereford's attack caused the German pilot to bale out. Hereford quickly broke off because he thought Marshall represented another German on his tail. (Louis Hereford returned alone with a rough running engine and he was finally forced to belly-land at Merrillville, France.)[21]

At Duxford 1st Lieutenant Richard H Spooner lived just outside the Officer's' Club in temporary wooden buildings and he called his room, 'Spooner's Greasy Spoon'. He had lots of guests for whom he fried potatoes,[22] none more so than on this day no doubt! Spooner got on the tail of another Bf 109. Closing to 200 yards he fired and the German baled out as his fighter spun in. As Spooner was trying to film this kill, another enemy aircraft appeared and he gave chase. Closing to 400 yards on the deck, Spooner ran out of ammunition so he decided to bluff the German. He closed to less than 100 yards and the German broke right and hit some power lines before crashing in flames. Captain Earl L Stier got into a tight right-turning duel with one of the Bf 109s hugging the ground heading east. When the German reversed his turn, Stier fired and caused a stream of coolant and oil. The German pulled up in a steep climb and baled out. Stier was just getting good strikes on another of six Bf 109s when 20 mm went flashing over his canopy and he broke from three Bf 109s on his tail. The last he saw of his second German the Bf 109 was gliding down in trouble. 1st Lieutenant Frank E Oiler's leader and his wingman went after two bandits going up a creek bed. A Fw 190 went between them firing, so Oiler turned on his tail. He lost him over some woods but picked up a Bf 109 and two Fw 190s being chased by a lone P-51. Oiler called to the P-51 to take one and Oiler and his wingman took the other. The Fw 190s broke opposite directions and the Bf 109 went straight up. Oiler got into a Lufbery circle at 1,100 feet with the Fw 190 and with the use of flaps got on his tail in two turns. He fired a three-second burst at about 35° deflection and he observed many strikes in the cockpit, fuselage and wing roots. Pieces flew off the Fw 190, which did a half snap and went in upside down. 1st Lieutenant Mark T Wilson closed astern of a Bf 109 and had little trouble shooting off its left wing three feet from the fuselage to send the German pilot spinning and snap rolling into the ground.

Having trouble dropping his right wing tank, 1st Lieutenant Willis H Lutz had been left above the fight by the rest of his flight. He tried to fire his guns to shake off the tank but none of the guns would work. Deciding to go home, he saw three aircraft exit from the forest shading and thinking they were P-51s, dived down to form on them. As he came closer he recognised them as Fw 190s. Looking back he saw three more enemy fighters diving down on him from five o'clock. Lutz tried to get away but they came in behind him. Pulling his left turn in tight, the four of them were in a Lufbery circle. Lutz pressed his gun-trigger as hard as he could and was delighted to find four .50s working. Gaining on the Germans in the turn, Lutz hit one and the pilot jettisoned his canopy and baled out. The American pilot gave another Fw 190 a long burst causing a fire in its right wing. The *Dora* flipped on its back at 100 feet and crashed. Looking about Lutz saw two Fw I90s coming after him from the north. They all quickly got into another Lufbery circle and again Lutz managed to outturn the enemy aircraft. After a couple of hits on a Fw 190 he ran out of ammunition and the German pilot disengaged. Lutz ran a bluff on the remaining Fw 190, which also turned tail and headed off to the east. Lutz resumed his course for England but patchy ground fog forced him to hug the ground. He crossed Allied lines south of Aachen and, recognising the area, he climbed to 350 feet for a better view. As he levelled off, Allied AA guns opened up and hit his P-51 with their first burst. Lutz baled out and landed safely but injured near Hauset, Belgium.[23]

Pete Keillor recalls:

On the fourteenth we were over Cologne and someone saw planes down against the snow. We dropped our external tanks to dive down but mine didn't come off till I had wasted some time firing my guns to shake them loose. When I got down I couldn't find anything to shoot at. My element leader, Frank Oiler, saw a Jerry on the way down and got it. We lost four pilots in January, Grimes, Spooner, Elin and Packer. Spooner was reported KIA having been seen to crash upside down. He survived but was badly burned. Packer was hit and baled out and became a PoW. Elin had instrument failure in clouds and crashed in England.[24] About that time we were having trouble with the '51's cooling systems. They used 70 per cent water and 30 per cent glycol and had a relief valve in case of too much pressure. The relief valves would pop off and not close again so that all the coolant escaped. That didn't give you much time to make a decision. It happened to someone nearly every day for a while and was very disturbing.

Several pilots were able to make it to Denmark and were helped to escape to Sweden where they sat out the remainder of the war.[25]

Because of strafing losses, pilot morale sagged during February, the costliest month during the whole period of operations from Duxford, with twenty-one pilots reported missing. Ten of the missing pilots, however, were taken prisoner and four more were later reported to have evaded capture. On 3 February the Group flew all the way to Berlin and back for their first time when they escorted the bombers from Zwolle in the Netherlands and left them two and a half-hours later near Ulzen in Germany. Every pilot logged over six hours on the mission.[26] Marshal Zhukov's Red Army was only thirty-five miles from Berlin and 'Big B' was jammed with refugees fleeing from the advancing Russians. The strike was therefore planned to cause the German authorities as much havoc as possible. The 8th Air Force lost twenty-one bombers over the capital and another six crash-landed inside the Russian lines. 1st Lieutenant William B Senarens was hit by flak over Wilhelmshaven on the way in and baled out to become a PoW. 1st Lieutenant Leon 'Lonnie' M Grisham, Pete Keillor's roommate, was shot down on his fourth pass while strafing Luneburg Heath airfield. Grisham was last heard over the R/T asking that he get credit for his three ground kills. The last thing he remembered seeing was the Packard Merlin engine bouncing away in front of him. He had a fractured hip but a German doctor took good care of him. 2nd Lieutenant Warren J Sawall was also shot down over Luneburg airfield and he too became a PoW. Further German disruption in the face of the Russian advance occurred on 6 February, when 1,300 heavies, escorted by fifteen groups of P-51 Mustangs, bombed Chemnitz and Magdeburg and the 8th resumed its oil offensive with raids on synthetic oil refineries at Lutzkendorf and Merseburg.[27] Three days later another raid by 1,500 heavies escorted by large numbers of fighters was attacked by Me 262s at 24,000 feet near Fulda. Seven of the jets were shot down and two more were claimed probably destroyed by 1st Lieutenant William E Hydorn and Captain Edwin H Miller. Miller recalled:

An Me 262 was approaching the box of bombers, which we were escorting. I called the bounce from approximately 22,000 feet, diving on the Me 262 which was flying 14,000 feet below. I began firing at extreme range, knowing that he would out-distance me the moment that my wingman and I were spotted. So on the first long burst the right engine began to smoke and the jet rolled over, falling through a cloudbank and we were unable to follow and confirm the victory. This was considered a 'probable' which appears on my record.[28]

On 21 February more than 1,200 heavies attacked military installations and communications targets at Nürnberg and thirteen other targets of opportunity in the area supported by ten fighter groups, which later strafed ground targets including Hitler's retreat at Berchtesgaden for the first time. On 22 February, George Washington's birthday, *Clarion*, the systematic destruction of the German communications network, was launched. More than 6,000 Allied aircraft from seven different commands were airborne this day and they struck at transportation targets throughout western Germany and northern Holland. All targets were selected with the object of preventing troops being transported to the Russian front, now only a few miles from Berlin. It was all part of the strategy worked out at Yalta by the 'Big Three' earlier that same month. Despite the low altitudes flown, five bombers only were lost. *Clarion* ripped the heart out of a crumbling *Reich* and the following two months would witness its bitter conclusion.

1   *Wandering Through World War II* by Pete Keillor (Privately Published 2003).

2   A total of 92 gallons was contained in each wing and this was supplemented by two 75-gallon underwing drop tanks and a fuselage tank, an 85-gallon design afterthought, behind the cockpit. Fuel was not the issue; commonality of equipment was one of the main reasons that Lieutenant General Jimmy Doolittle saw to it that the Mustang equipped all but one of the 8th Air Force Fighter Groups in England before the end of the war. Another chief reason was that the P-47's low-level performance made it better-suited for the ground attack role so the majority of Thunderbolts were better suited to equip the 9th and 15th Air Forces in England and Italy respectively. Their interdiction campaigns proved crucial for the ground forces on the continent of Europe.

3   *Wandering Through World War II.*

4   *Target of Opportunity: Tales & Contrails of the Second World War.*

5   At Fowlmere two PSP runways were also laid, one of 1,600 yards running NE–SW and the other of 1,400 yards on an E–E axis. Soon after Duxford was transferred to the 8th Air Force in 1943 Fowlmere became an airfield in its own right as Station 378 with P-51 Mustangs of the 339th Fighter Group stationed there and the 78th and 339th Fighter Groups were part of the 66th Fighter Wing with HQ at Sawston Hall. While the PSP matting was laid at Fowlmere the 339th Fighter Group was moved temporarily to Bassingbourn. At Fowlmere a T2 hangar was erected on the small RAF technical site which had grown up around the farm buildings on the northern perimeter. The 339th Fighter Group remained at Fowlmere for twelve months of operations, claiming 680 enemy aircraft destroyed for the loss of ninety-seven Mustangs. Soon after the end of the war Fowlmere airfield was returned to agriculture. It was retained by the Ministry of

Works until 1957 when the land was sold back to the former owners, the major part to EF Sheldrick & Sons Ltd of Manor Farm and the remainder to Mr F Pepper of Black Peak Farm. In 1975 the Sheldrick family re-clad the T2 hangar. Later a beautiful set of RAF wings painted on the wall of one of the buildings was restored also. *The Battle of Britain Then and Now* (After The Battle 1980).

6   *Eagles of Duxford: The 78th Fighter Group in World War II.*

7   His victim was a 78th Fighter Group P-47 Thunderbolt; the only P-47 lost this day. In all, the 8th lost four B-24s and fifteen fighters on the Hamburg raid. JG 1 lost twenty fighters (including eight in two minutes over Erfurt) and fourteen pilots killed in combat with the American fighters on 21 November. Four were wounded. *Defending the Reich; The History of Jagdgeschwader 1 'Oesau'* by Eric Mombeek.

8   On 14 September 1952 during the Korean War Major Hockery destroyed a MiG-15 flying an F-86F Sabre in the 39th Fighter Interceptor Squadron, 51st Fighter Interceptor Wing, for his eight victory of his distinguished career.

9   Just off Piccadilly, the famous Windmill Theatre took great pride in the fact that it never closed during the Blitz and 'We never closed' became its motto, although later it became, 'They Never Clothed' because the risqué shows with their nude girls became a wartime favourite. For many young GIs it was the first introduction to live theatre. 'The music was lively, the comedians were corny and GIs forgot why they were in England. There were three or four nude young ladies on the stage for almost every number. It seemed that women could appear nude on the stage as long as they didn't move.'

10   *Wandering Through World War II.*

11   Lieutenant Don R Freer and B-17G 43-38234 *Easy Does It* in the 322nd Bomb Squadron, 91st Bomb Group FTR, on 5 December 1944. Two men were KIA and seven survived to be taken prisoner.

12   *Target of Opportunity: Tales & Contrails of the Second World War.*

13   *Wandering Through World War II.*

14   *Target of Opportunity: Tales & Contrails of the Second World War.* Lamb eventually made a full recovery.

15   However, on 1 January 1945 four P-47s of the 84th Squadron led by Captain Wilbur Grimes escorted an *Aphrodite* mission directed at Oldenburg, south-east of Emden. Project *Aphrodite* comprised pilotless drone operations using war-weary B-17s. Each aircraft was packed with

18,000 lbs of Torpex, a nitroglycerine compound and was flown to a point over the English coast or North Sea where the pilot and co-pilot baled out. The drone would fly on and be directed onto its target (normally a V-1 or V-2 site) by remote control via a Lockheed Ventura 'mother ship'.

16   German production of fighter aircraft actually increased through 1944 into 1945. It had peaked in September 1944, when 1,874 Bf 109s and 1,002 Fw 190s were completed. (Though that same month, an average of three German fighters – and two pilots KIA – were lost for every B-17 or B-24 shot down.) The dispersed manufacturing plants were beyond the power of the 8th Air Force to seriously damage. Therefore, some post-war surveys concluded that the 8th Air Force bombing offensive was a failure. But the bombing was just good enough that the *Luftwaffe* fighters had to keep rising to attack and then the P-51s and P-47s mostly destroyed them.

17   Some 300 aircraft were lost, 235 pilots were killed and 65 pilots were taken prisoner.

18   On 13 June 1944 the first V-1 had started arriving in the London area. Of four 'Buzz Bombs' fired only one inflicted any damage, killing six and injuring nine others. V-1s killed over 6,000 civilians and nearly 18,000 were injured. Flying bombs travelled at 400 mph and only the British Meteor, a jet-propelled fighter, could catch one. Yet, with over 2,000 anti-aircraft guns, some with proximity fuses, nearly 2,500 of these weapons fell on London and the same amount on Antwerp, Belgium, after its capture by Allied ground troops.

19   *Wandering Through World War II.*

20   The 366th Fighter Group claimed two *Doras* shot down but none were in fact lost.

21   Hereford was KIA on 4 March 1945 probably as a result of oxygen trouble.

22   *Wandering Through World War II.*

23   (See *Eagles of Duxford: The 78th Fighter Group in World War II*). In all JG 26 lost seven Fw 190D-9s and four Bf 109G/Ks in the Cologne area. Among the dead and missing was *Ritterkreuzträger Oberleutnant* Gerhard Vogt, CO 5th *Staffel*, who had forty-eight victories. He was another 78th Fighter Group victim. His Fw 190D-9 was shot down SE of Cologne after he tried to escape in cloud near the ground. Major Anton 'Toni' Hackl returned to receive confirmation of a 78th Fighter Group P-51, his 175th victory and another downed 78th Fighter Group Mustang was awarded to *Gefreiter* Mittag for his first kill. A second mission flown by the 78th Fighter Group later in the day brought the kill tally to 14-0-14 when the 83rd Squadron's red flight bounced four Fw 190s in the traffic pattern of an

aerodrome north of Diepholz, Germany. See *The JG 26 War Diary Vol.2*. Anton 'Toni' Hackl scored 192 *Abschüsse*, 105 of which were on the Eastern Front and eighty-seven, which included thirty-two 4-*mots*, were on the Western Front. He was awarded the *Schwerten* (S) or Knight's Cross with Oak Leaves and Swords). *Luftwaffe Fighter Aces* by Mike Spick (Ivy Books 1996).

24   1st Lieutenant Herbert W Elin crashed near Bassingbourn and was killed. Spooner crashed east of Bruchstat strafing locomotives when he was struck by flak. 1st Lieutenant Allen R Packer was hit by flak at the target. In addition, the Group lost four other pilots in January 1945. On 2 January Flight Officer George W Morrison's engine quit twenty-five miles north of Saarbrücken and he baled out to become a PoW. 2nd Lieutenant Gerald F Boner ditched in the North Sea on 17 January after his engine quit fifty-five miles east of Great Yarmouth. He baled out at 5,000 feet and was seen to hit the water and his yellow life raft popped out. ASR arrived fifteen minutes later but his body was never found. On 20 January Flight Officer William E Bradley was KIA in the English Channel. That same day 2nd Lieutenant Kenneth J DeMaagd's engine quit and he crash-landed in a field west of the Rhine. He became a PoW. *Eagles of Duxford: The 78th Fighter Group in World War II*.

25   *Wandering Through World War II*.

26   *Eagles of Duxford: The 78th Fighter Group in World War II*.

27   Dick Hewitt, who in November 1944 had finished his second tour and had volunteered to stay for an extension of fifty more hours, finished his second fifty-hour extension on 6 February with a bomber escort to Merseburg/Leipzig, his longest mission to date (5.40 hours). 'The completion of 50 more hours would put me at 350 hours. The end of the war was barely in sight; the December winter blahs slowed things way down. I figured another 50 hours or less would wrap up the conflict in the ETO, so I went for it.' From 8 to 18 February Dick Hewitt spent R&R leave at a flak home but he noted that 'there were many bomber crew members there who quite obviously needed it a lot more than I did. They described seeing body parts blown about the interior of their aircraft. It made some all but lose their minds'. *Target of Opportunity: Tales & Contrails of the Second World War*.

28   *The Messerschmitt Me 262 Combat Diary*.

CHAPTER TWELVE

The Sky is Swept[1]

He crashed, skidding through a hedgerow, shedding the '51's wings and
debris flew so bad I figured he had 'had it'. I reported him as a probable
KIA at our mission debriefing. Turned out he survived the crash and was
taken prisoner. Later he was picked up by an advance Allied tank column
as the prisoners were being marched to a Stalag PoW camp. I attempted to
locate him after the war. Since my gun camera film failed, as it did quite
often, I never got kill credit. No eyewitnesses. I finally found him in the
early '60s but before I talked to him he died in a VA Hospital from a
suspected heart attack. My jet kills were never officially confirmed.
So be it.

Lieutenant Colonel Richard A Dick Hewitt[2]

During February 1945 the 78th Fighter Group pilots could claim no aerial victories but they did destroy fifteen aircraft on the ground as well as 105 locomotives, nineteen oil cars, thirty-five German soldiers and other targets. Duxford had two changes in commanding officers. Colonel Frederic C Gray, who had taken over in May 1944, went to 8th Air Force headquarters early in February and his place at Duxford was taken by Lieutenant Colonel Olin E Gilbert. He then became deputy commander when Lieutenant Colonel John D Landers took command. The twenty-three-year-old Oklahoman had completed two tours, the first in the Pacific in 1942 when he had destroyed six Japanese aircraft while flying P-40E fighters in the 49th Pursuit Group. After returning to the US 'Whispering John', as he was known, was promoted to major and he served as a flight instructor before joining the 38th Squadron, 55th Fighter Group, in late April 1944. Flying P-38J Lightnings he destroyed four German aircraft and damaged another before the Group converted to the P-51 Mustang. On 11 October 1944 he transferred to the 357th Fighter Group as Group Executive and on 18 November he scored his eleventh confirmed victory. Landers completed his second tour on 2

261

December and he returned to the US, before returning to the ETO to take command of the Duxford Outfit on 22 February.

On 1 March Major Dick Hewitt led the Group to the marshalling yards at Ülm where heavy flak 'damn near' got him. It blew him upside down at less than twenty feet off the deck but he escaped with no battle damage. 1st Lieutenant Ernest V Boehner of Glen Elder, Kansas, was hit just off his right wing in a strafing pass and went straight into the ground and blew up. The Group destroyed three locomotives on the five-hour fifty-minute mission. Next day, 2 March, Lieutenant Colonel John D Landers, flying *Big Beautiful Doll*, scored his first victories with the 78th Fighter Group when he downed two Bf 109s at Burg. By now the systematic destruction of German oil production plants, airfields and communications centres, had virtually driven the *Luftwaffe* from German skies and the Third *Reich* was on the brink of defeat. Despite fuel and pilot shortages Me 262 jet fighters could still be expected to put in rare attacks and during March almost all enemy fighter interceptions of American heavy bombers were made by Me 262s of JG 7 *Hindenburg*, Adolph Galland's *Jagdverband* 44, EJG 2, led by *Oberleutnant* Bär and I.KG(F) 54. However, the German jets and rockets had arrived too late and in too few numbers to prevent the inevitable.

One of the few occasions when *Luftwaffe* fighters appeared in some strength was on 19 March when 1,223 American heavies attacked marshalling yard targets at Fulda and Plauen and industrial targets at Jena and Zwickau. The forty-eight Mustangs in the Duxford Outfit, which was led by Lieutenant Colonel John Landers, were tasked with freelance bomber support for their withdrawal from Plauen-Ruhland. At first there was little indication of the fierce battle ahead as the Group was sweeping ahead of the B-17s of the 1st Air Division. In the vicinity of Hesepe three Me 262s attempted to bounce a Mustang squadron in a deliberate attempt to make them to drop their underwing fuel tanks. The Mustangs, however, immediately turned into their attackers without dropping their tanks and the jets soon flew off. Almost immediately, the 82nd Squadron, led by Major Dick Hewitt, was directed against four Bf 109s at three o'clock level at 8,000 feet in the Osnabrück area. Hewitt claimed two of the Bf 109s, both of whose pilots baled out and he hit two more but they were only damaged as he ran out of ammunition before he could finish them off. His No. 3, 1st Lieutenant Walter E Bourque, claimed another. More and more enemy fighters appeared until it was apparent that they numbered over 125 Bf 109s and Fw 190s, which had formed up for bomber interception over their airfields in the Hesepe-Vorden-Achmer area. There were five formations at *Staffel* strength between 7,000 and 14,000 feet, the topmost *Gruppe* in cirrus cloud presumably acting as top cover. A fierce battle raged and the Duxford Outfit claimed one of the highest single mission scores in 8th Air Force history with no fewer than thirty-two enemy aircraft destroyed, two probably destroyed and sixteen damaged for the loss of two pilots killed. Landers claimed a Bf 109 destroyed for his third Group victory and his fourteenth overall.

Among the other scorers was Bill Davis flying as 'Yellow 3' in the cockpit of *Twilight Tear*. He bounced a Bf 109 1,000 feet below him, then went through two turns before scoring hits in a 90-degree deflection shot. As the Messerschmitt spiralled down the pilot took to his parachute.[3] Major Harry Downing, who had just arrived at Duxford from the training command in the US and had been operations officer in the 82nd before taking command of the 84th Squadron on the 14th, was one of three pilots who were shot down and taken prisoner. The Shampoo White Leader was heard on radio saying, 'There's lots of meat here!' Then twenty Fw 190s encircled him and his last message was, 'I'm hit and I'm baling out. So long gang.'[4]

During the battle four of the Group's pilots set upon two low-flying jets identified as Arado Ar 234B-2 *Blitz* (Lightning) turbojet-powered bombers, which could have been used in the interceptor role to launch rockets at the American heavies.[5] Both of the twin-engined jets fell to the Duxford Outfit's guns. Allen Rosenblum and 1st Lieutenant James E Parker hit the first one, which smashed into a farmhouse and exploded, and they then picked out a second Arado 'stooging along on the deck', blasting the jet's tail, engines and fuselage. The German pilot had had enough and he crawled out of his cockpit to bale out but Parker's burst of fire knocked him forward over the wing.[6] Captain Winfield Brown and Huie Lamb applied the *coup de grâce* and the jet hit the ground in flames. All told the 8th Air Force P-51s flew 606 effective sorties and claimed forty-two enemy aircraft, including three jets, shot down.

On 20 March Dick Hewitt became 82nd Squadron CO. Just over 400 heavies bombed shipyards at Hamburg and an oil refinery at Hemmingstedt escorted by eight fighter groups who flew 298 effective sorties. Next day preparatory air operations for the forthcoming (23 March) crossing of the lower Rhine by Allied ground forces began. In morning raids 1,254 bombers, in conjunction with aircraft of the RAF and 9th Air Force attacking other targets, bombed ten airfields in north-western Germany, a tank factory at Plauen and a marshalling yard at Reichenbach.[7] In the afternoon ninety B-24s bombed Mülheim an der Ruhr airfield. US fighters flew almost 750 effective sorties in support of the two operations. Thirty-one Me 262s were among the *Luftwaffe* fighters that were despatched. Forty-three Mustangs led by Major Richard Conner were tasked with penetration and withdrawal support for the Third Air Division attacking the Ruhrland synthetic oil factory. They rendezvoused successfully with the heavies at 0840 hours above Nienburg and they headed with them to the Wittenburg area where a Me 262 made a pass on the Fortresses and downed two of them. Captain Edwin H Miller, who had scored a Me 262 'probable' on 9 February, spotted the 262 'leapfrogging' through the two bombers, shooting them down. The Me 262 pilot decided to make one more attack on a crippled B-17 and as the jet made a wide turn to come back again, Miller tried to scare him off with a 2,000 yard burst of fire, which scored a few hits in the enemy's wing. The Me 262 broke off and dived away for some clouds chased by Miller whose Mustang was clocking 500 mph as he pursued the jet through a thin overcast and cut him off in the turn. The Me 262 pilot tried to outrun Miller and his wingman but he could not shake them off.[8] Miller recalled:

> We broke through a scattered undercast and I was sitting right on his tail firing at 500 yards range until my guns were completely empty. By that time he was a 'Dead Duck' and veered off to the left just as he crashed into the ground.

21 March turned out to be a jet-feast for the Duxford Outfit, who claimed five Me 262s destroyed, three of which were caught at low level after taking off from Giebelstadt airfield[9] at 1215 hours. 1st Lieutenant Walter E Bourque and Mustangs of the 339th Fighter Group claimed one of these Me 262s destroyed. 1st Lieutenant Robert H Anderson also claimed one of the jets and 1st Lieutenant Allen A Rosenblum and Captain Winfield H Brown shared another. A fifth Me 262A, probably of JG 7, who lost four Me 262s in combat and two pilots killed and one damaged, fell to 1st Lieutenant John A Kirk III, who recalls:

> We were positioned at 28,000 feet and above and to the right of the bomber stream in the Meiningen area. Thus I was about 8,000 feet above the bombers as they neared the target. The first sighting of a Me 262 came when I saw a B-17 being attacked and bursting into flames. The jet broke off and went into a 45-degree dive straight ahead. I had peeled off and dove just about straight down as I was slightly ahead of him. My wingman followed me. The airspeed indicator rapidly advanced until it was in the red line. As I remember, it indicated that the plane was flying at about 550 mph. That must have been terminal velocity, however I had no problems handling my aircraft. He was in my K-14 gunsight, but out of range of my six wing guns. As we dove down to about 15,000 feet I knew I was not gaining on him, but he was not pulling away either. I decided to lob some bullets at him, although it was forbidden to fire your guns when your speed was in the red line, as vibration would tear the wings off. Having great faith in the strength of the Mustang, I pulled up the nose so that the gunsight was about one radius above the Me 262. One quick burst and a check on the wings showed them to be all right, so another fast burst was fired. My bullets must have hit his right engine, as smoke appeared. He slowed up and I anticipated his next move. I then pulled up from my steep dive, hoping to gain on him when he levelled out. He pulled up from his dive and we closed fast. Soon I was in perfect firing range. The guns were fired in long bursts as soon as he was centred in my gunsight. Strikes appeared all along his fuselage and wing roots. Suddenly the pilot seemed to 'pop out' of the cockpit and flew back very close to me. I could see him very well. To record the kill, I took a camera shot of the plane crashing in a ball of flame and the German pilot floating down on his parachute.[10]

Major Richard Conner made a strafing pass at three Me 262s waiting to take off from Alt-Lönnewitz airfield on the Czechoslovak–German border and got good strikes on two of them before firing a short burst into the third jet, which exploded in a fireball. Conner's Mustang was hit by light flak and he headed for Russian-held territory where he made a successful crash-landing on the east bank of the Oder River.[11]

Next day the Duxford Outfit claimed two more Me 262s to take the Group's total claims of twelve jets in air combat, the largest bag by a single 8th Air Force fighter group in March when a total of forty-three Me 262s were claimed overall. On 22 March 1,301 B-17s and B-24s bombed targets east of Frankfurt and ten military encampments in the Ruhr in preparation for the forthcoming Allied amphibious crossing of the lower Rhine. Lieutenant Colonel John Landers led the Jugs on ahead of the 2nd Air Division Liberators heading for Kitzingen, Giebelstadt and Schwabisch-Hall while more P-47s escorted the B-24s through the targets. The 8th Air Force bombed the Bottrop military barracks and hutted areas directly behind the German lines while 136 B-17s of the 15th Air Force attacked Ruhrland again and caused extensive damage to the plant. Twenty-seven Me 262s attacked the bomber formations and claimed thirteen B-17s shot down but only one Fortress was actually lost. Nine fighter groups strafed airfields and the 55th and 78th Fighter Groups claimed two of the jets destroyed and one damaged. One of the jets claimed destroyed near Giebelstadt airfield fell to the guns of Captain Harold T Barnaby. His victim was a Me 262A-2a.[12] of I./KG(J)54 flown by *Unteroffizier* Adalbert Egri. Barnaby recalled:

My attention was attracted to Giebelstadt airdrome because of its long runway and number of jet fighters dispersed around the perimeter. Four Me 262s were parked on the runway ready to take off. I saw one of the jets taking off from east to west. From 10,000 feet over the west end of the runway, I closed rapidly in a slight left turn as the 262 cleared the runway. I was indicating 425 mph and was about 400 yards behind when I reached his 1,000-foot altitude. He was going 400 mph in less than three miles flying distance. My first burst hit his left engine, which caused an explosion, blowing off parts. Hits in the wings and fuselage were making it unhealthy for the pilot. Using his speed he pulled up to 2,000 feet. He baled out. Unfortunately his jump was successful. The 262 half rolled to the right striking the ground vertically. The explosion made a spectacular sight about two miles south of the airdrome. The other jets were quickly dispersed after the tower fired a red flare.[13]

Near Ülm 2nd Lieutenant Milton B Stutzman picked up an Me 262 approaching the Liberator formations and he cut the jet off by turning into it. The enemy jet was Me 262A-1a 'White 12' flown by *Fähnenjunker-Oberfeldwebel* Helmut Reckers of 10./EJG 2. Reckers broke and headed south until he thought he had outdistanced his pursuers when he turned gently ninety degrees right. This allowed Stutzman and 1st Lieutenant Eugene L Peel to gain on the fleeing Me 262. North of Lake Constance Reckers led the pursuing P-51s across the southern perimeter of Lechfeld airfield where Stutzman and Peel opened fire, scoring strikes on the Messerschmitt. Pouring smoke, Reckers jettisoned his canopy and baled out. His parachute did not open before the Me 262 veered off left and crashed beside a small road and the German pilot was killed. Stutzman and Peel shared in the victory.

Next day, 23 March, 1,244 heavies bombed rail targets as part of the rail interdiction programme to isolate the Ruhr and cut off coal shipping. Since the loss of the Saar basin the Ruhr was the only remaining source of supply for the German war machine. On 23/24 March, under a sixty-six-mile long smoke screen and aided by 1,749 bombers of the 8th Air Force, Field Marshal Bernard Montgomery's 21st Army Group crossed the Rhine in the north while further south simultaneous crossings were made by General Patton's 3rd Army. Bomber groups flew two missions on 24 March, hitting jet aircraft bases in Holland and Germany. Approximately 6,000 aircraft, including gliders, transports and fighters, took part in the Wesel operation. The 78th Fighter Group flew three missions in support of the ground forces in the Lingen-Diepholz-Cloppenburg area making strafing attacks on enemy targets seen. Some 240 B-24s, each loaded with 600 tons of medical supplies, food and weapons, followed in the wake of transports and gliders ferrying troops of the 1st Allied Airborne Army. Grey-white smoke shrouded the battlefields and engulfed the city of Wesel. Smoke canisters, which had blacked out over sixty miles of the front for more than two days were still burning. The dropping zone was strewn with wrecked and abandoned gliders, smouldering haystacks and dead livestock. Spasmodic and highly accurate small arms fire and 20-mm cannon fire brought down several bombers and many returned with battle damage.

On 30 March the P-47s led by Lieutenant Colonel John Landers in *Big Beautiful Doll*, escorted the B-17s of the Third Air Division whose targets were at Hamburg. Near Rendsburg airfield Landers spotted a Me 262 1,000 feet off the deck heading south behind him. The CO and his wingman, Lieutenant Thomas V Thain, dived from 7,000 feet and bounced the Me 262, which possibly belonged to JG 7. The German pilot made some suicidal gradual turns which made things easier for Landers and Thain who queued up and fired into his cockpit almost at will. The German pilot tried to drop his landing gear and he put down on Hohn airfield but he crashed and burned without getting out. Landers and Thain shared in the victory, which took the CO's final tally to 14½ victories. Next day, 31 March, another Me 262 jet kill was claimed. Near Stendal Captain Wayne L Coleman was at 15,000 feet when he heard on the radio that jets were in the area. A short while later Coleman spotted one of the jets over the leading edge of his left wing. It was possibly the Me 262A-1 of 2./KG(J)54 flown by *Oberleutnant* Dr Heinz Oberweg, *Kapitän* of 2 *Staffel*. Coleman put his Mustang into a semi-split-ess, which brought him within range to blast the enemy's jet's cockpit and right engine. As Coleman broke left, the crippled Me 262 rolled right and went straight into the ground and exploded. Oberweg was reported killed after being shot down by a fighter near Halle.[14] 1st Lieutenant Paul S Ostrander perished in the North Sea after his Mustang was hit by light flak and set on fire. He baled out from 5,000 feet but his inflatable dinghy, which was a new type, fell away when his chute opened. 1st Lieutenant James E Moores, who stayed with him and circled the scene with two other Mustangs, saw Ostrander in the sea off the Dutch coast with his life vest. But the wind was strong and the water was rough and he lost sight of him before a RAF Warwick rescue aircraft of 280 Squadron from Beccles (Ellough) arrived. The body of the young pilot was never found. March had cost the Group nine pilots killed while four more were taken prisoner. Three pilots evaded capture after being shot down. Fifty-four air-to-air victories were claimed and nine locomotives and four aircraft were claimed destroyed on the ground.

Bomber crews were now hard pressed to find worthwhile targets and the planners switched attacks from inland targets to coastal areas. On 2 April the Thunderbolts made another sweep into north-west Germany but as Dick Hewitt noted, 'there were no Jerries; all gone to Czechoslovakia'. He could see Denmark from 32,000 feet in the CAVU conditions. This four-hour twenty-minute mission completed his third fifty-hour extension. He now had '400 and counting'. For two pilots in his squadron, 2 April was 'THE day' as Larry Nelson recalls:

I was informed that after 65 missions, my next mission would be my last. My friend Wayne Coleman was told it would be his last also. We joked about how they meant it would be our last! That morning we were roused very early. We went to the mess hall for breakfast. As usual we had our fresh egg, which was a treat. We walked across the road past the MPs where I got my salute and 'Good Morning Shorty Sir.' We gathered at the squadron flight room to hear what the mission was to be. It was to be a 'sweep' across northern Germany at low altitude to dive or skip bomb and strafe 'targets of opportunity'. These targets were defined as troop movements, airfields, flak towers, and railroad traffic – most anything that moved. Throughout the mission we could expect to be fired on constantly. After our briefing, we were taken to our planes which our crews had ready – full of gas and ammunition, with bombs under our wings and gun cameras loaded. We took off eight abreast, which was always a thrill and circled the field once to allow all 48 of us to get in formation. Then off we went thinking we were invincible, which we really weren't. Most every time we passed into German territory we were shot at with flak guns. Occasionally they hit one of us, but not this time. On command we dropped down to very low level. We shot up parked aircraft, skip bombed their hangars, chased locomotives and strafed them until they blew up. To me this was very impersonal. I could not see anyone being injured. I was just doing my job. I enjoyed working with my buddies setting up flight patterns to systematically eliminate our targets. Our flight training really paid off here. We had to stay out of each other's way.

After a couple of hours of this, it was time to go home – a sad time for me. I thought never again would I be able to do this. Before landing at our base, Wayne and I decided to put on an air show for our friends since we had some fuel left. We made high speed passes and executed rolls, loops, and close formation flying. It's a wonder we didn't kill ourselves! Upon landing the story changes. It was the squadron's habit to give each flyer a shot glass of Black and White Bourbon after each mission. Since I did not drink, I had always given mine to a friend. This being my last mission, they all got together and insisted I drink theirs. I started to chug-a-lug each of their drinks. Before long my head started spinning and I was in happy land. I left the flight line and went to the Officers' Club in my flying clothes, which was a no-no. I got hold of two fizz squirters and started spraying my friends. I was told I stuck the squirter in the ear of our CO who was talking on the phone. In general, I made a fool of myself. I went into the mess hall and ordered them to serve me a meal. Around that time I passed out. They gathered me up and carried me to my bed where I slept it off. It was a day to remember. Of this I had little or no recollection. I was more than happy to return home to resume my college studies at Ohio State University, which is where, within a month, I met my wife, Barney. But that is another story!

Next day Dick Hewitt led a five and a quarter hour Group mission to Kiel on bomber escort. Targets were fast running out. On 5 April the 8th Air Force's superiority was such that the B-17s assembled over France before flying to targets in the Nürnburg area. Everywhere the Allies were victorious but while the Germans kept on fighting, missions continued almost daily. In Germany the now desperate situation called for desperate measures to be taken against the all-powerful bomber streams and last ditch attempts were made by the *Luftwaffe* to try to stem the tide.[15] A plan conceived late in 1944 was the deliberate ramming of American bombers by converted Bf 109 fighters, called *Rammjäger*, flown by pilots of *Sonderkommando Elbe*.[16] On 7 April around 130 Bf 109s and their escort fighters took off from their airfields around Stendal and Gardelegen to ram bombers heading for underground oil refineries in central Germany but only an estimated twenty-five Messerschmitts and a few Me 262s, managed to break through the American fighter screen. Diving from a height of 33,000 feet, twenty-two bombers were rammed of which fourteen were B-17s and eight were B-24s, but *Rammkommando Elbe* lost thirty-one Bf 109s.[17] The 78th Fighter Group claimed five German fighters this day for the loss of one P-51 whose pilot survived to become a prisoner.

Next day, 8 April, the 8th Air Force was again out in considerable force. Fourteen of the fighter groups flew escort in areas north and north-west of Leipzig, south-east of and near Nürnburg and south-west of Chemnitz while more than

1,150 bombers hit their targets in the Leipzig, Nuremberg and Chemnitz areas. The Duxford Outfit flew their escort mission for the bombers attacking Plauen. On 9 April about 1,200 bombers supported by fifteen fighter groups hit ten jet airfields and other targets in south central Germany. Me 262s needed a big airfield with a runway of up to 2000 metres, which the pilots called *Silberplätze* or 'silver fields' but the situation had become so bad that they now had to operate from the Hamburg/Lübeck *autobahn*. Many German aircraft were grounded because of lack of fuel and they were sitting ducks on the *Luftwaffe* airfields. On 10 April over 1,220 bombers attacked eight airfields and two marshalling yards and other installations in north Germany supported by fifteen fighter groups who after providing close and area support, broke away to strafe ground targets.

Colonel Landers led an escort mission in support of the Third Air Task Force bombing for the jet fields in the Brandenburg area. After the B-17s had unloaded their bombs on Briest airfield, Landers gave the order to strafe jet airfields in the vicinity but the flak defences at Briest put up stiff resistance and 2nd Lieutenant Richard I Kuehl was hit. He baled out at Helmstadt and was captured for thirty-six hours until the advancing US 84th Infantry Division freed him. Five days later he was back at Duxford. Meanwhile, the rest of the P-51 pilots felt that discretion was the better part of valour and they flew on to Burg airfield near Magdeburg, which was still burning from bombing and strafing, Captain Foy C Higginbottom made a solo pass on a Me 262, which he claimed as damaged. At Werder south-west of Potsdam, Landers had spotted some P-47 fighter-bombers destroying about fifteen enemy aircraft on the airfield and he radioed up the 82nd Squadron with orders to attack. About seventy aircraft were parked close together on the perimeter and in the woods on the west side and they made an inviting target. But both hangars were on fire and heavy smoke rising from the burning aircraft made spotting targets and strafing difficult. Even so the Mustangs carried out about a dozen passes on the burning airfield and they left at least sixty aircraft burning or wrecked. Flak, which was described as 'moderate to meagre' downed two Mustangs. 1st Lieutenant Herbert A Stinson was killed and 2nd Lieutenant Roger A Spaulding baled out to be taken prisoner. On the way home the P-51 pilots used up the rest of their ammunition with some passes at Gardelegen and Hustedt airfields. Back at Duxford the Group put in claims for fifty-two enemy aircraft destroyed on the ground. The 82nd Squadron claimed thirty-three of these. Another forty-three enemy aircraft were damaged. Colonel Landers was credited with the destruction of eight aircraft on the ground and 2nd Lieutenant Edward J Carroll, Captain Huie Lamb and 1st Lieutenants Francis E Harrington and Henry R Slack were awarded four apiece.

As a result of the bombing of the jet airfields nearly all Me 262 units were forced to withdraw to the Prague area. On 16 April Orders of the Day No. 2 from General Carl 'Tooey' Spaatz ended the strategic mission of the 8th Air Force and only some tactical missions remained. Fifteen fighter groups again provided close and area support for the bombers over Germany and Czechoslovakia. The 78th

Fighter Group were tasked to provide area support to the 760 bombers of the First and Second Air Divisions bombing bridges and marshalling yards in the Regensburg-Straubing-Platting-Landshut areas. The *Luftwaffe*, however, was noticeable for its absence. Finding no targets in the air the 8th Air Force fighters dropped down and carried out strafing runs on over forty enemy landing grounds and installations. The 78th Fighter Group successfully attacked five enemy in Germany and in the Prague-Pilsen area of Czechoslovakia and wreaked havoc, some of the pilots making up to a dozen strafing runs on the airfields. The 78th Fighter Group, which was airborne for seven hours forty minutes, claimed no fewer than 135 enemy aircraft destroyed on the ground and a further eighty-nine damaged and was later awarded its second DUC for the long mission. In all the 8th Air Force fighter groups claimed a record 747 enemy aircraft destroyed for the loss of thirty-four fighters, which were largely downed by automatic AA weapons. Captain Manford O Croy was shot down by flak at Straubing airfield. He pulled up and baled out but he was too low and his parachute failed to open. 1st Lieutenant Eugene L Peel was shot down over Laudan airfield and he belly-landed near Frankfurt. Captain Robert B Holmes was last seen making a strafing attack on Ganacker airfield south-west of Platting before he was shot down and killed by flak. 2nd Lieutenant Fred R Swauger was shot down by small arms fire at Marienbad airfield and held prisoner for a time.

On 17 April when more than 950 B-17s and B-24s attacked eight railway centres, junctions, stations and marshalling yards and an oil depot in east Germany and western Czechoslovakia the German corridor was shrinking rapidly and the American and Russian bomb lines now crossed at several points on briefing maps. Eight B-17s and seventeen fighters were shot down, including six B-17s by Me 262s of JG 7. Eighteen US fighter groups flew support and they encountered about fifty fighters, mostly jets. Thirteen enemy aircraft including four jets were claimed destroyed. In the Prague area 1st Lieutenant Anthony A Palopoli destroyed a Me 262 on the ground at Cakowice airfield. All told the Group destroyed fifteen aircraft on the ground and damaged thirteen more. Two Me 262s were bounced by the flight led by Major Richard Dick Hewitt who chased the Me 262s for some distance before the jets ran low on fuel and they headed for Kralupy airfield. As the last jet was on its final landing approach Hewitt swept in and shot it down into trees off the end of the single runway. The first Me 262 was still rolling on the far end of the runway as Hewitt set it on fire with a burst of gunfire. By now flak was coming up furiously and his wingman, Allen Rosenblum, was hit as he crossed the airfield. Hewitt recalls:

> He crashed, skidding through a hedgerow, shedding the '51's wings and debris flew so bad I figured he had 'had it'. I reported him as a probable KIA at our mission debriefing. Turned out he survived the crash and was taken prisoner. Later he was picked up by an advance Allied tank column as the prisoners were being marched to a Stalag PoW camp. I attempted to

locate him after the war. Since my gun camera film failed, as it did quite often, I never got kill credit. No eyewitnesses. I finally found him in the early '60s but before I talked to him he died in a VA Hospital from a suspected heart attack. My jet kills were never officially confirmed. So be it.[18]

In total, the American fighters claimed over 250 aircraft destroyed on the ground. It was the last time that the fighter pilots were able to strafe enemy targets because on 20 April an order banning attacks of this kind was issued. On 21 April twenty plus enemy jets were spotted stationary on an *autobahn* south-east of Munch and the Group could not go down and strafe them. During the week 18 to 25 April, missions were briefed and scrubbed almost simultaneously. General Patton's advance was so rapid that at least on one occasion bomber crews were lining up for take-off when a message was received to say that General Patton's forces had captured the target the B-17s were to bomb! The last major air battles between fighter groups of the 8th Air Force and the *Luftwaffe* took place on 18 April when 1,211 heavies escorted by more than 1,200 fighters were sent to attack Berlin. Forty Me 262s of *Jagdgeschwader* 7 shot down twenty-five bombers with rockets. It was the final challenge by a dying enemy. The *Luftwaffe* was finished, destroyed in the air and starved of fuel on the ground. It was cruel luck therefore that with victory so close, three pilots were shot down and killed on 21 April. Lieutenant Colonel Leonard Marshall, the Group leader, was last seen flying inverted in overcast at 28,000 feet in the Mannheim area. His body and unopened parachute were later found twenty miles north of Strasbourg in France. In all probability he was a victim of oxygen or instrument failure. Shampoo leader, Captain Dorian Ledington and his wingman, 2nd Lieutenant John R Sole, were killed west of Koblenz. After failing to get into the Aviation Cadets, Ledington, who was from Kansas, had joined the Royal Canadian Air Force and flown Spitfires in the RAF before joining the 84th Squadron. His flight were flying on the deck desperately trying to find an airfield for Sole who had just ten minutes of fuel remaining when the weather closed down to zero. Sole's left wing clipped a treetop and he climbed calling for aid. Earl Stier told Sole to climb and bale out but he was at only 300 feet and his chute failed to open. Ledington had only recently returned from R&R for another tour.

The end came on 25 April 1945 in a fitting climax to Allied fighter and bomber operations. Some 282 B-24s were despatched to bomb four rail complexes surrounding Hitler's mountain retreat at Berchtesgaden in the south-east corner of Germany. The Obersalzberg, a beautiful mountainous region close to the Austrian border, was one that had long appealed to Hitler. Following the Munich Putsch and his imprisonment, Hitler had stayed in the Obersalzberg, writing part of Mien Kampf there. Royalties from the book's sale had enabled the German dictator to buy a house called the 'Berghof'. After coming to power the building had been rebuilt on a lavish scale and the best known addition was the dramatically named

'Eagle's Nest', a tea-house that had been built on Kehlstein mountain apparently as a isolated conference building. Hitler's home, referred to as the 'Chalet' by the RAF, was the target for 359 Lancaster heavy bombers and fourteen *Oboe* Mosquito and twenty-four Lancaster marker aircraft. Included in the mighty force were thirty-three Lancasters of Nos 9 and 617 'Dam Busters' Squadrons, each carrying a potentially devastating 12,000-lb *Tallboy* bomb in their long, rakish bomb bay. At least 126 Mustangs of 11 Group RAF and ninety-eight P-51s from two American fighter groups provided escort relays along the route, a round trip of 1,400 miles.[19] In the summer of 1940 11 Group's few squadrons of Spitfires and Hurricanes had held Hermann Göring's legions at bay, a defeat that had put in motion the gradual fall from grace for the rotund *Reichsmarschall*. By 1945 his beloved *Luftwaffe* existed in name only and he no longer had the ear of his *Führer*, who was safely tucked up in his bunker in Berlin while Göring now had to find shelter in one of the air raid tunnels under the remote mountain fortress.

Pete Keillor had the honour of leading the Group on the escort mission for the Lancasters. He guessed – wrongly – that the 'British bomber guys' wanted to fly in daylight 'once' so they loaded 'two bunches with 8,000-lb bombs' and sent then down to Berchtesgaden. 'Maybe they thought they'd catch Hitler there' he mused. In fact, ever since D-Day and on many days since, RAF Bomber Command had relinquished their nocturnal role and mounted many pulverising raids in the daylight hours. Traces of early morning mist and fog were in the air when the Mustangs lifted off from Duxford for the last time on a combat mission but 2nd Lieutenant Edward J Carroll fell at the first hurdle when he aborted shortly after take-off and he turned back towards Duxford. Near Sawston he hit trees in a dense fog and crashed to his death. He was the last 78th Fighter Group pilot lost on a combat mission. The remaining Mustangs, including a pair of unarmed two-seaters, one of which was called *Gruesome Twosome*[20] flew on over the sea and crossed into Belgium at 0630 hours but they missed the planned rendezvous with the Lancasters over Luxembourg, as Pete Keillor recalls:

> I reported in over the continent and ground control told me that my bombers were an hour ahead of where they were supposed to be. I put on extra power and finally caught up with them and escorted them to the target. I started counting them and saw that they were the wrong bunch. [They were the sixteen Lancasters 617 Dam Busters Squadron.] If I remember right there were a hundred and ten in the first bunch and eighty-eight in the second and the second was ours. American bombers all had tail markings so you could tell which was which but the Lancasters were just a bunch of planes, not even in real formation. So, after they'd dropped their bombs [on Hitler's 'Chalet' and the local SS guard barracks] I left them and hurried back to pick up the others.[21] Sure enough we found them and escorted them in and out. By that time we were getting low on gas with all the extra speeding around. I told everyone to drop their external tanks, but we still had to land

in France and get some. We had six hours and twenty-five minutes till we landed in France ands then another hour home. That was the prettiest scenery I ever flew over. It was perfectly clear – you could see forever – and we followed the north side of the Alps for hundreds of miles. Steep mountains went down to lakes in the valleys and it sure made you want to see it from the ground.[22]

Those who bombed the 'Chalet' mostly missed but the Berghof sustained much blast damage as a result of the bombs and the *Tallboys*. At the SS barracks one building and several others were damaged. Six of the 3,500 who had sheltered in the air raid tunnels were killed. Göring was not one of them but he was captured later and received his judgement at Nuremberg. However, a lethal suicide pill prevented his execution for war crimes. Soon after the raid the US 3rd Infantry Division won the race to occupy Berchtesgaden and share in the spoils of victory.

During the first week of May the German armies surrendered one by one to Montgomery at Lüneberg Heath, to Devers at Munich and to Alexander at Caserta. Finally, at 0241 on 7 May at a little red schoolhouse in Reims that was SHAEF headquarters, General Dwight D Eisenhower accepted the German surrender, which brought the war in Europe to a formal end. A simple cable announced the end to 'five years, eight months and six days of bloodshed and destruction' in Europe: 'The mission of this Allied Force was fulfilled at 3 am, local time, 7 May 1945. Eisenhower.' Sixteen war correspondents witnessed the German surrender. All except one of them agreed to a press embargo until an official announcement of the war's end could be made simultaneously by all combatants, including the Soviet Union who were planning a surrender ceremony of their own in Berlin. Edward Kennedy of Associated Press, 'a hard-nosed wire service correspondent' decided to telephone his report to his Paris office, which relayed it to New York via London and within the hour, news of the surrender broke but the only official announcement, ironically, was made by Hamburg Radio.

In Britain people were, in the words of the song, looking forward to 'getting lit up when the lights go on in London' but now nobody knew whether it really was time for celebrations to begin. In America officialdom appeared to do everything to stifle celebrations before they began. All bars were closed for twenty-four hours and flags were kept at half-mast in deference to the late President Roosevelt who had died in office in April. On 7 May Mayor La Guardia urged all the people of the City of New York who had 'thoughtlessly left their jobs' to go home and to be patient. Pete Keillor got orders on 7 May to go to London on TDY for thirty days, reporting to 8 Bryanston Square. He went, but had no idea what he was supposed to do.

This was the day that the Germans surrendered and my job was cancelled. However, I really lucked out by being on duty in London. Everybody was ordered back to base, but I just walked the streets along with the British. There was no traffic and not much noise. People just drifted around in a sort of bright daze. I missed the fun later that night. I heard that some women took their clothes off and tried to climb the statue in Piccadilly Circus. Next day I went to Buckingham Palace and stood outside until the Royal Family came out and waved. They did that every couple of hours. King George was still alive and the princesses were still girls.[23]

Prime Minister Winston Churchill used the 'secret line' to the White House asking President Truman that he bring forward the official announcement. Truman refused to do so without the approval of Joseph Stalin but Churchill knew that the Soviet dictator was playing power politics and he felt he could delay no longer. The British Ministry of Information announced that Tuesday 8 May would be VE (Victory in Europe) Day and a holiday in Britain. Washington finally lost patience with Soviet procrastination and in the early hours of 8 May President Truman held a news conference to announce the German surrender on all fronts to American, British and Soviet forces. Up to 30,000 New Yorkers gathered in Times Square but Truman's victory proclamation went largely unheard because no one had thought to have it relayed over loudspeakers.

At Duxford on VE day beer flowed free from spigots at Duffy's Tavern, the Officers' Club and the Sergeants' Club. The base was restricted for two days and work stopped almost entirely to celebrate. A formal review was held the day after VE Day and Colonel Landers read the official victory proclamation. Chaplain (Captain) Ellis R Veatch offered a prayer. After the ceremony the celebration began all over again.

In London crowds gathered early, encouraged by a change in the weather from storm clouds the night before to warm sunshine. Bells pealed. Flags flew from all the buildings. Shop windows were filled with red, white and blue clothes, flowers and materials. Aircraft flew overhead and streamers, ticker tape and paper poured out of every window and balcony. There was no traffic because the people of London and their children and thousands of visitors filled the streets and pavements and parks to celebrate victory in Europe. In Trafalgar Square the steps, lions and lampposts were 'coated with people'. Whitehall appeared to be paved with heads. 'This is it – and we are all going nuts,' wrote a *Daily Mirror* reporter.

There are thousands of us in Piccadilly Circus. The police say more than 10,000 – and that's a conservative estimate. In Piccadilly Circus a black bereted soldier in the Tank Corps climbed the little pyramidal Angkor Vat of scaffolding and sandbags, which was erected early in the war to protect the pedestal of the Eros statue after the figure had been removed to safekeeping. At the top he took a tiptoe Eros pose aiming an imaginary bow while the crowd roared. A paratrooper in maroon beret followed and once on top, reached down and hauled up a blonde in a very tight pair of green slacks. The Tank Corps soldier promptly grabbed her in his arms and, encouraged by ecstatic cheers from the whole Circus, for a moment seemed about to enact the classic role of Eros right on the top of the monument. GIs joined them and before long the pyramid was covered with servicemen and young girls.

The *Daily Mirror* report continued:

We are dancing around Eros in the blackout but there is a glow from a bonfire up Shaftesbury Avenue and a newsreel cinema has lit its canopy lights for the first time in getting on for six years. A huge V sign glares down over Leicester Square. And gangs of girls and soldiers are waving rattles and shouting and climbing lampposts and swarming over cars that have become bogged down in this struggling, swirling mass of celebrating Londoners. There had been great fear for the conduct of the Yanks but the spectacle of the staid and reserved English letting their hair down as it had never been down before so startled the Yanks that they were left without a leg to stand on. For once the British 'out-hollered' and 'out drank' the Americans.

On the American bases the average GI mirrored the confusion of the world outside. Pearl Harbor had yet to be avenged and rumours of redeployment to the Pacific abounded. It was 'Two Down and One to Go'. Italy and Germany had been 'licked' and while Japan was heading for defeat nobody was certain how long it would take. On Sunday 13 May a Victory Flypast was made over 'Widewing', the 8th Air Force headquarters where Lieutenant General James H Doolittle and his staff were housed. About 1,400 bombers and fighters were to take part but on course to High Wycombe the clouds moved in and the bombers had to abort. Final honours therefore went to more than 700 American fighters. Wave after wave flew over the old abbey, which before the war had been a school for girls. In the summer of 1942 when General Eaker had chosen 'Pinetree' to plan the future of his embryonic and untried force, some of the bedrooms still displayed a prim little card that said, 'Ring twice for mistress'.

Then came the newly announced point system for discharge, reconditioning of planes and equipment and regular Saturday inspection and reviews. It was almost like 'boot camp'. At Duxford on 1 July Lieutenant Colonel Roy B Caviness arrived from Little Walden where he had been commanding the 361st Fighter Group to swap places with Colonel John Landers. On 1 August an open day was held for 5,000 local people so that they could see the aircraft and meet the men before they started the long journey Stateside. By November all was quiet. A small party remained to tidy up, after which, on 1 December, Duxford airfield was officially handed back to the RAF. The sky had been swept, Shakespeare's 'sceptred isle' had been defended and the battle won.

1   The motto of RAF Duxford *Verrimus Cælum* – We Sweep The Sky.

2   *Target of Opportunity: Tales & Contrails of the Second World War.*

3   Davis flew the majority of his thirty-five combat missions in *Twilight Tear*, scoring three aerial victories and one damaged. Respiratory problems forced *Twilight Tear*'s early retirement from racing aged only four and she was retired to Calumet Farm, having won a staggering $202,165 in prize money and winning eighteen of her twenty-four races. She became a brood mare and went on to foal future champions before dying in 1954. Bill Davis returned home in July 1945 and left the service in 1946. Later that year, he married Patricia Sherman and they set up a successful real estate brokerage business in Setauket, New York, returning to Long Island in the summer months. Bill and Pat had three children, Robert, Louise and Virginia, and the family would take trips to Florida and Vermont and spend the summer months boating. Sadly, Bill Davis died from a cerebral haemorrhage in November 1967, just four days after celebrating his forty-eighth birthday. His famous Mustang was re-discovered in the 1970s and in March 1978 restoration to flying condition began. In April 2002 *Twilight Tear* returned to its wartime home, joining Stephen Grey's stable of famous fighters of The Fighter Collection at Duxford and he flew the P-51D at the Flying Legends show in 2006.

4   *Eagles of Duxford.*

5   The Arado 234 was the second jet-propelled aircraft to enter service with the *Luftwaffe* and the world's first jet bomber. Arado 234s of 6th *Staffel* KG 76 undertook its first operations during the Ardennes Offensive and I and III *Gruppen* joined the training programme during January 1945. III./KG 76 became operational in February but sorties were severely limited owing to lack of fuel. On 24 February 1945 following an attack by Me 262 and Arado Ar 234 jet bombers of KG 51 and KG 76 respectively, an Ar 234 of III./KG 76 was brought down by USAAF Thunderbolts near Segelsdorf, providing the Allies with their first Arado jet. From early March operations by KG 76 steadily increased. Perhaps the most vital mission was the attempted destruction of the American-held Ludendorf Bridge over the Rhine at Remagen, between 7 and 17 March, when the bridge finally collapsed, KG 76 made continuous and often almost suicidal attacks with SC 1000 bombs, supported by Me 262A-2 jet bombers of I. and II./KG 51. By the end of March 1945, Ar 234 bomber sorties had virtually ceased, KG 76 having about a dozen on strength. On 10 April KG 76 was transferred to the control of *Luftflotte Reich*. *German Aircraft of the Second World War* by J.R. Smith and Antony Kay (Putnam 1972).

6   *Eagles of Duxford: The 78th Fighter Group in World War II.*

7   The 21 March missions were the start of a massive four-day assault on the *Luftwaffe*, with 42,000 sorties being made over German airspace.

8   *Eagles of Duxford: The 78th Fighter Group in World War II.*

9   The pilots of Me 262A-2a 111605 9K+DL, *Unteroffizier* Heinz Erben, and Me 262A-2a 170118 PK+CK, *Leutnant* Erwin Diekmann, both of I./KG(J)51, were killed while taking off from Giebelstadt. In I./KG(J)51 Me 262A-2a 111973 9K+AL flown by *Hauptmann* Eberhard Winkel the *Staffelkapitän*, was also killed taking off from Giebelstadt. *The Messerschmitt Me 262 Combat Diary.*

10   *The Messerschmitt Me 262 Combat Diary.*

11   He returned to Duxford on 10 May.

12   11062 B3+DK. *The Messerschmitt Me 262 Combat Diary.*

13   *Eagles of Duxford: The 78th Fighter Group in World War II.* Adalbert Egri was wounded. Nineteen Me 262s of I and II,/KG(J)54 were bombed at Giebelstadt airfield and were badly damaged. *The Messerschmitt Me 262 Combat Diary.*

14   *The Messerschmitt Me 262 Combat Diary.*

15   One plan, in the autumn of 1944, had been Adolf Galland's *Grosser Sclag* (Big Stick). The *General der Jagdflieger* had worked out detailed plans to launch a mass-attack by 3,700 fighters in eighteen *Geschwaders* against a large-scale Allied daylight bombing raid in order to deliver a knockout blow. His assembled force however, bled to death during the Ardennes offensive and *Bodenplatte* and during raids like 26–27 November 1944.

16   Despite the losses to ramming attacks in the previous September American aircrew were still largely unaware of the nature of the attacks and most crewmen thought that the aircraft lost when the *Rammjäger* dived into the bomber formations were the result of collisions.

17   Twelve were shot down by Mustangs and P-47s, three by flak, five were lost in crash-landings and eleven were lost to unknown causes. Eighteen of the *Elbe* pilots were KIA or MIA, with seven others wounded. Total German fighter losses on the day were 133 aircraft destroyed. The determined onslaught by the *Rammjäger* and the Me 262 pilots did not stop 1,261 heavies dropping almost 3,500 tons of bombs on sixteen targets in Germany but many crewmen at de-briefings were apprehensive that the *Luftwaffe* might be resorting to *Kamikaze* tactics. In reality *Rammjäger* pilots were not suicidal. They were only expected to disable a bomber before baling out. At least seven, but probably more, *Elbe* pilots survived their ramming attacks to report their successful mission, although most of them were seriously injured in the process.

18   Hewitt was credited only with the Me 262 destroyed on the runway, a

decision that deprived him of five aerial victories and ace status. A Me 262A-1B of 3./JG 7 was shot down near Prague. *Unteroffizier* Fick was killed. (*The Messerschmitt Me 262 Combat Diary*). Another wingman, 2nd Lieutenant Alvin M Rosenburg, baled out after he was hit by flak west of Adorf, Germany.

19 *Barnes Wallis' Bombs: Tallboy, Dambuster & Grand Slam* by Stephen Flower (Tempus 2004).

20 Flown by Huie Lamb with Lieutenant Colonel Ben Pentecost, 66th Fighter Wing Flight Surgeon, in the jump seat – a flight lasting six hours thirty-five minutes.

21 At 1000 hours the Mustangs left the Lancasters and made a 180-degree turn back to Landshut where they rendezvoused with Second Air Division Liberators who dropped their bombloads on the railway marshalling yards. At 1045 hours the Mustangs broke off their escort and headed back over Belgium and the North Sea to Duxford for the last time.

22 *Wandering Through World War II*.

23 *Wandering Through World War II*.

INDEX

279

281